Arctic Alternatives

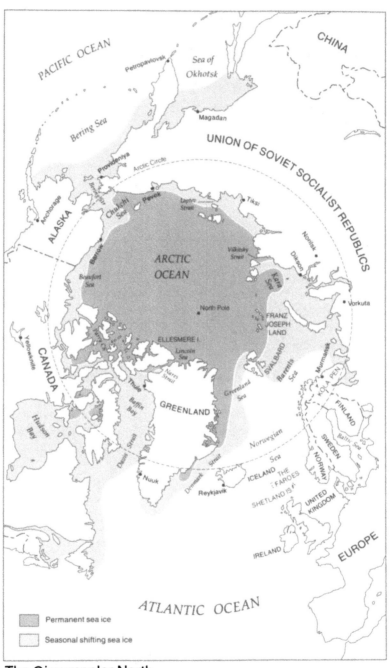

The Circumpolar North

Arctic Alternatives: Civility or Militarism in the Circumpolar North

Edited by Franklyn Griffiths

Canadian Papers in Peace Studies
1992 No. 3

Science for Peace / Samuel Stevens
Toronto

Canadian Cataloguing in Publication Data

Main entry under title:

Arctic Alternatives: civility or militarism in the circumpolar North

(Canadian papers in peace studies ; 1992 no.3)
Papers, revised in 1990, presented at a conference in Toronto, 1988.
Includes biographical references.
ISBN 0-88866-951-8

1. Arctic regions – Strategic aspects – Congresses. 2. Arctic regions – International status – Congresses. 3. Ecology – Arctic regions – Congresses. I. Griffiths, Franklyn, 1935- . II. Science for Peace (Association). III. Series.

G600.5.A73 1992   355'.033'98   C92-0984863-4

Science for Peace is a Canadian charitable corporation, registered in Ontario, funded by membership subscriptions and by individual and corporate donations. Its objectives include encouragement of research and education for peace as well as for the abolition of weapons of mass destruction.

Books submitted to the Publications Committee for this series (c/o Derek Paul, Department of Physics, University of Toronto, Toronto, Canada, M5S 1A1) will be considered on their merits, having due regard to the purposes of Science for Peace. In addition, the Committee seeks authors for books on topics that are thought to be of special importance at the time. The Committee has a general policy of submitting manuscripts to independent referees for comment but is not rigidly bound by this policy. It also seeks to avoid long delays when material of timely relevance is submitted.

The publications of Science for Peace are available from:

Science for Peace
University College
University of Toronto
Toronto, Ontario, Canada
M5S 1A1

Samuel Stevens & Co.
University of Toronto Press
5201 Dufferin Street
Downsview, Ontario, Canada
M3H 5T8

Printed and bound in Canada by Best Gagné Book Manufacturers

In memory of
John Dove and George Ignatieff

Contents

Preface

This book springs from a joint effort between Science for Peace and the Canadian Institute for International Peace and Security. Early in 1987 Science for Peace, an association of Canadians interested in applications of the natural and social sciences to address global challenges to humankind, decided to hold an international conference on Arctic military and civil problems that might be susceptible to co-operative solutions. Our underlying purpose was to identify and secure support for alternatives to what we regarded as the excessive reliance on military forces and military methods in the conduct of Arctic affairs. By October 1987 we had entered into a partnership with the Canadian Institute for International Peace and Security, a free-standing body established by the Parliament of Canada, which had offered to act as co-sponsor of the proposed meeting. In that month, too, Mikhail Gorbachev broke with past Soviet practice in an address calling for comprehensive Arctic co-operation. Departing from Moscow's perennial opposed-forces approach to the region's military and civil problems, the Soviet leader effectively altered the calculation of what was and is possible in Arctic international relations.

Subsequently, in October 1988, the conference we sought took place in Toronto. It gathered some seventy persons from all the regional countries, from Canada, Denmark/Greenland, Finland, Iceland, Norway, the Soviet Union, Sweden, and the United States. It also brought together an unusually wide variety of perspectives as representatives of the Arctic's aboriginal peoples joined with the individuals expert in military, scientific, environmental, and technical matters to discuss concerted responses to the region's problems. We learned a good deal about the need and opportunities for Arctic international co-operation. We also learned not a little about the difficulty of demilitarizing the affairs of the region even as the Cold War was brought to an end.

The volume in your hands collects the revised papers presented at Toronto. It aims to provide essential knowledge for those who would secure more harmonious and productive Arctic international relations in the 1990s. It also addresses the conceptual and practical problems that must be resolved if the peoples of the Arctic countries are to steer the development of their region away from militarism and towards civility. The central questions before us are the following: Why should the Arctic remain an arena of vigorous military competition and constrained civil co-operation when competition shows signs of giving way to military and civil collaboration in Europe, in other regions of the world, and directly between the world's two leading military powers? What can be done to end the discriminatory treatment of the Arctic by the populations and decision centres that lie to the south?

The fate of the Arctic is in the hands of southern majorities in the regional countries. We can continue to act with prejudice to the needs of the region and its inhabitants, or we can demand better of ourselves.

Although the editor is responsible for the intellectual framework and the selection of contributors to this book, little would have been accomplished without generous assistance from many quarters. Absolutely indispensable financial support was provided by the Canadian Institute for International Peace and Security. Help was also given by the Walter and Duncan Gordon Charitable Foundation and by Gulf Canada Resources Limited. The support of these institutions is gratefully acknowledged.

Many members of Science for Peace gave freely of their energy and imagination in preparing for and managing the conference in Toronto at which the papers collected here were originally presented. In their different ways Katherine Armstrong, Lois Dove, Lynn Trainor, and Robena Weatherley all made a particular difference. John Valleau provided rigorous accounting services for the project. Derek Paul assisted with the initial preparation of the manuscript and the final push to publication.

Lorraine Y. Smith showed unflagging good humour and initiative in the initial processing of the collected papers and Kit Pineau and Dieter Heinrich were extraordinarily dedicated and skilled in producing the final camera copy, following the customary meticulous technical editing of Marion Magee. Raul Cunha and Judy Kostilek prepared charts and figures with easy exactitude.

Two persons deserve especial mention. As president of Science for Peace, George Ignatieff offered powerful leadership and enthusiastic support for the project from its very beginning. Without his ardent desire to make the circumpolar Arctic a more peaceable place, the collective effort that resulted in this book would hardly have been possible. George died in Lennoxville, Quebec, in August 1989. John Dove gave without limit, as a board member of Science for Peace, in organizing the Toronto conference and making it the success it was. John died tragically in Botswana in May 1989. This book is dedicated to their memory.

Franklyn Griffiths / Toronto / June 1991

Arctic Alternatives

Co-operation and Security in a Militarized Region

Franklyn Griffiths

This book in itself is testimony to transition in the affairs of the north circumpolar region. Written in 1988 and updated to 1990, the papers assembled here have been overtaken by events. But by no means have they been outdated. When commissioned, the chapters to follow were to some degree ahead of their time in envisaging a more peaceable circumpolar region in which alternatives to militarization and the Cold War could be pursued through non-military or civil co-operation among the Arctic countries. As is made clear in the epilogue, which brings us up to February 1992, emergent realities in the Arctic have indeed begun to approach the basic aspirations, if not all of the assumptions, which governed the design of the book.

Perhaps most noteworthy in the onrush of events since 1988 has been the dissolution of the Soviet Union and its replacement in December 1991, not so much by the Commonwealth of Independent States (CIS) as by the Russian federation. Alone among the former Soviet republics, Russia faces the Arctic Ocean and retains effective control over the great bulk of nuclear and conventional weapons of the former USSR. By rights, all references in this book to the Soviet Union as an existing entity should be eliminated. And yet the larger part of the old Soviet infrastructure, its military assets included, has been reconstituted in the Russian federation. Nor, given the great uncertainty which surrounds Russia's internal political development in 1992, can it be assumed that Russia's ability to offer a renewed, if diminished, challenge to the liberal democracies is wholly a thing of the past. As well, not only Soviet communism but now the CIS could soon be a thing of the past. These and other considerations taken into account as they concern the dissolution of the USSR, it seemed appropriate to proceed with the set of essays as they appear here, and without a further revision which itself could be overtaken by events in Russia. The same applies to still more fundamental transformations associated with the end of the Cold War, which is now behind us but by no means wholly so in the Arctic.

Put yourself down at random on the shore of the Arctic Ocean in February 1992, stay a while, and you are unlikely to see any sign of armed force. But it's there. Well out of sight but in movement or poised for action there would be ballistic-missile-firing and nuclear attack submarines, land-based intercontinental missiles set for launch on or easily retargeted to transpolar flight paths, surface naval combatants, airborne anti-submarine warfare capabilities, strategic bombers now stood down from alert, air-launched cruise missiles with nuclear and conventional warheads, air defences against bomber and cruise missile attack, would-be strategic anti-missile defences, and still more. Arctic spaces continue, even in 1992, to be used for strategic deterrence, and for testing, training, basing, transit, surveillance, and still other military purposes. The Arctic is a militarized region.

The armed forces in question are those of the Russian federation and/or the CIS, on the one hand, and, on the other, those of the countries of the North Atlantic Treaty Organization (NATO) – principally but by no means exclusively the United States, Canada, Denmark, and Norway. (The remaining Arctic country in the alliance, Iceland, has no defence forces of its own.) Throughout the countries of the region, non-aligned Finland and Sweden included, a stance of defence preparedness and wariness is in greater or lesser measure institutionalized in military-industrial establishments, in the priorities of foreign ministries, and in the thinking of influentials. The effect is to maintain the sense of conflict and potential for confrontation in a region that deserves better.

As the chapters to come make clear – most notably those of David Cox, Steven Miller, Willy Østreng, and John Kristen Skogan – geography, politics, technology, and military doctrine long conspired to make the Arctic an arena of vigorous military activity. The militarization of the region was driven principally by the extra-regional security requirements of the Soviet Union and the United States. The Cold War endowed these requirements, defined very largely in military-technical terms, with great force. As indicated by the report in February 1992 of an underwater collision between an American and a Russian/CIS submarine in or near Russian/CIS territorial waters off the Kola Peninsula, the two key protagonists do remain opposed in the Arctic, even as the Cold War and the political rationale for confrontational military postures recede into the past. The terms "East" and "West" have now acquired a geographical meaning, but the guard has yet to be lowered in the North to the extent it has been in Europe and in wider dealings between Washington and Moscow.

However, as is reported in the epilogue, common understandings of Arctic environmental, social, and other civil problems have grown among the region's countries together with a willingness to co-operate in dealing with them. Shared requirements for multilateral co-operation arise from the striking similarity of physical conditions, occupancy problems, and transboundary processes experienced by these countries. The survival of aboriginal cultures, the effects of global warming, the elaboration of safe and efficient means of bulk transportation, the provision of health services, the co-ordination of scientific research, and any number of other civil problems all demand co-ordinated pan-Arctic responses if they are to be dealt with effectively. All of this was becoming evident when this book was conceived in the late 1980s. Equally evident was the fact that the evolution of multilateral civil co-operation in the Arctic was retarded relative to other regions of the world. This remains true today. Civil collaboration has in no small measure been constrained by the continued strength of military-strategic conflict in the affairs of the region. It is still inhibited by reliance on military force and military methods and by suspicion carried forward from the time, not so long ago, when the very thought of multilateral Arctic agreement seemed utopian.

Put the pieces of the puzzle together this way, add the unfortunate reality that the Arctic as such is more or less a peripheral concern for the southern majorities and decision-makers of the regional countries, and the outlook is not encouraging for those who would reverse the militarization of the region and its restraining effects on civil collaboration. Evidently, Arctic military problems must be addressed at source, which is to say not in talks among the ice states themselves but in extra-regional arms negotiations, primarily those between the United States and Russia/CIS. It would seem that much more will have to change on the outside before the course of militarism can be altered inside the Arctic.

Is there another and more enabling way of defining the problem? This was the basic question in the planning of this book at a time when the Cold War was not clearly a thing of the past and when the Soviet Union seemed likely to retain superpower standing for the indefinite future. It is still the question in 1992.

Bearing in mind the inherent difficulties of Arctic arms control and disarmament, it seemed as of the late 1980s that we might well explore the potential of an indirect attack on the problem of Arctic militarization.

Directness was and is of course indispensable. But by pursuing co-operation on civil questions, which deserved to be addressed in their own right, the Arctic countries could improve the outlook for military confidence-building and arms reduction agreements. If they were to collaborate on a steadily broadening array of civil matters, a variety of benefits could be expected. The sense of mistrust that attended a major preoccupation with opposed military forces could be reduced. New vested interests in Arctic co-operation could be created in the regional countries, as could new opportunities for diplomatic as distinct from military interaction. The result could be a more diversified Arctic international agenda, greater flexibility in the policy of individual states, and the evolution of a practice that built confidence in the belief that indeed there were workable alternatives to military-strategic confrontation.

In short, Arctic civil co-operation could in itself constitute a confidence-building exercise. It could contribute to regional demilitarization by spilling over into the negotiation of military confidence-building and, eventually, arms reduction agreements. All the while, the regional countries would be pursuing joint benefits through civil co-operation that should be sought on its own merits, irrespective of its potential to moderate military-strategic rivalry and improve security.

This book accordingly brings together a set of contributions that allow us to begin to see the affairs of the region in the round. In addition to military matters as viewed from the south, we consider aboriginal perspectives and needs on questions of culture (Aqqaluk Lynge), health (Jens Misfeldt), science (Milton Freeman), and militarization (Mary Simon), together with other elements of a comprehensive Arctic international agenda – the physical environment (M.J. Dunbar), industrialization and its consequences (Terence Armstrong), scientific co-operation (E.F. Roots), pollution and the greenhouse effect (Anders Karlqvist and Jost Heintzenberg), oceans management (Anders Stigebrandt), petroleum exploration (Melvin Conant), and marine transportation (Aleksandr Arikaynen). The intention was to begin to break through the confines of differing perspectives on the region and of professional specializations that still favour the consideration of policy problems in isolation. Hence the variety of expertise and idiom gathered in this volume. Hence also the variation in levels of practicality and sophistication with which various issues are considered: it fairly represents the state of affairs in Arctic international policy discussion as the 1990s begin.

But if this collection of papers helps to redefine the Arctic's military problems by viewing them in a broader regional context, the fact remains that they originate very largely from outside the region. Thus far we have taken only a first step towards a new understanding of alternatives to Arctic military confrontation. We have suggested that the route to more harmonious and productive Arctic international relations includes a substantial measure of civil co-operation and should not rely exclusively on measures of military confidence-building, arms control, and disarmament. Let us pursue this line of inquiry.

Those who would make military use of the Arctic are heavily concerned with the need to maintain security. Implicit in the notion that civil co-operation may contribute to Arctic demilitarization, and thus to regional security at progressively lower levels of force, is the thought that the meaning of security as such may be in need of redefinition. As Soviet spokesmen and commentators said with great good sense for several years, security is to be obtained on two planes: the political and (only secondarily) the technical. The latter is said to entail the balancing and structuring of armed forces at the lowest level required to avert war and otherwise ensure the defence of the nation. The political path to security is to be pursued through threat-reducing activity that serves to promote mutual reassurance and stabilizing collaboration among potential belligerents.

From this perspective, Arctic civil co-operation is not merely a form of confidence-building and a preliminary to regional military collaboration. It is an intrinsic element of Arctic security understood as a political as well as a military-technical condition. What seems at first to be an indirect attack on the problem of Arctic militarization turns out, on reflection, to be integral to the building of political security. Driven as it is by an intense concern with hardware and doctrine, the effort to maintain security defined in military-technical terms depends upon political judgments that make others into actual or potential adversaries. If civil co-operation in the Arctic can call adversarial assumptions into question, it may not only alter the conduct of regional affairs but also diminish the extra-regional sources of regional military interaction. Indeed, if there is one way that co-operation among the Arctic countries may most readily address the extra-regional political origins of Arctic military conflict, it is through civil co-operation. But civil co-operation may bear on security and our understanding of it in still other ways.

Growing awareness of the greenhouse effect and of the manifold challenges of sustainable development as reported by the Brundtland Commission has begun to alter notions of security on a planet with finite carrying capacity. Governments, expert panels, and individuals began in the 1980s to refer with ever greater frequency to environmental or ecological security and to economic security, to say nothing of energy security, security of human rights, and so on. Meanwhile, throughout the world, the Arctic very much included, aboriginal peoples had long been faced not merely with the need to make their cultures secure but also with the very question of cultural survival in the face of onrushing industrialism and modernity.

Non-military or civil requirements thus seemed to warrant a new and far more important place in our understanding of security. Civil co-operation, it appeared, was not merely a possible response to the problem of building political preconditions for security defined in terms of diminishing force levels and less threatening force postures, doctrines, and deployments. It was becoming the real business of security in a time of fundamental change in human affairs. Accordingly, in designing this book, it seemed appropriate to explore not only the potential of civil co-operation in countering the force of militarism, but the utility of a comprehensive conception of Arctic security in which military requirements were combined with an awareness of the need to act for political, environmental, economic, and social security as well. We shall see how these views fare, once we've had a look at the region and its problems.

Part I

Co-operation and Security

1

International Co-operation in the Arctic: Opportunities and Constraints

Oran R. Young & Arkady I. Cherkasov

In some international regions, like the Middle East, Southeast Asia, or Central America, regional conflicts threaten to escalate in ways that embroil outside parties and, in the process, trigger wider international conflicts. The essential problem in these regions is to devise codes of conduct to minimize outside interventions (especially competitive interventions), while seeking viable and preferably equitable solutions to the regional conflicts themselves. In other international regions, like the oceans, outer space, or Antarctica, outside powers are drawn to regional settings as attractive arenas in which to pursue their larger interests. In such regions, the central problem is to establish institutional arrangements or regimes regulating the interplay of outside actors in order to protect the integrity of the regions without seriously impeding the efforts of the outside parties to pursue their own interests.

The Arctic, we believe, belongs to the second of these categories. It is a sparsely populated, resource-rich region whose location makes it increasingly important in geopolitical terms. Because the Arctic offers an exceptionally favourable environment for the deployment of strategic weapons systems, like nuclear-powered submarines and manned bombers equipped with cruise missiles, the superpowers are steadily increasing their military presence in the region. About 20 per cent of the crude oil produced in the United States comes from the American Arctic. The comparable figures for the Soviet Union are much higher, with over 60 per cent of both oil and natural gas production coming from the giant fields of northwestern Siberia. The fact that the greenhouse effect is expected to produce temperature increases in the high latitudes that are two to three times those occurring in the mid-latitudes ensures that everyone concerned with global change will pay closer attention to the Arctic during the foreseeable future.

In contrast to the oceans, outer space, or Antarctica, however, the Arctic is a homeland for a sizeable collection of native peoples. What is happening in and to the region presents a growing threat to these peoples, especially those anxious to protect distinctive cultures or ways of life. As the international significance of the Arctic grows, decisions affecting the region's future are taken increasingly by outsiders who are seldom well informed about the concerns of Arctic peoples and who, in any case, have little reason to make choices that are sensitive to these concerns. But despite (or perhaps because of) this development, there is a pronounced resurgence in cultural awareness among the native peoples of the Arctic, which has unleashed a rising tide of interest in protecting their unique ways of life. The widening gulf between these two trends is a source of deepening concern among those desiring to maintain the integrity of the Arctic as a distinctive international region.

Opportunities for Arctic Co-operation

Co-operation in international society, as in other social settings, occurs when parties who are individuals in the sense that they make choices or select courses of action independently realize that there are joint gains to be achieved through co-ordination of their actions. Sometimes these gains are measurable in terms of the production of mutual benefits. The benefits likely to flow from scientific collaboration and joint economic ventures or enterprises are examples relevant to the Arctic today. In other cases, joint gains take the form of avoiding mutual losses. Arms stabilization or limitation measures as well as initiatives aimed at protecting the natural environment constitute examples of this type of co-operation which seem attractive under the conditions now prevailing in the Arctic.

Rising levels of human activity throughout the Arctic have increased interdependencies in the region and, in the process, enhanced the stakes of all the Arctic states in exploring co-operative arrangements for the region. An expression of American Arctic policy, for example, declares that the United States has "unique and critical interests in the Arctic region" and speaks explicitly of "promoting mutually beneficial international cooperation in the Arctic."[1] For their part, senior Canadian officials refer to international co-operation in the Arctic as a "trend of enormous importance" and state clearly that Canada wishes "to see peaceful cooperation among Arctic Rim countries developed further."[2]

Without doubt, however, the clearest and strongest expressions of increasing interest in international co-operation in the Arctic have come from the Soviet Union. In his Murmansk speech of October 1, 1987, for example, Mikhail Gorbachev laid out a six-point programme for Arctic co-operation and pledged the Soviet Union's "profound and certain interest in preventing the North of the planet, its polar and sub-polar regions and all northern countries from ever again becoming an arena of war, and in forming there a genuine zone of peace and fruitful co-operation."[3] In the ensuing months, the Soviet leaders acted vigorously to pursue this Arctic zone-of-peace initiative, as it has come to be called. They entered into co-operation agreements with Norway in the fields of scientific research and environmental protection, initiated discussions regarding co-operation with Canada, and expressed enthusiasm for the early establishment of the proposed International Arctic Science Committee. Even more significant for the longer run, the Soviet Union has established a State Commission on Arctic Affairs, which is designed to function as an inter-agency co-ordinating committee and is chaired by a first deputy prime minister. Under the circumstances, it will come as no surprise that Presidents Gorbachev and Reagan spoke specifically of Arctic co-operation during their spring 1988 summit in Moscow. The official statement released at the end of the meeting, in fact, states: "Taking into account the unique environmental, demographic and other characteristics of the Arctic, the two leaders reaffirmed their support for expanded bilateral and regional contacts and cooperation in this area."[4]

To be more specific, we wish to differentiate three sets of circumstances currently giving rise to opportunities for joint gains in the Arctic. There is, to begin with, a need for co-operation to protect the shared ecosystems of the region. The natural environment of the Arctic region is indivisible, unusually sensitive to anthropogenic disturbances, and linked to the ecosphere of the mid-latitudes in highly significant ways. Accordingly, air and water pollution cannot be confined to politically demarcated segments of the Arctic. Much the same is true of the effects of megaprojects that threaten the ecological balance of the region (for example, the hydroelectric development in northern Quebec or the currently shelved plan for diverting waters from Siberian rivers to the south). Because of the links between the Arctic and the mid-latitudes, especially with respect to the global climate regime, we must also expect that these northern effects will eventually make themselves felt on the earth's biosphere as a whole. It follows that all the countries of the Arctic stand to benefit from "the cooperation of the northern countries in environmental protection."[5]

There are, in addition, opportunities for co-operation in the Far North arising from the fact that the Arctic states have encountered many of the same problems in their efforts to develop the North while protecting the region's ecosystems and unique cultures. Some of these problems are essentially technical in nature; they are attributable to similarities in climatic conditions (for instance, the presence of permafrost) and in geographical conditions (for example, long distances and sparse populations) throughout the circumpolar North. Others are better characterized as economic and social problems. The high costs of extracting raw materials in the North and transporting them to distant markets, and the consequent lengthy wait for returns to be realized, constitute an important consideration in all investment decisions (whether under capitalist or socialist auspices). Similarly, the threats to the cultures of northern native peoples associated with participation in industrial development are much the same throughout the Arctic region. It would be both pointless and wasteful to adopt secretive policies in responding to these problems, thereby forcing scientists, engineers, and managers located in different parts of the Arctic to solve the same problems over and over again. Except in cases where the resultant products compete with each other in world markets (which are likely to be rare as far as the Arctic is concerned), therefore, co-operation in the exchange of problem-solving techniques and Arctic expertise will benefit all.

Yet another basis for Arctic co-operation involves joint ventures or enterprises designed to exploit complementarities arising from asymmetries in scientific, technological, and socio-economic development in the North. The Soviet Union, for example, leads in such areas as the construction of multi-storied buildings on permafrost, Arctic marine transportation, the provision of education for northern peoples in their own languages, and (at least in principle) arrangements designed to provide a measure of self-government for·northern peoples. Canada and the United States, by contrast, are ahead in the development of small dwelling units adapted to northern conditions, the use of specialized transportation technologies (snowmobiles, all-terrain vehicles), northern road construction, technologies for offshore oil and gas development, and the design and implementation of environmental safeguards for Arctic ecosystems. The Scandinavian countries have established the most effective systems of reindeer husbandry in the North and could assist in improving Soviet practice in this area and (together with the Soviet Union) in introducing reindeer husbandry into the North American Arctic. Each Arctic country leads in one or more spheres of northern experience. By pooling knowledge and resources through the establishment of joint ventures or enterprises, therefore, the Arctic states can generate mutual benefits exceeding the sum of what each country working alone would be able to produce.

Forms of Co-operation

Co-operation in international society, as in other social settings, takes a variety of forms. Co-operative arrangements may be bilateral or multilateral. The category of multilateral arrangements, moreover, covers a broad spectrum of cases encompassing three or more parties. Particularly significant for this examination of Arctic co-operation is the distinction between multilateral arrangements in which the participants are members of a well-defined region (for example, the Mediterranean Action Plan) and multilateral arrangements in which the participants are linked along functional lines (for example, the regimes for whaling and for trade in endangered species). In addition, international co-operation may be issue-specific or comprehensive. Here, too, there is a broad spectrum, ranging from highly restrictive arrangements (for instance, the co-operative management of polar bears) to those that encompass a wide range of interlocking issues (for example, the regime for the oceans set forth in the 1982 Convention on the Law of the Sea).

Three additional distinctions regarding forms of international co-operation are worth noting as background for this assessment of prospects for Arctic co-operation. Co-operation may be self-executing in that it involves interactions which are not recurrent or iterative in nature or ongoing in the sense of encompassing relationships of a continuing or repetitive nature. Co-operation aimed at the demarcation of jurisdictional boundaries, on the understanding that each party will subsequently exercise exclusive authority within its own jurisdictional zone, exemplifies such a non-iterative interaction. Regimes for continuing activities like high seas fishing or the use of the electromagnetic spectrum, by contrast, involve relationships of a continuing nature. In either case, the resultant co-operation may be explicit or tacit. Explicit arrangements, which constitute the form of co-operation we tend to think of first, are characterized by articulation of the terms of the relationships in formal agreements (that is, a treaty or a convention). Tacit co-operation, by contrast, requires only a de facto co-ordination of behaviour in order to realize mutual benefits or, more often, to avoid mutual losses. Parties engaging in tacit co-operation may, in fact, experience incentives (that is, the need to maintain public support in situations involving intense conflict) to deny publicly that they are doing so. Finally, co-operative arrangements of an explicit nature may or may not require specialized organizations to administer the interactions they govern. While the Antarctic Treaty of 1959 does not establish any specialized administrative apparatus, for example, the more recent Convention on the Conservation of Antarctic Marine Living Resources sets up a commission, a scientific committee, and a secretariat to administer its provisions.[6]

Those who approach international co-operation with the experience of the oceans or Antarctica in mind often take it for granted that co-operative arrangements should be multilateral, comprehensive, continuing, and explicit. Increasingly, moreover, they envision roles for specialized organizations designed to administer the provisions of these relatively complex co-operative arrangements. In these terms, the Arctic lags far behind Antarctica, the oceans, and even outer space with regard to its record of international co-operation. Yet there is no reason to accept this model as a general norm or, more specifically, as the appropriate paradigm to guide the search for co-operation in the Arctic. On the contrary, it makes better sense to think in terms of tailoring co-operative arrangements to the conditions prevailing in geographically demarcated regions or functionally defined issue-areas rather than of attempting to impose a uniform model of co-operation regardless of the circumstances.

Once we abandon the assumption that co-operation should always aim at creating arrangements that are multilateral, comprehensive, continuing, and explicit, it quickly becomes apparent that there is a substantial record of international co-operation in the Arctic. What is more, this experience runs the gamut from scientific and technical arrangements through environmental regimes to co-operation on matters relating to military security. The multilateral regime for Svalbard, which dates back to 1920, calls for the demilitarization of the Svalbard Archipelago and covers the exploitation of the area's natural resources.[7] The regimes for fur seals and polar bears are explicit, multilateral arrangements that are Arctic-specific in nature.[8] At the same time, there are numerous co-operative arrangements in the Arctic of a bilateral nature that encompass environmental protection (for example, the Canada-Denmark marine environmental conservation agreement covering Davis Strait and Baffin Bay or the new Norway-Soviet Union agreement on environmental protection in the area of their common border), the use of shared resources (the grey zone agreement between Norway and the Soviet Union), scientific research (the Soviet agreements with Canada and Norway, respectively), marine transportation (the Canada-United States agreement on Arctic co-operation dealing with the movements of icebreakers in the Northwest Passage), and economic development (the co-operative enterprises the Soviet Union has pursued with various partners to develop non-renewable resources in the Barents Sea).

We note as well that interest in devising a variety of co-operative arrangements for the Arctic is on the rise. The proposed International Arctic Science Committee has evoked enthusiasm throughout the region, and there is considerable optimism about the prospects for launching such a committee officially during 1990.[9] The Finns have taken the initiative in promoting the idea of developing an Arctic Action Plan (along the lines of those currently in place for the Mediterranean and the Baltic) to protect the marine environment of the Arctic Basin. As awareness of the links between the Arctic and the rest of the earth's biosphere grows, moreover, officials in all the Arctic countries are beginning to give serious consideration to proposals for international co-operation designed to protect Arctic systems that play critical roles in controlling the heat budget of the northern hemisphere and the global climate regime. There is evidence that tacit co-operation is emerging to reduce the risks of accidental or inadvertent clashes between strategic weapons systems deployed in the Arctic, a development of particular importance given the atmospheric irregularities that make command and control difficult under Arctic conditions. And numerous bilateral arrangements are now under consideration encompassing shared living resources (for example, Soviet-American arrangements for the Bering Sea), the development of non-renewable resources (Soviet-Norwegian joint enterprises for the Barents Sea), and general expressions of interest in exploring additional bases for Arctic co-operation in the future (the Canadian-Soviet agreement).

Obstacles to Co-operation

Nonetheless, international co-operation, in the Arctic as elsewhere, is not easy to achieve. While the prospect of realizing joint gains is a necessary condition for co-operation, it is by no means a sufficient one. One of the most robust findings of the social sciences is that parties behaving in ways that seem rational from an individualistic point of view regularly produce collective outcomes that are suboptimal (sometimes drastically suboptimal) for all concerned.[10] In this section we identify some of the substantive obstacles that must be overcome in efforts to take advantage of the growing opportunities for international co-operation in the Arctic. We then proceed, in the following section, to comment on several collective

action problems that may impede the process of arriving at agreement on
co-operative arrangements for the Arctic.

At the most general level, there is, as the Soviet prime minister, Nikolai
Ryzhkov, has put it, a "lack of trust that has built up in a region that is so
sensitive from the viewpoint of security interests."[11] Unlike the oceans
where there is a long-standing tradition of shared use or Antarctica where a
complex of co-operative arrangements in the area of science emerged
during the International Geophysical Year of 1957-8, the Arctic has been
plagued by a variety of expansive and often conflicting jurisdictional
claims during the twentieth century.[12] The growing geopolitical
significance of the region has combined with these jurisdictional conflicts
to heighten the sensitivities of officials in all the Arctic countries regarding
the strategic implications of new developments in the region. What is
needed, then, to reverse the resultant atmosphere of distrust is a broad
commitment to "mutual respect for each other's interests, and the
development of mutually useful cooperation, in the course of which trust is
born and strengthens, the 'image of the enemy' collapses, and its place is
taken by the image of a partner."[13]

We note as well a striking disjunction between the strategic perspective
on Arctic affairs and the point of view of those who approach the region in
cultural, scientific, or environmental terms. Military planners tend to think
of the Arctic as a theatre of operations for weapons systems and as a
potential theatre for actual combat. Such a perspective is antithetical to the
views of those who perceive attractive opportunities for collaboration in
scientific research in the Arctic and of those who sense a growing need for
co-operation to protect the shared ecosystems of the region. Even more to
the point, the perspective of the military planners is viewed with horror by
the permanent residents of the Arctic who regard the region as a homeland
rather than as a theatre for the interactions of alien powers. One response
to this situation is to seek a decoupling of military and civil issues in the
Arctic, concentrating on efforts to promote civil co-operation in the region
in the hope that co-operation regarding military issues will follow as
experience with civil co-operation grows. We are not convinced, however,
that this approach is the most fruitful one. An alternative response is to
broaden the conception of security to encompass economic, environmental,
and cultural concerns and to recognize the existence of reciprocal
relationships among the various aspects of security. In this regard,
Gorbachev may well have been on the right track in proposing a
multidimensional approach to Arctic co-operation in his Murmansk

speech, whether or not the individual elements of his six-point programme prove attractive to the other Arctic countries.

Another general obstacle to international co-operation in the Arcticarises from a lack of mutual knowledge and understanding among the Arctic states regarding each other's organizational arrangements and decision-making processes. While scientific research in the Western countries is ordinarily carried out by scientists based in the universities, for example, scientific research in the Soviet Union is spearheaded by scientists attached to the Soviet Academy of Sciences. Though the native peoples of the Soviet north share many problems with their counterparts in the North American Arctic, they are ethnically and culturally distinct so that they do not fit easily into organizations like the Inuit Circumpolar Conference. In the field of economics, moreover, there is a tendency to think in terms of efforts to promote international trade, whereas what is needed, in the Arctic at least, are exchanges of technologies and the development of joint ventures or enterprises. The solution to this problem, we believe, lies in a commitment to expand the flow of information and persons across all the Arctic's borders. Such a development would serve to increase mutual understanding of differing organizational arrangements and decision-making processes. In the process, it would help to break down the general atmosphere of distrust that prevails in the Arctic today.

Collective Action Problems

Quite apart from these general obstacles, we can identify a number of collective action problems that complicate efforts to realize joint gains in the Arctic, just as they do in many other social settings. Four such problems seem particularly critical to the prospects for international co-operation in the Arctic today. To make the discussion concrete, we illustrate our analysis with examples drawn from the negotiations regarding the establishment of an International Arctic Science Committee (IASC).[14] The effort to establish this committee has given rise to complex negotiations in which a number of interesting collective action problems have surfaced.

Negotiation Arithmetic

Even when joint gains are feasible, efforts to reach agreement on co-operative arrangements can easily founder on problems relating to the choice of participants and the configuration of issues to be included in the arrangements. In the case of the IASC, these problems have been reflected in the need to reconcile two distinct visions of the proposed committee. On one account, the IASC should be a non-governmental organization that concentrates on identifying and refining research opportunities and which is open to all parties engaging in Arctic research. Such a committee would resemble the Scientific Committee on Antarctic Research (SCAR) and might join SCAR in due course as a constituent element of the International Council of Scientific Unions (ICSU). An alternative approach envisions the IASC as an intergovernmental organization that focuses on the management and logistical support of Arctic research and which is limited in membership to the eight Arctic countries. Much of the discussion in the recent negotiations on the character of an IASC has centred on efforts to reconcile these competing visions.[15] The current plan envisions a complex hybrid which would deal with managerial issues as well as the design of scientific research and which would handle the problem of membership by establishing a two-tiered arrangement under which a board would be composed of the eight Arctic countries as "founding members," while an Arctic science conference meeting every third year would be open to all.[16] Under this plan, the participants would seek to play down the issue of whether the committee is to be a governmental or a non-governmental organization by avoiding the use of these terms altogether. It appears to us that this plan amounts to an uneasy compromise; it does not constitute a true reconciliation of the alternative visions of the IASC.[17] Because of the general enthusiasm for the establishment of an IASC, however, the treatment of this problem may well be shifted to the implementation phase in order to allow the parties to take the symbolically significant step of announcing publicly the formation of the IASC sooner rather than later.

Positional Bargaining

Co-operation and competition are by no means mutually exclusive. With rare exceptions, they occur simultaneously in interactions among the members of international society, a fact that has led many students of international affairs to describe these interactions as competitive/co-operative relations.[18] More specifically, parties endeavouring to reach agreement on the terms of co-operative arrangements seldom ignore concurrent opportunities to obtain the best possible outcomes for themselves. In the language of those who study negotiations, they engage in positional bargaining even while they are endeavouring to collaborate to maximize social or collective welfare. The negotiations regarding the creation of an IASC offer several illustrations of this class of collective action problems. The Soviet Union, for instance, has exhibited a distinct interest in orchestrating the negotiations in such a way that the formal establishment of the IASC would take place at a meeting in the Soviet Union, an occurrence that would reflect positively on its Arctic zone-of-peace initiative. The Americans, by contrast, have manœuvred to prevent such a development, precisely because the United States does not want the Soviet Union to gain credit for the establishment of co-operative arrangements for the Arctic. Not surprisingly, it now seems probable that the formal announcement of the establishment of the IASC will occur in Canada, an arrangement acceptable to the Soviet Union because of its interest in fostering co-operative relations with the Canadians regarding Arctic matters and to the United States because of the long-standing tradition of friendship between Canada and the United States. In the shadow of this positional bargaining on the part of the superpowers, the negotiations have also given rise to a positional pirouette among the Nordic countries over the locus of the secretariat for the IASC. The current proposal, which involves locating the secretariat initially in Norway but includes a provision allowing for its subsequent rotation among the Nordic countries, is easy to understand as a device to resolve the competing interests of the relevant participants. But it remains to be seen whether a rotating secretariat is an ideal arrangement from the point of view of those desiring to build a strong international Arctic science community or, for that matter, whether the locus of the IASC secretariat ever rotates in practice.[19]

Internal Divisions

As many students of international negotiations have observed, the parties to such processes are seldom monolithic entities behaving as rational utility maximizers as they interact with each other. Far more common are situations in which competing interest groups are active at the subnational level, seeking to influence the positions their countries adopt at the international level.[20] And the resultant intra-party bargaining regularly affects international negotiations, distorting the character of the co-operative arrangements that emerge and, in extreme cases, preventing the establishment of co-operative arrangements altogether. Once again, the negotiations regarding the proposed IASC offer interesting illustrations. Clear evidence has emerged, for example, of vigorous jockeying for position within several of the participating states over the composition of negotiating teams and, therefore, the interests emphasized in the negotiations. In the case of Canada, this has taken the form of a successful effort on the part of the Department of External Affairs to take the lead in negotiations regarding the IASC, shifting representatives of other departments, like Environment Canada and Indian Affairs and Northern Development, into a secondary role. In the United States, by contrast, the internal dynamics have centred on the roles of the National Science Foundation, the National Academy of Sciences, and the Arctic Research Commission, with the Department of State taking a back seat and the National Science Foundation increasing its influence in the negotiating process over time. Similarly, there are obvious conflicts of interest at the intra-party level regarding the choice of agencies to serve as official members of the IASC and to make decisions about national participation in the activities of the committee. The United States, for example, has frequently expressed the view that the IASC should be a non-governmental organization, a position suggesting that American participation in the committee should be handled through the National Academy of Sciences (as in the case of SCAR). But the National Science Foundation, which is clearly a governmental organization, has become the dominant participant in the American negotiating team, and there are unmistakable indications of conflicts of interest between the academy and the foundation in this area. In Canada, confusion reigns with respect to the issue of formal membership in the IASC. External Affairs, which is clearly not a candidate for formal membership, now dominates the negotiating team. The Canadian Polar Research Commission might become a candidate for formal membership.[21] And though no one has proposed the Royal Society as the vehicle for Canadian membership, it is probably the closest counterpart to the American National Academy of Sciences and the Academy of Sciences of the USSR. For their part, those engaged in the effort to negotiate the terms of the IASC at the international level have now adopted the sensible view that arrangements for national participation in the activities of the IASC are matters for each country to deal with according to its own preferences and procedures.

Political Will

Efforts to reap joint gains through international co-operation can and often do become bogged down in attempts to resolve the collective action problems we have discussed. Still, these problems can be overcome or swept aside in short order when the will to act is strong on all sides. Perhaps the most dramatic illustrations of this proposition have occurred in the realm of arms control. Negotiations over the reduction of intermediate-range nuclear forces, for example, dragged on for years in an inconclusive fashion. But when it became politically expedient for both the United States and the Soviet Union to conclude an agreement in this area, the two sides finalized and signed the Intermediate-Range Nuclear Forces Treaty of 1987 without delay. The point we wish to stress in this discussion, however, is that circumstances in which the will to act is present simultaneously on all sides are exceptional and almost always fleeting. Regardless of the issue-area, one or more of the key players will often be preoccupied with other concerns (for example, an election, a change of leadership, domestic turmoil) or find it expedient to drag out negotiations in the hope of benefiting from enhanced bargaining strength at a later date. In assessing the prospects for the proposed IASC, then, we must constantly ask whether the will to act on this matter is present in all the important parties. In our judgment, the will to make progress in this area is currently clear and strong in the Soviet Union. The desire to take steps towards the development of multilateral co-operative arrangements for the Arctic has been expressed repeatedly at the highest levels of the Soviet leadership. By contrast, it seems less clear whether the will to act is sufficiently strong in the United States or Canada to ensure success. In the United States, the unmistakable desire of the scientific community to press forward with the creation of an IASC has not been matched by unambiguous support from senior political leaders, and it remains to be seen what the attitude of the Bush administration will be on this matter. With respect to Canada, it appears to us that there is some division of opinion between those who would politicize the IASC and hope to use it to promote Canada's political agenda in the Arctic and those who would decouple this issue from the rest of the Arctic agenda and treat it as a worthwhile enterprise in its own right.

Conclusion: The Road Ahead

We have shown that a considerable network of co-operative arrangements in the Arctic already exists. It is also undeniable, in our judgment, that opportunities for new forms of international co-operation in this region have grown steadily in recent years as levels of human activity in the Arctic have risen. Yet it is equally apparent that the obstacles impeding efforts to realize joint gains through international co-operation in the Arctic are substantial. In this concluding section, therefore, we endeavour to pinpoint some key elements of a strategy designed to overcome these obstacles in the interests of linking together and building on the co-operative arrangements currently operative in the Arctic.

Above all, there is a need to reconcile two basic approaches to Arctic co-operation. On one account (which we may loosely describe as the Western approach to Arctic co-operation), it is desirable to decouple Arctic issues in order to promote co-operation regarding those issues that are not politically sensitive while setting aside the more sensitive issues in the hope that the growth of co-operation will make them easier to deal with at a later time. The critical implication of this approach is that the politico-strategic issues associated with the militarization of the Arctic should be passed over at this stage in favour of efforts to co-operate in areas like scientific research and environmental protection. The alternative strategy (which we may loosely describe as the Soviet approach to Arctic co-operation) rests on an extended conception of security, under which economic security, environmental security, and cultural security are inextricably linked with military security, and calls for a comprehensive approach to international co-operation in the Arctic region. Whatever the merits of its individual elements, it seems evident that the six-point plan articulated in Gorbachev's 1987 Murmansk speech is an expression of this broader approach to Arctic co-operation. It is not our purpose to say which of these approaches is more promising or ultimately correct. We wish only to point out that a mutual understanding of the bases of these alternative approaches seems necessary to achieve genuine progress towards enhanced international co-operation in the Arctic.

With regard to specific cases (for instance, the negotiations regarding the IASC), there is also a critical need for political leadership or entrepreneurship to overcome the collective action problems that threaten negotiations even when there is general agreement regarding the availability of joint gains. The role of the political entrepreneur is not to exercise power in the conventional sense, bringing pressure to bear on parties to accept particular forms of co-operation, but to package issues in ways that facilitate agreement, de-emphasize positional bargaining by highlighting the scope of feasible joint gains, and build transnational coalitions of supporters.[22] In our judgment, the lesser Arctic states (with Canada perhaps in the lead) are in the best position to assume this entrepreneurial role with regard to the growth of international co-operation in the Arctic during the near future. Regrettably, we feel compelled to conclude that the entrepreneurial efforts of the lesser Arctic states (with the partial exception of Sweden) in connection with the proposed IASC have not been particularly well conceived or effective. But this does not alter our view that these states must accept an entrepreneurial role if we are to solve the collective action problems arising in connection with the pursuit of international co-operation in the Arctic.

Finally, we note the role of organized groups and even persistent individuals in shaping the terms in which issues relating to international co-operation are framed and shifting the centre of gravity of public debate regarding these issues over time. It is hard to overlook the impact of the World Commission on Environment and Development (the Brundtland Commission), for instance, not only in pushing the issue of sustainable development to the forefront of the international agenda but also in providing the intellectual capital underlying efforts to broaden our thinking about security to encompass economic security, environmental security, and even cultural security.[23] With respect to the Arctic more specifically, similar comments are in order. There is no doubt, for example, that Karl Weyprecht and his associates played a role of enormous importance in launching the International Polar Year of 1882-3 and the growth of transnational co-operation in scientific research that flowed from this undertaking.[24] And it is already clear that a small group of well-placed individuals have been instrumental in stimulating the current negotiations concerning the creation of an International Arctic Science Committee. Those who choose to play such roles must feel comfortable in taking the long view. They cannot hope to supplant political entrepreneurs in solving immediate collective action problems, but they may exercise considerable influence over the longer run by shaping the way in which we think about international co-operation in the Arctic.

Notes

1 United States, National Security Decision Directive 90, April 14, 1983.

2 Joe Clark, secretary of state for external affairs, speech at the Norway-Canada Conference on Circumpolar Issues, Tromsø, Norway, December 1987. The text is printed in Canada, Department of External Affairs, *Disarmament Bulletin* (spring 1988), 22-4.

3 English-language versions of this speech have been printed in a number of places. See, for example, *The North: A Zone of Peace* (Ottawa: USSR Embassy 1988).

4 Communiqué issued following the Moscow summit, May 29-June 2, 1988.

5 *The North: A Zone of Peace.*

6 For a more extended discussion see Oran R. Young, *International Cooperation: Building Regimes for Natural Resources and the Environment* (Ithaca: Cornell University Press 1989), esp. chap. 2.

7 Willy Østreng, *Politics in High Latitudes: The Svalbard Archipelago* (London: Hurst 1977).

8   The regime for northern fur seals dates back to a 1911 agreement among Great Britain (on behalf of Canada), Japan, Russia, and the United States. This regime is currently in limbo, however, as a result of the failure of the United States to ratify a 1984 protocol extending the life of the agreement for another period of time.

9   For background on the proposed International Arctic Science Committee, see E.F. Roots, O. Rogne, and J. Taagholt, "International Communication and Co-ordination in Arctic Science: A Proposal for Action," discussion paper dated November 17, 1987. The committee was indeed established in August 1990. Founding documents are available in *Arctic Research of the United States*, 4 (fall 1990), 65-9.

10   For a general account, consult Russell Hardin, *Collective Action* (Baltimore MD: Johns Hopkins University Press 1982).

11   N.I. Ryzhkov, speech in Oslo, January 15, 1988. The text appears in *Foreign Broadcast Information Service*, Sov-88-011, January 19, 1988, 53.

12   We note with interest, for example, that Denmark and Norway, countries that are certainly on friendly terms in most respects, are about to initiate international litigation over an Arctic issue for the second time in this century.

13   Ryzhkov speech, Oslo, 51.

14   Some of the observations that follow represent the views of Oran Young. While Arkady Cherkasov does not necessarily disagree with these observations, he reserves the right to express separate views on the issues in question.

15   See Roots, Rogne, and Taagholt, 'A Proposal for Action,' for an argument that this problem should be dealt with by creating two distinct entities, an International Arctic Science Committee and an Intergovernmental Forum on Arctic Science Issues.

16   On the organizational structure of the committee, see the document proposed at a meeting in Stockholm in October 1988 and entitled "International Arctic Science Committee: A Proposal for an Organizational Structure."

17   To take a single example, consider the arrangement for the proposed Managers of National Arctic Programmes Group (MNAPG). Under the current plan for the IASC, this group would become an integral part of the committee (though it is clearly a governmental entity). This arrangement differs fundamentally from the analogous relationship between SCAR and the Managers of National Antarctic Programs (MNAP). As the National Science Foundation in the United States has recently put it: "MNAP and SCAR are separate bodies: in briefest terms SCAR frames research that is international in scope, and MNAP considers means of co-ordinating the implementation of meritorious projects." (Division of Polar Programs, *Newsletter,* no. 14, October 12, 1988, 2.)

18   For a seminal account, see Thomas C. Schelling, *The Strategy of Conflict* (Cambridge MA: Harvard University Press 1960).

19   The original arrangements for the SCAR secretariat contained a similar provision for rotation, but the provision has never been exercised, and the secretariat has remained in the United Kingdom.

20   Robert D. Putnam, "Diplomacy and Domestic Politics: The Logic of Two-Level Games," *International Organization*, 42 (summer 1988), 427-60.

21 See Canadian Polar Research Commission (Symons Commission), *The Shield of Achilles: The Report of the Canadian Polar Research Commission Study* (Ottawa: Department of Indian Affairs and Northern Development, May 31, 1988).

22 Oran R. Young, "The Politics of International Regime Formation," *International Organization,* 43 (summer 1989), 349-76.

23 World Commission on Environment and Development, *Our Common Future* (New York: Oxford University Press 1987).

24 On the history of co-operation in Arctic science, see E.F. Roots, "Co-operation in Arctic Science – Background and Prospects," keynote address to the Meeting on International Co-operation in Arctic Science, Stockholm, March 1988.

2

Political-Military Relations among the Ice States: The Conceptual Basis of State Behaviour

Willy Østreng

The militarization of the Arctic has been on the increase, both in geographical and in military-strategic terms. Prior to World War II, the region was a military vacuum, an area of absolutely no strategic utility to anybody. In the 1950s and 1960s the airspace over the Arctic Ocean began to be utilized for strategic deterrence, and today the Arctic's airspace, oceans, and indeed outer space are used for these purposes. This has taken place "in the absence of a concerted effort to check and reverse the process."[1]

Two measures have been proposed to counteract the trend towards militarization of the Arctic: first, "to develop an *integrated conception of Arctic security* in which military requirements are combined with an awareness of the need to act for environmental, economic and social security as well," and, second, to place "new emphasis on opportunities for *non-military co-operation* ... which may over time improve the outlook for confidence-building and arms reduction agreements in the circumpolar North."[2] These proposals seem to be founded on three assumptions: (1) to date, Arctic security has been conceived of solely in military terms; (2) conflict in one issue-area need not preclude co-operation in another – conflict and co-operation are linked to their respective issue-areas not to the relationship between them; and (3) co-operation in non-military areas can help to reduce the extent and content of military-strategic conflict. This paper discusses how these assumptions have manifested themselves in relations among the Arctic states in the postwar years. The aim is to shed light on the interplay between military and non-military issue-areas and to develop a conceptual apparatus concerning Arctic security and co-operation based on past and current political practice, both in the East and in the West.

Two intertwined questions need to be answered to understand the development of the concept of Arctic security after World War II: Which factors originally contributed to the choice of the Arctic as an area of strategic deployment? In what way have relations between military and non-military issue-areas been influenced by this choice?

Factors behind the Militarization of the Arctic

The interplay between and among three factors contributed to the postwar militarization of the Arctic:

- the East-West conflict, which created the political framework for superpower tension and bloc formation;
- developments in military technology, which produced the atom bomb and other nuclear weapons as well as long-range means of delivery; and
- geostrategic conditions, which indicated that the Arctic was a suitable deployment area for strategic, high-technology weapons systems.

While the first two factors were essential conditions for the Arctic being considered as a deployment area at all, the third factor explains why the choice was to fall precisely on this region. For that reason we shall focus our attention on geostrategic conditions.

A distinction can be drawn between two main types of geostrategic factors: *universal* ones, which place the same geographical constraints on the choice of action of several states in a given region; and *state-specific* ones, which place particular geographical constraints on the choice of action of individual states in the same region.

The universal features of the Arctic are well known: the shortest distance between three continents – Asia, Europe, and North America – is over the Arctic Ocean (see double arrow, figure 1). None of the major industrial areas in Europe, in the USSR, in North America, or in Japan lies more than 7,000 kilometres from the North Pole. Or, expressed in another way: 80 per cent of the world's industrial production takes place north of 30° North, while 70 per cent of the world's major cities (population over one million) are located north of 23.5° North. Equally important, the superpowers can almost be said to have a common border in this area, separated only by the narrow gap of the Bering Strait. In the 1950s, it was these geographical facts that suggested the Arctic as a natural route for any nuclear attack using strategic bombers. Only forward bases on the territory of other states could bring the opponent's territory so closely within reach of one's own weapons. The Soviet Union lacked such bases and thus had no alternative to the Arctic. The United States had the option of using both

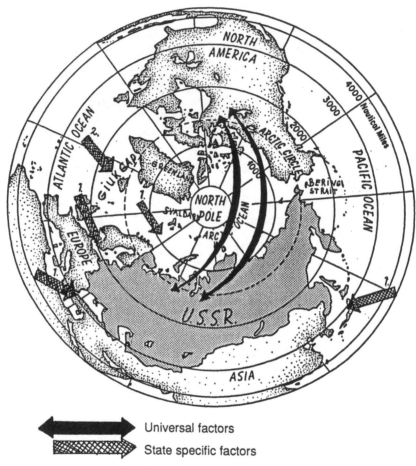

Universal factors

State specific factors

1. the general problem of access to the high seas
2. the GIUK-problem

FIGURE 1. Geostrategic factors contributing to the militarization of the Arctic in the postwar period.

forward bases and Arctic airspace. However, the United States preferred to make use of the Arctic because bases on the territory of other states could, depending on the political climate, be lost at any time. Polar attack routes were also inevitable because intercontinental ballistic missiles (ICBMs) follow great circles and thus, for many launch and attack points in the United States and the USSR, necessarily traverse the Arctic. In this way, geography laid almost equal constraints on both sides in their choice of strategy.

The state-specific factors, however, are solely a reflection of Soviet aspirations to be a naval power. As a land power, the Soviet Union suffers from clear geographical restrictions in its access to the high seas (arrow 1, figure 1). All of its fleets – the Baltic, the Northern, the Black Sea, and in part the Pacific – are dependent on passing through straits or narrow sea areas to proceed from home territory into the high seas, and vice versa. All these straits are controlled by powers or constellations with a tradition of tense relations with the Soviet Union. The Kremlin has historical experience to show how several of these straits have been closed to passage in wartime. The sole exception is the passage between Svalbard and northern Norway, which, even during the last world war, was not blocked for any appreciable period, despite major German efforts to do so. Geographically speaking, this passage is considerably wider than the others – 345 nautical miles (nm); in terms of climatic conditions it is also preferable because it remains ice-free throughout the year; and in politico-military terms it appears particularly attractive because its northern limit, Svalbard, is partly demilitarized, while its southern side, mainland Norway, is subject to self-imposed military restrictions (for example, on base and nuclear policy).[3]

Against this background, then, the Northern Fleet was gradually developed to become the most modern and potent of the Soviet fleets. Today it ranks second to none with regard to strategic retaliatory capability. At its disposal are 66 per cent of the USSR's nuclear-powered ballistic-missile-firing submarines (SSBNs), 67 per cent of its submarine-launched ballistic missiles (SLBMs), 76 per cent of its warheads, and 73 per cent of the megatonnage available to each fleet.[4] However, the country's general geographical handicap was to catch up with this fleet as well.

In the late 1960s and early 1970s, sea-based deterrence in the Northern Fleet was countered by Soviet Yankee-class submarines, equipped with short-range missiles. To reach targets in the United States, these vessels would have to sail through the GIUK gap between Greenland, Iceland, and the United Kingdom and then assume positions off the United States east coast (arrow 2, figure 1). However, the United States practised a barrier strategy in this area so as to be able to intercept Soviet submarines in transit in time of war. It was vital for the Soviet Union to counteract this threat because it affected its own retaliatory capability as well as the credibility of the balance of terror. The response came in 1972 with Soviet deployment of the first Delta-class submarine, equipped with SSN-8 missiles with a range of 4,300 nm. From then on, Delta submarines were capable of striking any target in Europe, North America, and China from a launch position in Arctic waters. By stationing its Delta and later Typhoon submarines north of the GIUK gap and under the polar ice, the Soviet Union avoided Western countermeasures that could cripple its strategic combat potential.[5]

The withdrawal of the Northern Fleet's strategic forces to Arctic waters, *the rear deployment strategy*, led the United States to follow suit and introduce military countermeasures in the same waters. In this way, the Arctic has gradually been transformed from a *military vacuum* prior to World War II, to a *military flank* in the 1950-70 period, and a *military front* in the 1980s.[6]

Thus, at an early stage, military necessity and geographical constraints marked the Arctic as a potential deployment area for strategic bombers and ICBMs. Here the universal geostrategic factors were equally relevant for both the United States and the USSR. It was the Soviet Union's state-specific problems as a naval power which led to diversification in the militarization of the region – first, with the need to raise the status of the Northern Fleet and its importance in relation to the other Soviet fleets and, second, with the need to use Arctic waters as a deployment area for SSBNs. Here political and military choices have had to be adjusted to an unchanging geographical reality. Geographical constraints have thus indicated that the Arctic, given the prevailing political and military-technological circumstances, was predestined for militarization. As a counter-factual hypothesis it may be maintained that the superpowers had no alternative but to put the region's geographical advantages to military use. Viewed in this light, it seems reasonable to conclude that any change in the situation in the Arctic could come about only as a result of fundamental changes in East-West relations, which long precluded the possibility of non-military co-operation.

Non-Military Issue-Areas in a Militarized Region, 1945-70

Non-military issue-areas in the Arctic may be split into two categories: *local* and *international*.

Local issue-areas are attended to only to a limited extent and are maintained to satisfy regional or national needs. Activity in such issue-areas touches the interests of other states only marginally, if indeed at all, and has little or no importance across national borders. Examples of such issue-areas include use of the Northeast and Northwest Passages, supplies to local outposts, mineral production in non-disputed national territories, and administrative measures concerning native settlements. The majority of the activities carried out by states in the Arctic region during the years 1945-70 involved such local interests. This meant that there was little overlap between the interests of the parties and thus only a marginal need for co-operation.

The second type of issue-area can be termed *international* in the sense that several states carry on the same type of activity and collectively either are affected by or have an interest in the others' involvement. Such issue-areas cut across national borders and thus provide a potential point of departure for co-operation. Up to 1970, this category in the Arctic region was concerned mainly with research efforts. Research was carried on by all, and scientists on both sides of the East-West divide expressed a desire for co-operation.[7] Among researchers there was the widespread belief that "science and scientists have a kind of objectivity which is congenial to co-operation. The nature of science is not only conducive to co-operation, but indeed demands it, for no man, no nation, has a monopoly of science."[8] Viewed thus, only two fields of activity in the Arctic could be termed *international* in this period – science and military strategy. Let us take a closer look at the relationship between them.

In the course of the 1950s the Arctic Ocean became an area of confrontation in the East-West conflict – a development which placed constraints on scientists. The few foreign scientists who carried out field studies in the far north of Canada during the 1950s and 1960s, for instance, were subject to security restrictions in their work. Similar restrictions were in place in Alaska and on Greenland.[9] The Soviet government took even more drastic measures, totally excluding foreign researchers from its northernmost regions. As Trevor Lloyd describes it: "It must be acknowledged that there has been a definite barrier between the scientists of the Soviet Union and associated countries and other countries. There has been no easy interchange between Western group members and the rest ... Although Polish and Czechoslovak scientists have worked with Soviet scientists in Antarctica, there is no record of this being done in the North, whether in the Soviet Arctic or elsewhere. The Soviet Arctic has not yet been opened to Western scientists, although a few individuals have made short visits there."[10]

This policy of exclusion applied not only to Soviet land areas but to its waters as well. When, on August 5, 1960, the Soviet Union extended its territorial waters to 12 nm, it declared that foreign vessels were "prohibited from carrying out hydrographic work and research in Soviet territorial and internal waters."[11] In addition, long before the 1982 Convention on the Law of the Sea was signed, Soviet authorities required foreign scientists wishing to work within the country's 200-mile zone to apply for permission to do so.[12] Furthermore, at an early stage, Soviet authorities prohibited their own scientists from participating in international organizations for Arctic research.

The sole area in the Arctic where all researchers have enjoyed somewhat the same freedom of research throughout the entire postwar period is on Svalbard. Here it has been Norwegian policy, in line with the spirit of the Svalbard Treaty of 1920, to offer unimpeded access and equal working opportunities to researchers of all political colorations.[13]

Everywhere else in the Arctic, research was to develop rapidly in a nationalist, somewhat chauvinistic direction. Research was organized mainly under the auspices of *national regimes,* only rarely *bi-nationally,* and even more rarely *multinationally* (for example, the International Geophysical Year of 1957-8). Prior to the IGY, most American Arctic research was initiated and funded by military authorities; after the IGY more research took place for civilian purposes, but military-strategic interests still carried great weight. Most probably, the same can be said for the Soviet Union. In other words, research served mainly military ends. It was used and consciously exploited in the superpower race to achieve military superiority in the region.

This trend reduced the possibilities of establishing co-operation across the East-West divide. After all, no one would wish to share with the enemy research results which might be put to counter-use in case of war. Nor would it be desirable, as a starting point for co-operative activity, to reveal to the opponent how much one knows, not to mention one's weaknesses. Likewise, each side would be wary of supplying the opponent with information which might promote its interests in the region. And politicians viewed any possible co-operation as something that might well lead to such undesirable results. Thus, the desire of researchers for scientific co-operation ran aground on the reef of politics. Scientists were mobilized for military purposes and were therefore unable to realize their own wishes for co-operation in basic research.[14]

In addition to the need of the state for applied knowledge, the co-option of scientists to a particular side in the Cold War arose from the decidedly *hegemonic* nature of the East-West conflict during this period. That is, it was a conflict between competing political systems – in ideological as well as material terms – which develops cumulatively, in that conflict in one

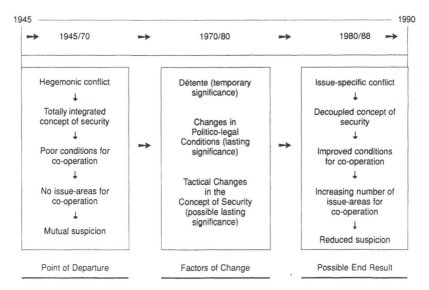

FIGURE 2. Schematic outline of the developments of conditions for scientific co-operation in the Arctic in light of security interests.

area automatically spills over into others. Purely hegemonic conflicts do not permit individual issue-areas to be kept outside the conflict realm; conflict is extended to embrace the entire range of interests and all points of contact between the parties. In times of crisis, hegemonic conflicts demand unambiguous national answers to what are interpreted as challenges from the adversary. No sector or segment, not even research, can free itself totally from conflicts of this type. Everything is included: the state, various sectors of activity, and individuals. The requirement of loyalty is absolute. The state has control of all sectors and formulates whatever actions are considered necessary to pursue the conflict. And these responses also bind the actions and behaviour of those actors whose own interests and priorities favour co-operation across national borders.

The hegemonic features of the Cold War contributed at an early stage to the creation of a *fully integrated multidimensional security concept for the Arctic*. The linkage between military and non-military fields became almost absolute, with few or no distinctions made between the various issue-areas.

All activity in the region became an expression of the conflict between the "good guys" and the "bad guys," between East and West. Conflict in one issue-area largely turned into conflict in others as well. Or, put differently, the conflict arose not primarily in the individual issue-areas of possible activity, but from the relations between the protagonists. This was true not only with regard to research but also in regard to various local issue-areas with an international element. For instance, there were no dealings between people from Alaska and those from the Chukotsky Peninsula just across the Bering Strait. Even those with close family on the other side of the strait were not allowed to visit each other.[15] The use of the Northern Sea Route was in practice closed to Western transit throughout this entire period.[16] However, there were certain exceptions to this general rule, such as the limited degree of fisheries co-operation which had gone on between Norway and Russia and then the USSR off the coast of Finnmark ever since 1830.[17] However, such examples carry little weight because they are few, are of relatively little importance, and attract attention solely because they are departures from the rule.

Development of the Security Concept, 1970-80

With the spirit of détente in the 1970s, there were more and more indications that the power and intensity of the hegemonic conflict was weakening. Linkages between military and non-military issues became less pronounced, and some cautious attempts at co-operative civilian ventures were initiated. For example, in 1972 a co-operative agreement was signed between the United States and the USSR on environmental protection in which the Arctic was included. The policy of détente was a contributory factor here. However, this was to have the reverse effect in the second half of the 1970s, when détente foundered. Two conditions helped to further the trends introduced by détente: (1) changes in the politico-legal conditions which strongly *suggested*, and even dictated, international co-operation; and (2) changes in integrated thinking on Arctic security which *increased* the number of potential co-operative issue-areas.

Changes in Politico-Legal Conditions
The Third United Nations Conference on the Law of the Sea (UNCLOS III), convened in 1973 after six years of preparation in the Committee for the Sea-Bed, was instrumental in the changes in politico-legal conditions. As early as in 1975, broad international consensus had been achieved concerning the right of coastal states to establish 200-mile economic zones (EEZs) and to administer the living and mineral resources in those zones. Such nationalization did not mean that the need for international co-operation ceased; it only changed in character. For example, an oil deposit

straddling the border between two countries' continental shelves will have to be exploited jointly, in order that both may extract their rightful share of the deposit. The same applies to the utilization of living resources.

This development was also to have consequences for co-operation in the Arctic's marginal seas. For instance, Norway and the Soviet Union have further developed their co-operation in the Barents Sea: in 1975 they established a joint fisheries commission; in the following year co-operation was expanded to include a new agreement, which in 1978 was further expanded through the so-called Grey Zone Agreement. The background for these arrangements was that the parties anticipated that the 200-mile zones would become a major element of the future law of the sea and that there would be no way of avoiding the formation of some kind of joint administration for the resources of the Barents Sea.[18] In 1977, both parties had established EEZs, without having agreed on a dividing line between the zones or on the shelf. This created problems for fishery activities in the area. The Grey Zone Agreement, which runs for one year at a time, therefore established a joint utilization zone for fishing in the disputed area. This arrangement has, in the main, functioned well.[19] In this connection, it is interesting that although the parties have not been able to agree on a dividing line because of security reasons amongst other things, they nevertheless manage to co-operate successfully on the non-military issue of fisheries administration. Here a non-military co-operative need has been decoupled from the demands of security policy. And in the Arctic this is something new, forced into being through changes in the politico-legal conditions following UNCLOS III.

Changes in Integrated Thinking on Arctic Security

On October 1, 1987, Mikhail Gorbachev gave a speech in Murmansk in which he signalled a desire to distinguish more sharply between military and non-military issue-areas in the Arctic. The aim was to bring about "a radical lowering of the confrontation level in the area. Let the northern part of the globe, the Arctic, become a zone of peace. Let the North Pole become a pole of peace."[20] The Murmansk initiative, consisting of six points, covered both military and non-military issues. Gorbachev spoke in favour of co-operation in the exploitation of natural resources and the establishment of a unified energy programme for the northern areas. Furthermore, he invited Norway and Canada to participate in joint ventures and projects for the exploitation of oil and gas on the northern Soviet continental shelf. Other states, too, were invited to negotiate such co-operative ventures. Moreover, emphasis was placed on co-operation on environmental issues and preparation of a common plan for protection of the Arctic environment. Additionally, the Northern Sea Route is, under certain conditions, to be placed at the disposal of foreign ships, which were offered the assistance of Soviet icebreakers. On all these points, Gorbachev decoupled non-military issues from the integrated concept of Arctic security which had dominated the postwar period.

With respect to research, a break was signalled with former policies. First of all, the importance of international co-operation was stressed, as was the need for an exchange of scientific experience in the Arctic. Furthermore, Gorbachev spoke in favour of adjacent states coming together at an international conference to co-ordinate future research and discuss the establishment of an Arctic research council. (This conference took place in Leningrad in December 1988.) The departure from the previous period is clear: the pursuit of "national self-sufficiency" is to be supplemented by international co-operation and co-ordination; national organization is to be supplemented by an international research council; secrecy is to be reduced through the exchange of Arctic research experience. There is much to indicate that Gorbachev was in earnest concerning these proposals.

To the amazement of many observers, the Soviet Union gave its approval to the 1986 initiative of the Scientific Committee on Antarctic Research (SCAR) to elucidate the possibilities for future scientific co-operation in the North. The resulting report favours the establishment of a non-governmental International Arctic Science Committee (IASC) to "promote international co-operation in scientific research in Arctic areas." It is further proposed that there be established an Intergovernmental Forum on Arctic Science Issues where "representatives of governments should discuss the feasibility of establishing a system of regular, structured discussions and liaison on Arctic science matters."[21]

It would appear that the Kremlin has also modified its policy of denying Western researchers access to Soviet soil. Both the Canada-USSR Arctic Science Exchange Programme of 1984 and the Norwegian-Soviet Agreement Concerning Technical-Scientific Co-operation on Exploration of the Arctic and the Northern Areas of 1988 provide for the establishment of co-operation which is to be balanced in terms of scholarly issues and geography. The parties are to take part in field studies on each other's territory.

These changes are especially interesting as they have come at a time when the Kremlin would, or so one might suppose, in fact have more to protect against prying Western eyes than ever before – not least in connection with the rear deployment strategy for Soviet SSBNs.[22] In the agreement with Norway, the Soviet State Committee for Science and Technology (GKNT) agreed that joint oceanographic studies are to be carried out in the waters between Franz Josefs Land and Svalbard and between Greenland and Svalbard. These are areas which, as early as the 1960s, were indicated in the Soviet media as routes for Northern Fleet submarines in transit between their bases on the Kola Peninsula and the Arctic Ocean.[23] When one recalls that naval strategists have claimed that "oceanography and its contribution to the knowledge of the environment are more important to undersea warfare than to any other warfare area,"[24] then it would certainly appear that such research co-operation in the North with Norway would run counter to Soviet security interests.

However, such a conclusion is somewhat premature, not least as concerns the waters between Franz Josefs Land and Svalbard. Here the ocean is shallow, the incidence of large submerged icebergs is high, and the seabed is characterized by depressions that lack an outlet to deep-sea areas. Under such conditions, submarines run the risk of becoming trapped between ice and seabed with no possibility of escape – the "valley of death" problem. Only small submarines, like those at the disposal of the Northern Fleet in the early 1960s, could utilize such a route, and only on an irregular basis. Today's SSBNs, which are up to 170 metres long and 28 metres high, have operational requirements of quite another kind.[25]

Thus, oceanographic studies in this area are more in the nature of basic than of applied research. Still, one should not underestimate the importance of basic research to military interests. As one United States naval commander stated: "Practical-minded naval officers often find difficulty in connecting basic research programs with fleet capabilities ... Admittedly, the connection often requires considerable imagination, but for the good of the Navy, we should not restrict our imaginative powers only to the subjects with which we are familiar. Progress is based on obtaining new knowledge, and this means probing the unknown. If a thing is truly unknown, its relations to such things as warfare capabilities must also be unknown."[26] Commanders of the Soviet Northern Fleet would, in all probability, agree with this view. Thus, oceanographic co-operation between the USSR and Norway cannot automatically be assumed to lack any naval strategic relevance. Such co-operation would certainly have been inconceivable during the 1945-80 period.

The straits between Svalbard and Greenland constitute one of the main sea routes for Soviet SSBNs on their way northwards to the Arctic Ocean and southwards to the Norwegian Sea. Oceanographic research co-operation across the East-West divide in this area can therefore be seen as a military risk. There is, however, a military advantage in getting to know what your opponent knows and thinks in areas of strategic relevance to both sides. From this perspective, co-operation becomes a means of obtaining access to the opponent's knowledge and insight – if you can't beat him, join him! Or, it may be that the Kremlin is consciously expanding the range of themes for research co-operation in order to achieve greater credibility for its rapprochement policies. Thus, co-operation is considered acceptable because the political gains are seen to outweigh the military disadvantages. No matter what the explanation may be, Moscow has taken a step in the direction of enlarging the framework for scientific co-operation with Western countries. This shows that political will and changes in political circumstances can in themselves provide the preconditions for international scientific co-operation, even in issue-areas formerly reserved for applied research under national auspices. However, there will always be a limit to how far the authorities can go in accepting research themes as the subject of international co-operation. The need will remain for privileged information meant solely for national use. What politicians can do is adjust these limits, either in a more liberal or in a more restrictive direction. What now appears to be happening on the Soviet side is an adjustment in a more liberal direction.

These changes indicate that the older conception of "totally integrated Arctic security" is breaking up, at least for those issue-areas which, in the strictly military sense, do not concern the military security of the state. If this process continues, the Kremlin will be left with a decoupled concept of security around a military strategic core. In other words, it seems that the period of meshing military with non-military issue-areas may be coming to an end in the Soviet Union. The Kremlin would seem to be endeavouring to identify issue-areas where the joint gains can be increased through co-operation and where the nature of the issue-area itself defines whether or not it is desirable to join forces with other nations. This is a functional approach in line with the general security thinking of Gorbachev. Just a few months after assuming power he voiced profound concern about the security of the USSR but highlighted the *economic* rather than the strictly *military* aspects of the danger. In his view, security was increasingly becoming a problem that could be resolved only by political means. The essence of his critique was that the Brezhnev leadership "had failed to gain the security benefits available through flexible diplomacy and compromise."[27] Decoupling became a prime instrument of Gorbachev's new policy, not only between military and non-military issue-areas, but also within the military field. In the course of 1987 he decoupled the issue of intermediate-range forces from the Strategic Defense Initiative and the talks on intermediate-range forces from those on strategic offensive and defensive arms. The heart of the "new political thinking" in the USSR now seems to be "the priority of common human values over class values in the nuclear age."[28]

What we are witnessing is by no means a repudiation of security as a comprehensive concept, but a *shift of approach* with regard to the *level of integration* between military and non-military issue-areas. By decoupling the two sets of issue-areas, non-military security may be achieved by employing, among other means, the co-operative potential of individual fields. This is consistent with and a corollary of the *perestroika* policy. Consequently, military conflict no longer seems to be the dominant factor in defining the content and pace of achieving non-military security. In this approach, comprehensive security may be achieved *asymmetrically*, in that the level of security in individual issue-areas at any one time may vary. However, by moving away from an *integrated* to a *comprehensive, decoupled* concept of security, the overall security of the USSR may be enhanced.

The indications are that the Soviet Union would appear to be consciously seeking to distinguish between military and non-military issues in its security policies. The non-military sphere is increasing; the military is being slimmed down. Whether this development will serve to improve the conditions for East-West co-operation will depend, among other things, on the Western concept of security.

Western Security Concepts

During World War II, the vice-president of the United States proposed that his country should lead the way in establishing an "Arctic Treaty" for, inter alia, scientific exploration and co-operation among the Arctic states.[29] However, the Cold War prevented the implementation of this proposal. During the IGY, time-limited co-operation was initiated in the region, but it was not until the early 1970s that the Western states again took serious initiatives in pursuit of co-operation with the USSR. In 1970, for example, the United States invited several nations to participate in "The Arctic Ice Dynamics Joint Experiment" (Aidjex), an ambitious project for studying thermal balances and the relationship between ice cover and atmosphere. However, this project was not warmly received; only two countries, Canada and Japan, accepted the invitation.[30] The Soviet Union refused because, among other things, "the economic and scientific reasons for investigating the Arctic Ocean are intertwined with military ones, which have elicited great interest on the part of the US Navy."[31] Two years later, however, Norway took the initiative on negotiations for a polar bear agreement between the United States, Canada, Denmark, the USSR, and Norway. The implementation of this agreement, which was signed in 1973, helps to illustrate the attitudes to co-operation held by the various parties. Among the Western signatories, the exchange of information has been profuse, and in line with the letter and spirit of the agreement. By contrast, the Soviet contribution has been so negligible as to give rise to the following Western reaction: "Whether only little research has been carried out in the Soviet Union, or whether the data exchange is being hampered by governmental red tape, it is difficult to say."[32]

Various co-operative initiatives came from the West in the course of the 1970s, and all of them were either rejected or accepted and implemented by the USSR only with reluctance. By the 1980s, however, the Soviet Union had begun to take the initiative, seeking to expand the range of co-operation and inviting increased economic, environmental, and other co-operation in the North. The West, while maintaining its open attitude to such co-operation, became less active. Against a background of Soviet invitations in the mid-1980s, the Norwegian government decided "to give the go-ahead to Norwegian firms to seek commercially viable ventures on non-disputed sections of the Soviet shelf."[33] Later, the Norwegian authorities also consented to letting Norwegian interests pursue involvements in the mining industry on the Kola Peninsula. West German and Finnish companies have also shown an interest in these ventures. In terms of research, it is worth noting that representatives from the United States, Canada, Denmark, Sweden, Finland, Iceland, and Norway have all supported the proposal to establish an IASC. Thus, there is reason to maintain that the Western Arctic states have remained open to functional co-operation in non-military issue-areas, especially research, throughout the past twenty years.

The interesting point about these examples is that they show how these Western states started amending their security concept a good ten years before the Kremlin did. The process proceeded along the lines later followed by the Soviet Union: non-military issues are identified and then peeled away and removed from those interests defined as pertaining to military security. Just how far these states, especially the United States, have advanced in this process, and how far they are willing to move in this direction, remains to be seen. The main point is that the tendency is the same in both East and West: towards decoupling the concept of Arctic security. This parallelism provides improved conditions for co-operation because the states are, during this process, constantly releasing new issue-areas for co-operative efforts.

In other words, the means by which to "check and reverse the militarization process" in the Arctic appears not to be "an integrated conception of Arctic security." Our discussion has shown that, on the contrary, to be in line with contemporary endeavours to co-operate in non-military issue-areas, the need is rather for a *comprehensive, decoupled conception* of Arctic security. It is this development which has, for the first time in the postwar period, laid a realistic foundation for co-operation. As long as military and non-military issues are combined into an integrated security concept, there is always the risk of militarizing non-military issues, as indeed happened during the years between 1945 and 1980. All the Arctic states now find themselves in a process of moving away from a *totally integrated hegemonic conflict* to a differentiated situation in which military-strategic conflict will come to exist side by side with non-military co-operation. The question then becomes whether this non-military co-operation can achieve dimensions and content sufficient to contribute to reducing and checking the continuing militarization of the region. In other words, can it be expected that the positive effects of non-military co-operation will spill over into the military-strategic conflict, and tone it down?

Non-Military Co-operation as a
Means of Regulating Strategic Conflict

Developments in the Arctic have not yet advanced far enough for us to be able to state whether co-operation in non-military issue-areas can help reduce the extent and content of the military-strategic conflict in the region. The quintessence of the policies of the Arctic states during the 1970s and 1980s has, however, been to distinguish sensitive areas from non-sensitive ones, so as to pave the way for co-operative efforts. There has been a certain amount of experience to show that co-operation in non-sensitive areas in the polar regions has yielded positive results, in the sense of reducing conflict between the parties.

In the Antarctic, conflict potential throughout the postwar years has remained bound up with unresolved sovereignty claims. Nevertheless, the states involved have managed to develop political and scientific co-operation that has stood as a model for the establishment of co-operation in other regions.[34] Such co-operation in the southern polar areas began in a modest way, dealing with issues that could not be seen as threatening sovereignty interests. In 1960, the parties were working together on themes that had no bearing whatsoever on matters of jurisdiction: for example, the registering of historical sites. By 1988, they were able to agree on the conditions for exploitation of mineral resources which had been consciously set aside in 1958 during negotiations concerning the Antarctic Treaty of 1959. This sequence of events demonstrates that it is possible today to co-operate on subjects which formerly could well have upset the co-operative "apple cart." How has this been brought about?

The fact is that, during the course of long-term co-operative efforts, the parties have gained so much that the costs of breaking off have come to exceed the costs of continuing. In other words, long-term co-operation on non-controversial issues seems to increase the tolerance limits for how sensitive an issue may be and still be taken up between the parties. What happened in the Antarctic was that co-operation promoted mutual interests rather than threatened particular ones. This increased confidence and trust between the participants in such a way that growth in trust led to growth in co-operation.[35] Experience from the South thus describes the process currently under way in the North: issues of conflict are gradually being reduced, while the range of possible areas of co-operation is on the increase.

The report presented by the SCAR group concerning the establishment of an IASC put it in this way: "The new developments should support national policies of Arctic nations with regard to Arctic science, and at the same time should help to increase international co-operation and communication, and facilitate the growth and exchange of scientific knowledge on a non-national basis."[36] This means that the parties will have to find research themes which meet both these criteria. In his Murmansk speech, Gorbachev identified aboriginal culture as one suitable theme for research co-operation. In the agreement between Canada and the USSR, the parties agreed to work together in four main areas: geosciences and Arctic petroleum; northern environment; northern construction; ethnography and education. The Soviet-Norwegian agreement defines biology, geology, oceanography, and geophysics as themes for co-operation. American scientists have noted that it is possible to work with their Soviet colleagues on such non-controversial issues as anthropology, archaeology, health, environmental protection, geophysics, permafrost, and wildlife.[37] With the possible exception of oceanography, all these are areas which may prove suitable for cautious expansion of pan-Arctic co-operation in the years to come.

The implementation of such a philosophy of co-operation requires step-by-step change, with the gradual expansion of co-operation to embrace more and more non-controversial issue-areas. This is quite in line with the current efforts of Arctic states to *decouple* the concept of security.

Conclusions

We began by suggesting that "an integrated conception of Arctic security" might provide a remedy for the militarization of the Arctic. Governments in both East and West would seem, however, to favour a "comprehensive decoupled conception of Arctic security," if their recent actions are any guide to their thinking. This policy seems to be yielding results, whereas a variant of the former (pursued in the period from 1945 to 1970/80) failed to show any results in terms of co-operation. Experience to date would indicate that a comprehensive decoupled security concept creates the preconditions needed to prevent conflict in one issue-area from affecting co-operation in another. Furthermore, the Antarctic experience shows that co-operation can be established and developed in those issue-areas which can be isolated from the conflict area. Whether this gradual change can succeed in dismantling or even curbing the conflict itself remains to be seen.

Notes

1 "International Conference on Arctic Co-operation," note on the purpose, problem, approach of the conference, Science for Peace, University College, University of Toronto, November 1987, 1.
2 Ibid. Emphasis added.
3 Willy Østreng, *Politics in High Latitudes: The Svalbard Archipelago* (Montreal: McGill-Queen's University Press 1978), 44-60.
4 Thomas Ries, *The Soviet Operational Command Structure and its Application to Fennoscandia,* NUPI Report (Oslo: Norwegian Institute of International Affairs, August 20, 1986), 61-2.
5 Willy Østreng, *The Soviet Union in Arctic Waters,* Occasional Paper 36 (Honolulu: Law of the Sea Institute 1987), 27-41.
6 Ibid., 43-5.
7 Willy Østreng, "Polar Science and Politics: Close Twins or Opposite Poles in International Co-operation?" in Steinar Andresen and Willy Østreng, eds.,

International Resource Management: The Role of Science and Politics (London and New York: Belhaven Press 1989), 88-114.

8   Hugh Odishaw, "International Co-operation," *Science and Technology*, unnumbered and undated, in the archives of the Fridtjof Nansen Institute, 28.

9   Trevor Lloyd, "International Co-operation in Arctic Science and Disarmament," mimeographed article in the library of the Canadian Institute of International Affairs, Toronto, March 1969.

10   Ibid.

11   William E. Butler, *The Soviet Union and the Law of the Sea* (Baltimore MD: Johns Hopkins University Press 1971), 83.

12   Tore Gjelsvik, "Science and Politics in Polar Areas," mimeographed article in the archives of the Fridtjof Nansen Institute, October 1985, 6-7.

13   Østreng, *Politics in High Latitudes*.

14   Østreng, *Soviet Union in Arctic Waters*.

15   T. Armstrong, G. Rogers, and G. Rowley, *The Circumpolar North* (London: Methuen 1978), 262.

16   There is one exception to this rule, and that was the offer of the Soviet government in 1967 to foreign shipowners to use the Northeast Passage on the condition that a fee was paid for Soviet services. Later the offer was withdrawn, probably due to the Six-Day War in the Middle East and the closure of the Suez Canal. The offer most likely was issued because of a pressing need for hard currency.

17   Brit Fløistad, *Hovedlinjene i utformingen av norsk sjøgrensepolitikk etter 1945, Interesseavveiningen: nasjonale og internasjonale*, Study R:022 (Lysaker: Fridtjof Nansen Institute 1982), 45.

18   Brit Fløistad, *Fish and Foreign Policy: Norway's Fisheries Relations with Other Countries in the Barents Sea, the Norwegian Sea and the North Sea*, Study R:005-1987 (Lysaker: Fridtjof Nansen Institute 1988), 31-73.

19   Willy Østreng, "Soviet-Norwegian Relations in the Arctic," *International Journal*, 39 (autumn 1984), 866-87.

20   For the Gorbachev speech, see appendix to *Sovjet-nytt*, no 26 (1987), 11.

21   E.F. Roots, O. Rogne, and J. Taagholt, "International Communication and Co-ordination in Arctic Science: A Proposal for Action," discussion paper dated November 17, 1987.

22   Willy Østreng, "The Barents Sea in Soviet Rear-Deployment Strategy," article in the archives of the Fridtjof Nansen Institute.

23   Willy Østreng, *Polhavet i internasjonal politikk*, study AA: H012 (Lysaker: Fridtjof Nansen Institute 1978), 178-209.

24   Charles Bishop, "Oceanography in Naval Warfare," *US Naval Institute Proceedings*, 85 (no 5, 1959), 82.

25   Helge Ole Bergesen, Arild Moe, and Willy Østreng, *Soviet Oil and Security Interests in the Barents Sea* (London: Pinter 1987), 79-83.

26   Bishop, "Oceanography in Naval Warfare."

27   Bruce Parrott, "Soviet National Security under Gorbachev," *Problems of Communism*, 37 (November-December 1988), 10.

28   For an excellent account of the security thinking of the Gorbachev regime, see Parrott, ibid.

29 Herman Pollack and Peter Anderson, "United States Policy for the Arctic," *Arctic Bulletin*, 1 (no 3, 1973).

30 *Aidjex Bulletin*, no 15 (August 1972).

31 A.F. Treshnikov, E. Borisenkov, N.A. Volkov, and E.G. Nikiforov, "The American Arctic Ice Dynamics Joint Experiment Project," in A.F. Treshnikov, *Problems of the Arctic and Antarctic* (Leningrad), 38 (1971).

32 Gjelsvik, "Science and Politics."

33 Nils Morten Udgaard, "Sovjetunionen som faktor i norsk sikkerhetspolitikk," *Norsk Statsvitenskapelig Tidsskrift*, no 1 (1985), 52.

34 Rodney W. Johnson and Philip M. Smith, "Antarctic Research and Lunar Exploration," in *Advances in Space Science and Technology*, 10 (1969), New York. See also: Gunnar Skagestad, "The Frozen Frontier: Models for International Cooperation," *Cooperation and Conflict*, 10 (no 3, 1975), 167-87.

35 Østreng, "Polar Science and Politics."

36 Roots, Rogne, and Taagholt, 'A Proposal for Action,' 15.

37 A.L. Washburn and Gunther Weller, "Arctic Research and National Interest," *Science*, August 8, 1986, 637.

3

Arctic Security

The briefing paper reproduced below was prepared by the Arms Control and Disarmament Division of the Department of External Affairs and International Trade in the Government of Canada and was released in December 1991 – Ed.

Issue

How best to promote peace and security in the Arctic.

Background

During the past several years, the Soviet Union has made a number of proposals related to security in the North. Perhaps the best-known are those made at Murmansk by Soviet leader Mikhail Gorbachev on October 1, 1987. These proposals (elaborated by Prime Minister Ryzhkov in a speech in Oslo on January 14, 1988) included the following:
- the creation of a Nuclear-Weapon-Free Zone (NWFZ) in Northern Europe;
- consultations between NATO and the Warsaw Pact on reducing naval activity in the Baltic, North, Norwegian and Greenland Seas;
- a meeting of "interested states" to consider banning naval exercises and concentration in agreed international straits and their approaches (i.e., the English Channel, Baltic Straits, Denmark Strait and the area between Iceland, the Faeroes and Scandinavia), important North Atlantic shipping lanes, and areas of intensive seasonal fisheries;
- a NATO-Warsaw Pact "Experts Meeting" to discuss maritime confidence-building measures in the Baltic, North, Norwegian[,] Greenland and Barents Seas;
- the banning of anti-submarine activity in the Northern and Western Atlantic;
- limiting NATO-Warsaw Pact major naval exercises in specified areas (not defined) to once every two years.

The Canadian government received no formal proposals from the USSR to follow up these ideas. Then Secretary of State for External

Affairs Joe Clark did, however, respond to the Murmansk speech in his address to the Norway-Canada Conference on Circumpolar Issues at Tromso, Norway[,] on December 9, 1987, and again in remarks at Carleton University in Ottawa on October 18, 1988. Among other things, he pointed out that proposals to declare the North a NWFZ or to restrict naval movements in areas such as the Norwegian Sea overlook the fact that the nuclear weapons threat is global, not regional. Such measures would do nothing to reduce the threat from these weapons and could be destabilizing for other regions. He also noted that Mr Gorbachev's proposals focused primarily on the Northern Atlantic and Western Arctic, without involving the Barents Sea or other waters adjacent to the USSR, and that the Soviet Union is the only country with major military deployments in the Arctic. Mr Clark emphasized that in Canada's view, the best prospects for progress toward enhanced security in the Arctic lay in supporting the negotiations then underway in Geneva on nuclear arms and in Vienna on conventional arms.

Renewed Soviet interest in Northern security was evidenced during a visit to Helsinki by Mr Gorbachev in October 1989. There he suggested that the USSR was prepared to come to an agreement with all of the nuclear powers and the Baltic states on effective guarantees for the nuclear-free status of the Baltic Sea. At the same time, he announced that the Soviet Union intended to unilaterally cut its nuclear forces in the Baltic, including several submarines. In May and October 1990, the USSR again proposed a Baltic NWFZ.

During Prime Minister Mulroney's visit to the Soviet Union at the end of November 1989, Soviet Foreign Minister Eduard Shevardnadze said that his government was prepared to declare that Soviet submarines would not enter the waters of the Canadian Arctic archipelago. Canada welcomed the declaration. At the same time, in private discussions with the Secretary of State for External Affairs, Mr Shevardnadze made very clear that he understood the preference for conducting any negotiations – as opposed to discussions – on Arctic security matters on an East-West basis. The Prime Minister and Mr Gorbachev agreed that Mr Shevardnadze and Mr Clark would explore further whether there were any Arctic security matters that could usefully be discussed between Canada and the Soviet Union. They also agreed that Canada and the USSR would consult regularly on Arctic questions.

As a result, a senior-level Soviet delegation visited Ottawa in mid-June 1990 for broad-ranging consultations with Canadian officials on Arctic cooperation. The question of arms control and disarmament was on the agenda and a useful discussion was held.

In addition to the Soviet Union, several Canadian non-governmental organizations (NGOs) have called for specific Arctic security measures. For example, the report of a non-governmental Panel on Arctic Arms Control released by the Canadian Centre for Arms Control and Disarmament (CCACD) in October 1989 proposed *inter alia*: the establishment of a Central Arctic demilitarized zone; Arctic "Open Skies" and other aerial confidence-building measures; limits on nuclear sea-launched cruise missiles (SLCMs) and the elimination of tactical naval nuclear weapons; the establishment of a Conference on Arctic Security and Cooperation [similar to the Conference on Security and Cooperation in Europe (CSCE)]; and the appointment of an Ambassador for Circumpolar Affairs.

Discussion

Discussion of security in the North sometimes reflects a perception that the Arctic is a scene of dangerous confrontation in which there is potential for inadvertent or accidental military conflict. The actual chances of such are remote. Except for bases in the Kola Peninsula region (where, for geographic reasons, the USSR is obliged to station its main naval forces), Arctic military installations are primarily defensive. This applies completely to Canadian defence assets in the region, which provide early warning and surveillance capabilities.

Proponents of Arctic-specific arms control and disarmament measures argue that such measures could address concerns of relevance to Canada as an Arctic nation. They argue that all of the circumpolar states, not just the superpowers, have a responsibility to ensure the peaceful development of the Arctic and that, as a major Arctic power, Canada is in a strong position to give leadership in the demilitarization of the region. They point to emerging civil cooperation among the circumpolar states in fields such as science and environmental protection, and suggest that Arctic arms control and confidence-building measures could help to insulate this cooperation from military competition.

While recognizing, in some cases, that the Arctic cannot be isolated from East-West rivalry, proponents of Arctic arms control measures believe that there is scope for agreements to channel and limit military developments in the region. They note that the Arctic is already relatively non-militarized when compared with other regions, and suggest that

Arctic-specific measures could help to keep it that way. The analogy is made to the Antarctic, which is subject to a demilitarization treaty. Arctic-specific measures are sometimes advocated primarily as a means of building confidence; it is argued that the benefits of increased cooperation and openness outweigh issues of comprehensiveness, verifiability, and military significance. It has also been argued that the Arctic presents Canada with an opportunity to take internationally-significant initiatives to prevent the deployment of destabilizing weapons systems.

Critics of Arctic-specific proposals argue that such measures would be virtually meaningless if they included only the Arctic regions of countries, leaving aside other areas. They note that there is no military threat peculiar to the Arctic; any threat to the rest of North America, however, tends to manifest itself in the North as well. They suggest that measures to limit or ban deployments in the Arctic would merely displace those deployments, not reduce or eliminate them, and could have a destabilizing effect on other regions. They argue that military developments in the Arctic are a symptom, not a cause, of past East-West security competition, and should be addressed – along with other military developments related to this competition – in the ongoing East-West negotiating forums.

Critics also argue that since many of the measures proposed for the Arctic would be essentially unverifiable, they could undermine rather than build confidence, because of doubts about compliance.

Canada's Objectives

To promote national and international peace and security.
To cooperate with other countries in the Arctic in a manner that complements arms control negotiations and security cooperation taking place elsewhere.

Canada's Position

Canada is interested in developing realistic measures aimed at enhancing peace and security in all areas, including the Arctic. Given the limited scope of military activity in the Arctic and this activity's fundamentally defensive nature, we see little point in Arctic-specific arms control negotiations. The weapons that pose a potential threat to Arctic security are primarily strategic nuclear ones. Most of these are not situated in the Arctic; in addition, they have ranges and targets far beyond the Arctic. Arctic security is not a special case and should not be treated in isolation from broader East-West military security issues.

Insofar as military activity in the Arctic has been a reflection of East-West security competition, enhanced military security in the region will rest on the continuing decline in East-West tensions and on continuing reductions in East-West armaments. The November 1990 Treaty on Conventional Armed Forces in Europe (CFE), the November 1990 Vienna Document on Confidence- and Security-Building Measures (CSBMs), the July 1991 USA-USSR Strategic Arms Reduction Treaty (START), and the USA and Soviet nuclear reduction initiatives announced in September and October 1991 have codified the recent improvement in East-West relations and dramatically lessened the likelihood of East-West conflict. Progress continues to be made in the CFE follow-on negotiations, the CSBM negotiations, the Open Skies negotiations, and the USA-USSR post-START working group talks on, *inter alia*, deterrence, stability and security. It is on negotiations such as these that Canada is concentrating its energies, as the best means of contributing to peace and security throughout the Northern hemisphere, including in the Arctic.

Only the Soviet Union has major deployments of military forces in the Arctic; only the Soviet Union bases nuclear ballistic missiles there. These weapons affect the security of not only the circumpolar countries, but of all the NATO allies. Just as Canada insists, because our security is involved, in taking part in the CFE and CSBM negotiations on forces in Europe, we would find it questionable to deal with Arctic-based weapons in a forum that excluded our non-Arctic allies. The Soviet Union has indicated that it, too, believes Arctic security is best dealt with in an East-West context. Although they have offered to discuss Arctic-based nuclear weapons in circumpolar forums, the Soviets are adamant that reduction of these weapons can take place only in the context of strategic nuclear arms talks between the USA and the USSR. Canada agrees with this approach. Since the presence of these weapons in the Arctic has been the result of East-West competition, the weapons should be reduced through East-West, not Arctic, mechanisms.

Canada will continue to effectively undertake early-warning and surveillance activities, which contribute to security in the Arctic. In addition, Canada is strengthening bilateral and multilateral cooperation with circumpolar states to enhance environmental and economic security in the Arctic. In November 1989, Canada and the Soviet Union entered into a comprehensive Agreement on Cooperation in the Arctic and the North, which provides a framework for scientific and technological, economic, and social and cultural cooperation. Canada also played a key role in the establishment in August 1990 of the International Arctic

Science Committee, which aims to promote scientific cooperation throughout the Arctic. In addition, Canada has been highly supportive of the "Finnish initiative" on the protection of the Arctic environment and joined the seven other circumpolar countries in signing in June 1991 a Declaration on the Arctic Environment. The accompanying Arctic Environmental Protection Strategy established a task force for an Arctic Monitoring and Assessment Program.

Speaking in Leningrad in November 1989, Prime Minister Mulroney suggested the creation of an Arctic Council as a political body of the eight circumpolar countries to coordinate and promote cooperation among them. At a conference in Ottawa in November 1990, Secretary of State for External Affairs Clark announced that Canada would formally propose such a council to the seven other Arctic countries and indicated Canada's willingness to host a council secretariat. An Arctic Council would provide a forum for the circumpolar countries to meet regularly and discuss issues of common interest related to the protection of the Arctic environment, the development of Arctic economies and the interests of Arctic peoples. Canada believes that the agenda of an Arctic Council should be flexible, allowing for growth as confidence increases. While we see no need to put formal limitations on the Council's mandate, we do not envision the Council addressing military security issues, which are more appropriately dealt with in other forums. Canadian officials have been discussing the proposal for an Arctic Council with representatives of the other circumpolar states.

Canada is concerned about the possible negative effects on the Arctic environment – including beyond Soviet borders – of the USSR's decision, announced in March 1990, to terminate nuclear testing at its principal test site in Soviet Central Asia by 1993 and conduct all testing after that date on the Arctic island of Novaya Zemlya. Mr Clark expressed these concerns directly to Mr Shevardnadze, as have Canadian officials to their Soviet counterparts. Canada intends to monitor the issue closely and to explore the possibility of multilateral cooperation in assessing the environmental impact. Although the Soviet moratorium on nuclear testing, announced in October 1991, means the Arctic test site will be closed for at least one year, we will continue to seek the assurances of Soviet authorities that stringent environmental safeguards will be imposed on any possible future testing. In Canada's view, nuclear testing in the Arctic appears contrary to the common aim of Canada and the USSR to protect the Arctic environment.

Part II
Aboriginal Priorities

Part II

4

Militarization and
the Aboriginal Peoples

Mary Simon

While its effects are not often visible, militarization is an increasingly compelling issue confronting aboriginal peoples throughout the world. Since World War II, the militarization of the territories of indigenous peoples has taken place in many parts of the globe.[1] Although the reasons for and circumstances surrounding these military activities may differ in different regions, indigenous peoples share a wide number of common concerns arising from them. These relate to the environment, culture, health, and human rights as well as to peace and security.

In some areas, such as the Marshall Islands in the South Pacific, there have been devastating environmental consequences during peacetime from nuclear testing and the dumping of radioactive wastes. In addition, the traditional economies and health of native peoples have been severely affected.[2] In too many instances which involve military activities, little or no respect is accorded by state governments to aboriginal peoples, their lands, or their fundamental rights and values. For example, every two years the United States Pacific fleet, along with the Canadian navy and other forces of the North Atlantic Treaty Organization (NATO), uses the sacred, uninhabited Hawaiian island of Kaho'olawe for target practice during military exercises. In 1986, and again in May 1988, Kaho'olawe was continuously bombarded as a part of a NATO war game, which included "simulated special [nuclear] weapons."[3] Insufficient concern is shown for the 544 archæological sites that are known to exist on the island even though these sites are "a link to 1,000 years of Hawaiian culture."[4]

In the circumpolar regions, nuclear tests have been conducted by the Soviet Union at five sites in Siberia among others.[5] In the early seventies the United States tested nuclear warheads at Amchitka in the Aleutian Islands off Alaska.[6] Although this particular test site is no longer active, it remains unclear what adverse environmental and health effects have resulted. The American Public Health Association Task Force on National Arctic Health Science Policy, appointed in 1983, concluded that there was an urgent need for continuous monitoring of radionuclides in humans, soil, and natural resources in Alaska. The task force also indicated that Inuit and Indian peoples are living in areas "with known exposures to high levels of fallout radionuclides."[7] Yet the essential health and related studies have never been done.

As these and other examples would suggest, there is cause for considerable caution and scrutiny of militarization. Aboriginal peoples in all parts of the Arctic can learn from the experiences of other indigenous peoples, whether they live in the northern or the southern hemisphere. As a general rule, in the face of military-related developments, the well-being and security of indigenous societies cannot be taken for granted. Militarization tends to undermine the self-determination of indigenous peoples. In many instances, it imposes costly and undesired policies, priorities, and activities within the boundaries of their territories, usually leading to a significant loss of control by native peoples over their lands and waters.

Although adequate information on defence policies and strategies is rarely furnished by governments to Arctic communities, such questions are increasingly being examined by a wide range of northern peoples. These include the Dene of the western Arctic in Canada, the Saami of Norway, Sweden, and Finland, and the Inuit of Alaska, Canada, and Greenland.

This paper focuses on the issues of Arctic militarization from an Inuit perspective. It includes: (1) a brief history of Inuit interest and involvement in defence matters; (2) the nature of military planning and activities in the North; (3) the consequences of militarization and related Inuit concerns; and (4) a proposed policy framework to ensure the peaceful use of the Arctic.

Inuit Interest and Involvement in Military Issues

Inuit have a solemn responsibility to be directly and actively involved in all major issues concerning the protection and development of the Arctic. This includes peace and security matters.

In view of the wide range of transboundary questions affecting the North, the Inuit Circumpolar Conference (ICC) was established by Inuit in 1977 at a meeting in Barrow, Alaska. The ICC, an international organization whose head office is currently in Canada, comprises Inuit from Canada, Alaska, and Greenland. The ICC continues to encourage the participation of Soviet Inuit (Yuit) within the organization and is optimistic that their vital input will become a reality.[8] Since 1983, the ICC has enjoyed non-governmental organization (NGO) status at the United Nations. The direct involvement of NGOs in the furtherance of disarmament and peace objectives has been repeatedly encouraged by the General Assembly and the United Nations Education, Scientific and Cultural Organization. As its charter states, the ICC is dedicated to the protection and advancement of Inuit rights and interests at the international level and to the promotion of international co-operation and world peace.

In considering the issue of Arctic militarization, it is important to take into account the transnational character of Inuit society and territory. For thousands of years, Inuit have used and continue to use the lands, sea-ice, and waters of the North. As aboriginal people, Inuit are the Arctic's legitimate spokespersons. Because Inuit northern lands and communities span four countries, we are in a unique position to advance peace and arms control objectives among Arctic states.

At present, there are approximately 105,000 Inuit in the polar region: 30,000 in Alaska, 42,000 in Greenland, 30,000 in northern Canada, and 1,500 to 3,000 in Siberia. This vast circumpolar region comprises the Inuit homeland. It transcends the geographical borders of both superpowers. Any military build-up in the North, whether by the United States or the Soviet Union, is not in the interests of Inuit.

The ICC firmly believes that extensive circumpolar co-operation (for example, international trade, polar research, environmental protection, cultural exchange) is a key factor in promoting Arctic and global peace. However, such co-operation would best flourish if it included meaningful and comprehensive arms control initiatives. For both defence and environmental purposes, state governments must look beyond geographical and political borders. They must begin to perceive the Arctic as a single entity, as Inuit do.

Inuit seek to decrease significantly the possibility of armed conflict, whether by design or by accident. We believe that Arctic demilitarization, in a gradual, balanced, and fair manner, is the most productive course to pursue at this time.

The Nature of Arctic Militarization

While circumpolar countries are currently advocating peace initiatives in various United Nations forums, military preparations and activities in the Arctic continue to increase at a significant pace.

In Alaska and the Soviet Union, military systems have been put into place over a number of decades. At Adak Island, Alaska, seventy nuclear depth bombs are stored.[9] Although Alaska ranks twenty-fifth among American states in the number of nuclear warheads deployed, it ranks second in nuclear infrastructure,[10] with forty-two facilities. It is said that in the event of war military forces will be deployed in Alaska as if to an overseas base.[11]

The nuclear weapons infrastructure in the Soviet Union is extensive and elaborate.[12] There has been a renewed focus on the Arctic by strategic analysts during the past ten years, in part as a result of the consistent build-up of Soviet military forces in the Kola Peninsula (adjacent to northern Norway and Finland). Today, the Kola Peninsula contains a huge arsenal of nuclear weapons, including the single highest concentration of submarine-launched ballistic missiles in the Soviet Union.[13]

In Greenland, there are four Distant Early Warning (DEW) radar sites. There is also a Ballistic Missile Early Warning System (BMEWS) station at the American air base in Thule.[14] Although a Home Rule government was established in Greenland in 1979, the island's defence and foreign affairs are still controlled by Denmark.

Canada ranks second (behind the Federal Republic of Germany) in the number of facilities it allows as part of the overseas nuclear infrastructure of the United States.[15] These include numerous radars as well as navigation stations for maritime surveillance. There are apparently over 70 treaties and 2,500 documents governing Canada-United States defence matters, so it is difficult to evaluate the degree of military integration of the two countries.[16] Evidence of accelerated military activity in the Canadian Arctic and sub-Arctic regions includes:

- initial discussions by Canada and the United States on a proposed joint naval defence pact or treaty that could provide United States nuclear-powered submarines with ready access to Canadian Arctic waters;
- establishment of "forward operating bases" for CF-18 fighter aircraft in five communities in Canada's North;[17]
- the North Warning System (NWS)[18] and other arrangements under the North American Aerospace Defence (NORAD) Agreement which may eventually be linked to the United States Strategic Defense Initiative (SDI);
- planned participation by Canada in research connected to the United States Air Defense Initiative, which, in the view of certain arms control experts, is clearly linked to SDI;[19]
- the proposed but now abandoned acquisition by Canada of 10 to 12 nuclear-powered submarines for use in the Arctic and other areas, at a cost of $8-$15 billion;[20]

.

- continued cruise missile testing by the United States over Canadian Arctic airspace; and
- increased low-level flight training involving fighter bombers, which has already had serious adverse effects on native communities and harvesting in Labrador and possibly in northern Quebec.

Like other organizations and governments, the ICC was encouraged by the signing of the Intermediate-Range Nuclear Forces Treaty in December 1987, the first treaty to abolish an entire class of nuclear arms. The treaty has also established new and significant precedents for co-operative methods of verification. Moreover, the climate for negotiating further arms control agreements has been considerably enhanced. However, it would appear that both NATO and the Soviet Union are studying whether and how to "modernize" their nuclear arsenals in the wake of the accord. Should other types of nuclear or conventional arms be conceived to replace those that are being eliminated, the positive objectives of the treaty could be largely defeated. It is also important that the removal of intermediate-range nuclear weapons from Europe does not lead to an arms build-up in other regions of the world, such as the North Pacific or the Arctic.

Consequences of Militarization and Inuit Concerns

The deployment of expensive air defence systems, cruise missile development and testing, and other military developments are proceeding apace in northern areas. Once in place, this arms build-up will likely be extremely costly and difficult to reverse. As in other arms races, the alleged need for new and improved weapons and support systems in the Arctic could well be never ending.

Unlike Europe, the Arctic has not yet become a focus of arms limitation talks. For example, no public request has been made by Canada to the superpowers for arms control negotiations to deal with the growing threat associated with cruise missiles. By default, costly defence and other military strategies are becoming the dominant theme and primary objective in circumpolar regions. Many of these strategies have adverse implications for true international co-operation, lasting peace, and real security for all peoples and all nations in the Arctic. Serious efforts should be made now to avert the aerial and naval[21] arms race that is gaining momentum in polar regions. It would appear that Canada and other non-nuclear Arctic countries are not taking measures to prevent and protect the North from becoming the new strategic military and combat zone for East-West competition and conflict. In the absence of regulatory measures, forward operating naval strategies may soon be implemented by both the United States and the Soviet Union in Arctic regions. For example, the Maritime Strategy of the United States navy is considered by many experts to be unnecessary and destabilizing.[22] Non-nuclear-weapons states, such as Canada, should not allow their Arctic territory to be used to launch offensive strategies that threaten other countries.[23]

While military activities continue to be justified by governments on the basis of defence and security considerations, such actions often serve to promote Inuit insecurity and may threaten the unique and delicate polar environment. These activities may also conflict with aboriginal uses of Arctic lands, waters, and sea-ice. Moreover, because of the confidential nature of military activity, the Inuit right to self-government would be more and more eroded or otherwise curtailed. Future policy options would be unnecessarily limited. Any adverse repercussions that might arise from excessive military strategies would most likely affect first and foremost those who live in the North. In many instances, our communities are near key military targets.[24] Also, any radioactive pollution, arising by accident or out of conflict, could easily devastate the Arctic environment and the traditional Inuit way of life.

Nor do Inuit support the introduction of unproven or unsafe technologies, such as nuclear energy,[25] in the Arctic. They are deeply concerned about possible accidents involving nuclear-powered submarines, including spillage of primary radioactive coolant.[26] Could the Canadian or any government respond effectively to such an emergency in the Arctic? Why risk the Arctic's environment?

It is a continuing injustice that governments still refuse to concede that military-related developments are "developments" and therefore subject to full environmental and social impact assessment prior to implementation. Too often, military projects are centralized undertakings that are unilaterally imposed on indigenous peoples and their territories. Such actions are inconsistent with the basic principles of aboriginal self-government. Inuit and other indigenous peoples must be directly involved in policy- and decision-making on defence and arms control matters affecting the Arctic. Timely access to relevant information must be assured.

Towards a Policy Framework for Lasting Peace

If the process of militarization is to be reversed, fundamental inadequacies in governmental approaches to Arctic defence and arms control need to be thoroughly examined. In view of the strategic position of the Canadian North and Canada's potentially influential role in this policy area, the activities of the Canadian government are the focus of the following comments.

Canada and other Arctic countries do not seem to have an adequate arms control policy framework to deal expressly with the mounting issues affecting the North.[27] It is true that, in the absence of crisis or war,[28] no nuclear weapons are permitted on the soil of Canada and other "middle power" countries in the North. However, such a policy does not render these nations "nuclear-weapons-free." In most instances, foreign vessels with nuclear arms are in fact tolerated in the ports and waters of these countries. Further, many states continue to allow a substantial infrastructure to be put in place within their national borders. This infrastructure will facilitate the use of nuclear arsenals in the event of real or potential conflict.

Too often non-nuclear-weapons states cite the need to maintain solidarity within the Western alliance as a reason for not adopting stronger positions on arms control within their respective territories. The ICC believes that concerted pressure must be brought to bear on both the Soviet Union and the United States by non-nuclear countries, if the weapons build-up in the Arctic is to be stopped and reversed.

While Canada produced a white paper on defence in June 1987,[29] there is no parallel policy on arms control with specific reference to the Arctic. This matter is increasingly urgent and at least one arms control expert suggests that the Canadian government "should be energetically pursuing negotiated measures of arms restraint in the region."[30] The development of a coherent Arctic policy was strongly recommended in the June 1986 report of the Special Joint Committee on Canada's International Relations. In its December 1986 response to that report, the federal government confirmed the need for a coherent set of Arctic policies, but to date no government paper on Arctic arms control has appeared for public review. The Special Joint Committee report also concluded that Canada, together with other Arctic and Nordic nations, should actively seek the demilitarization of the Arctic. In its response, the federal government indicates that "singling out the Arctic for demilitarization does not seem practicable." Moreover, it is suggested that "there seems no likelihood of the Soviet Union's co-operation at this time."[31]

In light of recent events, the Inuit Circumpolar Conference believes that Canada should reassess its position. In October 1987, Mikhail Gorbachev suggested turning the Arctic into a zone of peace and proposed

East-West talks to restrict military activity in northern seas.[32] Since Gorbachev's ideas were delivered in a nationally televised speech from Murmansk, it would be beneficial for Canada to solicit more concrete proposals from the Soviet Union in relation to the Arctic.

Other aspects of policy which should be considered by the federal government include the following:

- The need to revise the defence white paper to replace its Cold War military doctrine with more forward-looking strategies and concepts. For example, the threat facing Canada as an Arctic non-nuclear nation should be more accurately described in terms of a possible nuclear conflict between the superpowers, and not just in terms of a nuclear attack by the Soviet Union. The notion of security should be described in broad terms of collective security for all nations and not just as a matter of national, continental, or Western military security.[33]

- The need to integrate into defence and arms control policies and strategies comprehensive notions of "non-offensive defence."[34] Efforts should be made to examine seriously ways in which conventional forces could be restructured to defend rather than to attack.[35] Currently, both NATO and the Warsaw pact espouse the use of offensive strategies that many consider destabilizing. This situation perpetuates insecurity and a lack of trust.

- The need to promote internationally the illegality[36] of nuclear weapons and to seek constructive, non-nuclear deterrents on which security might be based.

- The need to undertake and support research efforts towards creating a transnational Arctic nuclear-weapons-free zone (NWFZ).[37] At its general assembly (July 1986) in Kotzebue, Alaska, the ICC was requested by Inuit delegates from three countries to explore the possibility of establishing such a NWFZ by international agreement or treaty. However, the project has faced financial shortages.

- The need to respect the fundamental values and rights of the Arctic's aboriginal peoples. A primary and explicit objective of Arctic policy (which is currently lacking) must be to ensure the well-being of these peoples in ways acceptable to them.[38]

- The need to incorporate impartial and timely environmental and social impact assessment procedures into all aspects of arms control and defence planning for the North. This is especially important because of the delicacy of the Arctic environment and the profound significance of northern lands, waters, and resources to Inuit and other indigenous peoples in the Arctic.

- The need to ensure the direct and continuous involvement of the Arctic's aboriginal peoples in policy- and decision-making with regard to defence and arms control matters.[39]
- The need to include emerging human rights in an evolving Arctic policy framework, such as the right to peace, the right to development, and the right to a safe and healthy environment.[40] In early August 1988, the ICC emphasized these rights in Geneva at the 6th session of the United Nations Working Group on Indigenous Peoples. Unfortunately, Canada's representatives did not at the time voice support for these vital concepts.
- The need to elaborate sufficiently, in an Arctic context, the relationship between military spending and social development.[41] Although northern economic opportunities are critically needed, militarization should not replace proper socio-economic development in the Arctic.

Conclusion

At the December 1987 Norway-Canada Conference on Circumpolar Issues, Canada's secretary of state for external affairs, Joe Clark, stated that "we must all learn from the Inuit and the Saami, the people who have lived for many centuries in the North. And we can learn lessons that are relevant far beyond the northern environment."[42] These words have yet to be put into practice by government.

Despite repeated requests, in-depth involvement of Inuit in Arctic defence and arms control matters has yet to be accommodated. If the future of our Arctic homeland is to be safeguarded, we must have direct input into government policy-making. Meaningful Inuit participation can make a vital contribution to circumpolar co-operation and should not be ignored.

Inuit believe that it is beneficial to promote both regional and global measures to scale down or reverse current plans to militarize the Arctic. They also support the concept of strengthening international controls. As compared with military purposes, too little effort and resources are devoted by governments to arms control and disarmament matters. This is especially true in the Arctic.

The mounting dangers inherent in new military technologies leave responsible governments little or no choice but to seek new "prescriptions" or approaches to Arctic and global peace and security. In this regard, governments and others should critically evaluate the existing alliances of East and West and encourage their reorientation where necessary.

Inuit have always viewed their circumpolar homeland as a delicate, life-supporting environment for present and future generations. The Arctic is a place for sharing and co-operation, sustenance, and peace. Whether it will continue to foster such qualities could well depend on the capacity of Arctic governments to alter their own priorities and share the continuing vision of Inuit.

We are convinced that now is the time to take unequivocal and committed actions to ensure lasting peace and security in the Arctic – actions that will clearly benefit all peoples and all nations. Indigenous peoples in the North demand and merit no less.

Notes

1   Independent Commission on International Humanitarian Issues (ICIHI), *Indigenous Peoples: A Global Quest for Justice* (London: Zed Books 1987), 76-82.
2   Ibid., 76-9.
3   J. Arkin and K. Fieldhouse, *Nuclear Battlefields: Global Links in the Arms Race* (Cambridge MA: Ballinger 1985), 187.
4   T. O'Hara, "Canadian Navy to Shell Hawaii," *Peace Magazine* (April/May 1988), 26. See also *Indigenous Peoples*, 78.
5   Arkin and Fieldhouse, *Nuclear Battlefields*, 68.
6   Ibid.
7   *The National Arctic Health Science Policy* (Washington: American Public Health Association Task Force, n.d.), 11.
8   After discussions in the USSR in August 1988 between members of the ICC executive council and high-ranking Soviet officials, a historic decision was reached by the Soviet government to allow Siberian Inuit to attend the ICC general assembly in Sisimiut, Greenland, in July 1989.
9   Arkin and Fieldhouse, *Nuclear Battlefields*, 172.
10   Ibid., 40 and 172.
11   Ibid., 172.
12   See, generally, ibid., 252-63.
13   R. Purver, *Arms Control Options in the Arctic,* Issue Brief 7 (Ottawa: Canadian Centre for Arms Control and Disarmament 1987), 3.
14   Arkin and Fieldhouse, *Nuclear Battlefields*, 220-1.
15   Ibid., 216.
16   J. Honderich, *Arctic Imperative: Is Canada Losing the North?* (Toronto: University of Toronto Press 1987), 117.
17   The five communities are Yellowknife, Inuvik, Rankin Inlet, and Iqaluit in the Northwest Territories, and Kuujjuaq in northern Quebec.
18   The North Warning System (NWS), a surveillance system which will replace the DEW line, consists of "a series of 13 long-range radars and 39 short-range radars situated across northern Alaska, northern Canada and down the Labrador coast." See H. Critchley, "Defence and Policing in Arctic Canada," in F. Griffiths, ed,

Politics of the Northwest Passage (Kingston and Montreal: McGill-Queen's University Press 1987), 210.

19 D. Cox, *Trends in Continental Defence: A Canadian Perspective* (Ottawa: Canadian Institute for International Peace and Security, December 1986), 29.

20 Canada's Department of National Defence maintained that the cost would be $8 billion, but the estimates of arms control and defence experts are considerably higher.

21 On the superpower arms race at sea, see the special issue of the *Bulletin of the Atomic Scientists*, 43 (September 1987).

22 B. Posen, "U.S. Maritime Strategy: A Dangerous Game," ibid., 24.

23 See also E. Regehr, "New Approaches to Security," in E. Regehr and G. Rosenblum, *The Road to Peace* (Toronto: Lorimer 1988), 123.

24 For example, it is said that the NWS would likely be destroyed by enemy action prior to the arrival of hostile forces. See Cox, *Trends in Continental Defence*, 36.

25 In regard to the problems with nuclear energy and uranium, see D. Orkin, "The Canadian Nuclear Industry: Regulation Forever," *Administrative Law Journal* (no 4, 1987-8), 50; K. Sanderson, "Aboriginal People Re-evaluate Uranium Mining," *Briarpatch Magazine* (Saskatchewan) (June 1988), 16.

26 Nuclear accidents on military vessels are discussed in J. Brightwell, "Unsafe Harbours," *Peace Magazine* (August/September 1988), 25.

27 This was the same conclusion reached with regard to Canada by the Consultative Group on Disarmament and Arms Control Affairs, which met in October 1987 to discuss Arctic peace and security issues. See *Disarmament Bulletin*, #8 (spring 1988), 25-6.

28 A secret arrangement in 1967 between Canada and the United States permits the United States, under certain conditions, to deploy 32 nuclear depth bombs to Canada for use against enemy submarines: Honderich, *Arctic Imperative*, 116.

29 *Challenge and Commitment: A Defence Policy for Canada* (Ottawa: National Defence/Supply and Services Canada 1987).

30 R. Purver, *Arctic Arms Control: Constraints and Opportunities* (Ottawa: Canadian Institute for International Peace and Security, February 1988), 80.

31 *Independence and Internationalism: Report of the Special Joint Committee of the Senate and of the House of Commons on Canada's International Relations* (Ottawa: Queen's Printer, June 1986), 127 and 135; *Canada's International Relations: Response of the Government of Canada to the Report of the Special Joint Committee of the Senate and the House of Commons* (Ottawa: Supply and Services Canada, December 1986), 85 and 87.

32 Mikhail Gorbachev, *The Speech in Murmansk* (Moscow: Novosti Press Agency 1987), 28-9.

33 R. Gifford and T. Creery, *Towards a World without War: The Defence Debate in Canada* (Halifax: Defence Research and Education Centre, January 1988), 8-9. See also Regehr, "New Approaches to Security," 104-28.

34 "Non-offensive defence" is also referred to as "non-provocative defence" or "mutual defensive superiority," because each side's defensive capability is superior to its potential enemy's offensive capability. See the special issue on non-offensive defence: *Bulletin of the Atomic Scientists*, 44 (September 1988). See also R. Neild

and A. Boserup, "Beyond INF: A New Approach to Nonnuclear Forces," *World Policy Journal*, 4 (fall 1987), 605.

35 In moving towards disarmament, the ICC believes that non-provocative defence concepts and extensive arms control measures should be applied to the Arctic. See Paul Rogers, "The Nuclear Connection," *Bulletin of the Atomic Scientists*, 44 (September 1988), 20: "Nonoffensive defense theories have dealt almost exclusively with conventional forces in Europe. But the same approach should also work on the global level, to eliminate offensive nuclear weapons and superpower intervention." Mutual and balanced reductions in weapons do not in themselves ensure stability or security, if new and more dangerous weapons and offensive strategies continue to be developed. See A. Kokoshin, "Restructure Forces, Enhance Security," *Bulletin of the Atomic Scientists*, 44 (September 1988), 35.

36 For views on the degree of illegality of nuclear weapons, see R. Weston, "Nuclear Weapons Versus International Law: A Contextual Reassessment," R. Falk, "Toward a Legal Regime for Nuclear Weapons," and D. Arbess, "The International Law of Armed Conflict in Light of Contemporary Deterrence Strategies: Empty Promise or Meaningful Restraint?" *McGill Law Journal*, 28 (July 1983), at 542, 519, and 89 respectively; L. Boyle, "The Relevance of International Law to the 'Paradox' of Nuclear Deterrence," *Northwestern University Law Review*, 80 (no 6, 1986), 1407; "Panel 5: Is There a Legal Basis for Nuclear Deterrence Theory and Policy?" in M. Cohen and M. Gouin, eds., *Lawyers and the Nuclear Debate* (Ottawa: University of Ottawa Press 1988), 173.

37 The government of Canada does not support a NWFZ for Canada or the Arctic. See "Canada's Position on Nuclear Weapon Free Zones," *Disarmament Bulletin*, 6 (summer-fall 1986), 12. For a more positive view, see E. Regehr, "The Way Out," in Regehr and Rosenblum, *The Road to Peace*, 168. As a first step, a NWFZ would not necessarily extend to all parts of the Arctic. Because the impact of Arctic denuclearization on the United States and the Soviet Union would not be identical, Arctic NWFZ proposals should include additional arms control measures in a fair and balanced manner. Efforts should be made to reduce significantly the large Soviet nuclear forces in the Barents Sea and Kola Peninsula in return for nuclear reductions by the Western allies.

38 For a similar view, see the conclusions and recommendations in *The North and Canada's International Relations: The Report of a Working Group of the National Capital Branch of the Canadian Institute of International Affairs* (Ottawa: Canadian Arctic Resources Committee, March 1988), 55, 66, 69.

39 Support for the direct involvement of the Arctic's aboriginal peoples in northern policy-making is expressed in F. Griffiths, *A Northern Foreign Policy* (Toronto: Canadian Institute of International Affairs 1979), 73, 79, 86. Support for the policy work of the ICC was urged by eleven Canadian church leaders on Canada's prime minister, Brian Mulroney: see *Peace-Building: The Church Response to Canadian Defence Policy* (Waterloo, Ontario: Project Ploughshares, February 1988), 11.

40 Principles pertaining to these rights are the subject of ICC policy work. See *Draft Principles for an Arctic Policy* (draft for delegates to ICC general assembly, Kotzebue, Alaska, July 1986), 19, 25. See, generally, B. Marks, "Emerging Human Rights: A New Generation for the 1980s?" *Rutgers Law Review*, 33 (1981), 435.

41 See, generally, R. Sivard, *World Military and Social Expenditures 1987-88* (Washington: World Priorities 1988); *Disarmament and Development: Joint Declaration by the Panel of Eminent Personalities in the Field of Disarmament and Development* (New York: United Nations 1986).

42 *Disarmament Bulletin*, 8 (spring 1988), 25.

5

Public Health in the Circumpolar North

Jens Misfeldt

During the last forty years the North American Arctic regions and Greenland have experienced a very similar development in health conditions. The early establishment of the concept of Arctic medicine or circumpolar health as a transnational geographically defined discipline is a consequence of several factors. First of all, Inuit in these regions share common cultural and genetic characteristics. Secondly, all Arctic communities have undergone a forced development of their societies – changes which have put great stress on the individual. Over a long period they may have caused alienation and a feeling of insufficiency because of lack of education and knowledge of the Western tradition.

In North America the exploitation of the circumpolar North started after World War II. About the same time the colonial status of Greenland was altered, and Greenland was awarded equal rights within the Danish realm. These changes led to social upheaval in the northern communities and considerable immigration of non-natives. Non-natives now constitute about 85 per cent of the population in Alaska and 42 per cent of the population in the Northwest Territories in Canada, while in Greenland the non-native population (that is, Danes) has only risen from 2 per cent in 1950 to about 17 per cent today. Thus the native population in Greenland has always been in the majority.

Disease Pattern

Tuberculosis was the major killer in all native communities in the period immediately after 1945, and the eradication of tuberculosis became the main task for the health services throughout the North American Arctic. The solution, however, was not merely medical. It required the improvement of hygienic conditions, particularly housing, and the reduction of overcrowding. These efforts proved successful, and since 1970 tuberculosis has played only a minor part in the region's disease pattern. However, communicable diseases are still a significant health problem, with high incidences of hepatitis B, early middle ear infections, and meningitis, in particular. Comparatively, the picture is alike in all Arctic communities, even if there are quantitative differences.

More recently, however, many of the original health problems of the northern native population have been largely replaced by socio-psychological problems resulting from acculturation.[1] Here, too, we find great similarities among the circumpolar countries. A high suicide rate is the most serious finding. But violence and violent deaths and promiscuity with venereal diseases and high abortion rates are other symptoms and consequences of the acculturative process in which alcohol abuse is both catalyst and symptom.

The pattern of chronic disease has been the object of much research, not least concerning cancer. Early studies have shown interesting differences between cancer rates in Inuit and other populations, and more recently a rise in the number of cases has been reported from all parts of the Inuit world. Large increases in the incidence of lung cancer in both men and women and in cancer of the cervix have caused special concern. These diseases can easily be attributed to cigarette smoking and promiscuity, respectively. Both may therefore be regarded as preventable.

Inuit cancer incidence is also characterized by a high frequency of nasopharyngeal and salivary gland tumours, presumably as a consequence of genetic predisposition and a prevalent virus infection (Epstein-Barr) in the Arctic. Diabetes and ischæmic heart disease occur only rarely in the Inuit population, but both are quite common in southern communities. The study of these differences is important for an understanding of the ætiology and pathogenesis of these disorders and for predicting their future development and finding preventive measures.

International Co-operation

In 1967 the former chief health officer in Alaska, Dr Earl Albrecht, invited representatives of the health authorities in the western Arctic to a meeting in Fairbanks. The provision of drinking water in Arctic areas was the main topic. This was the beginning of a series of Arctic medical symposia and congresses of which the seventh was held in 1987 in Umeå, Sweden. The ninth congress is to be held in 1990 in Whitehorse, Yukon. These international symposia have led to the establishment of separate workshops or working groups on particular subjects, as for example an international study group on cancer.

At the symposium held in Copenhagen in 1981, a first step was taken towards setting up an International Union for Circumpolar Health (IUCH), and in 1986 the organization was formally established. The objectives of the IUCH are to be a sponsoring group for international congresses, which have attracted a growing number of participants, and to act as a promoter of Arctic medical research. The union also intends to work with world governmental bodies such as the World Health Organization (WHO) by promoting joint health projects between countries. The union is made up of four core organizations: the American Society for Circumpolar Health, the Canadian Society for Circumpolar Health, the Nordic Council for Arctic Medical Research, and the Siberian Branch of the USSR Academy of Medical Sciences.

In 1969 the governments of Denmark, Finland, Norway, and Sweden founded the Nordic Council for Arctic Medical Research to facilitate co-operation among these countries in the field of Arctic medicine. The secretariat of the council is located in Finland, and the work is co-ordinated by the secretariat for Nordic Cultural Co-operation in Copenhagen. As well as promoting Arctic medical research in the Nordic countries, the council also aims to accumulate documentation on Arctic medicine and to make this available to research workers in the Nordic countries and the world at large. The council arranges workshops, symposia, and the like and publishes the only periodical dealing specifically with Arctic medical research. *Arctic Medical Research* is distributed in 17 countries and is indexed in *Index Medicus* and several databases.

At the seventh International Circumpolar Health Congress in Umeå, an Alaska-Siberian medical research agreement was presented. Since then joint Alaska-Siberian seminars have been held on both sides. Siberians and Alaskans have agreed that neither military funding nor work on any project that is military-related will be accepted. The aim is to make this agreement a model of how countries can work together peacefully on projects that are mutually beneficial.

Thus, in the medical field, international co-operation in the Arctic regions has been in progress for years. The new international union opens up new opportunities for international co-operative research.

WHO has shown an interest in circumpolar health but has not been able to make this a major programme because the population living in the circumpolar areas is very small and the countries concerned are wealthy. The most productive form of WHO involvement is through collaboration with other international organizations which focus exclusively on circumpolar health, such as the IUCH and the Nordic Council. In this respect, WHO worked with the Nordic Council to organize a working group on problems of family health in circumpolar regions in Ilulissat/Jakobshavn, Greenland, in 1985. In 1989 an International Circumpolar Meeting on Tobacco and Health took place in Yellowknife, jointly organized by IUCH and WHO. The latter is also developing guidelines for cold-climate water supply and sanitation as part of its work during the international drinking water and sanitation decade – a step towards the broad goal of Health for All by the year 2000.

Current Health Problems

I would now like to pinpoint a few major health problems in today's Arctic, and I will take as my point of reference conditions in Greenland with which I am familiar. Because there are great similarities among the Arctic countries, much of the information on Greenland holds true elsewhere.

Sexually Transmitted Diseases
Starting with medical conditions in a more restricted sense, I would like to stress that venereal and other sexually transmissible diseases (STDs) constitute a considerable health problem. Take, for example, syphilis

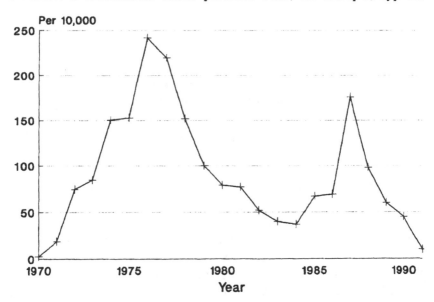

FIGURE 1. Cases of syphilis in Greenland per 10,000 residents (15-19 years of age).

(figure 1). This disease has been endemic in Greenland since 1970. Several hundred new cases are notified each year, and there have even been some epidemics reported. During the first quarter of 1987, for example, an epidemic of syphilis was reported in the southern four medical districts. This presented an opportunity for a mass examination by blood tests in which 2,557 males and 2,413 females, aged 50 to 60 years, participated. Previously unknown cases of syphilis were found in 2.5 per cent of the examined males and 2.2 per cent of the females. These extremely high rates indicated for a time an uncontrollable spread of this only moderately contagious disease. Unfortunately, the course of the disease is insidious. So far a few congenital cases of syphilis have been found, and serious tertiary cases may be expected in the future.

Gonorrhea and other STDs occur with an even higher frequency. Hepatitis B is a special concern. It is a viral disease which is transmitted sexually and by blood, and infection most often is transmitted by clinically healthy carriers of the virus. Fortunately vaccination is now possible, and vaccination programmes have been set up for risk groups. The international exchange of scientific information and views on strategies has been very valuable in this context.

Finally, there is AIDS. The AIDS virus (HIV) is also transmitted by blood and sexually, and infected persons may be carriers for years during which time transmission to another person may occur. Since 1985 we have known of HIV-positive persons in Greenland. The situation has been monitored by voluntary HIV testing of persons whose activities put them at risk and other groups. Today 13 persons in Greenland are known to be HIV-positive, and the real figure is probably not very different. Thus AIDS still seems to be a minor problem. However, it has to be remembered that while AIDS is a slowly spreading disease and its contagiousness is limited, the consequences of infection are disastrous.

In Greenland an epidemical, heterosexual spread of HIV infection may be foreseen, in light of both the known spread of sexually transmitted diseases and the experience with the disease in Africa. Therefore prevention of the spread of AIDS and other sexually transmitted diseases must be given a very high priority. Improving medical efforts in examination and treatment are valuable in relation to the classical venereal diseases. Vaccination programmes may be a good idea for Hepatitis B. Nevertheless the only measure that really counts, and the one that will attack the whole range of sexually transmitted diseases is a change in sexual behaviour. This cannot be implemented by the health authorities alone. A national and political effort, supported by the health

professionals, is necessary. Education, information, and positive attempts
to influence attitudes towards sexual behaviour are needed.

Non-Natural Deaths

The Greenland mortality pattern is characterized by a high mortality from
acute infections, accidents, and violence as well as by a high infant
mortality rate.

In the period 1980-5, suicide and marine accidents were the two most
prominent causes of death among males whereas stroke and chronic lung
diseases dominated female deaths. The average life expectancy for a
newborn was 58.5 years for males and 66.0 for females. Mortality rates
were higher in all age groups compared with corresponding figures from
Denmark, but the differences were most striking in age groups from 0 to
35 years.

These many early deaths explain the low life expectancies. Looking at
the modes of death, it is obvious that many of these fatalities are non-
natural deaths. For instance, in 1986, one-third of all male deaths and one-
quarter of all female deaths were classified as non-natural (accident,

TABLE 1. Suicides in Greenland, 1977-90

Year	Suicides total	Suicides Inuit	Suicide rate per 100,000 Inuit
1977	30	29	71
1978	23	23	56
1979	31	28	71
1980	41	40	98
1981	34	30	72
1982	49	46	109
1983	45	44	103
1984	53	52	120
1985	58	53	122
1986	58	57	129
1987	69	-	153
1988	48	-	105
1989	55	-	143
1990	66	-	143

Sources: Police reports, death-certificates,
Ministry of Greenland, Yearbook.

suicide, or homicide). The majority of these deaths involved young individuals. So the impact on life expectancy and the potential years of life lost from these causes is considerable.

Suicides constitute a special problem. In Greenland an exponential increase in the number of suicides has been registered since the early seventies, with 75 per cent occurring among young people under 30 years old, mainly males. Overall, about 10 per cent of all deaths in Greenland are due to suicide among young people. This is a very serious health problem, especially because these early deaths ought to be preventable.

Alcohol

No one in Greenland, I believe, will deny that the country has a drinking problem. In 1986 annual alcohol consumption per person aged 15 years or more was calculated to be 23.2 litres. This is an extremely high figure. The connection between casualties and alcohol intoxication has been demonstrated in several publications. It seems that more than 80 per cent of these incidents happen under the influence of alcohol. In cases of violence, both the perpetrator and the victim are frequently acting under the influence of alcohol.

Casualties caused by violence and homicides are obviously occurrences which involve the health service, and where the connection with alcohol will be examined. It has also been shown that most suicides are associated with alcohol. This does not, however, necessarily mean that they are caused by alcohol.

The social consequences of alcohol abuse should not be overlooked. Although statistics are not as easily available as for medical problems, every district medical officer and every social worker in Greenland can point to plenty of examples of families in which violence and child neglect are the sad consequences of alcohol abuse, throwing shadows on the conditions of the child while growing up and thus on the generation to come. Again, I would like to stress that alcohol abuse gives rise to and worsens many social problems without being necessarily the underlying cause of them.

I have focused on these three subjects – STDs, non-natural deaths, and alcohol abuse – because they are, in my opinion, the main public health issues in Greenland. This is not to minimize the importance of infectious diseases, cancer, and other acute and chronic disorders, but to emphasize that these socio-medical conditions are the main threats to people's health in the circumpolar North – and thus the major challenges to the health authorities as well.

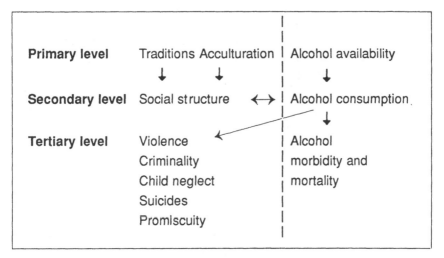

FIGURE 2. Pathogenetic interrelations with alcohol singled out as an important cultural factor. After Bent Harvald, "A Family Health Intervention Model," *Arctic Medical Research*, 40 (1985), 95-6.

In doing so I have also focused on some of the more tragic consequences of *acculturation* – defined as the process of cultural changes brought about by continuous firsthand contact between two cultural groups. Acculturation is an inevitable development in the circumpolar North. The consequences may be positive as well as negative. It is the obligation of the health authorities to call attention to the negative impacts on the health of the people of the North and to contribute to the development of preventive policies and programmes.

The negative consequences of acculturation in Greenland have been tremendous and will continue to be substantial. Therefore active intervention is urgent. In epidemiology we speak of different levels of prevention and disease control. At the *primary level* the injurious cause of disease is eliminated (for example, the eradication of the pox virus). At the *secondary level* the predisposition to disease is diminished (for example, by vaccination). The *tertiary level* refers to treatment of the symptoms.

Treatment of venereal disease cannot solve the problem of sexually transmitted diseases in general and has no influence whatsoever on the spread of AIDS. No treatment is available to counter the increasing inclination to suicide among young people, although early tracking of risk families and starting family therapy may be beneficial in individual cases. Treatment of alcoholics can solve the problem of alcohol abuse for a few individuals, but it will have no significant effect on the manifold serious consequences of alcohol abuse in society.

The only measures that really count in tackling these problems are primary and secondary prevention. Much effort has been expended in drawing attention to the spread of AIDS, and the WHO policy of education and information has been fully accepted in Greenland. In fact there are already some signs of success (that is, a reduction in the number of notified cases of venereal disease).

Concerning the suicide problem, we have not found the right approach so far. But a study has been started which it is hoped will create a framework for preventive measures. This investigation is part of an international study[2] on the effects of acculturation, which it is hoped will be of value for other circumpolar nations. However, the problem is urgent, and the Council on Health Promotion in Greenland is leaning towards starting a public discussion of the subject, as has been done in Alaska.

Concerning alcohol abuse, the Greenland Home Rule parliament set up an Alcohol Council in 1986. However, because of a political dispute on the approach to be taken, very little has in reality been done. In my opinion it is essential to act pragmatically on this problem, without making too many idealistic demands for scientific proof of causality. If, for instance, the consumption of alcohol is a serious problem in society, we need to do something about it, even if the acculturative process is to blame. Acculturation is an unavoidable process in Arctic societies where two different cultures have met for years. The outcome depends on how well those involved are able to integrate the original non-dominant culture with the dominant culture from outside. Alcohol abuse may be regarded as a negative way of trying to manage the situation. We cannot avoid the phenomenon of acculturation, but negative consequences such as the alcohol problem can be attacked, at both the first (availability) and the second (consumption) level.

In this context I wish to stress that heavy alcohol consumption may influence sexual behaviour in terms of favouring promiscuity and probably reducing attention to the practice of safe sex. Furthermore, alcohol consumption seems to be involved in the majority of cases of young suicides. Therefore it can be expected that measures to deal with alcohol abuse in society will have wide implications for control of the other two major health problems.

Conclusion

There has been international co-operation on circumpolar health issues for years and it continues to grow. A new joint Alaska-Siberian agreement has attracted much attention. Several national societies for circumpolar health have been at work for years and, recently, the International Union for Circumpolar Health has been set up.

Today the major health problems in Arctic countries seem closely linked to the acculturative stress caused by rapid changes in the Arctic societies. This is a process which occurs over time and in which the building of a new identity for people is essential. National educational and cultural efforts therefore play an important part in coping with this process.

However, to reduce the negative health consequences of acculturation, it is crucial to identify them and to take active measures against them promptly. In this article STDs, suicides among youth, and alcohol abuse have been pointed out as the main threats to the health of Arctic peoples.[3]

As these health problems are socio-medical in nature, the solutions are first of all political. Thus, it is the obligation of the health authorities to identify the problems and to convince the political decision-makers of the need for intervention.

Furthermore, as these socio-medical conditions are common to all Arctic societies, an international effort to change them might be a good approach. Maybe the Inuit Circumpolar Conference (ICC) could unite Inuit in seeking ways to combat the problems.

Notes

1 J. W. Berry, Psychology Department, Queen's University, Kingston, Canada: "Acculturation is a process of culture change brought about by continuous, firsthand contact between two groups. The consequences of this process for the individual are numerous, and may include disruption of familiar ways, identity confusion and loss, and perhaps a decline in physical and mental health":"Acculturation among Circumpolar Peoples," *Arctic Medical Research,* no 40 (1985), 21-7.

2 As presented at the 7th International Congress on Circumpolar Health, 1987, Umeå, Sweden, by J. Berry: "A collaborative project is being developed with the title 'Acculturation and adaptation among circumpolar peoples.' The general goal of the project is to gain an understanding about the process of acculturation in the Arctic, how it affects people living there, and what kinds of adaptions (mainly cultural and psychological, but also political and economic) are being made. The more specific goal is to examine the health outcomes (physical, social and mental) of this whole process, and to consider how policies and programmes may be

developed that will lead to more positive outcomes than have been observed up until now."

3   For further information, see: T. Bender, A. P. Lanier, et al, "The Evolution of Cancer as an Important Health Problem for Eskimos," *Arctic Medical Research*, no 33 (1982), 258-64; J. W. Berry, "Acculturation among Circumpolar Peoples" *Arctic Medical Research*, no 40 (1985), 21-7. B. Harvald, "Eskimo Disease Pattern – Genes or Environment?" *Acta Medica Scandinavica*, 212 (1982), 97-8, "Circumpolar Health," *Acta Medica Scandinavica*, 214 (1983), 97-8, and "International Collaboration on Circumpolar Health," *Arctic Medical Research*, no 42 (1986), 48; B. Jørgensen, L. G. Johansen, et al, "Accidents Due to Violence in Greenland," *Ugeskr Laeger*, 146 (1984), 3398-401; I. Lynge, "Suicide in Greenland!" *Arctic Medical Research*, no 40 (1985), 53-60; T. A. Mala, "The International Union for Circumpolar Health," *Arctic Medical Research*, no 42 (1986), 49-51, and "The University of Alaska-Siberian Medical Research Program: A Circumpolar Agreement," *Arctic Medical Research*, no 46 (1987), 35-8; J. Misfeldt, "Sexually Transmitted Diseases in Greenland," in *Circumpolar Health '87: Proceedings of the 7th International Congress on Circumpolar Health* (Umeå, 1988), 675-8; J. Misfeldt, B. Jørgensen, and S. Olesen, "A Serological Mass Examination for Syphilis in Greenland in 1987," *Arctic Medical Research*, no 47 (1988), 163-210; N. H. Nielsen, "Cancer Incidence in Greenland (thesis)," *Arctic Medical Research*, no 43 (1986); and P. Skinhoej, "Persistent Virus Infections in the Arctic," in R. Fortune, ed., *Circumpolar Health '84: Proceedings of the 6th International Symposium on Circumpolar Health* (Seattle and London: University of Washington Press, 1985), 195-8.

6

Ethnoscience, Prevailing Science, and Arctic Co-operation

Milton M.R. Freeman

In the early years of his presidency Ronald Reagan remarked that if Earth was invaded by hostile beings from another planet, the two superpowers would find no difficulty in working together. This was a prophetic remark. Progress on arms control followed on a welcome awareness on the part of the American administration that no nuclear war is winnable and that co-operation is indeed the best way to overcome the common threat posed by nuclear weapons.

The reduced prospect of global nuclear holocaust need not result in any reduction in East-West co-operative tendencies, for there are countless other shared challenges to our collective security and well-being. Many of these threats are global in scope and environmental in nature. It is particularly in the context of environmental research that I wish to speak about ethnoscience, or alternative rational approaches to understanding the natural world.

Science and Ethnoscience: Complementarity and Augmentation

The term *ethnoscience* is used here more because most people will know what the term means, and less because I think it an apt term. Just as one may question references made to *Arctic science* (which presumably is the same science whether practised in Toronto or Cambridge), it is possible to question the appropriateness of a term like ethnoscience. The investigative approaches used by some knowledgeable biological-resource users whose expertise is derived from non-academic sources may be remarkably similar to those employed by many academically trained scientists. Both groups utilize repeated sets of empirical observations to generate models of reality which are then tested and either accepted, rejected, or modified. Both groups may test their models of reality by means of experiments or critical comparative analysis. That the conclusions reached may sometimes vary is not remarkable. Disagreements are common in science and, indeed, they initiate and facilitate scientific advance. If the history of science tells us anything, it is that today's scientific truths will, given time, be replaced by different versions of scientific truth.[1]

This paper does not intend to attack science. But it does suggest that there may be alternative systems of knowing about those complex environmental realities that are the most difficult to comprehend using conventional scientific approaches. Indeed, it may be that science today has reached another of the several plateaux with which its history is studded and that in the best traditions of saltatory evolution, the next step will not be just "more of the same" but rather an unexpected change in the direction or pace of advance. Indeed, such an emerging shift has been discussed in Fritjof Capra's book, *The Turning Point,* which argues that in several fields of scientific endeavour, the linear reductionist model of classical science (which he equates with rational thought) can no longer be used to good effect. One area where it is not useful is in elucidating certain classes of complex environmental problems. As Capra puts it:

> It is now becoming apparent that overemphasis on the scientific method and on rational, analytic thinking has led to attitudes that are profoundly antiecological. In truth, the understanding of ecosystems is hindered by the very nature of the rational mind. Rational thinking is linear, whereas ecological awareness arises from an intuition of non-linear systems.[2]

> Ecological awareness, then, will arise only when we combine our rational knowledge with an intuition for the non-linear nature of our environment. Such intuitive wisdom is characteristic of traditional, non-literate cultures, especially American Indian cultures in which life was organized around a highly refined awareness of the environment.[3]

Capra is a theoretical physicist. It is understandable that he is concerned that physicists tell other scientists what they have discovered, namely, that reductionist and mechanistic thinking cannot be applied to all problem-solving situations and, further, that holistic and intuitive approaches to knowing are scientifically sound.[4] It is apparent from Capra's analysis that the discoveries of modern physics validate the holistic and intuitive approaches which are the basis of northern peoples' traditional understanding of their natural world.

Traditional Environmental Knowledge and
Adaptive Management

Quite independently of Capra's theoretical discussions, many other scientists have empirically demonstrated the utility of management approaches based on traditional knowledge for solving practical environmental problems.[5] It is also worth noting that biologists who are professionally involved with fisheries problems support tradition-based[6] and intuition-based[7] approaches to fishery management. Such approaches include that branch of renewable resources management known as adaptive management. It has grown out of a concern with practical problems involved in managing fishery, wildlife, and land resources and a recognition of the need to develop an alternative pragmatic approach based on understanding of how a "partially observed" system functions.[8]

In recognizing that the management of renewable resources is "done by man for man," adaptive management is concerned primarily with relationships occurring within a resource stock, between the population and its habitat, and between the population and its users. A basic assumption of adaptive management, therefore, is that socio-economic dynamics are inherent in the utilization of resources and must be taken into account if resource management problems are to be alleviated. Furthermore, scientists involved in adaptive resource management question the adequacy of the linear reductionist mode of inquiry, because there is no assurance that an understanding of how an ecological system functions at a given moment will provide insight into how it will function under changed circumstances in future. Moreover, the act of management itself alters relationships and causes unknown changes within an ecological management system, so that systems under study may be changing faster than they are being understood scientifically.[9]

Ecological systems are necessarily in a state of constant change, with annual cycles of growth and production in plants and animals as well as largely unpredictable and uncontrollable fluctuations in the size of animal populations. The aim of adaptive management, therefore, is to "work with nature" to assist population recovery if collapse should occur for whatever reason.[10] Subsequently, long-term management objectives focus on the identification of persistent changes in production processes that can serve as key indicators in assessing the health and status of a population under management.

As ecological systems are generally resilient and withstand

considerable stress before their structure is damaged – and this is true even in the Arctic[11] – the goal of management research is to understand the ecological process of stress and resilience in order to determine a range of alternative management options. In the course of research directed towards adaptive management, resource scientists, managers, and users learn about the potential of animal populations to sustain harvesting activities. This they do mainly through experience with management techniques rather than through the development of ecological theory or abstract modelling exercises.

Adaptive management represents a major paradigm shift in the resource sciences by actively seeking ways for dealing with uncertainty in the management of renewable resources. The key problem in renewable resources science is not how to gather more data or construct better models in hopes of making more accurate predictions, but how to develop a broader consensus among the individuals in the research, management, and user communities about the major uncertainties of a particular ecological system and the crucial role of management decisions in providing the empirical information needed to resolve the uncertainties.[12] The knowledge that traditional resource users have of the environmental variables to be assessed and their skill in collecting such data ensure their importance in implementing adaptive management regimes.

Recognition of Traditional Knowledge

Certainly in Canada, science-based institutions recognize that traditional knowledge systems have validity. Witness a workshop on the subject jointly sponsored by the Science Institute of the Northwest Territories, the Renewable Resources Department of the government of the Northwest Territories, and the Dene Cultural Institute. The government of the Northwest Territories, the Science Institute of the Northwest Territories, and various Canadian federal government departments[13] emphasize the importance of recognizing and utilizing traditional knowledge and of bringing scientists and traditional resource stewards into a better working relationship. There are good reasons for traditional knowledge to be taken very seriously in Arctic international co-operation.

First, much of what occurs in the international sphere is not decided by practising scientists or by decision-makers who consider issues according to any scientific methodology. In fact decision-makers may often despair of getting straight answers from scientists.[14] A recent report on the role of scientific knowledge in the work of the World Commission on

Environment and Development (Brundtland Commission) mentioned that although scientists frequently testified at the commission's public hearings, when the commission members referred back to what was said, "they almost invariably spoke of the testimony of the common people: youth, farmers, rubber tappers."[15] The results of several court cases and public environmental hearings on land-use conflicts in northern Canada and Alaska have clearly indicated that prognoses of the situation provided by knowledgeable local peoples often prove accurate in problem areas where outside experts so often disagree.[16]

A second reason for embracing traditional knowledge as an instrument for increased circumpolar co-operation arises from the fact that traditional knowledge is culturally based yet international. Its origins long predate and remain unaffected by those national ideological differences that often influence the behaviour of scientists involved in international affairs, and of negotiating teams in particular.[17] The Inuit Circumpolar Conference and Indigenous Survival International are two international aboriginal organizations in which culturally based concerns successfully transcend national differences that might impede co-operation. Significantly, both organizations have been effective in dealing with, and indeed influencing, national governments.

Lessons from the Antarctic

Antarctica has been called the continent of science and co-operation, whilst the Arctic is better known as the region of politics and conflict. In seeking to explain this interesting difference, Willy Østreng has identified three types of political utilities that scientific research may serve: (1) practical-instrumental, (2) symbolic-instrumental, (3) knowledge-instrumental.[18] Practical-instrumental utility is that found in applied science and technology-related research, directed towards the solution of immediate practical problems, whether in the industrial, civil, or military spheres of activity. The research sponsor, especially in the private industrial and military cases, will usually tend to regard the results of that research as *proprietary* or *classified,* and this secrecy creates an unfavourable climate for co-operation and sharing. At the other extreme is knowledge-instrumental utility resulting from basic science directed to a fuller understanding of reality. Such research does not claim to have any immediate practical utility, and the search for any such utility is left to other people working at other times and in other places. Sharing the information resulting from this type of research provides recognition and reward for the scientists and agencies supporting these research activities. Sharing the knowledge gained leads to openness rather than secrecy, and hence fosters co-operation. The conclusion, therefore, is that the less practical value research has, the more chance there is that international co-operation will be facilitated.[19]

In the Antarctic, incredible changes have occurred in international relations during this century. The early years, up until 1949, were the "nationalist era" in which scientific expeditions were dispatched to reinforce territorial claims to sovereignty in the region or to enhance international prestige by essentially competitive means. There was little international co-operation and, according to the earlier typology, these scientific activities served largely symbolic-instrumental functions. Symbolic-instrumental research serves primarily political ends. One of its main functions is to demonstrate that a scientific capacity exists and that there is a degree of political will to act, should some act of national assertion be required in the future.

However, in the 1950s evidence of international co-operation appeared, with the trinational Maudheim Expedition (1949-52) followed by the multinational International Geophysical Year (IGY) (1957-8). These endeavours contributed to the negotiation of the Antarctic Treaty (1959). The signatories agreed to full-scale international scientific co-operation and the banning of certain military and industrial activities in the region, activities that would tend to encourage those types of applied research fostering secrecy and unco-operative attitudes. This remarkable transition in the space of ten years, from lack of to full and friendly co-operation, required acts of political leadership. In the agreement it is expressly stated that nothing taking place in the region as a result of the treaty has any bearing on future actions that might be made or denied in connection with sovereignty claims.

These events in the Antarctic are both encouraging and potentially problematic. During the past several years pressure to exploit Antarctic resources has grown. Although such economic and industrial actions are governed by separate treaties, allowing such activity would certainly ensure that research of the practical-instrumental type would become increasingly prominent on the Antarctic research agenda. However, it is also important to observe that whereas any suggestions of full-scale economic exploitation of Antarctic resources would most probably have been soundly rejected in the 1950s, the various parties involved were able thirty years later to move to the initial stage of signing an agreement that would open the way for mineral and hydrocarbon exploration and development. It has been suggested that "long-standing successful co-operation seems in itself to widen the margins of tolerance for sensitive topics to be discussed."[20]

The contrasts to be found in the north polar regions as compared with the Antarctic arise in large part because the Arctic regions encompass strategically important northern extensions of the homelands of the opposing blocs.[21] Slowly, however, a thaw has appeared in superpower relations; notwithstanding the continued military importance of the lands and seas surrounding the Arctic countries, a series of East-West agreements has been signed. Mikhail Gorbachev's Murmansk speech (1987) also indicates a new Soviet willingness to move towards multilateral relations in the Arctic.[22]

Grounds for Optimism

What are the prospects for successful co-operation in the Arctic where military and industrial activities are well developed and, as noted earlier, promote the kind of practical-instrumental research that might be expected to impede, rather than encourage, co-operation and sharing? The experience in the Antarctic provides grounds for optimism, notwithstanding the evident differences between the two regions. In the Antarctic, the more sensitive areas of discussion, involving economic-industrial resource exploitation, may yet be successfully resolved after many years of international co-operation involving research in non-controversial areas of knowledge-instrumental utility. In the Arctic, there are already bilateral agreements. Expanding these research programmes to include other co-operating parties seems a distinct possibility following Gorbachev's Murmansk initiative.[23]

However, we do know that the terms of the Soviet-Canada agreement of 1984, of the Soviet-American agreement on Arctic medical research of 1986, and the 1987 Murmansk initiative[24] all include components that are certainly of a practical-instrumental nature. Might these create impediments to co-operation? That this need not be so can be argued by reference to the inclusion of both knowledge-instrumental and practical-instrumental research topics in each of the science agreements. It may also be that, as with President Reagan's remarks about alien invaders, both sides now recognize that certain problems in the northern regions deserve the urgent mobilization of the best available resources to meet a common threat. Just as nuclear holocaust threatens all, so too, in their own ways, do the depletion of the ozone layer, or changes to the thermal budget of the

Arctic Ocean, or transboundary pollution problems such as Arctic haze, to name just a few of the many commonly recognized northern environmental problems.

How can we better ensure that research agreements in the northern circumpolar regions foster this hoped-for international sharing and co-operation rather than working in contrary fashion? A retreat from co-operation may not stem only from the proprietary interest one party feels for practical-instrumental research. For example, such basic concerns as the choice of appropriate parameters, methodology, or equipment to be included in an environmental monitoring study can cause disagreement, especially where one party to an international agreement believes its level of participation is perceived as deficient or inadequate or its concerns are not given due attention by another party.[25]

In ensuring improved international relations as a result of joint research endeavours, ethnoscience or the traditional-knowledge-based approach has an important role to play. Just as science is international and therefore provides a recognized basis for common endeavours and shared understanding, so too is this traditional-knowledge-based system of knowing, despite the cultural diversity among the northern circumpolar peoples. An appreciation of the value of traditional-knowledge-based systems of understanding is widespread at the regional level throughout northern societies, whether these societies be Inuit, Saami, Chukchi, Dene, Yakuts, Tungus, Evenks, or others. And, as mentioned earlier, there is a growing appreciation of traditional knowledge among non-indigenous people whose work in the North exposes them to the depth of understanding that local resource users possess concerning the way in which northern ecosystemic relationships appear to function.

At a second level, traditional-knowledge-based understanding can be regarded as having knowledge-instrumental utility, for there are still extensive bodies of such knowledge that warrant collection and study in their own right. The appreciation of their practical value is relatively recent, so that much research needs to be done to ensure this long-standing human adaptational capability is not lost to future generations. Indeed, cultural diversity should be safeguarded throughout the noosphere with the same sense of urgency and purpose as is accorded the protection of biological diversity in the biosphere.

This, then, is a second strand in the web of relationships that circumpolar nations can establish to increase their mutual interrelatedness, one based on science co-operation, the other on a parallel system of traditional knowledge or ethnoscience. In the latter case, not only would ethnoscience serve to complement or augment scientific activities, but would itself be a subject for co-operative research. Insofar as traditional-knowledge-based activities are increasingly included in the discussions and investigative programmes of international science-based agencies, the web of co-operation extends not just in an east-west fashion around the Arctic, but in a north-south direction on a global scale. The potential therefore exists for Arctic and northern research to participate in the continued improvement of well-being on a global level.

Efforts to Ensure Traditional Knowledge Is Not Lost

Though an awareness of the utility of traditional knowledge in questions of environmental management, and especially the sustainable development of renewable resources, is growing, this understanding is by no means universally accepted. What is particularly helpful in efforts to further its wider acceptance is the endorsement that traditional-knowledge practitioners increasingly receive from science-based environmental management and conservation organizations and agencies. A few examples follow.

The Commission on Ecology of the International Union for Conservation of Nature (IUCN) has established a Working Group on Traditional Ecological Knowledge. The working group has stated its objectives as follows:

- to promote the synthesis and use of traditional ecological knowledge and resource management practices of rural communities as an effective basis for a modern and sustainable resource management system and for nature and natural resource conservation;
- to develop and promote effective ways of harnessing, recording, analysing, and applying traditional ecological knowledge for the conservation of nature and natural resources;
- to develop simple methods based on traditional ecological knowledge, for use by rural communities and others, for the assessment and monitoring of the conservation of nature and natural resources;
- to collaborate with groups with related interests in order to foster the achievement of conservation objectives through the application of traditional ecological knowledge.

The working group publishes a newsletter and is in the process of establishing international networks among interested individuals in the following areas: northern circumpolar regions, monsoon regions, Hawaiian islands, and Latin America. The newsletter reports on initiatives throughout the world involving the application and furtherance of approaches to environmental management using traditional ecological knowledge.

In regard to the northern regions, there is considerable interest. The bibliography compiled by Thomas Andrews provides many northern references.[26] The Dene Cultural Institute is to initiate a study in Fort Good Hope, NWT, and has undertaken to organize an international workshop (with participants from Africa and Oceania among others) to further the implementation of traditional knowledge approaches; this workshop is financially supported by the International Development Research Centre, Ottawa.

Elsewhere in the Canadian North, a community-based research study started in March 1989 in Sanikiluaq, an Inuit community in the Hudson Bay region, is directed towards developing a locally based management regime for a local wild reindeer population. This project aims to derive local and wider legitimacy by combining an adaptive management approach with traditional Inuit wildlife management principles. The community hopes to extend this approach to the resource management of marine mammals, wildfowl, and other locally important resource stocks.

On the international level, an organization based in northern Canada, Indigenous Survival International, has proposed a thorough revision of the World Conservation Strategy to embody recognition of the contribution to be made by greater use of traditional knowledge approaches; the strategy's sponsors (the IUCN, the World Wildlife Fund, and the United Nations Environment Program) appear to concur. The essence of the indigenous peoples' position is that they possess a substantial and detailed corpus of traditional environmental knowledge, including effective resource management systems that have ensured sustainable harvests over time. Further, aboriginal perceptions, ethics, and environmental knowledge have value at the present time when sustainable development is demanded, and when exchange of information and co-operative approaches involving indigenous peoples and environmental scientists and managers should be expanded. It needs to be recognized that even though denied recognition and rights, aboriginal people can play an appropriate role in environmental management by contributing to the common task of safeguarding valued yet vulnerable renewable resources.[27] There is an awareness, among both aboriginal people and many non-aboriginal environmental scientists, managers, and organizations, that co-operation and the exchange of ideas are timely and in order and that meaningful linkages should not be difficult to establish.

Social Concerns within the Environmental Problematique

This paper emphasized at the outset that the discussion was to be centred more especially on a consideration of environmental problems. In this regard two recent international initiatives have provided a promising framework for improving the critical human/environment relationship, namely the Brundtland Report and the World Conservation Strategy.[28] Both documents refer to the need for sustainable development, defined as development that meets the needs of the present without compromising the ability of future generations to meet their own needs.

In this quest for sustainable development, it is important to recognize that any preferred human interaction with the environment must necessarily be *socially* sustainable. For that reason the World Conservation Strategy recognizes that: (1) human life depends upon sustainable *and equitable* utilization of environmental resources; (2) the sustainable *livelihood* of people should be assured by governments; and (3) the active *involvement of local people* is necessary in developing and implementing sustainable development strategies.

A more widespread recognition of the appropriate part to be played by traditional knowledge in environmental programmes will contribute significantly to the goal of effecting sustainable social and economic development in the northern regions. It is nonetheless important to recognize that inter-group conflicts and tensions in northern regions do exist, not just across some international boundaries but within particular national jurisdictions wherever the local and the national interest may be differently perceived.[29]

This paper has argued that there is good reason to believe that traditional ways of knowing the North have a practical and positive role to play in effective and appropriate environmental management initiatives and that awareness of this fact is growing. Adaptive management is now a recognized means by which this new augmented approach, combining both science-based and tradition-based ways of understanding the problem, can be implemented. The eventual goal of an agreed circumpolar northern conservation strategy, which will address the full range of shared environmental management problems affecting the Arctic countries, needs all the support that governments, scientists, northern resource users, and residents in each country can supply. The contribution of traditional-knowledge experts is a barely tapped resource that is waiting to be called upon. The nature of the problem suggests the call should be made without further delay.

Notes

1   Nicholas Rescher, *The Limits of Science* (Berkeley: University of California Press 1984), 86.

2   Fritjof Capra, *The Turning Point: Science, Society and the Rising Culture* (New York: Simon and Schuster 1982), 24-5. In his book *Reconciling Man with the Environment* (Stanford: Stanford University Press 1978), 83, Eric Ashby wrote: "The technique of reductionism in science, although it has been enormously successful, does not (and cannot) illuminate the behavior of whole interdependent systems ... the techniques of reductionism are irrelevant for this order of [ecosystemic] complexity."

3   Capra, *The Turning Point,* 25. Fred Roots has written: "It is a truism to say that one of the most underutilized sources of information in many vital areas of Arctic development is the accumulated practical knowledge that the Inuit possess ... Southerners who have worked or studied in the Arctic for many years and know it well are those most conscious of the soundness and depth of traditional knowledge." "Basic Science and Its Relation to Arctic Marine Engineering," Sixth International Conference on Port and Ocean Engineering under Arctic Conditions, Quebec City, 27-31 July 1981, 23.

4   Capra, *The Turning Point,* 32. To quote from Roots again ("Basic Science," 22), in respect to mathematical modelling of environmental processes: "We should keep in mind that although we may dress up the estimates with numbers ... our general understanding of the overall relationships between Arctic weather and Arctic ocean behaviour is not demonstrably better than that of the Inuit who have a *feel* for it based on long and intimate observation."

5   For example, N. M. Williams and E. S. Hunn, eds, *Resource Managers: North American and Australian Hunter-Gatherers* (Boulder CO: Westview 1982); K. Ruddle and R. E. Johannes, eds, *The Traditional Knowledge and Management of Coastal Systems in Asia and the Pacific* (Jakarta: UNESCO 1985); B. J. McCay and J. M. Acheson, eds, *The Question of the Commons: The Culture and the Economy of Common Property* (Tucson: University of Arizona Press 1987); M. M. R. Freeman and L. N. Carbyn, eds, *Traditional Knowledge and Renewable Resource Management in Northern Regions* (Edmonton: Boreal Institute for Northern Studies 1988), especially T. D. Andrews, "Selected Bibliography of Native Resource Management Systems and Native Knowledge of the Environment," 105-24.

6   Fikret Berkes, "Fishermen and the Tragedy of the Commons," *Environmental Conservation,* 12 (no 3, 1985), 199-206, and "Common Property Resource Management and Cree Indian Fisheries in Subarctic Canada," in McCay and Acheson, eds, *Question of the Commons,* 66-79; Robert E. Johannes, "Traditional Conservation Methods and Protected Marine Areas in Oceania," *Ambio,* 11 (no 5, 1982), 258-61, and "Marine Conservation in Relation to Traditional Lifestyles of Tropical Artisanal Fishermen," IUCN, *Commission on Ecology Papers,* no 7 (1984), 30-5.

7   Shoiti Tanaka, "On the Practical Method for Stock Management" (Cambridge: International Whaling Commission, document SC/A86/CA6, 1986); Kazumi

Sakuramoto and Shoiti Tanaka, "Further Simulation Study on Management of Whale Stocks Considering Feedback Systems" (Cambridge: International Whaling Commission, Scientific Committee document, 1987).

8 *Adaptive Management of Renewable Resources* (Laxenburg, Austria: International Institute of Applied Systems Analysis 1986).

9 C. S. Holling, ed, *Adaptive Environmental Assessment and Management* (Chichester: Wiley 1978); C. Walters, *Adaptive Management of Renewable Resources* (New York: Macmillan 1986).

10 Walters, *Adaptive Management*.

11 Dunbar suggests that the term "fragiie Arctic" is catchy, widely believed, but ecologically unsound. He writes: "I can see little reason to suppose that Arctic ecosystems are any more or any less vulnerable to human interference than any other ecosystems ... In fact, the Arctic ecosystems appear to be as tough as others." Quoted from M. J. Dunbar, "The Arctic Marine Ecosystems," in F. R. Engelhardt, ed, *Petroleum Effects in the Arctic Environment* (London: Elsevier 1985), 26-7.

12 *Adaptive Management of Renewable Resources* (IIASA).

13 Nellie Cournoyea, "People, Policy and Practice: The Northwest Territories Approach to Renewable Resource Management," in M. M. R. Freeman and C. W. Slaughter, eds, *Arctic Science Policy and Development* (Washington: Man and the Biosphere Program 1986), 75-81; N. Sibbeston, "Economic Development and Renewable Resources in the Northwest Territories," in J. Green and J. Smith, eds, in *Native People and Renewable Resource Management* (Edmonton: Alberta Society of Professional Biologists 1986), 153-7; Robert R. Janes, "An Introduction to the Science Institute of the Northwest Territories," in W. P. Adams, ed, *Education, Research, Information Systems and the North* (Ottawa: Association of Canadian Universities for Northern Studies 1987), 72-5. Federal documents such as the 1987 Status Report of the Intergovernmental Working Group on Northern Conservation and the 1987 Canadian Arctic Maritime Conservation Strategy stress the part to be played by knowledgeable local resource users and traditional stewards of northern environmental resources. A recent discussion on environmental research in Alaska made a similar point: see *Arctic Research of the United States*, 2 (spring 1988), 60-1.

14 In a recent article, Frederick Seitz, a past president of the United States National Academy of Sciences, is quoted: "[When] issues related to science and technology [have] strong political content ... it was always relatively easy to find individuals with good professional qualifications to argue, even vehemently, in support of either side." Bruce L.R. Smith, "Odd Men Out: Why Presidents Ignore Their Science Advisers," *The Sciences*, 28 (September/October 1988), 50. Specifically in regard to biologists' opinions about one of the best researched Arctic animals, the caribou, see correspondence on the following pages of *Arctic*: 37 (September 1984), 293-5; 38 (March 1985), 53-7; 38 (June 1985), 154-6; 38 (December 1985), 344-5.

15 Lloyd Timberlake, "The Role of Scientific Knowledge in Drawing Up the Brundtland Report," *International Challenges: Newsletter from the Fridtjof Nansen Institute*, 9 (no 3, 1988), 12.

16 I have discussed this matter with respect to environmental/wildlife conflicts

15 Lloyd Timberlake, "The Role of Scientific Knowledge in Drawing Up the Brundtland Report," *International Challenges: Newsletter from the Fridtjof Nansen Institute*, 9 (no 3, 1988), 12.

16 I have discussed this matter with respect to environmental/wildlife conflicts elsewhere: in Jens Dahl et al, eds, *Native Power: The Quest for Autonomy and Nationhood of Indigenous Peoples* (Bergen/Oslo: Universitetsforlaget 1985), 265-81, and in E. Pinkerton, ed, *Co-operative Management of Local Fisheries* (Vancouver: University of British Columbia Press 1989), 137-53. In a paper entitled "Characterizing Uncertainty in Energy Policy Analysis," commissioned by the Brundtland Commission, Brian Wynn suggests that "scientific research may decrease our ignorance, but it also increases our uncertainty. Furthermore, if we attempt to resolve the issue by commissioning more research under an urgent timetable, even worse uncertainty results." Quoted in Timberlake, "The Role of Scientific Knowledge," 13.

17 See, for example, papers by Halldór Ásgrímsson, Per M. Bakken, and Jørgen Wettestad in *International Challenges: Newsletter from the Fridtjof Nansen Institute*, 9 (no 3, 1988).

18 Willy Østreng, "International Co-operation in Polar Regions," in *International Challenges*, 9 (no 3, 1988), 20-1.

19 Ibid., 21.

20 Ibid., 22.

21 See, for example, the analysis of Young and Cherkasov in this volume.

22 Arkady Cherkasov, "Prospects for Soviet-Canadian Co-operation in the Development of Northern Regions," *Northern Perspectives*, 16 (July-August 1988), 6-8; however, see Dan Hayward's more cautionary analysis of Gorbachev's Murmansk initiative in the same issue at pp 9-11.

23 There are many international agreements in the areas of science exchanges and environmental management co-operation among the Arctic nations. For example, the Canada-Denmark-Norway-United States-Soviet Union Agreement on the Conservation of Polar Bears (1973), the Soviet-American Agreement in the Field of Environmental Protection (1972), the Canada-USSR Protocol on Consultations on the Development of a Programme of Scientific and Technical Co-operation in the Arctic and the North (1984), and the Norway-USSR Science Agreement of 1988.

24 For details of the 1984 and 1986 agreements, see Walter Slipchenko, "Co-operation in Arctic Science," *Northern Perspectives*, 15 (May-June 1987), 12-13, and Theodore A. Mala, "The University of Alaska-Siberian Medical Research Program: A Circumpolar Agreement," *Arctic Medical Research*, no 46 (1987), 35-8. For the Murmansk initiative, see Cherkasov, "Prospects for Soviet-Canadian Co-operation."

25 Examples here are provided by global environment monitoring proposals. See Milton Freeman, "Dissent, Diversity and Biosphere Reserves," in J. T. Inglis et al, eds, *Research and Monitoring in Circumpolar Biosphere Reserves* (Edmonton: Boreal Institute for Northern Studies 1987), 71-2, and recent debates in the International Whaling Commission concerning disputed stock sampling methods

and single-species management approaches (Ásgrímsson in *International Challenges,* 9 [no 3, 1988]).

26 Andrews, "Selected Bibliography of Native Resource Management Systems and Native Knowledge of the Environment."

27 See a draft of the relevant rewriting of the World Conservation Strategy in issue no 6, *Tradition, Conservation and Development* (Occasional Newsletter of the Commission on Ecology's Working Group on Traditional Ecological Knowledge), 1-9, or write to Jeff McNeely, IUCN, 1196 Gland, Switzerland.

28 World Commission on Environment and Development, *Our Common Future* (London: Oxford University Press 1987); World Conservation Strategy (IUCN/UNEP/WWF 1980).

29 For example, see articles by Ole Henrick Magga, Odd Terje Brantenberg, Robert Paine, Georg Henriksen, Harald Eidheim, and others in Dahl et al, eds, *Native Power.*

7

Inuit Culture and International Policy

Aqqaluk Lynge

Members of the executive council of the Inuit Circumpolar Conference (ICC) from Alaska, Canada, and Greenland recently completed a trip to the Soviet Union, to the region of Chukotsky Peninsula where Inuit from Alaska met Yuit of the Soviet Union. It was a reunion of families and relatives who had not been able to see each other for more than forty years.

Inuit of Alaska, Canada, and Greenland had achieved something that they had been working for since the inception of the ICC in 1977. Years of diplomacy and extensive travel were honoured at a final meeting in Moscow with the vice-president of the Soviet Council of Ministers, Mr Masliukov, who agreed to send Yuit representatives to the next ICC general assembly in Sisimiut, Greenland, in 1989.

I think quite a number of people wonder why this small nation of Inuit is engaged in so many areas and on such sensitive matters as militarization and security questions. The ICC, with small regional offices in Alaska and Greenland and an international office in Canada, is in fact dealing with a broad range of issues, most of them stemming from the enormous pressures that come from outside.

Right now the Arctic peoples are facing the most critical situation in centuries. The threat comes not from the oil or gas companies, which is something that was faced several years ago, but from the environmentalists or animal rights groups, whose organizations are lobbying governments, international agencies, and various national organizations to take away the Inuit right to harvest their renewable resources.

In the 1970s Greenpeace started to campaign against seal hunting off the coast of Newfoundland, hunting done by non-natives in which only the skin and fur were utilized. The impact of that campaign has been devastating and disastrous for the people of the North. The livelihood of most of the hunters in the North, especially in Canada and Greenland, is heavily dependent on the seal hunt. If you don't sell your sealskins or your seal products, there is no cash. You become just a figure in the unemployment statistics of the government. Later we approached Greenpeace and tried to make them understand what they had caused. Although Inuit are against the industrial hunting of seals, we are not against our own hunting. Eventually, there was a better understanding by the Greenpeace people. They tried to apologize for what they had done to our traditional way of hunting. Everybody knows that the seal in the Arctic is in no danger of extinction. The way we have been hunting seals and using them has been the same throughout our history – we use the whole seal. The only thing we sell to the outside is the fur.

This is only one example of what can happen when environmentalists do not understand other cultures and their environments. Right now the lobbying efforts of animal rights groups in the European Parliament have almost succeeded in a ban on trapping, which is of most direct concern to Canadian and Alaskan Indians. And there is another effort in the European Parliament to stop all imports of sealskin.

Other areas where we are fighting and going to meetings all over the world concern problems created by conventions like CITES, the Convention on International Trade in Endangered Species. These conventions block our opportunities to trade our traditional products. Economic development between Alaska, Canada, and Greenland, based on our traditional products, becomes almost impossible. Even travel restrictions are in existence – import restrictions all over. It is illegal to bring any kind of sealskin clothes, which we still use in our area, from Greenland to Canada or from Canada to Alaska or other parts of the United States, although it's not illegal to bring other clothes from Alaska to Canada or Greenland.

These are only some examples of the difficulties facing economic and cultural co-operation among the Inuit – among the natives of the North.

One of the big issues the ICC has been dealing with for decades is whaling. We are involved in lobbying efforts here. The ICC has status as an observer at the International Whaling Commission, where we try to secure our traditional rights to hunt. It was in this forum that one of the first clashes of opinion between our small nations and the southern cultures occurred. A culture clash is a question about who you want to save. Do you want to save the environment as a whole, or do you want to save a species within the Arctic?

To my way of thinking, there is something wrong when the same amount of money is used to save the grey whales trapped under the ice off the coast of Barrow, Alaska, as the ICC has been using over the last ten years to organize themselves. There is something wrong with a human way of thinking when you do things that are against nature. Those grey whales will either live or become extinct, and that's the nature of things in the Arctic. But when the media with its one-second coverage show certain kinds of pictures, then it's almost impossible to have a different opinion. For instance, the Greenpeace campaign against sealing: when you see a picture on TV of a small, beautiful seal baby with its big eyes staring at you – what do you do? It sits back in your head for a long time and you never forget it. But the consequences for the people living up North – how do you make a picture of that!

The very core of the problem is the difference in philosophies between the ICC and indeed all the natives in North America, and the "Western" world. Somebody jokingly said that for every Eskimo there are three ethnographers. The ideal situation would be if for every Eskimo there were millions of people from the "South," including the scientists, who understood and supported the human aspects of our development.

One thing we have to be aware of is that Inuit are not the only native people living in the North. The northern peoples include the Indians, the Saami or Lapps, the Nenets, the Evenks, the Koryaks, and the Chukchi. But we didn't know anything about this twenty years ago when we began to organize. The only thing we knew about the Soviet Union was that there were a few Yuit left. The first Arctic conference on petroleum and gas development was in 1969 in Rouen, France. That's where Inuit, and for that matter also the Indians, met internationally for the first time. There was another conference in 1973 in Le Havre on these questions. I remember we were wondering what was going on. They were talking about gas and petroleum, marine transportation, icebreaking, pipelines, and … well, it took only four or five years before it was a reality, and there we were in the middle of a new world.

Our first conference was the Arctic Peoples' Conference in Copenhagen in 1973. And that was the very first time that the Canadian Inuit and the Greenlandic Inuit met with the Saami of Scandinavia. In 1975 in Vancouver Island, together with the National Indian Brotherhood of Canada, we arranged the World Council of Indigenous Peoples. That was the beginning of the realization that we, the Inuit of the Arctic, were dealing with problems that each group acting alone was not able to solve. That's why we gathered in 1977 in Barrow, Alaska, to see if a common language, a common culture, the same climate, and the same environment could produce something like the ICC – an organization that could speak for all natives in the North who, because they have the same language, are brothers and sisters. That is why the ICC was formed.

I should mention that although it might seem that native peoples all over the world have the same interests, the facts are different. Old stories tell that we and the Indians were enemies. In the present situation in Canada you can see how easy it is for the Canadian central government to divide these two groups, and it seems there will never be anything written in the constitution about the rights of Inuit or the Indians. That's the complexity of the situation. Another reason why it was easier to unite Alaska, Canada, and Greenland was the strategic situation of Western culture as a whole. Now we are very happy that the situation in the world has changed and we can have the Chukchi people and the other Arctic people of the Soviet Union join us in our efforts to internationalize the question of the human beings in the Arctic.

So how do we deal with all the challenges we face?

First of all we travel all over the world trying to educate others and tell what we stand for.

The ICC has worked on several issues for the last ten years. The main one is called the Inuit Regional Conservation Strategy, which is a programme being worked on in Alaska, Canada, and Greenland simultaneously. Its main goal is to make a map of all our renewable resources and try to build up a pool of knowledge so we can use it in our work, especially in the sound management of renewable resources. For many years we have been racing doped runners – everyone is in front of us. With the Inuit Regional Conservation Strategy we want to be ahead and want to be able to participate in international gatherings and conventions so we can secure our living resources. The strategy is mostly based on the United Nations Environment Program (UNEP), which not many governments have implemented yet. That's why we recently received the UNEP award, which we are very proud of. That's one of the small awards we think helped us in our work. The ICC is also member of the International Union for Conservation of Nature. The ICC is also working on completing an Arctic policy, which will serve as the foundation of the organization's work.

Among the few programmes I can mention is that we are working to develop a common writing system and a common writing language to promote an international Inuit concert on the issues we face. A principal aim on cultural issues is to work for the removal of travel restrictions – to ensure that ancient Inuit travel traditions are not hindered by contemporary political borders. An important aspect of Inuit heritage is cultural interchange among all the families throughout the Arctic. We are also promoting existing cultural and educational exchanges. We want access to research results of work done by scientists in our various areas. We also want that information to be given to all the nations involved in the ICC, so we can utilize that knowledge together.

Let me try to summarize what we think is happening. We have seen at this conference that there is not much intergovernmental co-operation among the Arctic states. There are some steps being taken now, and several Arctic nations are working on their polar programmes and Arctic legislation. But in the ICC we think there should be more governmental co-operation on both the regional and the local levels, so that the various treaties, for example on pollution or migratory birds, are not just forgotten afterwards. The Greenland Home Rule government has in the past ten years been able to co-operate with the Scandinavian countries through the Nordic Council. It is obvious that similar governmental co-operation could take place with other local or regional governments in Alaska, Canada, and Greenland.

A few moments ago there was an enthusiastic question about Canada and the USSR working together on "breaking the ice." One thing Eskimos are against is breaking the ice, because we know it's dangerous. But I don't know exactly what Arctic waters are concerned or where the USSR is operating. There must be some studies, but I don't know what kind of impact they have had on the environmental issues, and I don't know if the people in these areas are hunting on the ice. Greenlandic and Canadian Inuit do hunt on the ice and that's why they co-operated against the Arctic Pilot Project several years ago. If the governments of Canada and the USSR are going to co-operate, it must mainly be on matters of industrial development and not be focused on the people who traditionally live in the areas concerned.

If you don't recognize our rights to live there and to have access to your knowledge of these areas, then I don't know why people should gather to talk about the Arctic.

I see many possibilities and I'm not at all opposed to governmental co-operation. I just want to make a point on the essence of the model of co-operation – that you include regional and local governments. For instance, co-operation between the Northwest Territories and the Greenland Home Rule government should be on the agenda monthly. Even co-operation between the province of Quebec and Greenland should be developed. The Greenland Home Rule government is in a situation where it is able to co-operate much more than before, such as with the North Slope Borough in Alaska, with the Northwest Borough, the State of Alaska, and besides that, with the government of the USSR – the Chukchi area.

It's about time to develop a form of co-operation that includes all the nations and states of the Arctic. The ICC will be happy to consult with you on these matters.

Part III

Scientific, Environmental and Technical Issues

8

The Physical and Biological Environment

M.J. Dunbar

The first international Polar Oceans Conference dealing with both the Arctic and the Antarctic, sponsored by the Scientific Committee on Oceanic Research and the Scientific Committee on Antarctic Research, was held at McGill University in Montreal in May of 1974. It is appropriate to recall that meeting because the polar regions are undergoing active reassessment internationally from several points of view. Both regions may usefully be considered as vast scientific, economic, and social laboratories with impressive similarities and significant differences.

To begin with, their climatic and glacial histories are different, in terms of the growth of glacial periods. The cooling of the higher latitudes during the Tertiary period may or may not have involved a shift in the positions of the North and South Poles relative to the distribution of land and sea, but the position of the South Pole close to the middle of the Antarctic continent did mean that that cold land mass was surrounded by the only continuous circumglobal ocean current in the world, the Southern Ocean Current, which provides an enormous source of water vapour that is precipitated on the southern continent as snow, forming the Antarctic ice cap. This process appears to have begun some twenty million years ago, and the southern ice cap has existed without interruption since that time.

In the North, the North Pole is in the middle of an ocean, 4,000 metres deep, in contact with sources of heat carried by the Pacific and Atlantic oceans. This supply of heat to a large water body with a very large heat capacity and a reluctance to lose it meant, in contrast to the Antarctic land mass with very different heat characteristics, that the process of cooling in the central Arctic Ocean was a slow one. Precipitation of snow on the surrounding land, most of which lies in latitudes considerably lower than those of the Antarctic continent, was a seasonal event, meaning that for millennia the snow that fell each winter melted the following summer. The snow would not have begun to accumulate on land until the surface of the Arctic Ocean had cooled to a critical value, at which time the total heat carried in both atmosphere and hydrosphere had reached a lower steady state value. The precise time at which the snow began to accumulate on the surrounding land is controversial, but may be taken to have been somewhere between three and four million years ago, much later than in the South.

But the balance between sea and land in the northern hemisphere also meant that the glaciation in the north would be less stable than that in the south – to a large extent it would be discontinuous. When the cold winds from the land ice began to cause the surface of the Arctic Ocean to freeze, the supply of moisture to the system began to be reduced and was finally cut off. The deposition of snow therefore was reduced in winter, and the ablation of the ice in summer became greater than the winter precipitation. The northern ice caps on land thus began to dwindle, and the first interglacial period set in. So there began an oscillation between glacial and interglacial periods: when the ice caps disappeared, the winds over the Arctic Ocean warmed and, moreover, the water that had been locked up in the ice and which had caused a reduction in global sea level of something like 120 to 140 metres was returned to the sea. Heat from the Pacific and the Atlantic, and from the air, increased, and the surface of the Arctic Ocean became either free of ice or at least less heavily covered. Da capo – the process began again.

This, at least, is one version of what has been happening. Largely the work of geophysicists and oceanographers in the Lamont-Doherty Geological Observatory at Palisades, New York,[1] this very elegant theory has been challenged in recent years. The time-scale called for by the Lamont-Doherty group is about 100,000 years per cycle, but Emiliani, using the technique of oxygen isotope analysis of fossil shells of pelagic foraminiferan Protozoa in sea sediments, demonstrated a shorter cycle of hypsithermals in Quaternary time, closer to 50,000 years.[2] However, contemporary geophysicists seem to have forgotten the Emiliani paper and are happy with the longer cycle. One thing seems to be clear: temperatures as high as those of today occurred in the past for only about 10 per cent of the time during the last half million years.[3] Whether or not this is connected with the climatic changes of the present century is discussed below.

Global Interaction

An excellent stylization of the global pattern of the inter-relation between ocean, air, and land has recently been put forward by Broecker, also of the

Lamont-Doherty Observatory, from whose work figure 1 is taken. Broecker speaks of fairly sudden climatic changes in the past that brought about reorganizations of heat and transport cycles into patterns different from those of the immediate past (on the palaeontological scale). Such a reorganization occurred at the end of the last glaciation, about 13,500 years ago, starting off an oceanic conveyor belt in terms of heat and salinity. In the northern North Atlantic, in the region of southern Greenland and Iceland, the surface water is exposed to cold winds from Canada and Greenland and also from the Arctic Ocean. This removes heat and evaporates water from the upper water, both of which processes affect the climate of western Europe. The sea water, now cooled and more saline, sinks to form the North Atlantic Deep Water, estimated by Broecker to form a "subsurface river whose flow is twenty times the flow of all the world's rivers," which moves south to the Antarctic and eastward into the Indian Ocean and ultimately arrives in the North Pacific, the other end of the conveyor belt. Here the deep current rises to the surface under the advective influence of the North Pacific cyclonic (anti-clockwise) gyre and picks up heat and fresh water (atmosphere-carried). Broecker proposes that the water that freshens the North Pacific surface is "the same water that was distilled from the North Atlantic, which would require that it cross from sea to sea in the atmosphere" over the whole Eurasian land mass.[4] This upper water current formed in the North Pacific flows south and west,

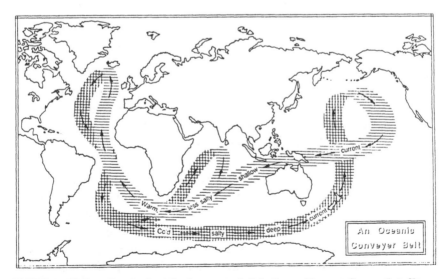

FIGURE 1. Wallace Broecker's stylized conveyor belt in the world ocean. Source: R.A. Kerr, "Linking Earth, Ocean and Air at the AGU," *Science*, 239 (1988), 259-60.

through the Indonesian-New Guinea region into the Indian Ocean, and so back to the North Atlantic.

This most recent, and perhaps most striking, demonstration of the unity of the global oceanic system extends our mental horizons. The world itself is an open system whether considered by the ecologist, the oceanographer, the meteorologist, or the climatologist. As one of my colleagues once remarked, "when walking on the ice of the Arctic Ocean one must remember that the very movement of that ice is in some way affected by events in Drake Passage, and vice versa." Before the European colonization of Greenland, the most important source of wood for the Greenlanders to use in building kayaks and umiaks was driftwood from the Siberian coast. And shortly after pesticides began to be used on land in the northern hemisphere they were found to be present in the marine fauna of Antarctica.

Surface Currents

Ocean currents are controlled by the wind system, by the effects of heating and cooling and of melting and freezing, and by the rotation of the earth. In this article, the atmospheric climate of the North as a whole cannot fully be covered. It is well described in summary by Lamb and by Hare.[5] Figure 2 shows the resultant pattern of surface flow and the interplay between the three water masses: Arctic, Pacific, and Atlantic. Transport values are given here in Sverdrups (1 Sv = one million cubic metres per second).

Arctic water escapes from the Arctic Ocean through Canada's Arctic islands and along Greenland's east coast in approximately equal volume. Some of it (about 0.05 Sverdrups) flows into Foxe Basin through Fury and Hecla Strait.[6] Some of it enters Baffin Bay directly from the Arctic Ocean by way of Nares Strait, Jones Sound, and Lancaster Sound. The East Greenland Current rounds Cape Farewell and enters the Labrador Sea as part of the West Greenland Current, which flows up the west coast of Greenland.

Atlantic water enters the system by two routes. The Irminger Current, a branch of the North Atlantic Drift, flows westward from the region southwest of Iceland and comes to lie beneath the East Greenland Current, forming a large wedge of warmer water underlying that cold Arctic current (the warmer water is denser by virtue of its higher salinity). This Irminger water and the East Greenland Arctic water flow together round Cape Farewell, the southern tip of Greenland. Considerable mixing of the two water masses takes place in this stormy region and also northward

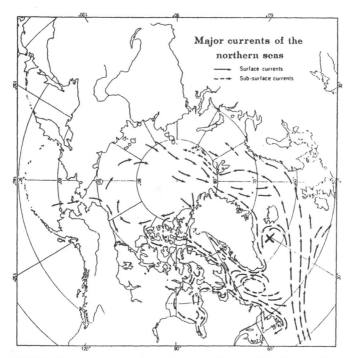

FIGURE 2. Major currents of the northern seas. Source: M.J. Dunbar, "Water Masses, Circulation, Ice Cover," in Kimble and Good, eds, *Geography of the Northlands* (New York: Wiley for American Geographical Society of New York 1955), 36-57.

along the western coast of Greenland, but the two water types remain distinguishable, and much of the success of the Atlantic cod's survival in the waters west of Greenland depends on how much of the Atlantic water flows over the banks off the Greenland's west coast. The second source of Atlantic water is in the Labrador Sea, the deep-water mass lying between the Labrador Current to the west and the West Greenland Current to the east. Labrador Sea water contributes very importantly to the West Greenland Current, to such an extent that the total transport volume of the latter may increase from about 3 to over 7 Sverdrups between Cape Farewell and Ivigtut.[7]

The West Greenland Current thus carries both Atlantic and Arctic water. As it flows northward from Cape Farewell it peels off water to the west, forming part of the Labrador Sea cyclonic (anti-clockwise) gyre, sothat there is a flow of West Greenland water south of Davis Strait towards Hudson Strait.

TABLE 1. Water, Salt, and Heat Budgets for the Arctic Ocean (annual mean)

Source	Volume transport Sv	Heat transport[a] 10^9 kcal S^{-1}	Mean temperature °C	Salt transport 10^3 tonnes S^{-1}	Mean salinity °/oo
Bering Strait					
Water	1.5	0.9	0.5	48.6	32.4
Ice	negligible	-0.4		negligible	
Arctic archipelago	-2.1	3.2	-0.7	-71.8	34.2
East Greenland Current					
Polar water	-1.8[b,c]	2.0	-1.2	-61.2[d]	34.0
Atlantic Water	-5.3[b,c]	-3.2	0.5	-185.0[d]	34.9
Ice	-0.1	8.0		-0.3	3.0
West Spitsbergen Current	7.1	16.3	2.2	248.9	35.0
Svalbard – Franz Josefs Land	-0.1	-0.3	2.7	-3.5	34.9
Franz Josefs Land – Novaya Zemlya[e]	0.7[f]	0.7	0.9	24.3	34.7
Run–off	0.1	0.5	5.0	0	
Total inflow	9.4		1.8[g]	321.8	34.6[g]
Total outflow	-9.4		00.1[g]	-321.8	34.6[g]
Total advective heat		29.7			
Total advective heat loss		-3.9			
Net exchange	0.0	25.8		0.0	

Source: K. Aagaard and P. Greisman, "Towards New Mass and Heat Budgets for the Arctic Ocean," *Journal of Geophysical Research*, 80 (1975), 3821-7; and H.E. Sadler, "Water, Heat and Salt Transports through Nares Strait, Ellesmere Island," *Journal of Fisheries Research Board of Canada*, 33 (no 10, 1976), 2286-95.

Positive values are inflows, or heat gains. Negative values are outflows or heat losses.

[a]Heat transport is relative to –0.1 °C.

[b]Calculated from required combined water and salt transports.

[c]The total value –7.1 is assumed in order to balance West Spitsbergen Current inflow.

[d]The total value –246.2 is calculated from salt continuity.

[e]Karskiye Vorota Strait is included in this source.

[f]Calculated from water continuity.

[g]Excluding run-off and ice transport.

North of Davis Strait the West Greenland Current continues northward, but much reduced in volume. It takes part in the cyclonic gyre in Baffin Bay, and as it continues northward it meets the flow of Arctic water from the Arctic Ocean entering through Nares Strait and Jones and Lancaster Sounds. The western side of the Baffin Bay gyre is the Canadian Current flowing south along the east coast of Baffin Island and over the Davis

Strait ridge. Together with the outflow from Hudson Strait and water from the West Greenland Current, it forms the Labrador Current.

Some of the outflow from the Arctic Ocean breaks off from the East Greenland Current to the eastward, forming part of the circulation of the Greenland and Norwegian seas and coming into contact with the North Atlantic Drift which brings warm water from the western Atlantic over the ridge between Scotland and Iceland, finally into the Barents Sea north of Norway and the northwestern Soviet Union, and into the Arctic Ocean. Entering the Arctic Ocean it sinks beneath the upper Arctic water layer and forms the 700-metre thick "Atlantic layer" found throughout the Arctic Ocean. Much of this Atlantic intrusion, however, is turned back north and west of Svalbard, to flow south again beneath the cold East Greenland Current.

Two large surface flows dominate the Arctic Ocean itself: the Beaufort Sea gyre, clockwise, north of Canada, Alaska, and eastern Siberia; and the broad flow from central Siberia towards the region between northeast Greenland and Svalbard. Pacific water enters the system in a northward flow of about 1 Sv through Bering Strait.

Table 1 summarizes the exchange of water, salt, and heat between the Arctic Ocean and the regions to the south.

Zonation and Biological Productivity

To understand the economic and political background pattern of the North, it is necessary to appreciate the climatic and biological zonation, not simply in terms of temperature, however important, but in terms of biological productivity and potential. In this paper I propose to pay minimal attention to non-renewable resources, because by definition they are of shorter term interest, and to ignore political boundaries because they are irrelevant to the natural system and tend to obscure the unified pattern of energy transfer and flow that allows us to treat the whole of the North as a subsystem of the global system.

In considering climatic and biological zonation in the North the land and the sea must be treated separately. This has been, and remains, a difficulty for those who follow the geographers rather than the oceanographers. Geographers are still apt to think that the root "geo" in the word really means the whole surface of the earth, as it did in the original Greek (and as it still should), whereas they in fact treat only of the land. Water, air, and land have very different mobilities and heat characteristics. Atlantic and Pacific ocean currents carry heat northward into the Arctic

Ocean, and Arctic currents carry cold water very far to the south. (Hudson Bay, for instance, is a penetration of Arctic Ocean water to the very heart of temperate Canada.)

First, however, we must deal with the Arctic Circle which the average person believes to be of serious climatic significance. It has in fact never been a helpful boundary. It is really not a boundary at all, except in respect of the north-south pattern of sunlight and the way in which that changes seasonally, a matter of somewhat limited concern. It is irrelevant to atmospheric and hydrospheric circulation, to faunal distribution, to climatic change, to the treeline or the limits of permafrost, and to general isotherm patterns. There is a strong case for removing the Arctic Circle from the atlases. The same, of course, goes for its Antarctic counterpart.

Productivity of Cold Salt Water

Arctic water is defined as the water of the upper 200 to 300 metres of the Arctic Ocean, the latter being defined as the central Arctic Basin only, bounded by the land masses of North America and Eurasia and its associated islands, including Greenland. This Arctic water mass is cold, -1.8 to 2°C or thereabouts and vertically stable, and it is therefore low in biological production. Vertical stability, caused by ice cover, lack of wind drag on water, and a freshened top layer resulting from ice melting in summer, leads to the absence of a vertical exchange of water and the lack of upwelling from below. Arctic water, in the strict sense used here, is therefore low in biological productivity. Coral reefs produce more living stuff in a day than Arctic water does in a year.

Sub-Arctic water, defined as mixed Arctic and non-Arctic (Atlantic or Pacific) water, is found in the region south of the Arctic water proper (figure 3). This zone is ice-free in summer, and, moreover, the mixture of the two water masses causes the density stratification typical of the upper layer of the Arctic water to break down, allowing for vertical exchange of water and upwelling of deeper water to the surface, carrying the plant nutrients to the sunlit (euphotic) layer. The term "nutrients" here is confined to the raw materials of the photosynthetic process: the inorganic salts (phosphates, nitrates, silicates) and other inorganic material required by plant life (phytoplankton, seaweeds, etc.) for growth. It is probably significant that the sub-Arctic zone coincides fairly accurately with the zone lying between the summer minimum of sea ice and the winter maximum (compare figures 3 and 4). The sub-Arctic zone is very considerably more productive than the Arctic water to the north.

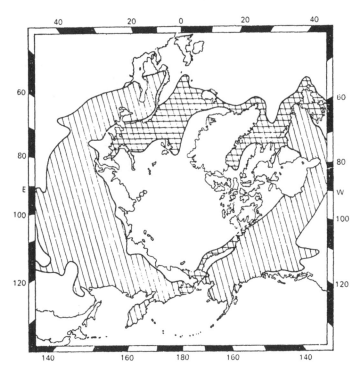

FIGURE 3. The sub-Arctic regions of the world: land and sea. Source: M.J. Dunbar, "The Arctic Marine Ecosystem," in F.R. Engelhardt, ed, *Petroleum Effects in the Arctic Environment* (New York: Elsevier Applied Science Publishers 1985).

Temperature. The global pattern, or map, of marine productivity demonstrates that temperature is not a decisive factor in that process. Great stretches of central tropical oceanic water are low in biological productivity compared with regions of sub-Arctic and temperate water; there are also areas in the tropics which, owing to upwelling of nutrient-rich water, are among the most productive regions in the world. The factor of greatest importance is the upwelling of deep water; another important factor is the establishment of a mixed stable layer, after the upwelling, of a density less than the water below the pycnocline. Thus both instability and stability, separated in time, are required.

The global pattern. Table 2 lists measured rates of biological production, expressed as grams of carbon fixed by photosynthesis per square metre of surface per year ($gC/m^2/yr$), the measure of the primary production by plant cells upon which all higher levels in the ecosystem

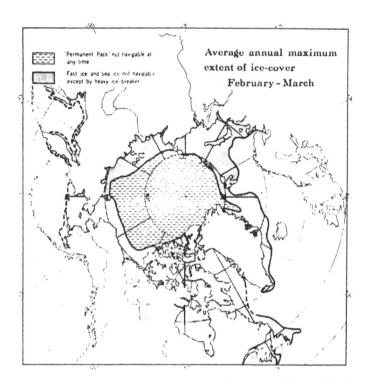

FIGURE 4. Average annual maximum extent of ice cover, February-March.
Source: *The Ice Atlas* (Washington: U.S. Hydrographic Office 1946).

depend. It should be noted that, especially in the northern waters, the pattern is sensitive to climate change. Climate change can, and does, alter the extent and position of the sub-Arctic mixed zone and of the ice limits. For instance, in west Greenland waters, the pattern of production and the species distribution has changed drastically since 1920.

The biological significance of ice. Much of the polar waters of the world should be called "ice-enriched" rather than the more common "ice-infested." Sea ice encourages both upwelling and the establishment of a stable mixed layer. This happens at the ice edge, at which wind-driven upwelling is a common phenomenon. As the ice recedes during spring and summer, the melting releases fresh water (the salt has leached out during the winter) which mixes with salt water and forms a stable layer above the halocline. The water at and near the ice edge, therefore, is normally rich in life. This was noticed consistently for centuries by the officers and crews of ships in both northern and southern seas; as soon as the ice edge is approached, the birds, seals, and whales appear, and if plankton nets had been used, they would have brought up a rich harvest of smaller creatures.

Polynyas. The polynya, an annually recurring area of open water, or of greatly reduced ice cover, can be looked upon as a special case of the ice edge phenomenon. Polynyas are found in both polar regions and range in size from very small (the smallest known is not more than a couple of hundred of metres in diameter) to giants of 150,000 square kilometres in the Weddell Sea of Antarctica. The largest polynyas in Canada and the Greenland Sea are of the order of 40,000 to 100,000 square kilometres. Although poor in ice, polynyas are in fact ice factories. Most are caused in the first instance by winds. The ice which is constantly formed during the winter at the surface is as constantly blown downwind. There is thus constant freezing of the surface water, and polynyas lead to the creation of much more ice than would occur if the polynya did not exist, so to speak. This new ice releases its salt, so that there is a sinking of dense saline water; this sets up a process of vertical exchange – salty water sinks from the surface and is replaced by water from deeper layers, which in the Arctic is normally warmer than the upper water. The heat advected upward helps to keep the polynya open, and it also must bring up nutrients. Polynyas may therefore be considered "biological hot spots," from which nutrients and possibly also phytoplankton radiate downstream to other regions. For instance, the North Water polynya in Smith Sound and northern Baffin Bay may be at least partly responsible for the striking spring and summer productivity of Lancaster Sound to the south. There is at present an international movement afoot to inaugurate intensive study of polynyas.[8]

Ice biota. For many years sailors in both the Arctic and sub-Arctic regions reported that sea ice turned over by the bow of a ship is often brown or green in colour. This was first studied scientifically in the mid-nineteenth century, but quantitative and detailed work on the matter did not start until 1960, when Apollonio in the North and Bunt in the Antarctic took up the study. The coloration is caused by diatoms – algal plants – that colonize the ice, forming a dense layer in its lowest few centimetres. The diatoms, together with other plant cells, live in the interstices between the ice crystals and are grazed by herbivores, notably copepods and amphipods. Nematode worms are also often very abundant. The diatoms form the basis for a specialized ecosystem in which the top trophic levels are fish (especially the two species of far northern cod), seals, and birds, and therefore ultimately polar bears, walrus, killer whales, and humans. This special system is found in the Arctic Ocean (Arctic water proper) as

TABLE 2. Primary Phytoplankton Production Estimates from Different Geographic
Regions

Region	Production (gC/m^2/year)
Arctic Ocean	0.6-5
Dumbell Bay, Ellesmere Island	9-12
Off Cornwallis Island	15, 32
Beaufort Sea	9-18
Northeast Chukchi Sea	18, 28
Frobisher Bay	41, 70
Bering Sea (shelf)	250
Bering Sea (oceanic)	75
"Sub-Arctic Pacific"	35-100
Gulf of Alaska	48
Barents Sea	25
Davis Strait	50
West Greenland, three locations	29, 95, 98
West Greenland (Disko Bay)	36
Jones Sound	20, 35
Gulf of Finland	30-40
Akkeshi Bay (Oyashio Current)	295
Sendai Bay, Japan	100
Suruga and Sagami bays, Japan	90
Seto Inland Sea, Japan	127
St Margaret's Bay, Nova Scotia	190
Gulf of St Lawrence (main gulf)	212
Gaspé Current, Gulf of St Lawrence	385
Lower St Lawrence Estuary	509 (?)
Strait of Georgia	120
Off New York	100-160

Sources: H.E. Grainger, "Primary Production in Frobisher Bay, Arctic Canada," in M.J. Dunbar,
ed, *Marine Production Mechanisms* (Cambridge: Cambridge University Press 1979), 9-30; K.
Hogetsu, "Biological Productivity of Some Coastal Regions of Japan," in ibid, 71-87; T. Nemoto
and G. Harrison, "High Latitude Ecosystems," in A.R. Longhurst, ed, *Analysis of Marine
Ecosystems* (New York: Academic Press 1981), 95-127; and LGL Ltd, *Biological Environment
of Eastern Lancaster Sound and Western Baffin Bay: Components and Important Processes,*
Environmental Studies 30 (Canada: Department of Indian and Northern Affairs 1983).

well as in the sub-Arctic seasonally ice-covered region. In the Arctic
Ocean, which is very poor in phytoplankton growth, this life-in-the-ice has
been estimated to account for up to 25 per cent of the total primary
production.

Chelation. Almost forty years ago it was discovered that the addition of ethylene diamine tetra-acetate (EDTA), which complexes with many metal ions (the process of chelation), to a culture medium together with metal ions which are normally present in sea water, greatly accelerated the growth of diatom cells. EDTA, a complex of organic carbon, is produced by the diatoms of the ice biota as an "external metabolite." Recently, Apollonio has gone a long way towards demonstrating that the release of the ice diatoms and the organic carbon compounds, when the ice begins to melt in the spring, has the effect of causing a sudden bloom of phytoplankton (including diatoms, but of species different from those of the ice biota) under the ice.[9] The process of chelation makes essential metal ions, some of which would otherwise be toxic, available to the phytoplankton.

Energy paths in the ecosystem. Recent work by Petersen and Curtis has revealed the interesting fact that the energy paths through marine ecosystems differ somewhat in tropical, temperate, and sub-Arctic marine environments.[10] Tropical systems favour the production of pelagic end-products (pelagic fish, for instance), temperate environments encourage both pelagic and benthonic fauna, whereas in the sub-Arctic (Disko Bay in their study), most of the energy goes into the benthos. There is much more work to be done in this new field.

Biological Production on Land and in Fresh Water

Although I have emphasized marine productivity, my own particular field, and have had to give production in rivers and lakes and on land rather short shrift, both land/fresh water and sea productivity are very significant. The Arctic zone of the land, north of the tree line, is poor in biological production, but the sub-Arctic zone as defined here (figure 3) includes vast areas of northern forest and marginal agricultural land and also very important fresh water resources such as salmonids and whitefishes.

Ecosystems

An ecosystem, or indeed any system, can be defined simply as an organized whole, as opposed to a random association of elements. Let us assume that such systems exist. To define an ecosystem more simply as "an organization" might be safer, because the "wholeness" is countered at every turn by the fact that ecosystems are open systems and, even at the global level, include extraterrestrial factors such as sunlight. This restriction has, however, the great advantage that it demonstrates, or demands, interdependence at all levels: "No man is an island."

Ecosystems are normally extremely complex. Ecosystems of the land in northern regions are simpler than elsewhere because they contain a relatively smaller number of species. But normally ecosystems are so complex both in space and time that it has been claimed by several leading ecologists that to model them comprehensively is impossible and a waste of time, the more so because life is not static but changes its reactions on all time-scales, from the annual to the evolutionary. Northern *marine* ecosystems are often as complex as those in more temperate regions. The marine system in Arctic and sub-Arctic regions is illustrated diagrammatically in figure 5. In contrast to this system, which demonstrates a considerable degree of complexity (the planktonic elements alone contain great diversity), the ecosystem of the tundra on land is relatively simple (plants, lemmings, predators); and even in the sub-Arctic forest zone the complexity is still much less than in the sea.

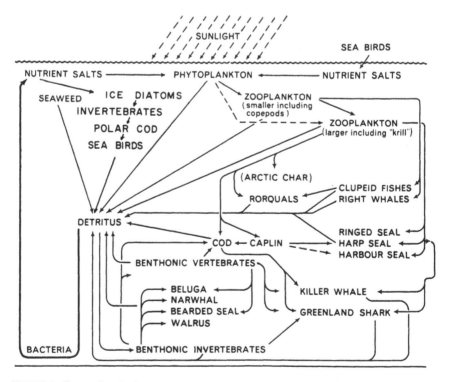

FIGURE 5. Energy flow in the northern marine ecosystem. Source: M.J. Dunbar, "Arctic Marine Ecosystems," in Louis Rey, ed, *The Arctic Ocean* (London: Macmillan 1982), 233-62.

The comparative simplicity of polar ecosystems has given rise to the belief that they are therefore more sensitive to perturbations and pollution in general than are systems of lower latitudes. On this subject I quote from Dunbar:

Ecological stability, diversity, and fragility have been exposed to so much discussion in recent years, both in the scientific press and in the popular press and other "media", that a sort of miasmatic atmosphere has been produced, from which it is necessary every now and then to escape into clearer and purer air. The phrase "the fragile Arctic" appears to have been coined and perpetuated not by scientists but by politicians and newspapermen. It is a catchy phrase and it has been greatly overworked. I can see little reason to suppose that Arctic ecosystems are any more or any less vulnerable to human interference than other ecosystems; and it seems from present developments that a really fragile system can be found in the tropical rainforest. It is true that Arctic systems are usually simpler than others, involving lower diversity of species, so that extinction of a given link in the food web might be serious. But on the other hand the individual numbers within species tend to be large, and moreover the same ecosystem extends over very large geographical areas, as on the tundra and in the sea, so that damage in one area can be repaired by immigration from adjacent areas. In fact, the Arctic ecosystems appear to be at least as tough as others. Small lakes, permafrost, and the sub-Arctic forest, are examples of terrestrial systems that one has to treat with care and understanding, but the marine systems do not show these special regions of concern.[11]

Climatic Changes in the Last 100 Years

Climatic change on the Pleistocene scale has already been discussed briefly. Of much greater significance in the present context is the behaviour of the atmospheric and hydrospheric climate during the present century and of climatic predictions for the next few decades. Here again it is necessary to treat the sea and the land separately, because the two biomes respond very differently to climate change. There has been a gradual movement of the fauna and flora of the land northward ever since the retreat of the ice of the last glaciation. That northward movement is still going on and appears to be largely independent of shorter-term changes in the atmosphere, including the large changes in the past hundred years. Response in the sea, however, may be said to be almost instantaneous, owing to the close-knit interaction between sea and wind. This means that whole marine ecosystems are shifted as their water masses are shifted. The interplay between hydrosphere and atmosphere controls, at the immediate level, the global climate, so that climate change on land as well as in the sea can best be followed by means of the marine events, the more so because the atmosphere is always in a hurry, roaring about in a

manner that makes the recognition of sustained patterns difficult. The sea
is slower, and it gains and releases its heat with reluctance.

It was pointed out by Berezkin that increased inflow to the Arctic
Ocean involves an increased flow of Arctic water from the Arctic Ocean.
In his words: "Assuming that the quantity of the water masses in the Polar
Basin remains constant from year to year, it may be inferred that an
increase in the intensity of the Atlantic Drift would inevitably bring about
a similar increase in the Polar Current that runs counter to it, and vice
versa. As a result, the whole circulation process of the waters of the Polar
Basin is expressed more intensely ... increased temperature of the North
Cape Current in August of any year is reciprocated by a greater amount of
ice in the Greenland Sea in July of the following year."[12]

The West Greenland Current, because it is composed of both Atlantic
and Arctic water, is peculiarly sensitive to climate change. So are the
waters of eastern Canada and of Iceland and the Norwegian Sea.
Beginning about 1920, there was a remarkable and sudden increase in the
heat carried by the West Greenland Current, illustrated in figure 6. The
upward phase of this event was described by Jensen and the later process
of cooling is summarized by Dunbar.[13] A similar curve was shown in
Canadian Atlantic waters, but the temperature peak there occurred about
1950, later than in west Greenland waters. In Iceland, the record of climate

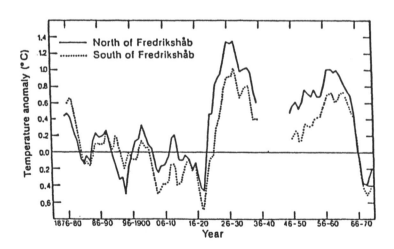

FIGURE 6. Sea surface temperature changes in the West Greenland Current.
Sources: Denmark, Referat af den Kongelige Grønlandske Handels Fiskerimøde,
mandag den 18 April 1977, 22pp., and M.J. Dunbar, *Twentieth-Century Marine
Climate Change in the Northwest Atlantic and Subarctic Regions,* NAFO
Scientific Council Studies, 5 (Dartmouth NS: Northwest Atlantic Fisheries
Organization 1982), 7-15.

change is closely associated with the behaviour of sea ice. Sea ice has played such a vital role in the economic and social history of that country that there are frequent references to it in the literature of the Icelanders. Consequently, the historical record of the severity of ice along the coast goes back to 976 AD, and the records of the number of days per year when ice affected the coast go back to 1590. By relating mean air temperature to ice cover for the years in which both are known (1846 to date), Bergthórsson estimated the mean air temperatures from 1590 onward (figure 7).[14] The pattern for this century resembles the West Greenland curve (figure 6), rather than the Canadian pattern.

The part played by the activities of mankind in this change is not clear, but is probably unimportant. Previous cycles of climate behaviour have been demonstrated; for instance, from analysis of an ice core taken at Camp Century, Dansgaard et al have been able to show an oscillation of cooler and warmer conditions on the Greenland ice cap with a mean period

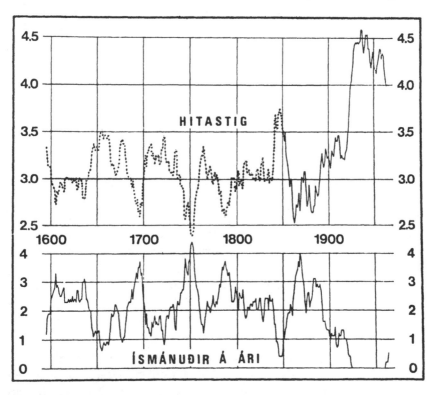

FIGURE 7. Air temperature as 10-year running means (upper) estimated from ice incidence (lower) at Iceland, 1590-1968. Source: P. Bergthórsson, "An Estimate of Sea Ice and Temperature in Iceland in 1000 Years," *Jökull*, 1969, and Dunbar, *Twentieth-Century Marine Climate Change*.

of about 76 years over the past 750 years.[15] Maksimov discusses an 80-year climatic cycle, and cycles of the same order have been recorded in an abundance of marine animals.[16] Other periods of natural climate oscillation have been suggested. There is evidence that the carbon dioxide "greenhouse effect" is finally showing up consistently in air temperature records, and there is no doubt that the carbon dioxide concentration in the atmosphere has been increasing in the last hundred years or so. But the twentieth-century event described here is apparently independent of the carbon dioxide increase, because the cooling has occurred simultaneously with the gas increase. We are dealing with a natural oscillation which will no doubt continue, no matter what the greenhouse effect does. Moreover, the supply of fossil fuels we burn is not unlimited, so it must be supposed that man-influenced climate change will not be permanent. The thinning of the ozone layer, much publicized and no doubt very serious, affects the penetration of ultraviolet light rather than the atmospheric temperature as such. Industrial haze reduces the penetration of sunlight and therefore counters the greenhouse effect. The complex situation is well described by Emiliani: "Because the hypsithermals represent such a precarious climatic balance, the effect of man on the course of the present hypsithermal assumes critical significance. Beginning from the time of widespread deforestation and accelerating toward the present time of industrialization and global atmospheric pollution, man's interference with the heat budget of the hydro-atmosphere is assuming alarming proportions ... Thermal, CO_2, and aerosol pollution produce contrasting effects, and so does urban development. Their relative magnitudes are poorly understood and the net effect is unknown, not only in magnitude but even in sign."[17]

The ecological and economic consequences of these climate changes are spectacular, involving as they do northward or southward shifts of whole ecosystems. Within the lifetime of people now in their sixties or seventies, for instance, the marine climate of western Greenland, between 1915 and 1940, and again up to the second peak in 1960, has warmed by some 2°C in the core of the West Greenland Current. This has had a decisive effect on the whole economy of the country, well described by Jensen and others, involving a change from a hunting to a fishing base. Iceland has experienced changes in the fishery of the same scale. Thórdardóttir has shown the close relation between primary production in northern Icelandic waters and the recent climatic changes, with production being much lower in the years of heavy ice.[18] Similar economic changes have occurred in the eastern North Atlantic segment of the sub-Arctic and Arctic, notably in the Svalbard region and in the Norwegian Sea. The history of the presence and absence of Atlantic cod in Spitsbergen waters is climate-related, and so apparently is the extent of salmon fishing in Davis Strait and the Norwegian Sea.[19] On land, the avifauna of Iceland changed drastically during the twentieth-century rise in temperature, and Vibe has made a special and classical study of the land and sea fauna of Greenland in relation to climatic fluctuation.[20]

Industrial Man in the North: Pollution, Disruption

The term "general disruption" is used in the Berger report on Canada's north to describe the disturbance of the native economy and way of life by the intrusion of industrial and political influences.[21] Close to it, or contained in it, is the term "environmental pollution." I am not sure whether these matters belong here, but they have been given so much publicity that they should be mentioned, if only in summary. They certainly apply circumglobally, therefore internationally. The literature on environmental problems and hazards in the North, as elsewhere, is now enormous and growing logarithmically, but the problems differ only in detail from the same problems everywhere. They are now recognized not only as political issues, but as international political issues.

Permafrost. The existence of permafrost (frozen subsoil) has led to surface damage of tundra areas owing to ignorance and carelessness. Damage of the insulating surface layer in summer, principally by heavy vehicles, causes a melting of the permafrost layer, a wound that does not easily heal (the so-called thermokarst effect). We have now learned to use vehicles with small area-loading, special tires, and so on and also to avoid the use of heavy vehicles altogether, if possible, during the brief tundra summer. It is also necessary to use special methods of building construction to maintain the frozen layer in its normal and natural condition. Of all the environmental problems of the North, this is the simplest to deal with.

Sewage. The disposal of sewage, domestic and other, including mine tailings, is a serious matter in Arctic conditions. The temptation to pour raw sewage and other refuse into streams and lakes, which is universal, is especially difficult to resist in the North because other means of disposal available in lower latitudes are not available in the Arctic. The shallow soil, or absence of soil, and the permafrost make burial of wastes impossible, and biodegradation is slowed down. The problem, superficial as it may seem in comparison with acid precipitation and oil spills, may turn out to be insoluble; consequently the northlands are becoming increasingly strewn with plastic debris, tin cans, and the other waste products of modern human habitation and industry.

Acid precipitation. Not yet thought of as an Arctic problem, the acid menace is nevertheless approaching. Certain sub-Arctic regions, such as the central Ungava Peninsula and northern Scandinavia, are directly downwind of industrial sources of sulphate and nitrate emissions in dangerous quantities, and pH values of 4.5 and lower are common, in the waters of these regions.

Airborne particulate matter. "Arctic haze," something new in our generation, is now well established and measured over the whole of the Arctic. The air circulation pattern shown in figure 8 explains why this should be. The same pattern, of course, also applies to the dispersal of acid rain and snow.

Oil. Most of the study of northern pollutants has been devoted to petroleum products. The literature is large, but the estimates of the damage that can be done by oil spills are still somewhat conflicting. There is no doubt that oil is a serious menace to seabirds, particularly in inshore waters. The short-term effects on the rest of the fauna and flora seem to be not very serious, but we know very little of the cumulative effects. The

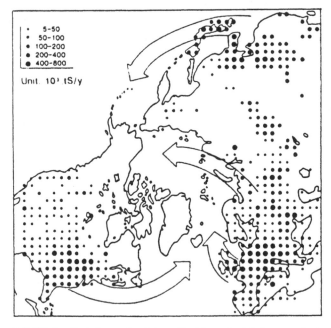

FIGURE 8.   Emissions of sulphur dioxide and global atmospheric dispersion. Source: Comité Arctique International, brochure, 1988.

BIOS (Baffin Island Oil Spill) experiment dealt at length with oil effects in a restricted marine area and is in general agreement with other studies.[22] The consensus is that oil is not by any means the most damaging pollutant in the sea or anywhere else. Of all the published accounts perhaps the most informative is that of the *Tsesis* incident in the northern Baltic Sea.[23]

Noise. Native populations, notably those of Greenland, have expressed keen concern over the effects of the propeller noise of shipping on sea mammals, especially whales, suggesting that it may interfere with their communication systems and have general disruptive effects on their behaviour. This concern appears to have subsided a little, no doubt because the potential use of the Northwest Passage-West Greenland route no longer looms so large, but it may be expected to revive if shipping increases. Canadian Inuit have expressed similar worries concerning the noise produced by seismic lines at sea. The general disturbance of sea ice conditions has also caused alarm. In the Beaufort Sea studies it was concluded that this was not a serious matter, but the Inuit in Baffin Island have pointed out that icebreaker traffic can greatly disturb hunting activities.

The emphasis in this paper has been on the sea rather than on the air or the land. This is not simply because the sea is my field of interest; it is because the sea is the unifying medium, in the North as in the rest of the world. The task of writing this sort of essay is often (usually) handed to a geographer, because mankind is land-based and mainly land-thinking. I am glad that this time an oceanographer got the job. Lighthouses, after all, are not there to warn us against the dangers of the sea; their purpose is to warn us against the hazards of the land.

Notes

1   M. Ewing and W. L. Donn, "A Theory of the Ice Ages," Science, 123 (1956), 1061-6; and W. L. Donn and M. Ewing, "A Theory of Ice Ages, III," ibid., 152 (1966), 1706-12.

2   C. Emiliani, "Quaternary Hypsithermals," *Quaternary Research*, 2 (1972), 270-3.

3   Ibid.

4   R. A. Kerr, "Linking Earth, Ocean and Air at the AGU," *Science*, 239 (1988), 259-60.

5   H. H. Lamb, "The Climatic Environment of the Arctic Ocean," in L. Rey, ed., *The Arctic Ocean* (London: Macmillan, 1982), 135-61; and F. K. Hare, "Weather and Climate," in George H.T. Kimble and Dorothy Good, eds., *Geography of the Northlands* (London: Chapman and Hall/New York: Wiley for American Geographical Society 1955), 58-83.

6   H. E. Sadler, "Water Flow into Foxe Basin through Fury and Hecla Strait," *Le Naturaliste Canadien*, 109 (1982), 701-7.

7   M. J. Dunbar, "Eastern Arctic Waters," Fisheries Research Board of Canada, *Bulletin*, 88 (1951).

8   See, for example, the proceedings of the Polynya Seminar/Workshop held at McGill University in October 1987, and the subsequent meeting in Bremerhaven under the auspices of the Arctic Ocean Sciences Board in February 1988. The most recent general description of polynyas is to be found in I. Stirling and H. Cleator, *Polynyas in the Canadian Arctic*, Occasional Paper 45 (Ottawa: Canadian Wildlife Service 1981).

9   S. Apollonio, 1989. Personal communication.

10 G. H. Petersen and M. A. Curtis, "Differences in Energy Flow through Major Components of Subarctic, Temperate and Tropical Marine Shelf Ecosystems," *Dana*, 1 (1980), 53-64.

11 M. J. Dunbar, "Arctic Marine Ecosystems," in Rey, ed, *The Arctic Ocean*, 233-62.

12 A. Berezkin, "Poteplenie v Arktike i usilenie tsirkuliatsii vod poliarnogo bassenina," *Morskoi sbornik*, 4 (1937), 105-32.

13 A. S. Jensen, "Concerning a Change of Climate during Recent Decades in the Arctic and Subarctic Regions, from Greenland in the West to Eurasia in the East, and Contemporary Biological and Geophysical Changes," *Biologiske Meddelelser* (Copenhagen), 14 (no 8, 1939); M. J. Dunbar, *Twentieth-Century Marine Climate Change in the Northwest Atlantic and Subarctic Regions*, NAFO Scientific Council Studies, 5 (Dartmouth NS: Northwest Atlantic Fisheries Organization 1982), 7-15.

14 P. Bergthórsson, "An Estimate of Sea Ice and Temperature in Iceland in 1000 Years," *Jökull* (Journal of the Iceland Glaciological Society), Report on the Symposium on Drift Ice and Climate, held in Reykjvaik, January 27-February 7, 1969, 94-100.

15 W. Dansgaard, S. J. Johnson, H. B. Clausen, and C. C. Langway, "Climatic Record Revealed by the Camp Century Ice Core," in K. K. Turekian, ed, *The Late Cenozoic Glacial Ages* (New Haven: Yale University Press 1971), 37-56.

16 I.V. Maksimov, "On the 80-year Cycle of Climatic Variation," *Doklady Akademii Nauk SSSR*, 86 (no 5, 1952), 917-20; M. J. Dunbar, "Cycles in the Sea," manuscript in preparation.

17 Emiliani, "Quaternary Hypsithermals."

18 T. Thórdardóttir, "Primary Production in North Icelandic Waters in Relation to Recent Climatic Changes," in M. J. Dunbar, ed, *Polar Oceans* (Calgary: Arctic Institute of North America 1977), 655-65.

19 M. J. Dunbar and D. H. Thompson, "West Greenland Salmon and Climatic Change," *Meddelelser om Grønland*, 202 (no 4, 1979).

20 C. Vibe, "Arctic Animals in Relation to Climatic Fluctuations," ibid., 170 (no 5, 1967).

21 T. R. Berger, *Northern Frontier, Northern Homeland: The Report of the Mackenzie Valley Pipeline Inquiry* (Ottawa: Supply and Services Canada 1977).

22 Special issue on BIOS, *Arctic*, 40 (no 1, 1987), supplement.

23 J. J. Kineman, R. Elmgren, and S. Hansson, eds, *The TSESIS Oil Spill* (Boulder, CO: U.S. Department of Commerce/NOAA 1980).

9

Industrialization and Its Consequences

Terence E. Armstrong

My object in this paper is to provide some background on the present and possible future level of industrialization in the Arctic. By industrialization I mean economic activity of all kinds, and by Arctic I mean, generally, north of the trees. The Arctic has become and will continue to be a significant source of raw materials, and mankind is going to press ever more strongly for their exploitation. It is not the last great reservoir on earth – there are several others still harder of access, such as the beds of the oceans and Antarctica – but it is the one for which the required technology is either available or likely soon to become so. The timing of any major development will probably depend mainly on factors external to the Arctic – advances in technology, fluctuations in world prices, changing relationships between nations – but the Arctic environment will always remain a powerful determinant of what is possible.

Resources Now Exploited

Perhaps the most important of the Arctic resources now being exploited are hydrocarbons.[1] As it happens, there are major occurrences in both Soviet and United States territory, with smaller discoveries and promising areas in other parts of the Arctic. The main Soviet petroliferous zone is in northwest Siberia, on the lower reaches of the Ob' and Yenisey rivers and especially in the region between them. In 1986, this general area of northwest Siberia which includes sub-Arctic as well as Arctic territory produced 65 per cent of Soviet oil and 62 per cent of Soviet natural gas – very significant fractions of national production. The prospects for further discoveries in this vicinity are good and include offshore sites in the Kara Sea. There is a network of pipelines for both oil and gas. This development has been under way since the early 1960s and will continue to be the heart of the Soviet oil and gas industry for the foreseeable future. The region is a very difficult one in which to work, from the point of view both of getting the product out of the ground and of building the necessary infrastructure, but the major problems appear to have been solved. In 1986 oil output was about 7.5 million barrels per day and the year's gas output stood at about 400 billion cubic metres. These figures may be compared with those for the whole output of the United States: about 8.6 and 400-500 respectively.[2] The Arctic contribution to the two figures at that date was two and nil, with Arctic oil being about 19 per cent of American production and 11 per cent of American consumption. Thus, Soviet production of hydrocarbons from northern sources is much greater than that of the United States, both as a proportion of national output and absolutely. The situation with regard to reserves is probably much the same, but the Soviet Union does not publish reserve figures. The Arctic region as a whole is the only one in the world that could rival the Middle East in respect of reserves.

By comparison with the hydrocarbons, other fossil fuel resources in the Arctic are quite small. The Soviet Union mines coal in the Pechora Basin, producing 30 million tonnes a year, and Norway, together with the Soviet Union, extracts about one million tonnes from three coal mines in Svalbard. Some other Arctic coal deposits are known, but few are worked because of the relatively low unit value of the commodity.

Other minerals are also mined. On the Soviet side the main ones are gold (Bilibino, Polyarnyy), tin (Pevek, Deputatskiy), nickel and platinum (Noril'sk), and iron (Olenegorsk). On the North American side there is mainly lead-zinc (Nanisivik, Polaris), which is also exploited in Greenland (Marmorilik), but the industry is much less developed. If we extend the boundary south to include the sub-Arctic, the Soviet north is found to provide, in general terms, all the country's diamonds and apatite, two-thirds of its nickel, and half of its tin and gold. The national dependence of the Soviet Union on the North is much more marked than in other national sectors of the Arctic, where there is at present little mining of significance.

Although it is the minerals which are attractive to industrializers, the North possesses certain renewable resources as well. The traditional resource was fur. The fur bearers of the tundra developed especially warm and opulent pelts, and in an age when fur was much more widely worn than it is today, these animals were highly prized. Both northern Eurasia and northern North America were explored by white men in search of fur. Two things happened, however, to reduce the scale of this trade. First, it was found possible to raise some of the fur bearers in captivity farther south and thus harvest the pelts more easily and more efficiently. Second, and much more recently, animal rights enthusiasts have stirred up public opinion in advanced societies (which are now the ones to buy furs) with the object of discouraging purchasers. Nevertheless, a northern fur industry does still exist, generating an income of some 200 million rubles a year (equivalent to Cdn$400-500 million) in the Soviet Union, though only Cdn$6 million in Canada. The Soviet fur trade has not suffered from adverse public opinion, and 42,000 more pelts went to auction in 1987 than in 1986. However, the market in the West for seal fur, a particular target of the animal rights movement, has slumped dramatically.

Another significant renewable resource is fish. Cold water is no deterrent to certain species, and the fringing seas of the Arctic Ocean are rich in them. The boundaries of the areas for which statistical records are published do not coincide with those of the Arctic, but using a generous interpretation of Arctic and sub-Arctic, one may say that the seas in these two zones yield about 14 per cent of the world catch of saltwater fish – in absolute terms, 3.3 million tonnes from the North Atlantic sector and seven million tonnes from the North Pacific sector (1983 figures).[3] Freshwater fisheries also exist, particularly in the large lakes of the Canadian Arctic and the great north-flowing rivers of the Soviet Union; but they are small-scale (though high-quality) operations compared with the sea fishery.

On land, there is little cultivation of the soil, although Soviet work on plant selection has identified a number of varieties that will in fact do well in harsh conditions. The most flourishing branch of farming in the North is reindeer husbandry. The USSR supports something over two million head of domesticated reindeer, Scandinavia about half a million, and Canada and Alaska some 15,000 each. Not many of the products of this industry (meat, hides, antlers) come south, but they are a helpful locally produced addition to the diet and needs of northerners.

If our southern boundary were to bend a little southward and include a part of the boreal forest, then one might expect a harvest of timber. But the size and growth rate of trees at these latitudes are so small that there has never been any commercial interest in the timber. There is plenty of excellent timber a little farther south.

Thus the North is currently producing, for the world, very significant quantities of oil and gas, certain valuable minerals, a good deal of fish, and some fur; and, for itself, very small quantities of food.

Infrastructure in Place

The most important component of infrastructure needed to effect the exploitation of Arctic resources is transport. The distribution of land and sea over the region offers the possibility of sea access to most parts of the

Arctic, but the presence of floating ice for some or all of the year requires special equipment and techniques. In this area, the USSR is easily the leader. Having made a sustained effort since the early 1930s to utilize the Northeast Passage, or the Northern Sea Route in Soviet terminology, Soviet activity has reached a fairly high level of operation.[4] Employing some twenty icebreakers of Arctic capability, four of them nuclear-powered, and a fleet of ice-strengthened freighters and tankers, shipping operators are capable of carrying millions of tonnes (the exact figure is not revealed, but it could be around six million tonnes a year) on the Northern Sea Route. A notable advance in the last ten years has been a lengthening of the shipping season. Different sections of the route used to have different seasons, varying from about two months in the most ice-infested parts to five in the southwest corner of the Kara Sea, but now the southwest Kara Sea is navigable virtually year-round, and there are plans to extend operations in the rest of the route in the 1990s. Key factors in achieving the advances so far made were the deployment of nuclear-powered icebreakers and the introduction of a new class of shallow-draught icebreakers for use in estuaries.

Thus far, the Russians have used this capability to service remote areas of northern Siberia, reached by way of the northward-flowing rivers. The stimulus towards year-round operation, for instance, was provided by the need to take nickel ore from the mining centre of Noril'sk to the refinery near Murmansk. There has been almost no use of the through route connecting the Atlantic and the Pacific, although current levels of skill and technology are sufficient to do so. They would also permit the operation of surface ships in the central Polar Basin itself, something which began to look feasible when the Soviet nuclear-powered icebreaker, *Arktika,* went to the North Pole in 1977. The shortest distance between the Atlantic and the Pacific would be along a route passing close to the Pole, so the ability to use it could influence international sea transport networks. One must note, however, that despite striking advances in technology, no ship has yet been built, or even designed, that would be capable of going anywhere at any time. Certain ice conditions can halt even the most powerful vessels so far contemplated. A Canadian paper of 1986 argues, however, that advances in hull design will allow the achievement of a "go anywhere any time" capability at a much lower engine power rating than had been previously supposed.[5]

Complementary to the operation of ships in coastal waters and farther out to sea is the development of efficient river shipping. The most useful advances here have been the introduction of a new class of river icebreaker, built in Finland (like the other non-nuclear-powered icebreakers), which has allowed a significant lengthening of the navigation season; and the development of ships capable of operating in both sea and river.

All movement in ice-infested waters is critically controlled by the natural history of the ice cover. Conditions may deteriorate from natural causes, and there is reason to believe this is happening in the eastern sector of the Northern Sea Route.[6] Up to now improvements in ship design and technology have appeared to offset this deterioration, but there is no guarantee that they can do so indefinitely. Sea-ice conditions off the north Eurasian coast are thought to have been better this century than at any time in many earlier centuries. Whether this could also be said of other Arctic waters is hard to determine because of a paucity of evidence. What is important to bear in mind is that the situation is constantly changing.

The clear pre-eminence of the USSR in the whole field of Arctic shipping does not mean that other countries lack any capability: Canada, the United States, and the Scandinavian countries all have some capacity. The most striking new development would have been the construction of a Canadian icebreaker capable of moving through eight feet of solid ice at a steady three knots (class 8). Although plans for the ship have now been cancelled, it would have been the world's most powerful icebreaker at 100,000 shp (compared to 75,000 shp for the Soviet Arktika class). The Western countries are especially weak in ice-strengthened freighters, without which cargo carriage in Arctic waters is severely constrained.

Besides the physical ability to sail in these waters, any would-be navigator in the Arctic must also be aware of the legal position. Outside territorial waters – generally twelve nautical miles – are the high seas, which should be open to all, but the presence of floating ice has led to some argument about this, because high seas with a solid surface allow people to do things – live, build, drive around – which cannot be done in normal high seas. Still more contentious is the regime of the Northwest and Northeast Passages: are they international waterways or not? There is fundamental disagreement between Canada and the United States on this point in relation to the Northwest Passage. And there are other, relatively minor, maritime border disputes, or failures to agree: between the United States and its neighbours in the Beaufort and Bering seas, between the USSR and Norway in the Barents Sea, between Canada and Denmark/Greenland in the Lincoln Sea. Most of these have little effect on navigation, however.

Air transport is of course the main medium for passenger and light freight movement. in the Arctic. Aircraft need little in the way of special design or modification to function in the North. In sparsely populated areas there is likely to be a shortage of landing strips, but generally this lack is not hard or particularly expensive to rectify. There is therefore an extensive network of airways in the Arctic, both within sovereign territory and internationally. Light aircraft operation is very widespread in the North American Arctic, and a number of international airlines follow great circle routes to cross parts of the Arctic Ocean, especially when flying between western Europe and western North America. Aircraft can fly over foreign territory only with the permission of the sovereign power concerned, but air boundaries in the Arctic are well established and recognized, and incidents rarely occur. All commercial flying is controlled by flight centres and the various sectors of the Arctic Ocean fall under one or other of these.

Land transport in the Arctic comes a poor last. There are few roads and fewer railways, for both are very expensive to build. The development of cross-country vehicles has begun to make a difference. The inventive North American car industry has come up with a number of models, while in the USSR there has been some emphasis on airscrew-driven passenger vehicles. The ubiquitous snow machine has had a profound influence on social life in the Western world and is no doubt having the same effect in the Soviet Union, where it has recently been introduced. There remains plenty of room for further development.

Resources for the Future

Many more Arctic mineral deposits are known than are at present exploited, and no doubt many more exist than are now known. Future exploitation will depend on many factors. The rarer the resource, the higher the value, and the greater the incentive to overcome problems. Vast deposits of iron and coal are known, but expense, largely for transport, precludes any action now. More valuable resources will no doubt be discovered when the demand for them reaches a level which will justify the expense of exploration in remote areas. But one may note in passing that the Soviet Union is perhaps less likely to be motivated by world price movement, since its motive for resource development has generally been to achieve independence of foreign sources of supply rather than to save, or make, money.

A low-value resource in abundant supply is fresh water. Arctic water can be used for many things: irrigation, fisheries, power generation, transport, or a combination of these. It is in use already, but the most ambitious projects have remained projects. These were a diversion of water from the Mackenzie River system of Canada's Northwest Territories southwards to arid parts of the American west and, most notably, the grandiose Soviet plans for diverting water from the Ob' and Yenisey rivers into central Asia. The main purpose of both these projects was irrigation, but there were also to be substantial benefits in power generation and transport. The Soviet plans were apparently cancelled by Mr Gorbachev in 1986, but it still seems possible that one variant of the proposal may be further investigated in relation to a possible attempt to restore the level of the Aral Sea.

There might be some expansion in production of biological resources, especially marine ones. A relatively recent example is the growth of a shrimp fishery based in western Greenland. The constraints on similar developments are more likely to be environmental than technical. On the whole, food industry techniques are straightforwardly applicable in the North, requiring no special modification, although the remoteness of sites is always apt to create or enlarge difficulties.

The Labour Force

The kinds of industrialization under discussion have been southern-inspired and operated largely by southerners. The economy of the native peoples before white contact was, of course, self-contained. But the interest from the south has led to a great change in the population structure. In the 1920s (which may be taken as the starting point of industrialization), the human population of the Arctic and sub-Arctic was of the order of 2.3 million, of whom 0.9 million (40 per cent) were native peoples; by the mid-1980s the total was 10 million, of whom 1.1 million (11 per cent) were natives.[7] The southerners had multiplied by four, while the natives had increased by only 20 per cent. Over half the total population and 90 per cent of the native population of the North are to be found in the Soviet Union, but the vast size of the Soviet north (11,000 sq. km.) means that it is not the most densely populated sector – northern Scandinavia is four times more thickly settled. We are considering, then, an area of the earth's surface in which several million people live, but in which there is only one inhabitant to every 2.5 square kilometres (even when the Greenland ice sheet is left out of account).

While all the industry, except some of that based on living resources, is primarily the concern of the immigrant population, a point of particular interest is the extent to which the native population is or should be involved. There are strongly held opposing views on this. From the natives' point of view, industry, whatever it may be, is likely to be quite alien to their culture and may cause side-effects which are markedly harmful to that culture. Still, it may provide jobs of a kind and thus offer employment in an area where other possibilities do not exist. The immigrants, however, see in the natives a possible source of local, hence cheaper, labour, though one not likely to have many of the skills required. But the natives are the unquestioned experts on living in their own environment, and the white man can learn much from them, if he will. In the USSR the policy seems to be to keep the natives employed in their traditional pursuits (hunting, fishing, reindeer herding) on the grounds that this is the way they can contribute most to the general welfare. But the Soviet Union is fortunate in having native populations big enough to do this; other countries would (and some do) find it more difficult to pursue that policy.

Industrialization and preservation of native culture are often seen as mutually exclusive. But it is not clear that this need always be so. Industry can act with sensitivity, and a native culture which stands still will simply fossilize. But what is, or ought to be, clear is that any expansion of industrial activity must be put in train with the knowledge and, if possible, the active co-operation of the native peoples. The use of intermediate technology, with its requirement for lower-level skills, may be a fruitful line of advance.

Environmental Concerns

Industrialization inevitably brings risk to the environment. The remoteness and inaccessibility of the Arctic confer both advantages and disadvantages in the area of environmental control. There are fewer humans to create pollution (or to notice it), but once created the damage may be harder to rectify. The Arctic countries have their own national legislation, but the centre of the Arctic is high seas, and there is no agreed environmental regime for this area. What may be interpreted as a start in this direction was made by Canada with its Arctic Waters Pollution Prevention Act of 1970. The intention was to institute controls over shipping within a 100-nautical-mile belt off Canada's Arctic shores. Horror was expressed at the time over the magnitude of the belt, but soon afterwards the related concept of the exclusive economic zone of 200 nautical miles gained wide acceptance, and the Canadian action seemed relatively mild. The area of high seas remaining after all Arctic rim countries have claimed their EEZs is of course much diminished, and the problem might be reduced to some extent if each country applied relevant legislation to its zone. Some international co-ordination would, however, be very desirable.

Atmospheric pollution, particularly Arctic haze, is a problem that has been identified in many other parts of the world. Its effects can be both unpleasant and harmful and its control is no easier in the Arctic than anywhere else.

Another aspect of the environmental problem is endangered species of wildlife – no respecter, obviously, of national boundaries. There have been some successes here. In the case of polar bears, regulations for their protection were agreed by all the relevant countries in 1973. This agreement could serve as a model for future action of this kind.

Looking Ahead

There can be no doubt that industrialization of many kinds will continue and grow in the North. Population increase will lead to more pressure on resources, and inaccessibility will become less of a barrier. The impact on the environment and on the local residents, whether native or immigrant, will be great. It is necessary to examine ways in which its harmful effects can be minimized or mitigated. There should be opportunities for co-operation in this endeavour, for all participants have to face similar harsh natural conditions.

The stimulus to action being economic, one may expect a certain measure of co-operation to come about of its own accord. If specialized skills and knowledge are available for sale, they will surely be bought by those needing them. Oil industry engineers exchange ideas and know-how, even if there are constraints in particular topics at particular times. Commercial secrets exist in an atmosphere of friendly rivalry, but in the longer term knowledge is shared. There is much unofficial networking – a method well suited to Arctic work because those involved tend to know each other anyway. The question is to what extent can moves towards greater co-operation be helped by organizational frameworks? The answer in most cases of this kind is the rather obvious one: a good framework will be helpful, a bad one will be unhelpful. International co-operation for its own sake is not necessarily a good thing, but it may increase confidence in other contexts and that perhaps is the most important point for us now.

In certain areas, such as the central Arctic Basin, it is very desirable to have some measure of international understanding in order to minimize the

risk of unintentional clashes. One might think of an agreement along the
lines of the Antarctic Treaty, which has functioned so successfully for
nearly thirty years at the other end of the world. But conditions in the two
areas are only superficially similar, and it would not be easy to gain
unanimous agreement (the basis for the Antarctic Treaty) for an
international Arctic regime. A more modest goal might be easier to attain,
and co-operation might be achieved by building on such uncontroversial
accords as the polar bear agreement.

But making agreements to limit action in various ways inevitably
causes dissatisfaction to some. Instead, the stress should be on the broad
opportunities for co-operation in the sphere of research which all Arctic
industrialization requires. Co-ordination of scientific effort, joint
programmes of many kinds, pooling of data – there are many levels of
possible co-operation which should not provoke objections or
antagonisms. There are many successful examples of such schemes. The
easiest to set up are bilateral agreements in a particular subject area.
Multilateral projects are obviously more complicated to organize. The
International Geophysical Year of 1957-8 set the tone for Arctic research
in the postwar world. Although not exclusively polar, it had a polar
ancestry, being the descendant of the First and Second International Polar
Years of 1882-3 and 1932-3. Other large multinational programmes have
followed, some wholly Arctic. More recently, there has been a tendency to
set up a continuing organizational structure which is not limited to a
particular project. One of these is the Arctic Ocean Sciences Board, with
membership from ten countries, established in 1984. Another is the Comité
Arctique International (1979) which has organized some very successful
conferences. The most recent – formally established in August 1990 – is
the International Arctic Science Committee, with membership from all the
Arctic nations. Most of these organizations are non-governmental, though
they probably attract government money. More institution-building is
possible and will surely be closely linked to any development of
industrialization.

The subject of this conference is Arctic co-operation. The reader will
have noted that there are many areas in which co-operation could take
place: in the exploitation of resources, in the organization of transport
systems, in the framing of international agreements, in the pooling of
scientific effort. Opportunities abound. I have tried only to raise some of
the issues and point to some of the possibilities. But will these
opportunities be pursued? If this is to happen, several things are necessary.
All co-operating parties must be convinced that there will be a real gain,

and the political framework and implications must be favourable. That there is potential gain is probably rather widely agreed on; the difficulties have mostly been, and still are, political. Such difficulties are likely to diminish only as a result of events totally unrelated to the Arctic and taking place far from it. But it does seem that such hopeful developments are happening, and all those interested in the Arctic should be ready to react to them. The idea of humans standing together and pooling their resources in order to master (but not to fight) the environment is surely an appealing one.

Notes

1 Most of the information in this section is taken from the standard statistical handbooks of the countries concerned.
2 J. Hannigan, "Oil and Gas Development in the Soviet North," *Northern Raven, 7* (summer 1987), 2-5.
3 *Yearbook of Fisheries Statistics* (Rome: Food and Agriculture Organization, various years).
4 See summaries of activity published annually in *Polar Record.*
5 B. M. Johansson and C. R. Revill, "Future Icebreaker Design," in A. Cassidy, ed, *Proceedings of the International Polar Transportation Conference* (Vancouver: IPTC 1986), I, 169-200.
6 A. Arikaynen and G. Burkov, "Ukhudshayutsya li ledovyye usloviya v Arktike?" *Morskoy flot* (no 6, 1985), 36-7.
7 Terence E. Armstrong, George W. Rogers, and Graham W. Rowley, *The Circumpolar North* (London: Methuen 1978), 280-3 (updated from same sources).

10

Co-operation in Arctic Science: Background and Requirements

E.F. Roots

In nearly every scientific subject or field of activity, careful research and data-gathering in Arctic regions has an important international component.

Most science in northern regions today is carried out for domestic or national reasons, even though some is the Arctic element of national participation in global or international activities. Nevertheless, it is a characteristic of studies in high latitudes, both in pure science and in applied sciences and engineering, that they are in many ways more closely linked to and dependent on the scientific activities of other countries in similar latitudes than is the case for most science in temperate and tropical regions. There are many reasons for this. Perhaps the principal one is that Arctic geophysical and environmental characteristics and processes are distinctive and related on a circumpolar basis but are in many ways different from those in lower latitudes. Thus, despite strong national interests, scientific activities of all kinds in the Arctic, including resource development and environmental studies, take on a polar rather than a national character. There is in addition a very important human reason. The cultures and societies of the Arctic regions have connections that are not confined by present national boundaries but are boreal or circumpolar in nature. Any careful study of Arctic peoples and their development, even within a single nation, has many international aspects. Finally, simple polar geography, bringing Arctic nations closer together today than many of them felt they were before the advent of modern technology, has led to a shared need for applied and pure sciences connected with circumpolar and transpolar communications, transportation, weather and space phenomena, and oceanography.

It is obvious that the Arctic nations share many problems that require research and scientific data from other Arctic regions. In fact, in many fields of study important to Arctic countries, there is more in common between the Arctic regions of different nations than there is between the Arctic and the more southerly parts of each respective nation. Therefore, it is no surprise that many Arctic countries have taken a similar or common approach to Arctic science and that many arrangements and practices have developed through which countries share or co-operate in Arctic scientific work.

Arctic research is difficult, both physically and scientifically or intellectually. It requires specialized techniques and equipment, much of which is of little use in other parts of the world except the Antarctic. And it is very costly, both in money and in the amount of effort and organization that needs to be expended to produce a given amount of data or new scientific results. But the scientific results of Arctic research are increasingly of vital importance – nationally, internationally, and to the northern peoples themselves.

For all these reasons, there is a strong incentive to achieve increased international and circumpolar co-operation in many fields of Arctic science.

Experience has shown, however, that the established mechanisms for international scientific co-operation, which have been developed through the growth and pursuit of modern science in other parts of the world, do not operate very well for achieving co-operation in Arctic research. The difficulties are of many kinds – political obstacles, reasons of national policy and differing priorities, problems of cost and the availability of research facilities and ice-going research ships, and reasons related to the nature of modern science itself. We will want to look at some of the scientific and managerial difficulties that stand in the way of effective international Arctic scientific co-operation.

Although there have been many examples of effective international collaboration in specific areas of Arctic science, the lack of a means to foster continuous international communication and co-operation on a broad basis has been seen by many as increasing the cost and decreasing the value of Arctic research and data-gathering in the modern context. The absence of effective international co-operation is a handicap in particular to the smaller northern countries in their pursuit of Arctic science and technology. It also makes more difficult the interrelation between modern science and the contributions that indigenous northern societies can make to the social, cultural, and economic development of their respective countries.

Co-operation in Arctic science activities has become ever more necessary because the advance of science itself has greatly increased the global and international importance of Arctic research. In this context, the value to science of Arctic research is measured by its benefit to the whole world, not just by the benefit to the nation where the research was done or which did it. And yet in nearly every case science in the Arctic is undertaken by national agencies for purposes that are of importance to the sponsoring nation. International co-operation and co-ordination are necessary if these separate national studies are, together, to produce scientific results of global importance.

Another consideration is that, taken overall, despite its importance to many countries and to world science, Arctic research is only a small and specialized fragment of world research. The volume of science and the number of scientists engaged in Arctic studies are just too small to maintain, spontaneously, the vigorous flow of information, criticism, and interchange that is essential for healthy scientific progress, using the institutions and mechanisms that are in place for most of world science. Many are convinced that intellectually as well as operationally or managerially Arctic science will benefit if there can be put in place an imaginative yet practical scheme for improving international co-operation. There have been repeated expressions from scientists, from administrators, and from those concerned with Arctic policy of the need for improved co-operation, liaison, and communication among Arctic countries on topics related to Arctic science and research.

This paper discusses how, in the light of these problems and opportunities, we can achieve improved co-operation, liaison, and communication in Arctic science.

Historical Setting

The issues surrounding co-operation and sharing of knowledge of Arctic regions, of international rivalry and protection, and of international schemes for working together are not new. They have had a long history of ups and downs, and there have been times in the past when those concerned with Arctic investigations have faced opportunities and frustrations not unlike some of those that lie before us today. It may thus be useful to note briefly some incidents in the history of co-operation in Arctic investigation and knowledge as a background to our discussions.

When, about the year 860 AD, Othere of Halgoland made the first recorded voyage into the Arctic Ocean and sailed around North Cape "to find what lay beyond the wasteland," he started a pattern of exclusive possession of Arctic knowledge and information that has left traces today. For several generations after this voyage, only Othere's family knew how, or had the right, to sail around the Kola Peninsula and into the White Sea and to extract tribute from the Finns. When Othere made a business trip to England in 895 to bargain with King Alfred the Great and exchange his secrets of sailing directions to the White Sea in return for a portion of trading rights to Britain, King Alfred welcomed him but firmly refused.[1] Thus, from an early date, the sharing of Arctic scientific and technical knowledge was mixed up with national priorities, international relations, and economics.

The fullest expression of the *mare clausum* or closed sea approach to Arctic knowledge was in the royal proclamation, or bann, issued by the king of Norway in 1294, which forbade any foreign ship to sail north of the latitude of Bergen without the king's permission or the king's emissary on board.[2] The bann appears to have been surprisingly successful for a couple of centuries; and the main force in ensuring its success appears to have been that the Bergen pilots had exclusive knowledge of how to pass safely through the reefs and whirlpools and how to avoid the terrifying sea monsters and the threatening mountains of ice that beset the minds and the ships of northern travellers in those days.

Suppressed information will, however, escape. In 1360 a book was published in Italy entitled *De inventione fortunata* which took more than a century to circulate but which forever altered the international aspect of Arctic knowledge. The book was attributed to Nicholas of Linne, "a Minorite from Oxford," and bore the subtitle "qui liber incipit a gradua 54 usque ad polum" ("which book begins in the description at latitude 54 degrees and goes as far as the Pole"). No copies are known to exist today, but for the next two centuries this book was widely quoted, often at length, and it was the acknowledged source of information about the geography of the Arctic Ocean region. It was used by cartographers of the day in several countries – Rysch (1508), Mercator (1539, 1569), and Ortelius (1570), for example – in compiling national and international maps and atlases. Although the details of the geography, apparently derived from the stories and legends of Scandinavian and British sailors, were in many respects fanciful, the international spread of the information from *De inventione fortunata* and the many maps that incorporated it were important elements in the evolution of a uniform geographic information system for all of Europe. From the beginning of the sixteenth century there began to be developed, in effect, an international Arctic data base. Even rival countries and opposing interests worked thereafter from, and added information to, this integrated data base.

In 1494, the Treaty of Tordesillas, given international sanction two years later by a papal bull, divided the right of exploration and acquisition of the unknown world into two domains. The portion west of a line 470 leagues west of the Azores was granted to Spain, and areas east of this line were assigned to Portugal. Although the treaty extended from pole to pole, it excluded lands already in possession of a Christian power and did not prevent northern nations from exploring the coasts of lands that they already claimed.[3] Holland and Britain, and to a lesser extent France, Sweden, and Denmark, concentrated their efforts on exploration of the Arctic regions, searching for northeast and northwest passages to circumvent the Portuguese and Spanish restrictions. Thus, indirectly, the Treaty of Tordesillas provided a strong political incentive for the increase of Arctic knowledge and to the intentional sharing, even among rival countries and companies, of Arctic geographical and technical information.[4]

In the enthusiasm that characterized the sixteenth-century sharing of ideas about the Arctic regions, not all the information was correct. Christopher Columbus himself subscribed to a then-current notion that sea ice could only form near coastlines and could not cover the polar ocean, and in 1500 he wrote to his patron proposing a voyage to China by way of the North Pole. This misconception about sea ice, and the erroneous ideas about Arctic Ocean geography with four central islands and mythical straits joining the North Atlantic and North Pacific that were derived from *De inventione fortunata*, persisted for nearly three centuries and cost many lives and fortunes in failed and tragic expeditions.

The open sharing of Arctic scientific information and practical knowledge received a further stimulus when, during the seventeenth century, the concept of *mare liberum* – that the world's oceans away from the coastlines were free for access and travel by all countries – came to be generally accepted. Except for the closing of the North Pacific by Russia (1824-70), all countries engaged in Arctic science have since followed the principle of the freedom of the seas in Arctic regions in peacetime, and most information has been freely exchanged. In recent years, however, the principle has been challenged by various mostly unofficial but influential statements of a "sector principle" for the Arctic Ocean.[5] Legal jurisdictional issues have also arisen in recent years with respect to the use of the sea ice for travel, hunting, and temporary occupancy.[6] Whether these developments will have an influence on the control and exchange of Arctic scientific information remains to be seen.

One of the most interesting examples of the tradition and benefits of international co-operation in Arctic scientific research is provided by the expedition of Constantine John Phipps in 1775. This was perhaps the first major Arctic expedition whose primary goal was scientific research. Because discovery of new lands, a new trade route, or other overt national advantage was not its primary purpose, Phipps's expedition has been largely ignored by geographers and historians. But it provides many insights into the differences between scientific research and national exploration in Arctic regions. The expedition had a genuine international background. The plan was proposed by the French round-the-world explorer, Louis de Bougainville, who presented it to the Académie royale des Sciences. The French turned him down, so de Bougainville took the proposal to the Royal Society of London, of which he was a fellow. After considerable discussion and influenced strongly by the urgings of the eminent Swiss geographer, Samuel Engel, the Royal Society accepted the proposal for "a voyage made towards the north-pole to be of service to the promotion of natural knowledge."[7] In the preparations for this multidisciplinary expedition, authorities in many fields were consulted throughout the scientific world. A senior scientist and officer of the Royal Society, Joseph Banks, himself went to the Netherlands to interview Dutch sea captains and obtain detailed information on ice conditions and ocean currents north of Svalbard, information which was freely given and which turned out to be quite accurate. Similarly, the results of this scientifically fruitful expedition were reported throughout the specialist scientific literature and not simply treated as appendices to the story of a national exploration. In this instance, at least, international communication on Arctic science worked very well.

The clearest expression of the benefits of international co-operation in Arctic sciences, and also one of the most successful examples of international scientific co-operation that the world has yet seen, took place a little more than one hundred years ago. Arctic science, and Arctic international relations, owe a great debt to Karl Weyprecht. Weyprecht was a physicist and an officer in the Austro-Hungarian navy with a special interest in studies of magnetism and the aurora. When co-leader of the German North Polar Expedition of 1872-3, he became convinced that geographical exploration should be replaced by international scientific research carried out according to an openly agreed plan. Weyprecht launched a campaign throughout academies and scientific institutions in Europe, stating that the Arctic regions offered opportunities unparalleled anywhere on the planet for scientific studies of the earth's physical and natural processes. He promoted the concept that co-operation among nations was essential to the successful accomplishment of research in the Arctic.[8]

Weyprecht made the first strong statement of the need for international co-operation in Arctic science. Some of his arguments apply with equal force today. He said:

- The earth should be studied as a planet. National boundaries, and the North Pole itself, have no more and no less significance than any other point on the planet, according to the opportunity they offer for phenomena to be observed.
- Science is not a territory for national possession.
- Small nations must be able to take part in Arctic research.
- Unco-ordinated observations can have only relative significance.
- Scientific knowledge of lasting value can result from co-ordinated and co-operative studies undertaken according to an agreed plan, with the results of the observations freely shared without discrimination.

Weyprecht's ideas were radical for their time, but persuasive. They gradually became endorsed by leading institutions concerned with the study of natural history and the physical phenomena of the earth. They led to the creation of the International Polar Commission in 1879, and then to the International Polar Year of 1882-3.

The International Polar Year was one of the greatest steps forward, in any subject or any part of the world, towards international communication and co-operation in science. Not only did 11 nations, sponsoring 14 simultaneous polar research expeditions, together with 39 permanent observatories in 25 countries co-operate in a detailed circumpolar and global research programme, but the observations and data were reported to a central commission and made available to the whole world. This example also led to broad acceptance of the view that the standards of accuracy and objectivity in science must be set through review by scientific peers and not through political favour or personal prestige. The freeing of scientific results from political influence, which has meant so much for the progress of science for the past one hundred years, came about to an important degree through the achievement of international co-operation in Arctic science by the International Polar Year.

The International Polar Year was followed by a marked advance in world-wide scientific co-operation. Aided by advances in communications technology, geophysical observatories developed global networks of co-ordinated observations, weather observations became synchronized, and tidal readings were harmonized. Fifty years later, in 1932-3, the Second International Polar Year marked another co-ordinated international study of high-latitude phenomena. Twenty-five years later still, in 1957-8, the geophysical sciences were ready to spread the concept of co-ordinated study over the whole world, with the International Geophysical Year or IGY. The IGY was truly global, but it paid particular attention to the polar regions, Arctic and Antarctic, and brought them for the first time into the mainstream of international world science. Sixty-seven countries, and more than 25,000 scientists took part in the IGY, and its success has influenced subsequent thinking on the need for and benefits from international co-operation in science. Nowhere is this more evident than in the Arctic.

The International Council of Scientific Unions, which was responsible for the organization of the International Geophysical Year, gave careful consideration to the best way to achieve international co-ordination of scientific activities in polar regions. At the 1957 meeting of ICSU in Brussels, a proposal was made for a scientific committee for Arctic and Antarctic research, dubbed SCAAR, which would serve as an international centre for communications and joint planning for Arctic and Antarctic research. Several countries were in favour of a SCAAR. But because several northern countries already had institutions concerned with Arctic research and were already involved in Arctic studies and because the need for co-ordinated scientific planning was obviously greatest in the Antarctic, it was agreed that it was easier and more logical to form a special committee for the Antarctic first. Therefore in 1958, the Special Committee on Antarctic Research was created by ICSU, and later changed in name to the Scientific Committee on Antarctic Research (SCAR). It has functioned ever since as a body for international communication and co-ordination of scientific activities in the southern polar regions.

Co-operation since the IGY

The success of the International Geophysical Year, not only in advancing scientific knowledge but also in demonstrating the advantages and feasibility of large-scale international co-operative scientific endeavours, led naturally to a number of somewhat similar programmes in other fields of scientific enquiry. Within a few years, the International Hydrological Decade, the International Biological Programme, and the International Upper Mantle Study were under way; each was global or planetary in scope but with important specialist attention to the Arctic region. Other international programmes, direct offshoots of specific IGY research, set out to investigate particular phenomena whose study in different parts of the Arctic was essential. The International Year of the Quiet Sun and the International Magnetospheric Study are examples.

All of these developments demonstrated the circumpolar unity of Arctic science and the essential linkage between science in the Arctic and science in lower latitudes. At this stage, there was little "nationalism" in the leading scientific research projects in the Arctic regions, and indeed in many areas scientific leadership in Arctic research was taken not by scientists from Arctic countries but by scientists and institutions from other countries who were leaders in global research.

While the large integrated research programmes achieved a remarkable degree of international co-operation and sharing of results related to Arctic regions in the period from 1958 to 1972, international developments of a different nature also affected science and technology in Arctic regions. Advances in communications and instrumentation, and a better understanding of the science involved, led to greatly improved high-latitude circumpolar networks for weather observation and reporting, radio transmission, and magnetic observation. The management and co-ordination of these networks led to the refinement and increased importance of international scientific and technical organizations whose principal role was the co-ordination of technical activities and the exchange of technical information. The importance of international professional organizations in facilitating co-operation on specific ongoing technical activities in the Arctic regions led to a desire in some quarters for an effective international body to enhance co-operation in Arctic research in general.

During the same period, developments in three other areas had a profound effect on the directions taken by international scientific co-operation in the Arctic.

Advances in technology made the Arctic regions – on land, in the sea, and in the air – accessible in a new way. The repercussions of the new technologies were profound. Arctic natural resources (petroleum, metals) became potentially important in world commerce and in geopolitics and led to new national policies about northern development in most Arctic countries. But these developments also led to international or multinational sharing of many Arctic technologies and to the development of transpolar transportation and communication. As well, the role of the Arctic regions in defence and military strategy was profoundly changed. These technological developments have had a mixed effect on Arctic science co-operation. Distance and a harsh environment are no longer a barrier to research. But neither do they provide national safety or protection. There is now little exclusiveness in scientific knowledge in the Arctic regions; rival technologies, both civilian and military, rapidly converge. There is a great increase in shared information, but little systematic way of sharing it. In all northern countries, most current national policies concerning the Arctic are strongly based on the state of scientific knowledge and technology, but the knowledge and the development of technology are rarely controlled nationally.

A second development is the emergence of environmental concerns to prominence among the most important Arctic issues, politically and with the public. These issues concern both northern residents and large numbers of people who live in more southerly regions. The concerns are in part economic, in part related to heritage and the need to preserve a vulnerable and valuable land for the future, and in part related to what Arctic regions can tell us about the condition of the planet as a whole. The nature and substance of these concerns depends directly on scientific knowledge and the communication of that knowledge, and on the scientific ability to detect trends and predict changes in the natural environment. The Arctic environment is vulnerable to change, not only from natural causes and activities in the Arctic itself, but from developments originating in other parts of the planet. Anticipated changes in world climate will be greatest in Arctic regions and will affect the natural environment and renewable resources of Arctic regions more than those of more southerly latitudes. These questions have obvious international and national dimensions. Environmental issues are increasingly a part of national policies of all northern countries, but the issues themselves are rarely national; they are mainly circumpolar or world-wide in nature. This situation has intensified the importance of international co-operation in Arctic science.

Finally, social and political developments in the Arctic regions have altered the demand for scientific knowledge and exchange of information. The northern regions of all Arctic countries have experienced profound socio-economic and educational changes. The indigenous people, whose culture and heritage are not restricted to national boundaries, have in many parts of the Arctic a more circumpolar outlook than most of the public in the countries of which they are citizens. Increasingly, the aspirations and activities of northern peoples focus on the local or practical application of the results of research and technological development – on resource management, environmental protection, the construction of settlements, or the improvement of transportation and public services. The need to incorporate modern international science into educational programmes in the Arctic is widely recognized. Local or national socio-economic questions increasingly provide policy and economic justification for national investment in Arctic science. However, the science undertaken to study these issues must often be international in scope.

Mechanisms for Co-operation in Arctic Science

A wide variety of mechanisms and arrangements have been developed in the past three decades to facilitate international co-operation in research, data-gathering, and technological development in Arctic regions.[9] Let us look at some of the more important which should be kept in mind during consideration of what is needed for the future.

Multilateral intergovernmental agreements. There are few multinational intergovernmental agreements dealing directly with Arctic science, although some international treaties and agreements have led to shared research. An obvious example is the 1973 international Agreement on the Conservation of Polar Bears. Some other treaties, such as the Svalbard Treaty, do not mention science but have been used to open the door to equal access, thereby facilitating international co-operation if the countries concerned wished it.

Bilateral intergovernmental agreements. There is a large number of bilateral intergovernmental agreements between northern countries, or between Arctic countries and non-Arctic countries that have Arctic interests. Some of these, such as the USSR-Canada Agreement for Co-operation in Science in the Arctic and the North, or a similar agreement between Norway and the USSR, are focused directly on Arctic science. Others, such as the co-operative agreement between the USSR and the United States, are broader in scope but contain specific clauses dealing with the Arctic. The range of subjects covered by these bilateral agreements is very wide, from the upper atmosphere to medicine to environmental protection.

International scientific organizations and programmes. There are a number of international scientific organizations whose principal purpose is to provide communications and exchange information directly related to Arctic science: the International Union for Circumpolar Health, the International Permafrost Association, the Comité Arctique International, and the Arctic Ocean Sciences Board are examples. More common, and on the world scene perhaps more influential, are international scientific organizations that are global in scope but include specific units or programmes dealing with Arctic topics. Most of these have a fairly well defined disciplinary focus, and many represent the Arctic component of the global interests of the parent body. Prominent among these are the numerous organizations of the International Council of Scientific Unions. Typical examples from among many such bodies are the International Commission on Polar Meteorology of the International Association of Meteorology and Atmospheric Physics and the Northern Research Basins Network of the International Association of Hydrological Sciences (both these associations are components of the International Union of Geodesy and Geophysics), or Working Group 82 of the Scientific Committee on Oceanographic Research, which deals with "polar deep sea palæo-environments." Other examples, outside the ICSU family, are the Northern Science Network of UNESCO's Man and the Biosphere Programme or the polar sub-programme of the World Climate Research Programme.

International participation in nationally organized Arctic research activities. Several of the best examples of international Arctic scientific co-operation in recent years have been activities sponsored or organized primarily by one country but involving scientists or institutions from other countries as well. Well-known recent nationally sponsored Arctic studies in which scientists from several countries took part include the Swedish Ymer expedition, the Norwegian PRO MARE programme, the American MIZEX and Fram research projects, and the Canadian LOREX and CESAR studies. The success of these studies when they have gone well and the great effort required to plan and achieve genuine international co-operation for a single expedition have been among the principal motives for the repeated desire that there should be a continuing, formally recognized international mechanism to facilitate co-operation in the future.

The Lessons Learned

The varied recent examples of international co-operation in Arctic science reviewed above, and many others that have been noted and reviewed elsewhere, prompt us to ask some searching questions. How successful have the present mechanisms for co-operation been? How well have they served science? How well have they served the national interests of the participating countries? How well have they served the cause of international relations in general? Has international and multinational science in the Arctic regions been a positive factor, a difficult obstacle, or a passive victim in the development of Arctic bi-national and international relations and in defining the role that the Arctic plays in world affairs?

It is necessary to ask these questions and to try to answer them frankly – not all answers will be the same – before considering the questions of today. **Do we need something else?** And then: what can be devised or constructed in the modern context that might succeed where the present mechanisms have failed to serve either science or national interests?

Those involved in Arctic science today are called upon to search for an international mechanism that would not displace or discredit the various bilateral and specialized arrangements for Arctic co-operation that exist, that would truly represent varied national and international interests and could be supportive of national policies, and that still would meet the need for effective co-ordination of important science and keep it at arm's length from political interference. To accomplish this will not be easy, but the persistence and good will with which the question has been addressed in all the circumpolar countries in the past few years, despite difficult political and administrative obstacles, has led to a widespread belief that it will be done.

Parallel developments

During the past decade, while the various arrangements for international involvement in Arctic research programmes have been evolving, there have been developments in other areas that have a bearing on the need for, and the likely political acceptability or scientific usefulness of, an international mechanism for Arctic scientific co-operation. Some of these may be noted.

Developments in **Antarctica** related to regimes for resource management (living resources and minerals), tourism, and the challenges in the United Nations General Assembly that the Antarctic Treaty is too "exclusive" have led to much discussion and clarification of the relationship between intergovernmental policy and positions (dealt with through the treaty) and non-governmental but government-endorsed scientific co-operation (dealt with by SCAR) in polar regions.

Developments related to international co-operation in **studies of the world's oceans and regional seas**, consequent upon national and international discussions concerning ratification of the 1982 United Nations Convention on the Law of the Sea have similarly had important implications for the relationship between national and international policies and international co-operation in research. Involved in these discussions are not only United Nations bodies dealing with science – United Nations Environment Programme (regional seas), UNESCO (Intergovernmental Oceanographic Commission) – but independent intergovernmental organizations (International Council for the Exploration of the Seas), informal international groups of agencies supporting Arctic science (Arctic Ocean Sciences Board), and non-governmental scientific members of the ICSU family (Scientific Committee on Oceanographic Research and others). Many of the principles and arrangements being developed in these discussions will apply directly to international co-operation in Arctic regions of which the Arctic Ocean is a vital and central part. In addition, like the discussions of the co-operation in Antarctica and in space research, the evolving arrangements for co-operative oceanographic research are relevant in the broader sense of illustrating the problems, trends, and possibilities for international co-operation in research in areas that are both politically sensitive and of economic and environmental importance to all nations. It is very important to ensure that any arrangement for international scientific co-operation in the Arctic, which includes research on the Arctic Ocean, is compatible with arrangements or mechanisms for co-operation in oceanographic research.

In the **social sciences**, important international developments include the influence of the Inuit Circumpolar Conference (ICC) and the growing recognition of it by governments of several Arctic countries as a legitimate voice for the concerns of and knowledge about northern peoples. The ICC has become an active promoter of international scientific research on social issues, history and heritage, economic planning, and Arctic political sciences. Its concerns and activities have found support in much of the scientific community and in the policies of several Arctic nations, and it will undoubtedly (some will say belatedly) influence the future character and style of international co-operation in Arctic science.

There is as well a new wave of **global-view scientific programmes**, international in nature and participation, which necessarily include the Arctic regions as a normal but essential part of their activities. The International Geosphere-Biosphere Programme of ICSU, the World Climate Research Programme of the World Meteorological Organization, and the World Ocean Circulation Experiment are examples and there are several others. International co-operation is an essential element of such global-scale studies, and this co-operation must be extended to the Arctic regions. Any specific mechanism developed for co-operation in Arctic science must be compatible with the co-operation necessary for these major global programmes.

Several countries, including some that do not possess Arctic territories (for example, Germany and Japan) have responded to the newly recognized importance of Arctic science and the polar sciences generally by revising their policies with regard to the Arctic or by strengthening their facilities and resources for Arctic research. Most Arctic countries have recently given national attention to the adequacy of Arctic science as seen from their own national perspectives. While the emphasis and focus have differed from country to country, one feature common to all has been the recognition that enhanced international co-operation in Arctic science is in the national interest of each Arctic country, as some highlights of current and recent developments in these countries show.

Canada. The study, "Canada and Polar Science," stresses the importance of international participation in polar science and the need for Canada to improve its organization for support and improvement of high-latitude science. The government of Canada has recently announced its intention to establish a polar commission whose tasks will include the furthering of international co-operation in Arctic science.

Denmark. A new Danish Polar Institute has been created which, while focusing on the need to strengthen national polar activities, gives strong attention to the international dimension of Danish science. Also, discussions connected with the establishment of a Greenland University and a research centre at Nuuk have been carried on in an international context.

Finland. The developing programme of the Arctic Science Centre at Rovaniemi has envisaged participation by foreign scientists as an integral part of its activities. Finland's initiative for intergovernmental action to protect the Arctic environment has been an important step in promoting international communication on Arctic issues and has led to co-operative assessment of the state of Arctic environmental knowledge.

Norway. Both the parliamentary review of the Norsk Polarinstitutt and the approved programme of the Norwegian Research Council, which supports important Arctic research, refer to the essentially international nature of Norwegian polar science.

Sweden. The enlarged and supported mandate of the Polar Research Secretariat charges it with maintaining liaison and co-operation with other countries in polar research and states specifically that "polar research ... calls for collaboration, often in an international setting."

United States. The Arctic Research and Policy Act defines international co-operation in science as one of the goals in Arctic research and charges the United States Arctic Research Commission to see that this is accomplished. Its five-year plans include a section on international co-operation.

USSR. In a speech delivered at Murmansk on October 1, 1987, Mikhail Gorbachev stressed the importance of international co-operation in Arctic science, and he referred to it again during the Washington summit meeting on January 13, 1988. The USSR took the first major step in modern times in bringing together scientists from various countries and many disciplines to discuss the findings of Arctic research by organizing an international conference on the co-ordination of research in the Arctic, held in Leningrad in December 1988.

An Arctic SCAR?

The most common question raised in discussions of the feasibility of establishing a comprehensive and multinational circumpolar arrangement for improving scientific co-operation is: "Why cannot we establish an Arctic equivalent to SCAR?" In my own experience, such a suggestion has been put forward at about five-year intervals since 1960. A little reflection and examination has nearly always led to the conclusion that, at least in recent decades, the geopolitical, national policy, and research support situation in the Arctic is sufficiently different from that in the Antarctic that an international committee patterned directly after SCAR does not seem feasible for the Arctic, unless (which has until recently seemed politically most unlikely) there was an intergovernmental political instrument equivalent to the Antarctic Treaty to provide some sort of policy umbrella. We should recall, however, that SCAR was established as a non-governmental international scientific body of ICSU before the Antarctic Treaty came into existence. And so initially it did not have the benefit of the treaty to help keep it clear of policy entanglements.

In full realization of the different situations in the Antarctic and the Arctic, a number of serious proposals have nevertheless been made to re-examine the question of whether an "Arctic SCAR" in the ICSU sense would be useful and feasible. In 1986, during the SCAR meeting in San Diego, an informal meeting to reconsider this question was chaired by Dr J. H. Zumberge, at that time simultaneously the chairman of SCAR and the chairman of the United States Arctic Research Commission. Representatives of several countries at that meeting felt that the time was propitious, in light of both the international political situation in the Arctic and the needs of science. It was decided to explore the issue further.

The Norsk Polarinstitutt in Oslo offered to host an informal meeting of persons from Arctic nations who were familiar with the complex history of scientific co-operation in the Arctic and with national policies and international relations to discuss the feasibility of a new and forward-looking mechanism for international co-operation that would take into account modern realities. I was asked to prepare a discussion paper for the meeting; Odd Rogne of the Norsk Polarinstitutt commented on it and graciously consented to let his name also be attached to it.[10]

In our review of the points to be taken into consideration with regard to the need for, feasibility of, and possible role of a mechanism for improving international co-operation in Arctic science, we stressed the following points which continue to be relevant today.

Caution. It was important not to be carried away with the enthusiasm of the moment and to make a decision that a new international Arctic science committee is needed and feasible before looking carefully at all the angles and implications. With such a rich history of attempted and occasionally successful examples of co-operation in the past, why was something new needed and why had the previous attempts not developed into a lasting mechanism?

Issues. We identified four main issues to be dealt with. First, different countries had different domestic priorities and different international priorities, and all had a science component. Second, the Arctic interests of Arctic states often differed from the Arctic interests of non-Arctic states, and this influenced their respective approaches to Arctic science. Yet the data base of scientific knowledge was for the most part shared and non-national. Third, to an increasing extent in several countries, the kinds of scientific information most needed by government or industry in the short term called for research quite different from the research that was most important from the point of view of major scientific questions in the Arctic or of the needs of world science. The degree of desired international involvement and collaboration could also differ. And, finally, the level of scientific or political authority at which international co-operation would be most effectively organized needed to be carefully considered (scientist-to-scientist, institution-to-institution, programme-to-programme, government-to-government). The problem was to retain desired flexibility and yet have sufficient control and influence to achieve true co-ordination.

Comparison with the Antarctic. In the Antarctic, the continued success of international co-operation in research is facilitated by as clean as possible a separation of political and policy issues from the issues of science.[11] Was this same separation possible or desirable in the Arctic? Would the two mechanisms to which the different issues were separately addressed need to be developed simultaneously? If not, to what degree was the SCAR model appropriate for the Arctic today?

Recent experiences. What lessons could be learned from the experiences of different organizations that had been involved in international scientific Arctic activities, in planning, evaluation, operation, or communication? Among the most valuable were the Comité Arctique International, the Arctic Ocean Sciences Board, the Committee for High Arctic Research Liaison and Information Exchange (CHARLIE), the Man and the Biosphere Northern Science Network, and the polar-related ICSU bodies.

"Sticky" problems. Though not major conceptual issues, these questions would have to be dealt with or else they could become major obstacles: (1) What countries would be included? What would be the "qualifications" for membership? (2) How would a balance be kept between "big science" (the global and regional programmes), "modest science" (the facilitation of co-operation or team work between individual scientists or universities on small projects), and "national science" (mission-oriented science according to national priorities)? Was a "balance" necessary or desirable? (3) How would the desired range of disciplines or subject areas be enhanced through international co-operation? In particular, how would the mechanism promote or achieve co-operation in the area of human and social sciences? (4) Would the mechanism facilitate the Arctic component of international global scientific programmes? If so, would there be a risk of conflict of interests and procedures? (5) How would the mechanism deal with commercial science and military science, much of which was already characterized by co-operative participation, but not on the same open terms as public science?

The 1987 paper also made some suggestions. They remain relevant and are worth repeating.

- To achieve effective international co-operation in Arctic science, there should be continuing consultation or communication at various levels: between scientists; between science managers and administrators; and between ministries or those responsible for Arctic policies. How, and whether, to bring these together or keep them separate would determine the nature and the success of any international Arctic science committee.

- Any body or mechanism created to facilitate international co-operation in Arctic science must support, and not weaken or supplant, the bilateral and multilateral mechanisms already in place.

- The practical results of an international co-operation mechanism would depend upon the resources and interest that can be sustained over a period of years and not be tied to the support for a particular scientific project. Therefore, the question of continued support had to be carefully considered before any decision was made to form a new body.

- Full co-operation or partnership among all circumpolar countries in any field of research was an unrealistic expectation. It was necessary to start with practical goals in a few areas where circumpolar agreement already existed.

- Despite its complex ramifications, the idea of a means to achieve improved international co-operation in Arctic science needed a simple and clear description and identity, so that it could be widely discussed in all northern countries before commitment to its establishment.

The meeting held in Oslo on February 13, 1987 was a historic one. It was the first time that senior people from all countries with territories north of the Arctic Circle had come together expressly to discuss co-operation in science. As of April 1990, senior people from all the Arctic countries continued to meet, and there was open and careful discussion of the necessity to ensure that non-Arctic countries as well as Arctic countries continued to play an important role in, and benefit from, Arctic science, while ensuring that the special interests and priorities of Arctic countries were protected. In August 1990 these discussions and meetings succeeded in establishing an International Arctic Science Committee that has the endorsement of governments of all Arctic countries, is satisfactory to the governments of non-Arctic countries with an interest in the Arctic regions, and should be seen by Arctic scientists throughout the world and by the residents of northern regions as practical, helpful, and something they can use and benefit from. With such an international mechanism now in place, there can be little doubt that it will be put to use – for the good of the Arctic and world knowledge.

Notes

1 N. Lind and C.E. Fell, *Two Voyagers Othere and Wulfstan at the Court of King Alfred* (York: William Sessions 1984).

2 G. A. Blom, "The Participation of the Kings in the Early Norwegian Sailing to Bjarmeland (Kola Peninsula and Russian Waters) and the Development of a Royal Policy concerning the Northern Waters in the Middle Ages," *Arctic,* 37 (December 1984), 385-8.

3 B. Johnson-Theutenberg, "Mare Clausum et Mare Liberum," *Arctic,* 37 (December 1984), 481-92.

4 J. R. Weber and E. F. Roots, "The Arctic Ocean Region – Historical Background: Exploration, Concepts and Observations," *Decade of North American Geology,* vol 50 (Boulder CO.: Geological Society of America 1989), chap 2.

5 B. Johnson-Theutenberg, *The Evolution of the Law of the Sea: A Study of Resources and Strategy with Special Reference to the Polar Regions,* Natural Resources and Environment Series, vol 17 (Dublin: Tycooly 1984).

6 A. Cook and E. van Alstine, eds, *Sikumiut: The People Who Use the Sea Ice* (Ottawa: Canadian Arctic Resources Committee 1984).

7 Royal Society (London), *Minutes,* 6 (1769-1782), 158.

8 N. H. de V. Heathcote and A. Armitage, "The First International Polar Year (1882-1883)," *Annals of the International Geophysical Year,* vol 1 (London: Pergamon 1959), 6-100; and E. F. Roots, "International and Regional Co-operation in Arctic Science: A Changing Situation," *Rapport fra Nordisk Vitenskapelig Konferanse om Arktisk Forskning* (Tromsø: University of Tromsø Press 1984), 127-56; reprinted in *Musk-Ox,* no 34 (spring 1986), 9-27.

9 See Roots, "International and Regional Co-operation."

10 E. F. Roots and O. Rogne, "Some Points for Consideration in Discussions on the Need for, Feasibility, and Possible Role of an International Arctic Science Committee," mimeo (Oslo: Norsk Polarinstitutt 1987).

11 Polar Research Board, *Antarctic Treaty System: An Assessment* (Washington: National Academy Press 1986). See, in particular, J. H. Zumberge, "The Scientific Committee on Antarctic Research and the Antarctic Treaty System," 153-68, and E. F. Roots, "The Role of Science in the Antarctic Treaty System," 169-84.

11

Arctic Pollution
and the Greenhouse Effect

Anders Karlqvist & Jost Heintzenberg

Most of us would like to think of the polar regions as pristine places unspoiled by man. It is an attractive idea that there might be places which bear witness to an original state of the globe and which could serve as references against which to measure the human influence on planet Earth. There once seemed to be no better candidates for such a place than the most remote areas of the world – the Arctic and the Antarctic. This idea was shattered when it was discovered that pesticides and man-made radioactive material had spread all the way to Antarctica and could be found in the tissues of penguins. Since that time in the late sixties, only some twenty years after DDT had come into general industrial use, we have reluctantly come to accept that there are no pristine refuges on the globe. We cannot escape our responsibility for the world as a whole.

This situation is historically quite new. Human impact on the global environment dates back only to the dawn of industrialization less than two centuries ago, and most of the significant changes in the environment related to human activities have emerged in the last few decades. This is an extremely short time span, when viewed in the perspective of geological or even biological time. Thus, there are very good reasons to pay attention to these matters right now. The management of the global environment is an issue for our generation. There is no time to lose. We cannot afford to wait and hand the problems over to our children or grandchildren.

Global Pollution – A Problem for Our Time

There are several good reasons to place global pollution on any Arctic research agenda. First, the world has changed dramatically. Population, production, and emission of substances into the atmosphere have risen to unprecedented levels. Table 1 shows some typical figures in a forty-year time perspective. Many of the chemical substances which are produced

TABLE 1. Population, Production, Emission of Substances

	1950	1985	
World population	2.5	5.0	(billions)
Gross world product	2.9	13.1	(trillion 1980 dollars)
World fossil fuel consumption	3	12	(billion tons, coal equivalent)
World carbon emission from fossil fuels	1.6	5.3	(billion tons)
Synthetic organic chemicals production in United States	(approx.) 8	105	(million tons)

Based on information from Worldwatch Institute Reports 1987-88.

today and eventually released into the environment were not even known in 1950. Other more familiar substances such as carbon dioxide (CO_2) and methane (CH_4) are now generated by human activities in quantities that far exceed previous records.

Another reason for attending to this matter now lies in our improved capability to observe and measure substances even in very small quantities and to register minute but significant changes over time. Modern isotope techniques have greatly enhanced these possibilities. "Clean" ice or air was discovered to be far from unaffected once the sensitivity of our measurement instruments improved and analyses became more accurate. Great progress has also been made in the scientific study of complex global systems with the advent of powerful computers and new mathematical techniques. Scientists have begun to understand the interaction between the atmosphere, the oceans, and the ice caps, to express these relations in quantitative terms, and to appreciate the complexity of the chemical cycles involving both the biosphere and the geosphere. Large-scale simulation models reveal cause-effect links which are far from obvious. Yet at the same time it has become evident how difficult it is to use this theoretical knowledge and historical data to make predictions. The discovery of the thinning of the stratospheric ozone layer over the Antarctic in the mid-1980s is a dramatic example of this problem.

The progress of science has demonstrated the importance of widening the scope of the analysis to include complicated temporal and spatial interdependencies. It is also evident that global problems necessitate co-operation across national borders. Major environmental changes caused by human activities can be neither studied nor influenced effectively by individual countries operating independently of each other.

In all of this research, the polar regions have a very special role to play. Remote from major population centres and by and large unaffected by local pollution, they provide early warning signals of change at the global level. Moreover, the effects of climatic change are likely to be more dramatic at higher latitudes than in the temperate areas of the world. The extreme conditions prevailing in the Arctic and the Antarctic accentuate the risks of damaging life conditions and upsetting the polar ecosystems. Generally speaking, these systems are more vulnerable to disturbances and less resilient in responding to damage. This is especially important for the Arctic which is not only a habitat for many species of animals and plants but also a home for people who have lived in the North and subsisted on its living resources for thousands of years.

Baseline Monitoring

To understand global changes in the atmosphere and the possible man-induced impacts on climate, reference measurements are needed. Obviously, global monitoring should not be influenced by local or regional pollution sources. Hence, remote sites in the polar regions provide suitable conditions for atmospheric baseline monitoring. At the beginning of the 1970s several international monitoring programmes were set up, such as the GMCC (Global Monitoring for Climatic Change) programme of the United States and the World Meteorological Organization's Background Air Pollution Monitoring Network. Atmospheric baseline monitoring stations were established to measure certain background parameters such as carbon dioxide concentration and atmospheric turbidity.

To draw conclusions about global trends requires observations made over long periods of time. Unfortunately, direct observation of the atmosphere's composition has a rather short history, less than twenty years for most substances. For earlier records we have to rely on palæo-climatological data drawn from sediments and ice cores.

During the past decade sampling and analytical techniques have improved greatly, and it is now possible to determine the levels of a large number of trace substances in polar air masses, water columns, and ice caps. Hence, a much more complex picture of the composition of the atmosphere and the changes which it undergoes has emerged.

For long-lived gases, such as CO_2 which remain in the atmosphere for several years, the geographical distribution can be assumed to be smoothed out and measurements (taken not too close to local sources) will well reflect global conditions. CO_2 has been a major focus of interest as the key factor in anthropogenic influence on the global climate. Recently the effects of other gases such as methane and chlorofluorocarbons have been added to the scenario for the future, a scenario which is dominated by global warming.

The Greenhouse Effect

The physical explanation underlying the prospect of a global warming is captured in the so-called *greenhouse effect*. The shortwave radiation from the sun during the day is balanced by continuous black-body radiation in the infrared spectrum out from the earth. Some of this energy is radiated back by the atmosphere to the earth. In this process gases such as CO_2 and methane act as *reflectors*. Hence the term greenhouse gases.

The interaction between the global climate system and CO_2 is convincingly corroborated by the data. Probably the most complete continuous record of temperature has been derived by isotope analyses of the ice from the Vostok core.[1] It covers some 160,000 years. This ice core, which is more than 2,000 metres long, was drilled out of the ice cap at Vostok, the Soviet station in Antarctica in 1980. The data go back before the most recent ice age and hence cover major shifts in the global climate. Besides the changes between glacial and interglacial periods, spectral analysis also revealed periodic shifts, the so-called Milankovitch cycles in climate with intervals of 20,000 years.

The data in figure 1 show the striking correlation between temperature and concentration of carbon dioxide in the atmosphere. Although there are no simple causal links between CO_2 and temperature, there is a common understanding that CO_2 in the atmosphere together with certain other gases amplifies temperature changes. The greenhouse effect plays a prominent role in this positive feedback loop. The Vostok core and records from other ice cores in Greenland and the Antarctic show very consistently that the concentration of CO_2 has increased. During the last ice age the level of CO_2 in the atmosphere was around 200 ppm (parts per million). During the warmer interglacial period it rose to 270 ppm and today it is 350 ppm. A look at recent data (figure 2) reveals a steady increase in atmospheric

Anders Karlqvist & Jost Heintzenberg

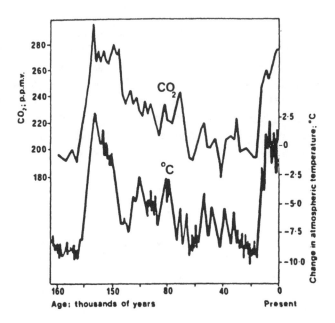

FIGURE 1. CO_2 concentration against age in the Vostok record and atmospheric temperature change derived from the isotopic profile of deuterium. Source: J.M. Barnola, D. Raynaud, Y.S. Korotkevich and C. Lorius, "Vostok Ice Core Provides 160,000 Year Record of Atmospheric CO_2," *Nature*, 329, October 1, 1987.

concentrations. The cause of this recent development is quite clearly linked to human activities and, in particular, to the large-scale use of fossil fuels. The detailed long-term effects of the increase are difficult to assess, but there seems to be a strong consensus among scientists that the net general effect will be a global warming. The extent of the temperature change and its geographical distribution is less certain. According to most theoretical calculations, the polar regions will be most affected. It is likely that the warming at higher latitudes will be higher than in areas closer to the equator by a factor of five to ten.

It should be stressed that the climatic system is extremely complex. The greenhouse mechanism is only a part of its overall dynamics in which regional geographical variations in snow cover (albedo), cloudiness, precipitation, and biosphere also play roles. It is also crucially important to understand the complex interaction of the atmosphere with the ocean's circulation system (on a much longer time-scale), because the oceans act as a major reservoir for CO_2. These circulation patterns are major

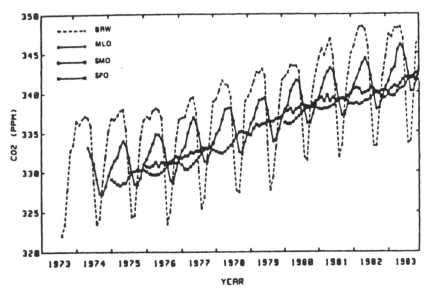

FIGURE 2. Annual cycles and long-term trends in atmospheric concentrations at Barrow, Alaska, Mauna Loa, Hawaii, Samoa, and the South Pole Observatory. Source: J.M. Harris and E.C. Nickerson, *Geophysical Monitoring for Climate Change* (Boulder: NOAA Environmental Research Laboratories 1984), 12.

determinants of climate. There is serious concern that perturbations in ocean circulation caused by a gradual change in temperature can cause dramatic shifts and actually flip the system from one mode to another (that is, by reversing ocean currents). There are indications of such swift shifts in climate in the ice core records, and similar events cannot be excluded from future scenarios. We are dealing then with a time-scale which is alarmingly short, if we are thinking in terms of political and industrial decision-making.

Methane is generated by biological activities and, like CO_2, the concentration of CH_4 has increased over time (figure 3). The amount of methane has risen from about 600 parts per billion before industrialization to 1700 ppb today with an increase of almost 1 per cent a year. Methane is known to play a significant role in the greenhouse effect and may contribute up to 30 per cent of the global warming due to greenhouse gases. It is a long-lived gas and remains in the atmosphere for five to ten years.

Another group of substances of human origin which have caused a great deal of concern during recent years are the chlorofluorocarbons (CFCs). These gases have gained prominence in connection with the

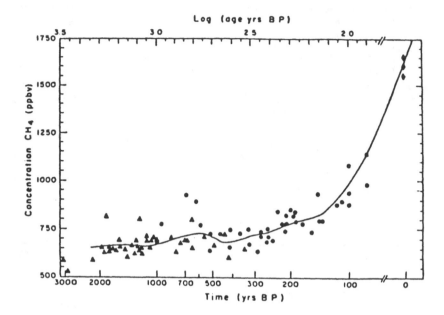

FIGURE 3. Methane concentrations obtained from ice cores in Greenland (circles) and Antarctica (triangles). Present concentrations of methane are shown on the right (diamonds). Source: M.A.K. Khalil and R.A. Rasmussen, "Causes of Increasing Atmospheric Methane: Depletion of Hydroxyl Radicals and the Rise of Emissions," *Atmospheric Environment*, 19 (1985), 397-407.

depletion of ozone in the stratosphere over Antarctica, but it is important to note that CFCs also play a role in the greenhouse effect. It was recently reported that the emission of CFCs into the atmosphere through anthropogenic usage has modified the long-wave radiation budget of the atmosphere by around 0.1 per cent. The irony is that gases like CFCs have been found to have useful industrial applications and to be harmless to use precisely because they are highly stable and non-reactive. These very properties mean that the gases will remain in the atmosphere for a very long time, more than one hundred years. The problems created by today's emissions will be with us for a long time, making the overall situation potentially much more dangerous.

Ozone Depletion

Much has been written about the ozone hole over Antarctica. Indeed, it is probably the most widely discussed global atmospheric problem of today. There are good reasons for this interest. While a general stratospheric ozone depletion had been predicted since the early seventies, the discovery of the Antarctic ozone hole was a surprising and unforeseen event. The first reports, published by scientists with the British Antarctic Survey in the middle of the 1980s, showed a dramatic decrease in stratospheric springtime ozone over Halley Bay.[2] Between 1977 and 1984 the amount of ozone had decreased by more than 40 per cent. Subsequent measurements have confirmed that the depletion has continued and the lowest values ever were recorded in austral spring 1987.[3]

The time-scale of ozone depletion is dramatically short compared to any other climate-related processes. The effect was not foreseen in any predictive models even though the physical processes which cause the destruction of the ozone layer are fairly straightforward and well understood in theory. When the threat to the stratospheric ozone layer was first identified in the early 1970s, the concern was linked to the expected introduction of supersonic air traffic. The emission of nitrogen oxides and water vapour at high altitudes was considered a major risk element. The debate died along with the grand plans for supersonic transport planes. Now the risk element is found to be the chlorofluorocarbons used on the ground in air conditioners, refrigerators, aerosol sprays, and agents for producing foam and for cleaning electronic parts. It is well known that these CFC compounds act as catalysts in destroying ozone. The active component is the chlorine atom which is freed by the energy in the ultraviolet radiation which hits the CFC molecule. In very simple terms, a chlorine atom can steal an oxygen atom from the ozone molecule. This oxygen atom can then combine with another oxygen atom to form oxygen molecules (O_2). The chlorine atom can then engage in another catalytic cycle.

This chemically based explanation does not provide a complete answer to the appearance of an ozone hole because there are other processes which interfere with the catalytic cycle. To explain the events over Antarctica, it is important to understand how these counteractive processes involving, for example, nitrogen oxides are impeded by the unique meteorological conditions in Antarctica. Such conditions involve the formation of high altitude clouds in the winter when the absence of sunlight leads to very low stratospheric temperatures. The polar stratospheric clouds may act as chlorine reservoirs from which active chlorine is released in early spring with the return of sunlight.

These proposed explanations do not preclude the possibility that atmospheric dynamics themselves play a key role in the formation of the ozone hole. The special circulation pattern over Antarctica and the polar vortex would prevent the ozone-rich air from the north from moving into the Antarctic atmosphere until late in the spring when the polar vortex dissipates. To explain the rapidity of the change over the last decade, it is necessary to assume that the dynamic patterns have changed. Such a change is possible, but it raises new questions about what causes these extraordinary shifts in atmospheric circulation.

Although there is as yet no firm and universally accepted theory of ozone depletion, a balanced view based on the available information on the topic could be summarized in the following way: "Taken together, recent data add weight to the growing suspicion that chlorofluorocarbons do contribute importantly to the ozone hole. The findings also indicate that the phenomenon is affected by the region's unique meteorology (the polar vortex, frigid stratospheric temperatures and PSC's [polar stratospheric clouds]) and probably by a shift in airflow patterns in the Southern Hemisphere."[4]

The cause of the ozone hole is of great importance for global science and not just for Antarctic science. Is this phenomenon peculiar to the Antarctic atmosphere, or is it an early warning of an environmental problem that will spread to the rest of the world? Can we expect something similar to happen in the Arctic? The evidence from investigations in the North is less conclusive. However, a recent review of data collected at monitoring stations in the northern hemisphere has revealed a reduction in the ozone layer in winter of around 6 per cent since 1969 at latitudes between 53°N and 64°N. The effects are less pronounced than in the South, and fluctuations in climate and sun activity make trend extrapolations and predictions more difficult. Still, the indications of disturbances in the chemistry of the ozone layer in the Arctic are serious enough to warrant close monitoring.

Global Climate and International Co-operation

It is trite to say that global problems call for international solutions. Atmospheric science is probably one of the best examples of extensive international co-operation in data collection and research. The implications of the problems of global warming and ozone depletion require more than routine international responses. Moreover, these problems have a strong polar component. It is therefore most relevant to discuss these matters in the context of polar, or more specifically, Arctic co-operation.

The palæoclimatic records found in the ice cores from Greenland and the Antarctic, together with the sediment cores from the deep oceans, are the best evidence we have of the atmospheric history of our planet. The actual drilling and retrieval of cores is a major undertaking which requires many resources and much technical machinery. Suitable sites for drilling are often far from ports and airfields and transportation and infrastructure are very costly. These practical considerations favour international co-operation.

The Vostok drilling is a good example of such collaboration, in this case primarily between French and Soviet scientists. The deep ice core drillings in central Greenland have typically been joint efforts by the United States, Denmark, and Switzerland. The drilling on the Renland glacier in eastern Greenland in recent summers is a Nordic project with participants from Denmark, Iceland, and Sweden.

In future, several new drilling operations are needed to complete the palæoclimatic picture. As a matter of fact, this research is given high priority in many national and international research organizations. Consequently, the new European Science Foundation initiative in polar science has been focused on palæoclimatological studies. Deep core drilling on the crest of the Greenland ice cap and drilling on Berkner Island in Antarctica have been proposed as prime objectives.

Much of this work will be impossible to carry out unless resources are pooled and international efforts concerted. The same is true of ocean drilling where the technical arrangements with a dedicated vessel and drilling equipment are extremely costly and in practice beyond the reach of almost any single country. The Ocean Drilling Programme now under way is organized as an international co-operative venture. The extension of drilling into the central Arctic Basin is a great challenge for the future. The formidable problems of operating in the heavy pack ice of the central Arctic, a region which is almost inaccessible even with the strongest icebreakers in the world today, mean that this challenge could be met only with a truly international effort .

The international attention given to the ozone problem has also spurred research co-operation. The Airborne Antarctic Ozone Experiment in 1987 drew on resources from four countries and involved some 150 scientists from 19 different organizations. Ozone measurements in the Arctic are about to generate similar co-operative efforts.

The crucial step, however, is to find the means to co-operate internationally in taking action to reduce the emissions which actually contribute to the problem. As noted above, the cause-effect links are neither simple nor undisputed. Even if it seems clear that the anthropogenic factor is important and that the burning of fossil fuels and the release of halocarbons into the atmosphere should be limited, it cannot be demonstrated convincingly, at present, that this will provide a definitive solution. The complexity of the chemical interactions and the time lags involved in change make it virtually impossible to calculate the effects of any remedial action. Furthermore, how is the responsibility to be shared? The atmosphere is a common asset, but it is no longer a free good. Without a consensus that action needs to be taken and international agreements at the political level, the warnings from the scientists will not be heeded. Without commitments from most or all countries to respond to the problem, the outcome is more likely to be a "tragedy of the commons."

The Arctic has a special position in this global drama. Key information is provided by Arctic research and baseline monitoring at high latitudes. The effects of a global warming will likely be very pronounced in the Arctic. Some of these effects might be favourable – better conditions for fishing and increased productivity on marginal lands, for example. Any change in the pack-ice cover in the Arctic Ocean would certainly have implications for marine transportation. Taking into account the sensitivity and strategic importance of the Arctic Basin, improved access to the area would have important implications for national sovereignty and international relations in the region. However, the whole global climate system would be upset at the same time because of the severe consequences for energy transport in the system.

Arctic Haze

So far, we have discussed substances which remain in the atmosphere for a long time. In general the effects of these man-induced emissions have a rather even geographical distribution. Specific transport processes play only minor roles compared with the overall circulation system and the large-scale cycles and interaction between ice, ocean, and atmosphere. However, many air pollutants are short-lived and their occurrence is strongly dependent on source location and transport pathways.

In the 1950s it was observed that the visibility over large parts of the Arctic region was reduced during the winter months.[5] This phenomenon, called Arctic haze, turned out to have an anthropogenic origin. It has been studied intensively during the last decade, but many factors contributing to the problem are still poorly understood. The sources of the haze are found in industrial areas at mid-latitudes in the northern hemisphere. It takes about five to ten days for the air masses to carry the substances to the Arctic. During that time particles of smaller size (less than 0.1 µm in diameter) have coagulated and most coarse particle material (bigger than 2 μm) has been eliminated by sedimentation. The result is a narrow particle size distribution around an average of 0.26 μm in diameter.

The major components of Arctic haze are sulphates, nitrates, and elemental carbon. Still, about 60 per cent of the particles are unidentified but believed to have an organic origin. The haze itself is essentially created by water droplets which form on hygroscopic sulphate particles or sulphuric acid. Winter concentrations are 10 to 20 times higher than those in the summer, and interannual variations up to a factor of 3 have been observed. During the summer, the frequent occurrence of low stratus clouds over the Arctic Ocean provides an effective wet-scrubbing process whereby most of the pollutants are deposited. In fact, summer concentrations of aerosols are as low as any obtained anywhere, as the measurements of the Ymer expedition in 1980 show.[6]

Although no systematic picture exists of the vertical distribution of Arctic haze in the atmosphere, exploratory studies have demonstrated that it is predominantly a boundary layer phenomenon, that is, most of the pollution burden is confined to the lowermost two kilometres of the atmosphere.

Elemental carbon which originates from combustion processes is a chemically inert component in soot particles. This component is of importance for the effect of Arctic haze on the radiative balance. The radiative balance, as noted above, is determined by the net effect of incoming short wavelength radiation from the sun and thermal radiation emitted from the earth. The haze particles affect the radiation in both spectral regions. The net effect – cooling or warming – depends on the mixture of the black elemental coal with sulphates and other substances in haze particles. At present it is not possible to predict with any certainty whether the effects of Arctic haze are positive or negative, in other words whether this form of pollution adds to the greenhouse effect or contributes to a cooling of the atmosphere.

We have already noted that Arctic haze is an aged anthropogenic aerosol transported from the industrialized regions of Eurasia and North America. The chances of pollution from these sources reaching the Arctic is strongly influenced by prevailing meteorological conditions and the distribution of source trajectories. The seasonal difference in circulation over Europe and the Arctic, arising because the Arctic is blocked from receiving most of the direct pollution from the south in the summer, is reflected in the great difference between summer and winter pollution levels in the Arctic. Interannual differences can also be explained by meteorological variations. These variations are more pronounced in the North than in Antarctica.

In addition to meteorological data, it is also possible to relate pollution to distant sources by identifying a chemical *signature* for the particular matter and matching this signature to receptor sites and source regions. Unfortunately, the amount of signature information is not very complete, and data from many nations, especially from sources in the USSR, are missing. Nevertheless, attempts have been made to identify and quantify the sources of Arctic haze. According to Lowenthal and Rahn,[7] more than half of the pollution aerosols originate in the USSR, particularly in the winter. Trajectory calculations support these findings. Aerosols from sources in the USSR seem to predominate in the boundary layer. The relative contribution of European sources increases with altitude. At altitudes above 3 to 4 km, sources in North America may also play a role in the formation of Arctic haze.

In spite of the scientific interest in Arctic haze and its importance, many problems remain unsolved. Heintzenberg has set out a list of some important issues in the following set of questions:

- What is the horizontal distribution of Arctic haze (the central Arctic and the region north of the Soviet Union are not covered)?
- What is the vertical distribution (no systematic geographical coverage and no systematic picture of seasonal variations exists)?
- What are the components and how are they mixed chemically?
- How are we to quantify the physical and chemical transformations during long-range transport?

Most importantly, the long-term trends of key components such as heavy metals and soot have yet to be established. The relation between Arctic haze and climate change cannot be estimated, although this effect might be of critical importance in the future.[8]

This list of questions can readily be interpreted as an agenda for research. It is also evident that this research programme cannot be realized without close international collaboration involving all the countries around the Arctic Basin. An observational network is needed which gives systematic coverage of the Arctic. Detailed information about sources and emissions should be provided and shared among the countries concerned.

Concluding Remarks

There are few Arctic research problems in which the transnational aspect is more striking than the case of atmospheric pollution. It is in practice impossible to approach the problem of airborne Arctic pollution without an international commitment to co-ordinated research. It is well known that Arctic co-operation is not an easy and straightforward affair. There are many national and regional interests which need to be taken into account. The Arctic is *not* a no man's land where science can set the rules. Parallels with Antarctica are therefore misleading when the political aspects of research co-operation are taken into account. However, all research results are relevant to the peoples of the Arctic region, and this interest is shared across national boundaries. Concern for environmental degradation on a regional and even on a global scale is a fairly recent development. With the present political climate of increased openness and contacts between East and West, with greater political awareness of the importance of dealing with environmental problems – on a large scale and with a long-term perspective – and, finally, with a renewed desire and action in many countries to strengthen and co-ordinate their Arctic research, the prospects are better than ever before in history to address major Arctic research issues together. Airborne pollution, both as a specific Arctic problem and as the Arctic component in a global problem, is probably the best candidate for a truly co-operative effort in the North.

Notes

1   J. M. Barnola, R. Raynard, Y. S. Korotkevich, and C. Lorius, "Vostok Ice Core Provides 160,000 Year Record of Atmospheric CO_2," *Nature,* 329, October 1, 1987, 408-14.
2   J. C. Farman, B. G. Gardiner, and J. D. Shanklin, "Large Losses of Total Ozone in Antarctica Reveal Seasonal ClO_x/NO_x interaction," ibid., 315, May 16, 1985, 207-10.
3   R. Stolarski, "The Antarctic Ozone Hole," *Scientific American,* 258 (January 1988).
4   Ibid.
5   J. M. J. Mitchell, "Visual Range in the Polar Regions with Particular Reference to the Alaskan Arctic," *Journal of Atmospheric and Terrestrial Physics,* spec. suppl. 1 (1959), 195-211.
6   H. Lannefors, J. Heintzenberg, and H. C. Hansson, "A Comprehensive Study of the Arctic Summer Aerosol," *Tellus,* 35B (1983), 40-54.
7   D. H. Lowenthal and K. Rahn, "Regional Sources of Pollution Aerosol at Barrow, Alaska, during Winter 1979-80 as Deduced from Elemental Tracers," *Atmospheric Environment,* 19 (no. 12, 1985), 2011-24.
8   J. Heintzenberg, "Arctic Haze: Air Pollution in Polar Regions," *Ambio,* 18 (no. 1, 1989, 50-5.

12

Knowledge Requirements for Ocean Management

Anders Stigebrandt

The Arctic Ocean and its surrounding rim of land constitutes an area which is of vital interest to a variety of groups. A current list of these parties and their main Arctic interests has the following appearance. Mankind: the area is believed to be important for the global climate, including the climate of the world ocean. Indigenous peoples: it is their home and the source of most or all of their material needs. The scientific community: the Arctic offers many challenging scientific problems, both specific polar problems and problems of global interest. Nations and/or smaller groups: industrial exploitation of renewable and non-renewable natural resources. The superpowers: military use.

The indigenous peoples around the Arctic waters possess an extensive and sophisticated knowledge permitting them to adapt to the extremely harsh climate. However, their way of life is threatened in several ways. Industrial exploitation may, among other things, spoil local natural food resources.

Systematic descriptive scientific exploration has revealed important natural resources in the area. Albeit generally sparse, those ocean data which exist are increasingly used in quantitative scientific work. Knowledge about the functioning of the physical, chemical, and biological systems on different temporal and spatial scales in the Arctic Ocean accordingly increases. But scientific achievements have also paved the way for the industrial and military use of the Arctic. Much of modern scientific research in the Arctic in some way or another has been promoted or initiated by industrial and military users. These uses also require the development of infrastructure with respect to communications, transportation, housing, social services, and so on. All these human activities have an impact upon the Arctic natural environment.

The initiation of the International Geosphere-Biosphere Programme (IGBP) arose from a growing awareness of possible global changes in the climate and the chemical composition of the biosphere.[1] Expected changes are thought to be caused by the extensive use of fossil fuels (the greenhouse effect) and by the leakage of different chemicals into the environment from the production, transportation, and consumption of a large number of industrial products. Because Arctic waters are an active part of the global atmospheric and oceanic circulation system, changes caused by activities at lower latitudes will ultimately influence this area. The extent of possible climate changes is commonly believed to be greatest in the polar areas. If this is true, climate changes should be seen first in the polar areas.[2] Certainly, air- and waterborne waste products from modern civilization are known to reach the Arctic ice and waters. Thus, a global perspective is necessary when studying many aspects of the state of Arctic waters.

It is probably true that care is often taken to protect the local environment when natural resources are exploited. This usually means that toxic substances and nutrients are partly removed and deposited in "safe" locations from which they are unlikely to leak. However, a certain fraction of these substances is almost always discharged into the sea. For example, the discharge may be diluted with sea water to low concentrations in order to reduce local harm. As well, accidental discharges must be taken into account. It appears likely that there will be an increasing exploitation of the Arctic's renewable and non-renewable resources. The Arctic natural environment will certainly also receive increasing amounts of waste products from human activities at lower latitudes. In future, imports from lower latitudes and emissions from the exploitation of Arctic resources as well as from an increasing Arctic human population may together change the chemical composition of the Arctic's surface waters. Such a change would likely disturb the area's ecosystems. Both this potential situation and future climate changes may require more active management of Arctic waters.

Successful management of a system generally requires a good model for that system. Model construction in turn requires extensive qualitative and quantitative knowledge about the system including its interaction with neighbouring systems. Much knowledge about general processes can be utilized in Arctic models. However, some specific polar processes, in some way or another due to ice, call for field investigations. The construction and verification of models of the Arctic system also require that the state and the forcing of the system – the forces at work upon and within it – be known. This will necessitate major field measurement programmes in Arctic and adjacent waters, in the atmosphere, and in rivers discharging into the area to be modelled. To ensure the best possible data coverage as well as a free data flow to all interested parties, the required field measurement programmes should be promoted and co-ordinated by a proper international committee for scientific co-operation in the Arctic. As well, multinational intergovernmental bodies, organizing high-quality routine field measurements at fixed positions for purposes such as climate and environmental watch in a broad sense, would be desirable.

This paper continues with a brief outline of system models. These may constitute efficient tools to synthesize existing knowledge as well as to identify areas where research is needed. In the following section an example of a system model for the Baltic Sea is presented and the use of such models for ocean management is discussed. Subsequently, knowledge requirements for applying Arctic system models are discussed. Similar requirements are also considered for the inclusion of the Arctic Ocean in global models. Some scientific areas where research is urgently needed are pointed out. The paper concludes with a short discussion of existing international co-operation as it serves to generate needed knowledge, together with some thoughts on what could be done to improve such co-operation. It is suggested that the expanding and rather extensive scientific co-operation on the Baltic Sea could serve as an example for co-operation in the Arctic.

On Ocean System Models

In grappling with the wide field of ocean management, it is necessary to use knowledge from several academic branches of oceanography. We will discuss ocean management within the framework of ocean system models. An ocean system is in general defined as a certain volume of water, that is, the whole world ocean or a part of it, with its content of energy and matter and the processes acting in it. The state of a system may be described by any number of variables. These describe the distributions in time and space (fields) of the different kinds of matter and energy. The exchange of energy and matter with the surroundings, the external forcing, is vital for most systems.

A model offers a concise description of the functioning of a system. Because most real systems are extremely complex and contain a large number of processes, it is usually necessary to simplify or idealize the description of the system to comprise only a reduced set of variables relating to energy and matter and the processes of importance for the turnover of these factors. A qualitative model of the system may be described when all processes of major importance in the transport and biochemical transformations of actual substances have been identified. If all the processes concerned can be described mathematically (parameterized), a quantitative (mathematical) system model can be produced. The verification of the model requires observed data from the real system. In addition, the forcing of the system has to be known.

We should perhaps mention some traditionally much utilized state variables in ocean systems. For computations of the physical dynamics of the system, the mass distribution may be described by three variables: salinity, temperature, and sea level. In addition there is need for variables describing advective and diffusive motions. Arctic applications also require a number of state variables describing the ice field. The optical and acoustical properties of the sea further depend on certain chemical and biological variables. In Arctic waters the moving, unhomogeneous pack-ice field may be a dominating factor for some optical and acoustic aspects. Examples of variables traditionally employed in biological oceanography are concentrations of carbon, different nutrient species, oxygen, and different species of plants and animals. In chemical oceanography one may also be interested in a variety of trace elements.

An attempt to show how the distribution of substances in a system depends on external sources or sinks (forcing) and on physical and chemical/biological processes is made in figure 1. On the left are listed external forcing fields. The exact contents of this list depend of course on what substances the model is going to describe. At the bottom of the box marked "system" is a sample list of individual or groups of state variables. For most of the variables both physical and biological/chemical processes are of importance. Changes of one or more components of the forcing field would result in changes in many (or all) of the variables. Provided a good system model is available, the actual response of a real system to a change (caused for example by the introduction of anthropogenic substances) may be computed.

It should be evident that only the distributions of chemically and biologically inert substances can be predicted from purely physical theory. Such a prediction obviously requires a good mechanistic model for the circulation and mixing of the system. An additional prerequisite for reliable prediction is that the external sources can be quantified. The circulation and mixing model must be able realistically to simulate time-scales at least on the order of the residence time for inert substances (e.g. sea salt). For ocean systems this usually means time-scales from tens to thousands of years. For the prediction of distributions of chemically and/or biologically active substances it is also essential that the relevant chemical

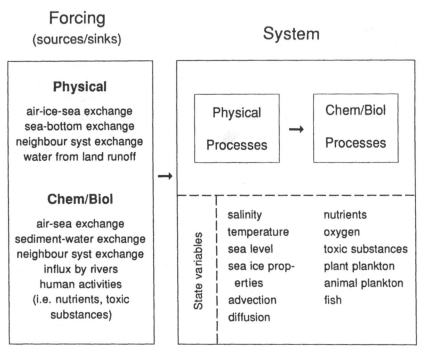

FIGURE 1. Sketch of an ocean system. The system is forced by the fields listed in the box to the left. The state of the system is described by the distribution of the variables in the system. Physical, chemical, and biological processes are responsible for the transport and transformation (between different variables) of matter and energy within the system.

and biological processes can be modelled. Even if sources and sinks can be well specified as functions of time and space, it is usually a considerably more complex task to compute the distributions of such substances than to compute distributions of chemically and biologically inert substances. For substances which may be tied to particles (for example, nutrients in plankton), one has to account for transport by sinking particles in addition to ordinary advective and diffusive transport. For several biochemically active substances transport by sinking particles may be of the same order of magnitude as advective and diffusive transport.

One major use of system models is to predict the state of the system with respect to the various variables when the forcing is specified (the management mode). I have constructed a simple two-layer (system) model for the Arctic Ocean using variables and processes only from the domain of physics.[3] The purpose of the model was to provide a means to study the thickness and salinity of the upper Arctic Ocean as functions of the fresh-water supply from land, the supply of low salinity water from the Bering Sea, and ice export (the forcing). Thus the model can be used to study the effects of diversion of riverborne fresh water which enters the Arctic Ocean naturally. The steady state response of the ice cover to a changed heat balance was also investigated. The only physical "processes" explicitly considered in this model are the upwelling of sea water from below (that is, Atlantic water) into the surface layer and the geostrophical outflow of surface water to the Greenland Sea and Baffin Bay. Although the model may seem crude, compared for instance to the numerical Baltic Sea model described in the next section, it does exemplify a simple analytical system model.

We have not discussed the possibility of verifying predicted changes with time. Since the aim of a management model is to predict future changes in the state of the system as a consequence of forcing, it is of course essential that the time-dependent properties of the model be verified. Most natural ocean systems have time constants on the order of hundreds of years. However, reliable measurements of ocean state variables only cover a fraction of this time. Thus, even if small changes in forcing have occurred during some decades, the existence of a great time constant of a system implies that the resulting state changes would be very small and therefore hard to detect. However, it is known that large changes in climate have occurred on the time-scale of one hundred thousand years (glaciations). The bottom sediments of oceans and lakes contain records of these climatic variations. One of the goals of the IGBP will be to assess the time evolution of a number of variables for the whole earth during at least the last 20,000 years. When this work is completed, the time evolution of at least some state (the palæo-oceanographic signal) and forcing variables for the ocean will be available for (at least partial) verification of the time-dependent properties of ocean models including that for the Arctic Ocean.

An Example of a Simple Ocean System Model

A more complex but still relatively simple ocean system model has been developed for the vertical circulation of the Baltic Sea.[4] The model, which has very high resolution with respect to depth and time, quite realistically predicts the horizontally averaged fields of temperature, salinity, nutrients (different nitrogen species), oxygen, hydrogen sulphide, and plant plankton. The model is forced by air-sea interaction, the water exchange with the ocean (through the Danish sounds), and the fresh water and nutrient supply from land. Such a system model can be used to compute the response of Baltic Sea state variables to changes in the different forcing components. Accordingly, the model can be used for some aspects of ocean management.

Work is in progress to expand the Baltic Sea model to include additional biochemical state variables. This requires, however, that the relevant biogeochemical processes are understood and can be parameterized. In future greater realism in the description of the Baltic Sea ecosystems may be realized in the model. Such a model might be used, for instance, in some way to optimize fish catches. Another management application of the model, which may be attempted soon, is to compute the response of Baltic Sea nutrient concentrations to changing discharges of nutrients from the different countries bordering the sea.

There has been some discussion about using the Baltic Sea model to simulate the fate of toxic substances entering the sea from industrial and agricultural activities. However, to use it in this way requires that the metabolic processes in, and the paths of the substances between, the different participating organisms are known. This is at present not the case, but discussions are continuing on using the model and may stimulate research to develop the knowledge needed by the model. This example points to what is perhaps the main research use of system models, namely, to synthesize existing knowledge from many scientific fields as well as to identify needed research within "neglected" fields of science.

It should be mentioned that for the Baltic Sea there is a wealth of organizations (about 20) for international co-operation on scientific marine research, environmental monitoring and protection, and on fishery matters.[5] The Baltic countries (neutral nations as well as from the two major political blocs) have agreed upon fixed networks of measuring stations. Data obtained at these stations are reported to two intergovernmental bodies, ICES (International Committee for the Exploration of the Sea) and HELCOM (the Helsinki Commission). Two non-governmental bodies, the Conferences of Baltic Oceanographers and the Baltic Marine Biologists meet biannually for seminars and discussions of scientific problems concerning the Baltic Sea. Intercalibration of measuring methods is regularly performed. Joint field experiments are carried out. The latest grand experiment, PEX (Patchiness Experiment in the Baltic Sea), was conducted in 1986 and engaged about 150 scientists, representing 15 marine research institutions, on board 14 ships from 6 countries. Thanks to international co-operation throughout the years, a reasonably good basic set of forcing and state data is available for the

Baltic Sea. It might be worthwhile to look more closely at the successes of Baltic Sea co-operation when considering co-operation in the Arctic.

Knowledge Needs for Arctic System Models

The work with the Baltic system model emphasized some potential difficulties that could become great obstacles for the modelling of other areas of the ocean. For model verification, field data on the actual state variables are needed. For the Baltic such data were available. The fact that the actual model contains only a few variables is of course an important factor in this respect. The Baltic Sea is one of the world's most extensively probed systems, and the data flow is reasonably free, although some countries certainly release more of their data than others do. However, data coverage of the Arctic Ocean is poor or even non-existent with respect to both essential state variables and the geographical distribution of data.

Data for the forcing of a system model is another potential bottleneck. Here one requires atmospheric data permitting computations of the air-ice-sea exchange of energy and matter, data on the riverborne contributions of fresh water and biochemically active species, and data from adjacent seas permitting the computation of the exchange of energy and matter with these seas. To measure and assemble good data-sets describing the state of Arctic waters and the forcing will require concerted efforts among, at the very least, the Arctic countries.

A system model of the Arctic Ocean requires that a number of physical, chemical, and biological processes be described mathematically. Many of the processes involved occur globally and can be studied elsewhere in the ocean. Within the domain of physics there are a number of processes connected to the presence, growth, melting, deformation, and advection of sea ice that probably best can be studied in the Arctic Ocean. However, a model focusing upon ice as a mechanical obstacle to shipping would probably require different parameterizations of ice processes than a model for studying long-term balances of heat and matter where ice definitely is an oceanographic factor.

For routing ships in ice-covered Arctic waters – of primary interest for industrial and military applications – one is interested in knowing the exact positions of open leads and areas of thin ice. Their prediction requires very high resolution models describing ice advection and deformation forced by precision weather forecasts. Such ice models should be initialized as often as possible, preferably using satellite information. For the modelling of, for instance, the response of Arctic Ocean vertical salinity stratification to long-term changes of the forcing of the system, however, the focus would be on properties of the ice field relevant to the seasonal melting and growth of ice and the ejection of salt. Here the seasonal distribution of ice thicknesses, of melt ponds in summer, and of other properties of importance for the albedo would be central, as would salinity distribution, especially on shallow shelves. The latter application will no doubt allow a coarser temporal and spatial resolution of the ice state variables. However, so far, this application seems to have attracted relatively little attention. Available ice data could meet the data needs for an initial development of this type of ice model for use in long-term system models for the Arctic.

Perhaps the most urgent research need with regard to physical processes of oceanographic importance in the Arctic Ocean concerns the complex convective vertical circulation, which is ultimately due to the ejection of salt during ice growth. We have as yet only vague information about the flow rates and depths of interleaving in or below the Arctic Ocean halocline.[6] A whole chain of processes needs to be studied before it is possible to compute the impact of changes in the forcing fields upon annual flow rates and their distributions among different salinities. More specific questions concern the importance of the salinity field at the start of the ice growth season and the importance of shelf topography (water depth, width of the shelf, significance of canyons and ridges). Does dense water form intermediary bottom pools from which leakage may be computed by simple methods?[7] What is the mixing of ambient water into sinking dense plumes?

These are only a few of several important questions within the domain of physics which have to be answered before truly mechanistic models for the long-term circulation can be produced. Other important areas, where knowledge is also meagre at present, concern the exchange of matter and energy with surrounding seas and the eternal global problem of the mechanics of vertical mixing below the mixed layer at the sea surface. Within the biological and chemical domains there are many unresolved processes as well.

Conclusions

For the purpose of Arctic Ocean modelling and possible future management, it is important that the best possible set of state and forcing data be assembled and continually updated. It is essential that the Arctic state and forcing data bank be made freely available to any scientists regardless of nationality who want to study this area of the ocean. The data-set will also be indispensable for future use in global models. Truly international co-operation should certainly stimulate the research necessary for the understanding of the large-scale functioning of the Arctic system (the reverse may also be true). This is thought to be of special benefit for the first two parties on the list in the introduction: mankind and indigenous peoples.

An International Arctic Science Committee (IASC) has now been established. One would also hope for future intergovernmental bodies to deal with climate change, living marine resources, environmental protection and monitoring, and so on, as well as SCOR working groups on specific scientific topics with participants from both of the major political blocs. Scientific co-operation in the Baltic could to some extent serve as a model for the work of multi-organizational co-operation in the Arctic. Returning to the IASC, one may hope that this organization will be able to assess how a future Arctic state and forcing data bank should be created, to co-ordinate the observational efforts of the countries involved (a fixed net of observational sites should probably be established), and to work for intercalibration of methods and comparison of methodologies and, hopefully, a free flow of Arctic state and forcing data. The latter could be encouraged by the establishment of an Arctic data centre, possibly linked to the IASC secretariat. The IASC should regularly organize scientific meetings and support joint field experiments on major Arctic physical, chemical, and biological processes.

Notes

1 Report 3 of the International Geosphere-Biosphere Programme, a report from the Second Meeting of the Special Committee, Harvard University, Cambridge, MA, 8-11 February 1988.

2 D. K. Hall, "Assessment of Polar Climate Change Using Satellite Technology," *Reviews of Geophysics & Space Physics*, 26 (1988), 26-39.

3 A. Stigebrandt, "A Model for the Thickness and the Salinity of the Upper Layer in the Arctic Ocean and the Relationship between the Ice Thickness and Some External Parameters," *Journal of Physical Oceanography*, 10 (1981), 1407-22.

4 A. Stigebrandt and F. Wulff, "A Model for the Dynamics of Nutrients and Oxygen in the Baltic Proper," *Journal of Marine Research*, 45 (1987), 729-59.

5 I. Dybern, "The Organizational Pattern of Baltic Marine Science," *Ambio*, 9 (1980), 187-93.

6 G. Björk, "A One-Dimensional Time-Dependent Model for the Vertical Stratification of the Upper Arctic Ocean," *Journal of Physical Oceanography*, 19 (1989), 52-67.

7 A. Stigebrandt, "Computations of the Dense Flow into the Baltic Sea from Hydrographical Measurements in the Arkona Basin," *Tellus*, 39A (1987), 170-7.

13

Perspectives on Arctic Petroleum

Melvin A. Conant

It is commonly believed by petroleum geologists, investors, speculators, governments, and peoples of northern regions that the on- and offshore oil and gas resources of the Arctic constitute a source of vast future wealth. Projections are in a range of 100 to 200 billion barrels of oil and a possible upper limit for natural gas approaching 2000 trillion cubic feet (tcf).[1] It is also commonly believed that the Soviet Arctic may contain the largest hydrocarbon deposits as the Soviet Union possesses a continental shelf greater than those of all the other Arctic nations combined.

These are exciting observations which imply an Arctic future in which revenues from petroleum to governments, and profits from petroleum to companies, will bring unprecedented monies from the sale of petroleum into world markets. They also spell further intensive modernization of the life styles of northern peoples, their more extensive and intensive incorporation into industrial activities, and, over many years, a highly probable near extinction of their unique way of life. The impact of still greater changes in the Arctic from the widely anticipated increase in the development of petroleum reserves will present, on an ever larger and inescapable scale, the already familiar predicaments northern peoples face.

Geology and Economics of Arctic Petroleum

The excitement from estimates of petroleum reserves is not yet as well founded as one might believe. Interest in Arctic oil and gas is not more than twenty years old, whether it be in the Soviet Arctic, the United States, Canadian, and Norwegian North, or Greenland. In that comparatively brief period only one very large discovery with a potential for large-scale production has seemingly been made: Alaska's North Slope. Since then, while exploration activities have increased greatly, as have the technologies for production, there has been no comparable development anywhere else in the Arctic proper, on- or offshore.

In short, the estimate of 100 to 200 billion barrels of oil and 2000 tcf of natural gas may, in time, prove to be accurate, but at this moment, and for another twenty to thirty years, we will not know whether the reserves exist, where they really are, or how costly they will be to exploit. Nor will we know what their comparative production costs are in contrast to those for the prolific fields of the Middle East or, at the other end of the cost range, the "unconventional" crudes of Alberta.[2] Yet comparative production costs are of critical importance. Whether a discovered field is produced depends upon anticipated demand and price levels and on the size of the field. (An Arctic find may have to be between one and two billion barrels to be truly commercial, depending on whether it lies on- or offshore, and counting exploration, drilling rigs, infrastructure, and pipeline costs.) In deciding whether to develop a discovery, an oil company will assess its other options; it may have other, less expensive reserves nearer to markets. A government, however, may choose to subsidize some portion of development costs for reasons of the national interest. The government may be looking for revenue, for foreign exchange from export sales, or to limit the growth of its own oil imports.

For example, current and prospective production costs for North Sea oil range from US$12 to US$20/barrel; for United States oil, the range lies between $5 and $10/barrel; while for the Middle East current development costs range from Kuwait at 13 cents/barrel to Saudi Arabia at 32 cents/barrel to Abu Dhabi at 98 cents/barrel. There are no comparable cost estimates for Soviet oil production from western Siberia but these are almost certain to be similar to those at the higher end of the range for North Sea oil.

If one estimates *proved reserves* in the Middle East at 565 billion barrels, that total is about four times the estimated *as yet undiscovered* oil reserves of the Arctic. The known reserves of unconventional crudes in Canada measure some 265 billion barrels (75 per cent of the world's total). There has to be a very large incentive for private sector investment, or a large government interest, or both, for exploration and development to occur in the Arctic.

A barrel of oil produced in the Arctic has to meet a current (1988) market price of about $15/barrel; ten years from now that price could be $25/barrel (in 1988 dollars). It takes seven to ten years to develop a field, so long-term anticipations of price help determine the decision of a company or a government about whether to exploit a discovery. There is also the estimated life expectancy of the world's spare producing capacity,

TABLE 1. Barrels Discovered Per Drilling Foot

Region	1950	1960	1970	1980	1987
Middle East	100,000	100,000	70,000	11,000	10,000
Latin America	2,000	700	500	5,000	4,000
Africa	600	2,000	3,000	5,000	4,000
Far East	1,000	1,000	800	700	600
West Europe	50	200	500	500	400
North America	80	60	200	50	45

which in 1988 approaches 14 million barrels per day. It will be many years before that is reduced to a more manageable 2 to 3 million barrels per day. These are all serious issues which can confound high hopes for the exploitation of Arctic petroleum discoveries.

The situation is similar for natural gas. Figures on gas exploration and development costs are not so generally available as those for oil, but it is likely that they are of the same order of magnitude. One should certainly not assume they will be less. There is a growing interest in the search for natural gas as such, rather than gas being merely a somewhat unwanted resource discovered in the search for oil. The extraordinary Soviet effort to exploit its huge west Siberian gas discoveries, as well as the anticipation of declining oil production from many regions outside the Middle East, have changed the outlook for gas as a fuel in virtually all uses for which oil has hitherto provided the energy. (Transport is still dependent on oil but major research and development efforts are under way to find ways to use processed natural gas.)

Opinions vary about the recoverable natural gas reserves of the Arctic; it may even prove to be the case that recoverable energy in the higher Arctic will be largely, or mainly, natural gas, not oil. We do not know and

TABLE 2. Oil Well Productivity

Region	Barrels per Day per Average Well
United States	14
Canada	29
Latin America	164
Far East	305
Western Europe	519
Africa	1,239
Middle East	3,247

have little way of knowing until many years have passed and a lot of extensive and expensive exploration has taken place.

To make these comparative costs of exploration and development as clear as possible, it should be noted that finding and development costs, region by region, reveal an Arctic barrel of oil to be much more costly. As of 1987, approximate worldwide development costs per barrel varied widely: United States, US$5.80; Canada, US$3.80; Europe, US$2.50; Latin America, US$1.90; Far East, US$1.75; Africa, US$.80; Middle East, US$.40. Moreover, a potential investor (public or private sector) in the Arctic must also consider the historical record of discovery in evaluating the probability of success in what is now considered to be a classic "frontier" region of highest cost and (outside the United States at least) an area in which discoveries to date have been disappointing.

Table 1 sets out comparative data on barrels discovered for various regions. Another factor to be considered is oil well productivity. Assessment of this aspect of the analysis completes the argument which dispels any expectation of the likely economic competitiveness of even successful Arctic discoveries (see table 2).

Given these basic observations which are taken into account in deciding whether to pursue exploration and development, one has to look for the motivations which might lead the private sector to consider investment in a high-cost frontier region such as the Arctic. There are two particularly important factors. First, from 1975 to 1986, world proved reserves *remained* at about 675 billion barrels while consumption averaged 22 billion barrels a year or a total of 264 billion barrels. In each of those years the oil consumed was about equal to discoveries. That is not a desirable situation. Thus, if substantial Arctic discoveries could increase reserves, it could only be good news in terms of the ratio between consumption and proven reserves. Moreover, 75 per cent of the world's oil is in 320 known "giant" fields, each with over 500 million barrels of recoverable crude. Discoveries of such giants dropped from 100 fields in the 1960s to 56 fields in the 1970s and became even rarer in the 1980s.[3] This drop occurred despite industry claims of far-reaching improvements in technology and very high real oil prices.

A second reason for interest in the Arctic (or such other regions as western China, the United States west coast, and the Gulf of Mexico) is that current projections reveal increasing dependence on Middle East Gulf oil to meet the rising import needs of Europe, North America, and Japan.

There is still another consideration affecting prospects for Arctic oil: the sensitivity of oil exploration and development in areas which today are strategically important to one or another of the two world powers.[4] For the Soviet Union, the pertinent region is the Barents Sea (which includes for the purpose of this discussion offshore exploration and possible production off northern Norway). For the United States, it is the Bering Sea. In both areas there is a mix of interests in potential oil production and submarine operations. Canada's intention eventually to use nuclear-powered submarines (conventionally armed) in its Arctic passages for peacetime "watch and track" did not appear to conflict with oil production or maritime logistics of importance mainly to natural gas supplies from the eastern Arctic. The concern related mainly to the possible use of oil production rigs or surface bottom production units for the detection and tracking of submarines and, in a few instances, to the location of rigs in particular areas used for submarine passage.

Another aspect of this problem, currently of particular importance to the United States but eventually likely to affect the Soviet Union as well, is the vulnerability to attack of important supplies of oil and gas from Arctic locales. This is an important defence problem, but it is not likely that giant discoveries of petroleum will go unexploited because of security considerations.

There are no particularly difficult international legal issues likely to affect petroleum prospects in the Arctic.[5] Where issues do exist, their settlement, or temporizing with, involves political-security compromises. These issues include the Norwegian-Soviet boundary differences off northern Norway, the differences in view as to the extent of Canada's jurisdiction over maritime passage through the archipelago, the Beaufort Sea boundary, and a boundary issue between the Soviet Union and the United States in the Bering Sea. On each of these there is a potential for further contention. It is likely, however, that these are all susceptible to compromise and adjustment, once petroleum interests and operations are engaged. There are many oil-producing regions of the world in which a common interest in production revenues has overcome differences which might be less easy to resolve in other circumstances. The management techniques for common or joint exploitation are well established.

In the particular case of Canadian-United States differences over the Northwest Passage, it is altogether possible to arrange for acceptable commercial use as long as care is taken to avoid situations which would cause either nation to take umbrage. Canadian responsibility for protection of its claimed waters through application of its Arctic Waters Pollution Prevention Act is now accepted by maritime interests as an eminently sensible and necessary precaution.

The adequacy of the international legal aspects of protection of the Arctic environment from petroleum accidents is less important than the efficacy of the measures taken by oil companies and by governments. This is a matter which must be constantly monitored and tested. The Occidental disaster in the North Sea is a terrible reminder of what can happen even in a presumably prepared offshore station. It would not take more than one similar experience in an on- or offshore Arctic rig to bring a halt to exploration, at least until the damage done to the environment had been assessed with greater actual knowledge of the consequences. Still, the on- and offshore record of the oil industry in difficult sea conditions has been excellent. The state-of-the-art technologies used by the oil industry were assessed in 1985 by the Office of Technology Assessment of the United States Congress and found acceptable.[6]

Petroleum Prospects of the Arctic Nations

What follows is a distillation of estimates prepared by companies and governments as to the outlook for Arctic petroleum interests in the Soviet Union, Norway, Greenland, Canada, and the United States. Some is known, much is guessed at, and all reports are usually infused with an optimistic spirit to be discounted, if at all, with greater experience. So much depends on sheer projections. The energy-consuming industrial nations with their awesome appetite for energy, more energy, and still more energy are interested. Some of the northern peoples, recipients of very large amounts of oil money, face a future which is not at all secure. If the constellation of petroleum issues – volumes, costs, and the forecast market price – are not in the right order, nothing could happen almost in spite of the right geology, and that is as uncertain a factor as those of volume, cost, and price.

Alone among ice states, the **Soviet Union** has for many decades sought actively to develop substantial commercial interests in its Arctic region as a matter of high national interest.[7] It is well known that immense discoveries of natural gas and oil dominate the energy production of the near Arctic regions of the USSR in western Siberia. About 60 per cent of total Soviet oil production comes from Tyumen province alone. More than half of Soviet gas production also comes from western Siberia (Urengoi and Yamburg), and it is there, mainly close to the Arctic Circle, that the greatest additional finds are anticipated. The USSR has further expectations offshore in the Barents Sea and eastward to the Arctic regions of eastern Siberia. Nothing very useful appears to have been learned about prospects in the Kara, Laptev, and East Siberian seas, but there is evidence and hope that eastern Siberia (on- and offshore) will prove to be a geologic counterpart of the prolific energy fields of western Siberia.

While virtually all Soviet Arctic oil and gas appears to be transported to market by pipelines, Moscow's deep interest in building vessels for the Northern Sea Fleet dwarfs the efforts of other ice states.[8] It is likely that in time, petroleum (and other) supplies will be conveyed by tanker through the whole Northeast Passage. If it is not yet open to ordinary commercial traffic, it will probably reach that point by the end of the 1990s, if not before, especially if east Siberian supplies become important.

At the moment, the USSR lacks extensive experience in offshore regions. The Norwegians, British, Canadians, and Americans have most of the engineering and operational experience, and the Soviet Union thus appears to be moving towards common or joint ventures with them.

For **Norway**, the Barents Sea frontier is the focus of interest in the Arctic where preparations for offshore exploration are accelerating.[9] These were long delayed in the region because of the dispute between Norway and the Soviet Union. While this issue has not been resolved, it is now possible for exploration to begin. It is in the western portion of the Barents Sea that initial efforts are under way. Depending on discovery rates, exploration may later move to the central and eastern areas, bringing operations close to the disputed area.

The Norwegians require technical and operational assistance from countries with frontier experience, so joint venture companies are likely to be used. The Norwegians possess very large quantities of natural gas and therefore are hoping to discover oil, but there have been significant finds of oil in the exploration efforts under way. In the view of oil companies, the Norwegians have shown greater awareness of the conditions in which the private sector prefers to operate. Norway thus has less difficulty in encouraging foreign private sector companies to participate in what may be one of the larger Arctic exploration ventures.

Despite several tentative exploration efforts, there is now thought to be no petroleum resources in western **Greenland** large enough to warrant further exploration and later development on a scale which would bring in revenue from exports.[10] No one can be certain, but it is doubtful that even domestic requirements could be met without large subsidies from the Danish government. Whether evidence from some prospective areas in Melville Bay and farther south in the Davis Strait will prove interesting is still highly speculative. There are no longer any intractable boundary issues with Canada which would hinder petroleum exploration. However, Greenland is especially sensitive to environmental change from oil work, including the Canadian Arctic Pilot Project which would have put Greenland fisheries at risk from marine transport. The issue remains, pending further Canadian investments in its islands in the High Arctic.

Canada has the second largest continental shelf among the polar states. Canada's Arctic exploration efforts have been concentrated in the Mackenzie Delta and the Beaufort Sea and in the eastern islands of the High Arctic. While the hope is still for oil, it is increasingly likely to be natural gas that is discovered. Despite claims to the contrary, no giant commercial discoveries of either oil or gas have been made anywhere in the Canadian Arctic. Nevertheless, prompted in part by the knowledge that the Canadian government is improving its terms, companies have persisted in exploration and production investments.

It now appears as if renewed efforts are under way to complete the construction of a major logistics system to move Canadian and United States Arctic gas southward to increase the supply in the lower 48 states. Long delayed, this logistics system would move gas from Prudhoe Bay and the Mackenzie Delta and the Beaufort Sea to the Yukon and then Alberta to meet the anticipated needs of the United States market a decade hence, a measure of the size and expense ($5 billion) of the undertaking. If the application to Canada's National Energy Board is approved, the American and British oil companies involved would then become the largest private landowners of North America. The route to carry Arctic natural gas could take one of two options. It could either carry Canadian Mackenzie Delta-Beaufort gas to Alberta or link with the long-postponed Alaska Natural Gas Transportation System. (While the magnitude of either project has long frustrated companies and governments, it is worth noting that the Soviet Union has been completing comparable gas pipelines every 15 months.)

Environmental concerns (on the North Slope of the Yukon) have long plagued pursuit of the Alaskan link through Canada, but even more difficult perhaps has been the question of the division of revenue between the northern peoples and the Canadian government. This issue and others relating to the Canadian North await a redefinition of territorial rights and status: in effect, the long-needed Northern Accord with its implied changes in constitutional arrangements.

No estimate of potential petroleum reserves or production is more difficult than that for Alaska in the **United States**,[11] because of corporate secrecy and the expectation of all players that the North Slope bonanza must surely be repeated. North Slope is the largest discovery to date in the United States. It provides 2 million barrels of oil per day or some 24 per cent of total domestic supply. Every forecast warns of an approaching decline in production. Of all the discoveries of relatively large and small fields since 1968, the only prospective huge field is that of West Sak whose oil is of poor quality and will be expensive to produce. West Sak is said to have oil in place in the range of 15 to 25 billion barrels, but how much of it can actually be recovered depends in large measure on enhanced oil recovery techniques, the prospective world oil price, and whether a United States administration will subsidize development.

Taking North Slope fields as a whole, at the 1988 price of $15/barrel, possibly 5.25 billion barrels are likely to be recovered. If the price rises (or is subsidized) to $24/barrel as it was before 1986, perhaps 10.5 billion barrels might be produced (or less than two years of current United States consumption).

The prospective importance of the Alaska National Wildlife Refuge is now much debated. The estimates are a total of 3.2 billion barrels (with a 19-per-cent chance of any recoverable oil being found), that is, about 20 per cent of current American consumption. That discoveries in the Bering or Chukchi seas will change this picture is highly doubtful but not, of course, impossible. Preliminary data from the Geological Survey and the Minerals Management Service of the Department of the Interior have led to greatly reduced estimates of undiscovered, economically recoverable oil. (While such a calculation is wholly beyond proof or even discussion, this shift is indicative of the pessimism now widely shared.) Chukchi Sea prospects, previously thought to be the less interesting, suddenly underwent a change in late May 1988. The oil and gas lease sales drew bids totalling nearly $500 million in what was described as the most active offshore lease auction outside the Gulf of Mexico. The Chukchi Sea is a most forbidding environment and its reserves (if any) would lie off the northwestern coast. Royal Dutch/Shell was the most active bidder.

There may be at least 30 tcf, and possibly much more, natural gas in Alaska. For fifteen years it has been locked out of the United States market because of a mix of expense, environmental concerns (pipeline and habitat), and lack of demand. However, by century's end, the United States is likely to welcome Alaskan gas. Consequently, there has been a revival of talks on completing the pipeline logistics system.

Conclusion

Enough has been said about oil prospects in the Arctic to make it clear that apart from uncertain geologic considerations, the economic forces of the world oil market – outside global trends – greatly influence the pace of exploration in the first instance and very largely determine whether development takes place. In discussing these forces which lie beyond the control of anyone in the Arctic itself, the key word is *competition*.

It is competition for oil markets in the last analysis, but before that stage is reached, it is competition for money to do exploration in the Arctic (there are other less costly frontiers), competition for skilled manning of rigs, competition for better technology, competition for acreage on which to explore, and competition to obtain the best possible terms – taxes, royalties, and related fiscal regimes from host governments or other owners of prospective fields. Much of what a company is doing and why is normally held close. Secrecy is inherent in competition.

In times of relatively low oil prices and a sizeable world surplus in producing capacity, there is not much about the Arctic to attract a private sector company which has other options. In such a competitive environment, the reputation of ice states for observing agreements and their familiarity with the support needs of exploration and development and the logistics required to move oil to markets are crucial to petroleum interests. It is never enough to have bright geologic prospects and sufficient money and experience. Without a host government accustomed to stable long-term energy policies and practices, prepared to resolve conflicts in accordance with legal principles and the practice of law, an oil company runs considerable risks.

This is not a scene to which the term "co-operation" seems immediately appropriate. It is certainly not a familiar word, nor is it heard every day except perhaps in the fuzzy sense typical of public relations releases. Co-operation in the carrying out of Arctic exploration generally, or in the sharing of technology to build rigs and manage production except in the context of specific agreements (such as joint ventures), is rare indeed.

Is more co-operation needed in atmospheric sciences? Yes. Co-operation in ice research? Yes. Co-operation in air, sea, and land rescue? Yes. Above all, co-operation in precautions against oil spill damage? Yes. Co-operation in clean-up? Yes.

Co-operation between ice states can be important in encouraging exploration and production.[12] Examples are the settlement of boundary disputes or agreements on common activities in a disputed territory to obtain revenue rather than to forgo it. Co-operation is important among ice states on government policies and actions regarding the conditions for maritime passage or access across another's territory. The objective is not only agreement but uniform standards common to the Arctic as a whole. An example: when oil moves by tanker west of the Canadian border, or to the east, will tanker operations involve different standards, different procedures, different laws, and different means of policing and of redress? Organizations such as the International Maritime Organization work towards the uniformity of effective standards, and the provisions of the Law of the Sea Convention have also helped. And these are useful. To the extent that oil companies can contribute to the work of effective and uniform standards and practices, well and good; they are already involved but the pace is often maddeningly slow.

Finally, without coherent, durable Arctic policies on the part of the ice states to guide resource developments and other uses of the region, very little can be accomplished nationally or internationally. The Soviet Union has long had such policies; more recently, Canada and Norway defined their interests; those of Greenland and the United States are still in the formative stage.

There is, therefore, a place for co-operation among host ice states utilizing the experience of oil companies. Still, it is often true that calls for co-operation reveal a misunderstanding of the circumstances in which oil companies (or gas interests) do their business. Co-operation is not or should not be a pejorative term, however. It is the essence of an activity which will be of very great importance to the economic and social well-being of northern peoples and to the fuel needs of distant societies.

Notes

1 Oran R. Young, "The Age of the Arctic," *Foreign Policy,* no 61 (winter 1985-6).
2 Conventional crudes are those which flow or are pumped to the surface; unconventional crudes have to be heated or chemically treated before being pumped or mined and then processed before further use. There is a large difference in production costs for the two categories.
3 L. F. Ivanhoe, "The Permanent Oil Shock," paper delivered at AAPG Conference, Los Angeles, California, June 9, 1987.
4 See Helge Ole Bergesen and others, *Soviet Oil and Security Interests in the Barents Sea* (New York: St Martin's Press 1987). Also William E. Westermeyer and Kurt M. Shusterich, eds, *United States Arctic Interests: The 1980s and 1990s* (New

York: Springer-Verlag 1984); and Clive Archer and David Scrivener, *Northern Waters* (London: Croom Helm 1986). A major source on submarine operations is George Lindsey, *Strategic Stability in the Arctic*, Adelphi Papers 241 (London: Brassey's for the International Institute for Strategic Studies 1989).

5   See "The U.S.-Canada Arctic Policy Forum," *Journal of the Arctic Institute of North America* (December 1986); Bergesen, *Soviet Oil and Security Interests;* Westermeyer and Shusterich, eds, *United States Arctic Interests;* and Franklyn Griffiths, ed, *Politics of the Northwest Passage* (Montreal: McGill-Queen's University Press 1987).

6   United States, Congress, *Oil and Gas Technologies for the Arctic and Deepwater*, Report OTA-0-270, May 1985.

7   See the energy map and text on the Soviet Union, in *Petroleum Economist* (London) of April 1985, and also Bergesen, *Soviet Oil and Security Interests.*

8   Lawson W. Brigham and Ellen M. Gately, *The Soviet Maritime Arctic* (Woods Hole, MA: Woods Hole Oceanographic Institution 1987).

9   See Archer and Scrivener, *Northern Waters*, and the *Oil and Gas Journal* for September 21, 1987.

10 H. C. Bach and Jorgen Taagholt, *Greenland and the Arctic Region – Resources and Security Policy* (Copenhagen: Information and Welfare Service, Department of Defense, 1982).

11 See William E. Westermeyer, "Future of Oil Production on the North Slope of Alaska," *Geopolitics of Energy* (September 1988) and the study by the Office of Technology Assessment of the United States Congress, *Oil Production in the Alaska National Wildlife Reserve* (Washington 1988).

12 See "The U.S.-Canada Arctic Policy Forum."

14

Experience in Arctic Marine Transportation

Aleksandr Arikaynen

For a long time the ardent desire to know the Arctic derived inspiration from three great aims: to discover and develop the Northern Sea Route; to discover and develop the Northwest Passage; and to reach the North Pole. These aims became a sort of *perpetuum mobile* urging man into the Arctic, and two of them, as we see, were directly connected with Arctic navigation. In the development of the latter we can clearly trace three stages: discovery of sea routes; a period of Arctic sea expeditions; and the development of cargo transportation first during the summer and, finally, in Arctic winter ice conditions.

The Northern Sea Route was traversed by Russian pioneers early in the eighteenth century and mapped by 1824. About three hundred and fifty years elapsed, however, between the 1497 voyage of John Cabot, who was the first to formulate the idea of a northwest route to China and India, and McClure's voyage on the *Investigator* (in 1850-1), which confirmed the existence of a sea route to the north of North America. Thus, the discovery of Arctic sea routes took a long time. This seems quite natural in retrospect because the problems of Arctic navigation could not be easily solved with wooden sailing vessels. We must, however, admire the courage and heroism of these pioneers who did everything possible to prove the existence of a Northern Sea Route and Northwest Passage despite extreme difficulty.

A lot of time and effort was subsequently spent on development of these sea routes. Half a century elapsed between the first complete voyage along the Northern Sea Route (1878-9) and the organization of regular sea operations in the summer (late 1930s). It took about the same time to develop the Northwest Passage: the first complete transit took place in 1903-6, but regular cargo traffic did not start until the early 1950s.

While American and Canadian polar explorers sought to solve the problem of Arctic navigation in ice conditions, the USSR pursued a variety of specific means and services which together form the complex scientific

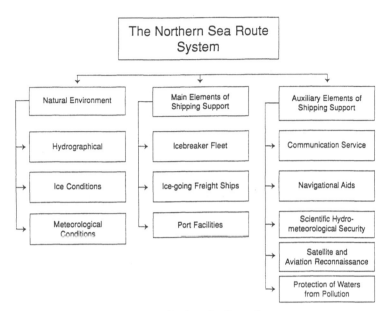

FIGURE 1. The Northern Sea Route System.

and technological system of the Northern Sea Route (figure 1). In fact, this system's elements represent major areas of potential international co-operation in modern Arctic shipping. Traditional research into the sea transport system was pursued along six interrelated lines to determine an Arctic navigation strategy (figure 2). Each of the lines is equally important and requires constant attention. However, in the current stage of development, increases in Arctic expenditure and the greater urgency of winter navigation heighten the significance of research in engineering (figure 3) and economics (figure 4).

In the framework of engineering research, the design of icebreakers and ice-strengthened ships (figure 5) as well as Arctic ports (figure 6) has first priority. One may suppose that optimization of the air reconnaissance of ice conditions and methods of combating ice water floods are also likely to be of mutual interest. In the framework of economic research, the exchange of experience in elaborating methods for the economic assessment of icebreaker and transport fleet growth may be an important area of international co-operation. Of equal importance may be methods of optimization and simulation of the functioning of Arctic fleets and ports. My colleagues and I would especially welcome an exchange of experience and information on modelling methods. Our own experience may be of use to our foreign colleagues, and that is why I would like to say

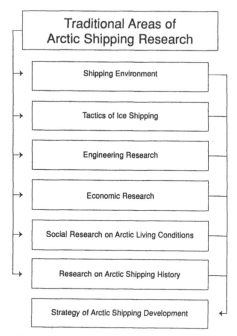

FIGURE 2. General scheme of research that determines shipping strategy.

a few words about our simulation model of Northern Sea Route
transportation. It aims to identify the rational limits of extending the
navigation period. It consists of six functional blocks (figure 7), one of
which gives a detailed description of the ice conditions on the route (figure
8). The management block contains a set of decision-making rules with
respect to the fleet's operation depending on the specific conditions.

Much more could be said about the general usefulness of international
co-operation in the Arctic, but it seems more productive to speak in
concrete terms. I would like to lay the first brick of our common house of
co-operation and tell you about two important aspects of navigation on the
Northern Sea Route (NSR). The first relates to the ice sheet in Soviet
Arctic seas and the limits it places on navigation for icebreakers and ice-
strengthened ships and the second concerns the problems faced by Soviet
sailors in winter navigation of the Kara Sea.

Characteristics of the Ice Sheet on the NSR

The central part of the Arctic Ocean, somewhere close to the relative
inaccessibility pole (the point equidistant from all Arctic basin shores, at
latitude 77° N and longitude 150 W), contains the core of the ice sheet —

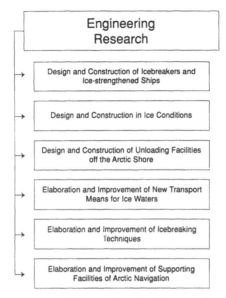

FIGURE 3. Structure of engineering research on Arctic shipping.

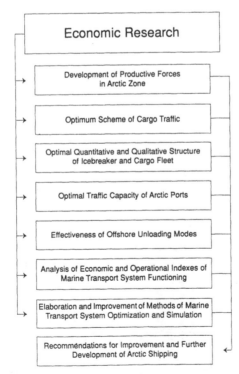

FIGURE 4. Structure of economic research on Arctic shipping.

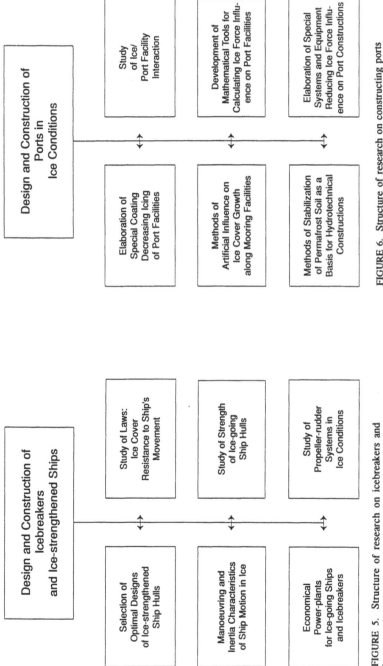

FIGURE 5. Structure of research on icebreakers and ice-strengthened ships.

FIGURE 6. Structure of research on constructing ports in ice conditions.

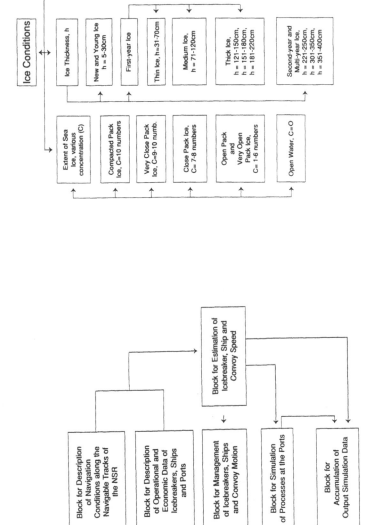

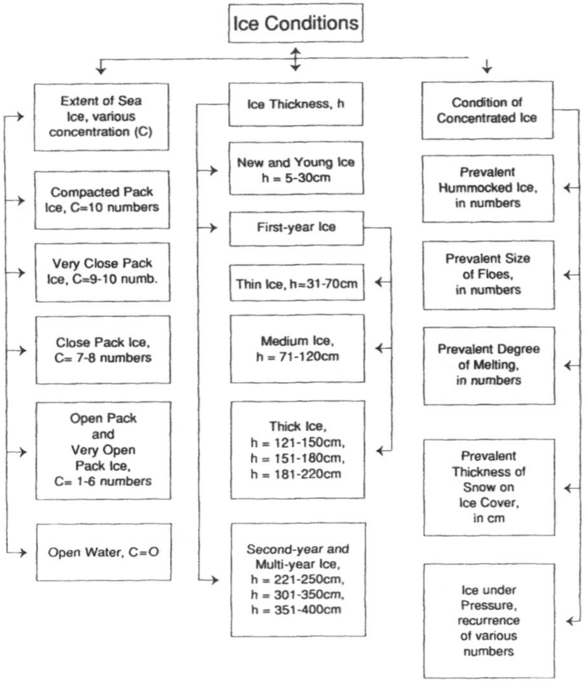

FIGURE 8. Vector description of ice conditions along main navigable tracks of the Northern Sea Route.

FIGURE 7. Main blocks of adaptive simulation model of transportation process along the Northern Sea Route.

multi-year and second-year very hard ice more than 2.5 or 3 metres thick. On the outer edge of the multi-year ice field there is a belt of first-year pack ice that begins to form in autumn. By the end of winter that ice is over 2 metres thick. Typically, these belts of first-year pack ice are seldom found in pure form. As a result of winds and steady currents, second-year and multi-year ice from the transarctic current system usually shifts towards the Arctic seas. Therefore, in real conditions, the arrangement of ice is rather patchy: first-year ice zones alternate with second-year and multi-year ice zones.

In Arctic waters the general ice arrangement pattern depends on the formation of fast ice whose external boundary is located within an isobath of about 20 or 30 metres. Between the zone of first-year pack ice, second-year ice, and multi-year ice, and the zone of fast ice, there is an intermediate zone where sea ice actively forms. Here polynyas of young ice are likely to evolve. The probability of their formation and spreading in the flaw polynya zone depends on the direction and strength of winds. The seaward winds contribute to, whereas the landward winds prevent, formation of polynyas beyond the fast ice edge. Depending on the distribution of atmospheric pressure during the winter, polynyas are more likely to form in the western area of the NSR than in the eastern area.

Thus, by the end of the winter, the ocean-bound ice arrangement pattern is as follows: a fast ice zone, an intermediate flaw zone of young ice formation, a predominantly first-year ice zone, a second-year zone, and a multi-year ice zone. As a result, at the end of May directly beyond the fast ice edge there is a zone of ice-free water, then a zone of ice 70 cm thick. The vast sea surface is covered with ice which formed in the October-December period of the preceding year, where one can find small local formations of younger ice. Thus, in winter, the thickness of pack ice varies greatly within each sea.

There is another characteristic that varies even within a comparatively small section of the sea – the thickness of the fast ice. Fast ice, whose thickness is typically described as uniform, turns out in reality to be far from uniform. Calculations at the end of winter show that the maximum thickness of the ice that formed naturally averages 120 to 130 cm in the Kara Strait, 160 to 170 cm near Dikson Island, 190 to 200 cm in the Straits of Vilkitsky and Dm. Laptev, and 160 to 170 cm in Long Strait. Analysis also shows that average ice thickness may vary by 30 to 50 cm, depending on whether a winter is warm or cold. Ice thickness also grows considerably in some areas, because of hummocking. The height of hummocks ranges from 1 to 3 metres on average.

In the spring and summer the Arctic sea ice begins to melt. First to melt is the ice in the southwestern part of the Kara Sea and the southern part of the Chukchi Sea, which are subject to the warm currents of the Barents and Bering seas, respectively. From there melting spreads to the central part of the NSR. Melting not only decreases the thickness of the ice, but also its strength, a change which is particularly important for navigation.

Arctic navigation is dependent on the melting rate of the fast ice, that is, the steady transition of the fast ice into pack ice. This occurs under the influence of the wind and sea level fluctuation, mainly after ice thickness drops to 1 or 1.5 metres and its strength decreases accordingly. Fast ice begins to fracture in June (figure 9), spreading from the Kara Strait to the east and from the Bering Strait to the west, with the majority of the Arctic zones becoming completely free of fast ice in July. The periods of ice fracturing vary greatly from year to year: the fluctuation is from one to three months. And in years of unfavourable weather conditions, some high latitude locations are not totally freed of fast ice. Owing to the melting between June and September, there is a gradual reduction in the overall ice area of the Arctic seas. Figure 10 shows the minimal, average, and maximum extension of ice-free water boundaries. The two extreme isograms show the fluctuation in the ice edge over several years. One can see that it is widest in the Kara Sea and in the Laptev Sea, and that it increases in all the seas in the period from June to September.

Ice conditions at sea are expressed by ice cover – the area of a sea or part thereof occupied by ice irrespective of its concentration. The ice cover of the Arctic seas gradually decreases from late June or early July until mid-September (figure 11) but the rate of seasonal change differs from year to year. The greatest problem for ships comes from close pack ice (7 to 10 units) rather than from very open or open pack ice. Time and space characteristics of pack ice arrangement in Arctic waters greatly resemble

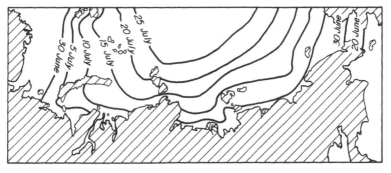

FIGURE 9. Dates of onset, melting of ice in Arctic Seas.

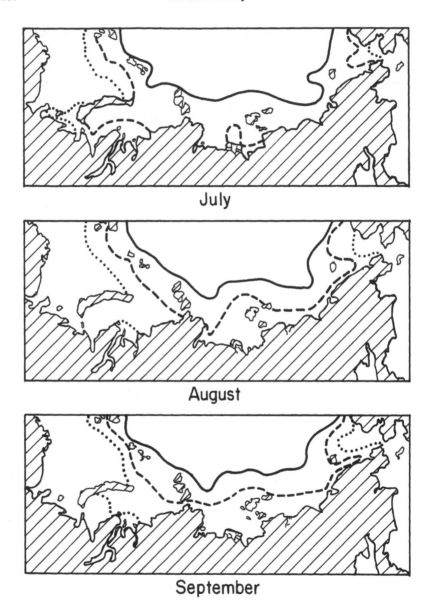

July

August

September

FIGURE 10. Boundaries of minimum (————), average (– – – –), and maximum
(•••••••) ice cover in the Arctic seas, July through September.

those of figure 10, differing only in that they are more seaward than very open pack ice. The seasonal variation in the concentrations of various types of ice is shown in figure 12.

Observations show that close pack ice forms more frequently in certain areas of the Arctic seas than in others. Such fields of close pack ice are called ice massifs. There are nine such massifs (figure 13). The Novozemelsky, Severozemelsky, Yansky, and Novosibirsky massifs are formed largely from local fast and pack ice. The Taimyrsky, Ayonsky, and Vrangelevsky massifs are ridges of the ocean ice massif and are characterized by a higher concentration of ice, a lower degree of melting, and the presence of second-year and multi-year ice. These three massifs exert the most unfavourable influence on icebreaker and ship movement. The Novozemelsky massif provides the least obstacle to navigation because even in unfavourable conditions it melts completely in the course of the summer (figure 14).

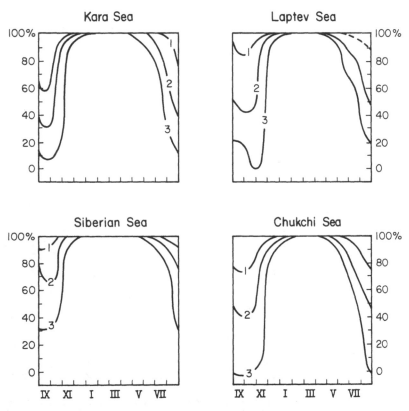

FIGURE 11. Change of ice cover in Arctic seas, creating unfavourable (1), average (2), and favourable (3) conditions for navigation.

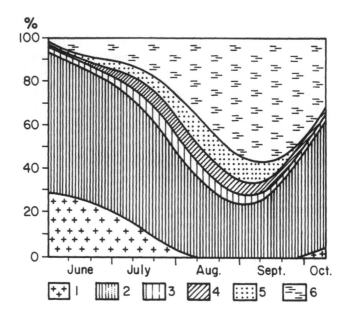

FIGURE 12. Change in total areas of concentration for various types of ice, summer season, in Soviet Arctic seas: 1 - compacted pack ice; 2 - very close pack ice; 3 - close pack ice; 4 - open pack ice; 5 - very open pack ice; 6 - open water.

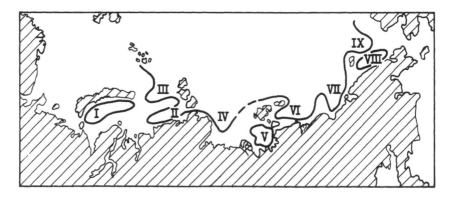

FIGURE 13. Main ice massifs in Soviet Arctic seas: I – Novozemelsky; II – Severozemelsky; III – Severny Karsky; IV– Taimyrsky; V – Yansky; VI – Novosibirsky; VII – Ayonsky; VIII – Vrangelevsky; IX – Chukotsky Severny.

Analysis of seasonal changes in the ice massifs indicates that only six of the massifs melt completely in favourable conditions. The greatest changeability is found in the Novozemelsky and Vrangelevsky massifs, whose areas are from 4.7 to 5.6 times larger than their average multi-year value in years of unfavourable conditions. Least changeable is the area of the Ayonsky massif: in unfavourable conditions it exceeds its average multi-year value only 1.5 times.

Analysis of the data shows that in the first half of the Northern Sea Route, the longest strip of close pack ice is observed in the area between the mouths of the Lena and Kolyma rivers. This circumstance determines the timetable of sea operations in the summer navigation season. Freight shipping is first undertaken on the flanks of the NSR. Then, as the ice in the Novosibirsk area begins to melt, operations are expanded into the central sections of the NSR. By September navigation conditions are almost the same in all sections of the route. However, this is only an average picture. In specific transits it may vary considerably, depending upon the combination of easy, medium, and heavy ice in different sections of the NSR. Both on a multi-year and seasonal scale, the length of close pack ice strips varies greatly in each section of the NSR, with changeability increasing towards the flanking sections. Given favourable hydro-meteorological processes, each section allows navigation without icebreaker support (in flanking sections – throughout the summer

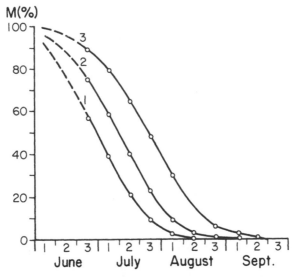

FIGURE 14. Changes in Novozemelsky massif area, June through September, under favourable – 1, average – 2, and unfavourable – 3 conditions.

navigation season). Conversely, with unfavourable hydrometeorological processes, conditions may require icebreaker support during the entire summer navigation season. Fortunately, the hydrometeorological processes develop in such a way that heavy ice is not formed simultaneously in all the sections of the NSR. This allows the icebreaker fleet some flexibility for manoeuvre and allocation along the NSR.

Thus, from the standpoint of potential navigation, the ice conditions along the NSR are characterized by the following.

The cycle of ice cover formation in the Arctic seas is divided into two periods: accumulation of ice from October through May, and melting in June through September. Depending on the hydrometeorological processes, the time limits of these periods vary. In the first period, the water areas of the Arctic seas are filled with ice of varying thicknesses, which requires icebreaker support for navigation in all hydrometeorological conditions. Taking into consideration the thickness of first-year ice, the minimum icebreaker capacity required is 2.5 metres; to deal with hummocked and multi-year ice the maximum capacity is about 3.5 metres. Naturally, these capacities are sufficient only if there is continuous movement along the route. In the second period, the water areas of the Arctic seas are gradually freed from ice. The beginning of summer navigation was traditionally determined by when melting and fracturing of the fast ice began. Summer navigation ended when the autumn ice phenomena set in. During the summer, the length of the close pack ice strip decreases considerably, which makes it possible to reduce the number of icebreakers required compared with the winter period. Multi-year and seasonal fluctuations of easy and difficult navigation in different NSR sections in the summer also make it possible to reallocate the icebreakers. The most essential feature of the ice in summer is its reduced strength, allowing icebreakers with a lower capacity to convoy ships in that period. Taking ice strength into account, the maximum icebreaker capacity needed in summer may amount to 1.4 to 1.6 metres. This will ensure continuous movement in low-hummocked and non-pressurized ice.

These figures for icebreaker capacity in the summer and winter periods do not take into account the pressure of ice, a characteristic of ice that also affects Arctic navigation. Once ice pressure is taken into account, a higher icebreaker capacity may be required, with the degree depending on the probability of ice pressure in each section of the NSR in a particular season of the year. Given a higher probability of ice pressure in larger areas of close pack ice, its occurrence is substantially more probable in the winter than in the summer. The increases in the velocity of wind and in ice strength as winter approaches also make it more likely that stronger ice pressure will occur in winter. The predominant pack ice motion varies in different sections of the NSR in the winter period of navigation and therefore the probability of increased ice pressure is higher in the eastern areas than in the western ones. The space and time characteristics of ice pressure determine marginal icebreaker capacity. They exert a strong influence on the economics of ice navigation and, in the final analysis, on the development of Arctic navigation.

As our data show, the most favourable ice conditions along the NSR occur in the southwest section of the Kara Sea. It is not accidental therefore that the pioneering of sea operations in the winter took place in this particular region.

Major Problems of Winter Navigation

In the course of winter operations, specific problems arose that exerted an influence on navigation in ice and led to certain technological developments with respect to sea transport.

To begin with, in winter the probability of ice pressure is higher as there is more ice in the sea. At the same time, higher wind velocity in the transition period from summer to winter creates the likelihood of stronger pressure which handicaps icebreaker activity. One should also bear in mind that ice pressure in winter is more dangerous. In this period of accumulation, the ice possesses more strength and can exert pressure on relatively small sections of the ship's hull. This circumstance makes ice-inflicted damage more probable in winter. The ice pressure effect is much smaller in summer because the protruding pieces of ice, which are comparatively *warm,* and consequently plastic, during the melting period, disintegrate when pressed against the hull of a ship. Moreover, during the summer, ice pressure zones are local and captains may pass round their epicentres. In winter, however, favourable conditions for ice pressure exist over a large area, and selection of a navigable route becomes more difficult.

In winter and in the presence of 1-to-3-point ice pressure, an ice *cushion* develops along the ship's hull just at the waterline. Created by the freezing of small particles of fractured ice to the ship's body, the cushion may be from 4 to 50 metres long, and its effect may be an immediate and rapid decline in speed. A snow-ice cushion on an icebreaker increases the probability of damage to the ships following the icebreakers at the instant of their unexpected stop.

During the polar night there is little or no daytime light and horizontal visibility deteriorates. Ships and icebreakers must possess powerful artificial lights to illuminate their route. Polar darkness coupled with low clouds, storm winds, and snowfalls complicates air reconnaissance. Therefore artificial lighting of the surface to be explored was provided by the aircraft. It turned out that in situations of limited visibility, air reconnaissance complemented by instruments contributes to faster movement during the polar night by identifying leads and fractures hidden from the icebreaker by darkness and frost vapours.

On the whole, limited winter visibility is a most unfavourable factor. If a convoy loses the lead and gets locked in the ice, freeing it is extremely time-consuming. During autumn-winter navigation in the lower Yenisey River and Yenisey Bay, it turned out that in order to convoy ships in a lead it was necessary to have icebreakers clean the latter regularly – *rejuvenation* of the lead. The effectiveness of winter navigation is determined by the predominant thickness of the small ice floes and their degree of consolidation, which depends on the frequency of ship movement and the air temperature. *Rejuvenation* of the lead every 2 or 3 days is considered to be optimal. This regular cleaning activity by the icebreakers increases their operating time, however, resulting in higher overall costs for icebreaker services. However, there finally comes a moment when most of the ice in the lead becomes *cemented,* no matter how often the lead is rejuvenated. Navigation should then be stopped. This moment usually occurs in January, but in unfavourable winters, it will be in December. About a month later, the lead in the fast ice should be reopened. Given the comparatively narrow strip of water on some sections of the Yenisey, and taking into account the width of a lead, there are serious difficulties here for the fleet in reopening the passage. The situation is aggravated by the fact that in some instances of navigation in fast ice, one may observe the phenomenon of thermic pressure – convergence and hummocking of the lead's edges due to expansion of ice when the air temperature soars. In such situations one has to make another lead. With due consideration of the narrowness of the strip of water available, this again is no simple task for icebreakers.

Sailors and port operators work in the open air in severe frost and bitter winds, creating a need for special seasonal clothing which is warm, light, comfortable – possibly, artificially warmed. This problem is being given serious attention now.

During transportation of ore from Noril'sk it was discovered that at low temperatures the ore becomes frozen and consolidated in the ships' holds.

The same is true for ships' moorings. This necessitates loosening the moorings before loading which requires additional effort.

In the winter the ice in the port of Dudinka is constantly in a fractured state because of non-stop navigation. Its thickness gradually increases owing to the consolidated layers and hummocking. This process is especially common in the mooring area. Thus, by the end of winter navigation, ice thickness may amount to 4 metres. Ice may get frozen to the mooring structures and protrude 3 to 6 metres into the water area. During freight handling operations, the ice coating a ship's hull may also get frozen to the ice on the mooring. Therefore, during the loading operation the ship's draught does not change gradually as it should. Then suddenly the ice bond breaks instantly and the vessel may list. On certain occasions this may lead to an accident and damage to both the ship and the mooring. In Arctic waters one should also take into account the fact that the time required for the mooring of freighters increases between twofold and fourfold. These operations also reduce the life of expensive mooring structures because of washout of their bases and blows from the ice.

Research on winter navigation in the Arctic showed that working conditions for the crews of ships and icebreakers also change substantially. Reduced natural light in autumn and the complete absence of sunlight in polar winter leads to monotony of visual perception. This is aggravated by monotonous work, as unfavourable climatic conditions may make the crew members stay inside all day round. Crew members may experience low emotional activity, dissatisfaction with the situation, depression, etc. In ice conditions, such stress reduces the reliability of the personnel which may be a danger in emergencies. In response to this observation, the Murmansk navigation administration, in agreement with medical staff, has developed a pattern of changing the crews of ships and icebreakers three times a year. This operation is assisted by other vessels, planes, and, in certain cases, trips of passenger ships.

The higher level of damage inflicted by ice in the autumn-winter period in the western part of the Arctic shows in the relative accident rate and the amount of damage caused. The average accident rate in winter amounts to 25 per cent of the total summer accidents. This is quite a lot, if one takes into account that the level of winter activity is only 5 to 10 per cent of total summer transportation, and that in winter ships of the ULA and UL type were used, whereas in summer the predominant type of ship was LI. On the whole, however, the extended navigation period on the Dudinka route resulted in a growth of ship tonnage used as a consequence of reduced freighter speeds and less intensive loading operations compared with those in the summer periods: in November-December, 1.3 times; in January-February, 1.8 times; and in March-May, 3.0 times.

By the end of the winter season (compared with a summer season), the performance of the fleet decreased more than twofold, and the cost of transportation per one ton of freight increased 3.3 times. The profitability of the fleet's operation in the period from January to May was about 3 times lower than in the summer period. But, on the average, the operation of transport vessels in this period is still profitable for the Ministry of Merchant Marine because of tariff structures for these routes.

With increased tonnage, the need for icebreaker support has grown considerably, particularly for more powerful (and more expensive) icebreakers. In comparison with the summer period, the specific cost of icebreaker support (per one ton of transported freight) grows as follows: in November-December, 2-2.5 times; in January-February, 7-12 times; and in March-May, 17-25 times. However, despite powerful icebreaker support, the speed of convoys decreased 1.5-2.5 times.

These problems force us to weigh more carefully all the *pros* and *cons* with respect to the development of winter navigation on other cargo traffic routes.

The solution of these and other problems of Arctic navigation may well be effected more fruitfully within the framework of international co-operation. I would hope that this idea will receive some stimulus in the near future. But it will take more than hope. Therefore, it seems appropriate to begin the preparation of a collective monograph on the state of the art and on problems of Arctic navigation. Of no less importance, in my opinion, is a collective publication of Soviet, American, Canadian, and other experience in important fields such as methods of using ships in ice. Solution of this and other urgent problems will make possible new contributions to international co-operation in the Arctic.

Part IV

Militarization and Confidence-Building

15

The Arctic as a Maritime Theatre

Steven E. Miller

Many in the countries that border on the Arctic rim hope that a wide-ranging framework of co-operation can be constructed for this region.[1] There are even some signs that progress towards Arctic co-operation may be possible. In matters such as pollution control, economic development, scientific exploration, and transportation, there is considerable room for mutually beneficial co-operation, and many of the region's governments have indeed expressed an interest in moving forward on some of these issues. Mikhail Gorbachev, in particular, galvanized international interest by proposing, in his now-famous Murmansk speech of October 1, 1987, that discussions be undertaken on all these issues.[2] However, Gorbachev also raised another subject – arms control – that drew attention to a more difficult reality, one in which military competition seems likely to prevail over prospects for co-operation. While co-operation may prove to be attainable with respect to the other issues, in the realm of military affairs hopes for a co-operative solution collide with the growing military importance of the region.

The Arctic emerged as a region of military significance initially as a consequence of the rise of air power during the Second World War, which drew attention to the potential use of Arctic airspace for transportation routes and attack corridors. This led the United States and Canada, during the 1950s, to invest in capabilities to provide air defence against attack from the north. With the arrival of the missile age in the late 1950s, another strategically significant role for the Arctic was added to that of air defence. Because ballistic missiles would be fired across the pole, the Arctic became a critical region for early warning and anti-ballistic missile capabilities. By 1960, the Arctic was playing an unprecedented and extremely important, if circumscribed, role in the strategic relationship between the United States and the Soviet Union. Although this role has changed in character and urgency over time, it has become a familiar and accepted feature of contemporary strategic thought. Indeed, during the 1980s, it acquired additional prominence as a consequence of the renewed interest in ballistic missile defences and the initiative to improve air defences in response to the modernization of bombers and cruise missiles.[3]

More recently, still another dimension has been added to the strategic importance of the Arctic: it has become a factor in the naval interaction between the two superpowers. This has come about as a result of three related technological developments. First, the *nuclear-powered submarine,* the earliest versions of which were deployed only in the late 1950s, made it possible to patrol for long distances under ice and hence brought the entire Arctic Basin into the operational purview of the Soviet and American navies.[4] Second, the development during the 1970s of *long-range sea-launched ballistic missiles,* which are deployed on nuclear-powered submarines, turned the Arctic into a potential deployment area for Soviet sea-based nuclear forces. Third, the emergence of the *nuclear sea-launched cruise missile,* which is currently being deployed on American submarines, further increases the likelihood that waters of the Far North will be used as a deployment area and firing station for superpower nuclear forces; both of the superpowers can fire long-range sea-launched cruise missiles from Arctic waters and strike targets in the opponent's homeland. These several considerations have caused the Arctic to become a *maritime* region of considerable strategic importance.

Two decades ago this was not the case. A decade ago it was beginning to come into view.[5] Now all indications are that the Arctic has become an area in which the superpower navies do intend to operate.[6] This is likely to become ever truer in the future as the Soviet and American navies acquire capabilities that are designed and optimized for Arctic operations. In what follows, I will examine the characteristics of the Arctic as a maritime theatre, discuss the role it is coming to play in the strategic and naval competition between the Soviet Union and the United States, and finally explore whether arms control can play a role in defusing military developments in the region.

The Arctic as a Maritime Theatre

Viewed as a theatre of military operations, the Arctic has a number of distinctive characteristics which must be considered if we are to understand how and why the Arctic has emerged as an arena of superpower naval competition. There are at least five broad points to be emphasized. For the most part, they are quite obvious, but the implications are often overlooked.

The *first* critical point is the proximity of Arctic waters to the Soviet

Union. The most casual glance at a map reveals that the USSR possesses an Arctic coastline measuring thousands of miles. More importantly, however, some of the most important Soviet naval installations (as well as air bases and other military facilities) are located on this coastline in the area of the Kola Peninsula.[7] This is the home of the Soviet Union's most powerful fleet, the Northern Fleet. It is the home base to more than half of the Soviet strategic submarine force. It represents the largest increment of naval power that the USSR could bring to bear in the North Atlantic. And it is the most accessible of all Soviet naval facilities to the high seas. These facts mean that this area is militarily vital to the Soviet Union. Moreover they serve to guarantee the militarization of the Arctic; given the inescapable need of the USSR to exploit its Arctic basing infrastructure, the presence in the region of substantial naval capabilities and significant numbers of nuclear weapons is likely to be a fact of life for the indefinite future. Those who regret the militarization of the Arctic forget that it has, in this way, long been militarized. Those who hope that the Arctic can be demilitarized must come to grips with this reality.

The implications of this immutable geographical situation are several. The peripheral waters of the Arctic Basin – notably the Barents and Kara seas – are the natural *home waters* of the Northern Fleet. It is here that the strongest concentrations of Soviet naval power, complemented by land-based air power, are to be found. These waters are, further, essential to the *defence* of Soviet bases and territories in the North.[8] They are also an important *transit* area for Soviet naval forces seeking to reach the high seas of the North Atlantic or the icy deep of the central Arctic.

As important as these considerations may be, two others are the most significant. The most critical military fact about the Arctic is that it now serves as the *deployment* area for a large number of (and a large fraction of) Soviet ballistic-missile-carrying submarines (SSBNs). Indeed, it is thought by most Western experts that the primary aim of Soviet naval strategy is to turn at least some portion of the Arctic into a protected bastion in which its SSBNs can safely operate. This makes the Arctic a consequential element of the strategic nuclear relationship between the superpowers. Insofar as the Soviet Union views its SSBNs as the most survivable component of its strategic forces, or considers its sea-based nuclear forces to be an essential strategic reserve, the military situation in the Arctic can be said to bear on some of the most vital interests of the Soviet state.

The other especially critical consideration is that the Arctic can serve as an *attack corridor*, because the naval forces of the United States and the

North Atlantic Treaty Organization (NATO) can threaten Soviet bases, forces, territory, and SSBNs with conventional or nuclear attack *only* by frontally assaulting the bastion in the Barents Sea from the south *or* by coming in the back door via the central Arctic Basin. One reason that attention has been drawn to the military competition in this region during the 1980s is the fact that the United States made clear, in publicly articulating its naval strategy, that it intended to undertake precisely this sort of action in the event of war.[9] Indeed, the central strategic dynamic at work in the Arctic region is the strong Soviet desire to protect, and the explicit American desire to threaten, Soviet submarines. The interplay of these two instincts accounts for much of the controversy and concern associated with military developments in the Arctic.

In short, the geographic proximity of the Arctic Ocean to the USSR and the Soviet need to exploit these nearby waters for basing and deploying its naval forces guarantee that the Arctic is a region of strategic significance. That these bases and forces serve as a magnet for American naval power makes this all the more true.

The *second* broad point to be emphasized about the Arctic Ocean as a maritime theatre is that it is to a considerable extent a closed sea. There are only three points of entry into the Arctic: through the Bering Strait in the Pacific, through the Canadian Arctic Archipelago via Davis Strait west of Greenland, and through the Norwegian Sea. The first two of these are narrow and confined routes that are quite vulnerable to closure. Closing off the Norwegian Sea is much more difficult because it is a rather large body of water and not easily choked off.[10] The Soviet Union does have, however, a considerable quantity of naval forces to devote to such an effort.

Obviously, from the Soviet point of view, the ideal situation in the event of war would be to close off the Arctic so as to deny access to Western naval forces (especially, of course, submarines). Such an outcome would provide the best security for its bases and forces in the region. Hence, it is not surprising to find indications that this is just what the USSR would like to be able to do and will attempt to do if war comes. As an analysis from the United States Center for Naval Analyses concluded: "Almost certainly, then, the Soviets will attempt to impose a blockade of the Arctic Ocean's gateways – probably at the outset of hostilities – aimed at barring additional enemy forces from access to the theater."[11] This operational concept implies not only strenuous efforts to contest Western naval forces in the Norwegian Sea, but also Soviet moves to block the Bering Strait and the Canadian Archipelago. What this suggests, of course, is that the entire Arctic, and not merely those portions of it closest to the USSR, represents a potential area of superpower naval operations, for a struggle to close off (or, from the Western point of view, to break into) the Arctic brings the waters of the Canadian and Alaskan Arctic into play.[12] In short, understanding the semi-enclosed character of the Arctic illuminates some of the operational naval possibilities that might obtain in war and makes clear the way in which conflict might spread across the region.

A *third* broad point to consider is the size and remoteness of the Arctic. The primary task of the Soviet navy is to hide and protect its strategic submarines and a major objective of the United States navy is to search for, and in war to destroy, those submarines. The fact that the Arctic is a broad and relatively inaccessible ocean area gives the Soviet Union a number of deployment options for its SSBNs, while complicating the strategic anti-submarine warfare (ASW) problem for the United States. Here again is a circumstance that provides the USSR with an incentive to exploit Arctic waters beyond those of the Soviet continental shelf.

American discussion of Soviet SSBN deployments is often preoccupied with the Barents Sea. This is understandable because the Barents is a fairly large area (500,000 square miles), is adjacent to the USSR, and is heavily protected by the Soviet Northern Fleet. Moreover, the Barents is a relatively shallow, noisy sea, which increases the problem of detection by acoustic means; it is a good environment in which to hide submarines. For these reasons, the USSR almost surely deploys some of its SSBNs in the Barents. But there are good reasons for believing that it may deploy SSBNs elsewhere as well.

The Barents Sea, for all its advantages, has limitations as an SSBN deployment area.[13] Shallow water and seasonal ice limit the size of the area in which SSBNs can be comfortably stationed. Also, if all Soviet SSBNs were deployed in the Barents during crisis or war, this could create undesirably high densities and thereby a "target-rich" environment for American attackers. In addition, the presence of Soviet SSBNs in these waters might inhibit the activities of Soviet ASW activities aimed at the threat from American attack submarines; it is possible to imagine many circumstances in which a Soviet commander could not be sure whether the submarine he had detected was Soviet or American. Another consideration is that the USSR may prefer to reserve the nearby waters of the Barents for SSBNs that would need to surge from port in a crisis while sending routinely deployed SSBNs to more distant stationing areas. Østreng concludes: "All in all, it therefore seems that operative SSBNs primarily use the Barents Sea for transit to other stationing areas ... The Barents Sea does not have a primary function as stationing area. Dispersion of SSBNs to a larger Arctic area will reduce the innate problems which the Northern Fleet otherwise would be confronted with."[14]

There is one final reason why the Soviet Union will have an incentive to deploy at least some SSBNs across the widest possible area: to do so greatly compounds the difficulty of hunting for them. Once Soviet SSBNs are stationed in the open ocean – that is, assuming that they are not destroyed or trailed as they leave port – pursuing them involves area search. In the Arctic, this will be more or less random, because the region is (at present, in any case) virtually free of sensors which might provide attack submarines with information about potential targets. The chances of successfully detecting a target under such circumstances are heavily influenced by the size of the area that must be searched.[15] Because the Arctic is more than ten times the size of the Barents alone, it is obvious that the possibility of Soviet SSBN deployments throughout the Arctic Basin greatly compounds the area search problem for the United States. The assumption that the Soviet Union will want to make it as difficult as possible for the United States to threaten its strategic submarines leads naturally to the conclusion that it will exploit as much of the Arctic as it reasonably can in order to stress the American ASW capability.[16]

A *fourth* broad consideration, which reinforces the third, is the fact that the Arctic Basin is covered with ice; the edge of the ice-covered area expands and contracts with the seasons. This may seem an obvious point, but it has a number of implications for military operations that should not be overlooked and which may influence Soviet incentives for deploying SSBNs outside the Barents Sea. For one thing, ice cover constrains the use of naval forces because some naval assets simply cannot operate effectively in ice-infested environments. This is true, clearly, for surface forces. It is also true, at least for the time being, of ASW aircraft, whose sonobuoys and weapons are designed to be dropped in water, not on ice. From the Soviet perspective, in short, it might appear that submarines operating in ice-covered waters are exposed to fewer threats than those deployed in ice-free waters where combined Western naval assets – air, surface, and subsurface – may be able to operate together. A naval battle in the central Arctic would thus be limited to a hidden and quiet duel between nuclear-powered submarines.[17] Another consideration, already mentioned but worth stressing, is that ice-covered Arctic waters are virtually free of sensors compared with other nearby ocean areas. Efforts to develop or discover effective detection techniques are under way,[18] but the inhospitable conditions, the lack of basing infrastructure, and the vulnerability to attack of remote and exposed facilities are unlikely to change the situation in the near future. Meanwhile, current fixed sonar arrays provide very little coverage of the Arctic, while air-dropped sensors or surface-towed arrays, in wide use elsewhere, do not come into play in ice-covered areas. Presumably this reduces the chances of detection for submarines deployed in these waters and hence constitutes another way that submarines deployed in the deep Arctic are exposed to fewer threats. As one analyst has put it, operating in the ice-covered Arctic "enables Soviet missile-firing submarines to escape detection by hiding under the north polar ice where the US has little or no ability to detect and counter them."[19]

Another advantage conferred by ice is that the marginal ice zone, at the edge of the solid ice pack, is a very noisy environment and is further marked by sharp temperature and salinity gradients – all factors which complicate ASW operations.[20] Hence, it is a good place to hide submarines.[21] The area of the marginal ice zone is quite circumscribed, constituting less than one per cent of the ocean area in the Arctic. Consequently, it is not sufficient to serve as the sole, or perhaps even the primary, deployment area for SSBNs, for the difficulties of searching under these conditions would be offset by the reduced search area if only the marginal ice zone had to be searched.[22] But if the Soviet Union wishes to maximize the stress on American and NATO ASW capabilities, it could deploy some portion of its SSBN force in the marginal ice zone and thereby compel the United States to try to deal with the difficult ASW conditions found there.

The SSBN has advantages under the permanent ice as well. It can, for example, exploit the deep ice keels that form on the bottom of the ice layer. Hiding among ice keels (which can be as much as 200 feet in size) can provide protection against torpedo attack. It also causes distortions in the propagation of sound and disturbs the performance of active sonars. Atkeson writes, for example: "The ice pack's underside is highly irregular, and an SSBN hugging the 'ceiling' could readily select a spot ... that would provide her with downward projecting ice 'curtains' of protection on one or more sides."[23] Furthermore, an SSBN operating under the ice could move very slowly, or not at all, thereby minimizing the amount of noise it generated and thus reducing the likelihood that it would be detected. As Lindsey explains: "a tactic suggested for SSBN, called 'ice-pick', is to stop engines and use gentle positive buoyancy to nestle up to the under-surface of the ice, perhaps behind a pressure ridge under rough, multi-year ice. Acoustic detection and torpedo attack against a boat in this position would be extraordinarily difficult, and the hunted would probably hear the hunter approaching."[24] In such a scenario, the American attack submarines would find themselves in the position of hunting targets that are nearly invisible to current means of detection, while their own presence could be betrayed by the noise generated in the process of searching. The availability of advantageous tactics such as hiding amongst ice keels and/or "ice-picking" is yet another reason why the USSR might be inclined to operate at least some of its SSBNs in the ice-covered reaches of the Arctic.

It is also possible that the ice can be used against the SSBN, by serving as a platform for sensors or for mines or torpedoes. But these same opportunities are afforded the Soviet Union in attempting to defend its Arctic-deployed submarines. Indeed, a case can be made that the defender would be more likely to benefit than the attacker. The Soviet Union, for starters, has the advantage of proximity, which means that it could insert SSBNs quickly into the Arctic and then seek to maximize the defensive possibilities offered by the ice. An SSBN could, for example, be protected by mines suspended from the ice, or by acoustic decoys that hide the SSBN behind a shield of noise, or by a combination of mines and decoys that serve as a kind of baited ambush, with the noise of the decoys luring attack submarines into dangerous minefields.[25] Furthermore, the Soviet Union will know where it is sending its SSBNs, while the American attack submarines must try to search anywhere that an SSBN might be deployed. This raises the possibility of the Soviet Union creating killing zones, heavily laden with mines and homing torpedoes, which Soviet SSBNs would know to avoid but which American attack submarines might stumble into. And then, of course, the defender has an advantage by the very fact the hunter must move to search, and this means that the defender's sensors, mines, decoys, and so on are more likely to be useful than those of the attacker, who is seeking a foe whose primary purpose is to avoid detection. In short, while both attacker and defender can attempt to exploit the ice as a platform for weapons and sensors, the net effect seems to favour the defender.[26]

There are, of course, disadvantages in deploying SSBNs to the ice-covered Arctic. It is, after all, a difficult and unforgiving environment. Ice may prevent SSBNs from being in a position to fire, for example, resulting in some loss of military flexibility (though it should be pointed out that there is open water in the Arctic and, furthermore, that submarines are reported to have the capability to surface through at least six feet of ice.[27]) There can be navigation problems caused by icebergs or ice keels, notably in shallower waters such as those found in the Barents and Kara seas. It can be difficult to communicate with submarines operating under ice. And in some parts of the Arctic under some conditions, the acoustic environment is not particularly advantageous from the perspective of hiding SSBNs.[28] There are, in short, some disincentives to operating submarines in the ice-covered Arctic. Nevertheless, on balance it appears that the advantages are sufficient to outweigh the disadvantages.[29] Consequently, it would be very surprising if the USSR did not want to preserve at least the option of deploying SSBNs in the Arctic Ocean, if only as insurance against the possibility that SSBNs deployed elsewhere might become excessively vulnerable. And from the point of view of posing the maximum challenge to American ASW, it is certainly in the Soviet interest that the United States expect some Soviet SSBNs to be in the Arctic.

To summarize, the presence of ice-covered or ice-infested waters is one of the distinctive features of the Arctic as a maritime environment. This has a number of significant implications for naval forces: it limits the forces which can be used, controls tactical options, inhibits intelligence efforts, and generally complicates military operations in the region. While some of these factors can work both ways, the net advantage seems to lie with the defender, that is, with the Soviet navy seeking to reduce the vulnerability of its ballistic missile submarines.

Thus far we have explored the military import of the fact that the Arctic is a large, semi-enclosed, largely ice-covered body of water much of which lies near the Soviet Union. The inescapable major conclusion is that the Arctic is an area of considerable strategic significance, with direct links to the strategic nuclear balance and with major implications for the naval interaction between the superpowers.

There is, however, a *fifth* broad consideration to keep in mind: this conclusion does not apply uniformly to the entire Arctic. Rather, the maritime environment in the Arctic region (including the Arctic Ocean and adjacent seas) subdivides in a number of ways, some physical and some geostrategic, and these subdivisions help to determine the relative importance of different portions of the Arctic and shape the character of military activities. One subdivision is between ice-free waters (such as the northern Norwegian Sea or portions of the Barents), ice-infested waters (such as portions of the Barents or the Greenland seas), and ice-covered waters (predominant in the Arctic Basin). As noted, this factor heavily influences the strategies, tactics, and forces that might be brought to bear in a naval engagement in this region. A second physical subdivision is between shallow water and deep water. Most of the water above the vast Soviet continental shelf in the Arctic, for example, including the Barents and Kara seas, is quite shallow, whereas the central basin is extremely deep. Militarily, this distinction is significant. Sound propagates quite poorly in shallow waters, making ASW sensors substantially less effective.[30] This provides one reason for regarding the shallow waters of the Soviet continental shelf as potential SSBN deployment areas. Another point is that the difficulties and dangers associated with under-ice operations increase in shallow water.[31] Some waters can, of course, be too shallow for submarines to operate in safely or comfortably. This leads to an additional observation: submarine transit through shallow waters can be channelled by the presence of excessively shallow water, resulting in what might be called underwater choke points – areas in which an adversary might reasonably predict submarine passages.[32] For reasons like these, water depth is clearly a salient consideration.

Perhaps even more important are the geostrategic subdivisions within the Arctic. There are at least two of note. First, in those areas close to the Soviet basing infrastructure on the Kola Peninsula the highest densities of military capability will be found. Especially in the ice-free reaches of the Barents, the Norwegian, and the Greenland seas, there will be not only submarine activity but a considerable number of surface vessels from the Soviet navy as well, often operating under cover of land-based air power. This is the heavily militarized core of the Soviet Arctic bastion, and certainly one of the primary targets of American military efforts in the area. Although this is not the only source of military activity in the Arctic, to a large extent it is true that the militarization of the Arctic radiates outward from the Kola and attenuates with distance. Thus, it is possible to envision an enormous naval battle in the north Norwegian Sea, involving dozens of vessels on each side and accompanied by a fierce battle in the skies involving hundreds of aircraft, whereas in the central Arctic the more likely scenario is one, two, or three Soviet SSBNs being pursued by a like number of American attack submarines. In short, while there are, as has been suggested, reasons for thinking that the whole of the Arctic would be an active naval theatre in the event of war, military capabilities are quite likely to be unevenly distributed across this large area.

The other notable geostrategic subdivision has to do with the distinction between choke points and open waters. It is the choke points that are, for obvious reasons, the most critical spots from the perspective of naval strategy and operations. Consequently, they are a primary focus of all thinking about superpower naval deployments and interactions in the

Arctic area. And while the Bering Strait in the Pacific and the passages through the Canadian Arctic Archipelago are certainly relevant, the spotlight is on the Norwegian and Barents seas. Indeed, it is in these waters that most of the factors discussed here come into play: high densities of forces, the presence of strategic nuclear assets, enormous stakes for both superpowers in waters whose domination allows control of the main gateway into (or out of) the Arctic.[33] For the United States and its NATO allies, dominance of the southern reaches of the Norwegian Sea bottles up the Soviet navy in northern waters, away from NATO's important Atlantic sea lanes, while projection of naval power northward is thought to pin down Soviet forces which might otherwise attempt to break out into the North Atlantic, to jeopardize the Soviet bastion, and to threaten the Soviet SSBN force.[34] For the Soviet Union, achieving dominance of the north Norwegian Sea would largely secure the Arctic for Soviet naval use, especially but not only its bastion in the Barents Sea; this would provide protection for both Soviet bases and Soviet SSBNs. In this portion of the Arctic, if nowhere else, there is reason to expect that war would certainly result in large-scale naval operations on both sides.

To summarize, the Arctic is an important and, in a number of ways, a distinctive theatre for naval operations. The strategic role of the Arctic produces uneven effects across the region, but nevertheless it is plausible that the entire Arctic Basin could be brought into play in the event of war. This conclusion can be illustrated by imagining rational (and feasible) Soviet behaviour in the region in the event of crisis or war. It would, of course, immediately put its bastion protection forces (constituting most of the Northern Fleet) into place for the seemingly inevitable battle for the north Norwegian Sea. So long as United States naval strategy calls for breaking open this bastion, it is hard to see how a battle can be avoided. Beyond this, the Soviet Union might well deploy attack submarines forward in the Arctic to attempt to control the Bering Strait and passages through the Canadian Archipelago. It makes little sense to make strenuous efforts in the north Norwegian Sea to deny the United States access to the waters of the Far North but allow it free entry through these "back doors." And a major, if not the major, target of American naval efforts in the Arctic is obviously and explicitly the Soviet ballistic missile submarine force. Consequently, the Soviet Union should be strongly motivated to make it as difficult as possible for the United States to threaten this force. This incentive could easily manifest itself in the wide distribution of Soviet SSBNs. Some would surely be deployed in the heavily defended Barents Sea. Some could be deployed in the relatively inaccessible waters of the

Soviet Arctic shelf east of the Barents, in the Kara Sea, for example. Some could be deployed in the marginal ice zone in the Greenland Sea, where the high level of ambient noise and the complex oceanography render ASW extremely difficult. And some could be deployed under the ice in the central Arctic, thereby requiring area search of a relatively large ocean area.[35] This deployment scheme would be sensible if the Soviet Union was sufficiently concerned about the survivability of its SSBNs that it wanted to pose the greatest possible challenge to American strategic ASW.[36] When one adds this all up, it is apparent that the whole of the Arctic Basin could, with varying degrees of intensity, feel the impact of a large-scale East-West war.

The Future of the Arctic as a Maritime Theatre

What is true today need not be true tomorrow. Therefore, it is important to ask: Will this analysis hold true in the future? Or is there any hope that the military salience of the Arctic will decline with time? There are some trends that might lead to a decline in the maritime importance of the Arctic, but I will argue that the forces of continuity are stronger and that the Arctic is likely to remain strategically significant for the foreseeable future.

There are at least two reasons why some may hope that the Arctic will recede into the strategic background. First, the fortunes of the United States navy have faded somewhat since its heyday in the mid-1980s. Growing pressures on the defence budget have cut into the navy's resources, and it is already clear that the ambitious shipbuilding plans of the peak Reagan years cannot be sustained.[37] The 600-ship navy, the goal that symbolized the revitalized navy of the 1980s, will not be attained. The navy's high-priority objective of preserving 15 carrier battle groups has fallen in the face of the need to make cuts in the defence programme. The navy will not, in short, be as large or as powerful in the 1990s as it hoped and planned to be.

A closely related point is that the navy's aggressive Maritime Strategy and the concerns it raised, a source of considerable controversy just a short time ago, are no longer in the spotlight.[38] There are several explanations for this. One is that the individuals most closely identified with the strategy and its most outspoken public champions, the former secretary of the navy, John Lehman, and the former chief of naval operations, Admiral James Watkins, have passed from the scene. Another is that the navy, chastened by the controversy it provoked and stung by the criticism it attracted by articulating the Maritime Strategy, has adopted a lower public profile with respect to its strategy.[39] And, of course, mounting budget constraints may have led many to conclude that the navy simply will not have the forces necessary to implement the strategy.

The second reason why one might conclude that importance of the Arctic as a maritime theatre might diminish is that effective ASW is growing ever more difficult with each new generation of submarine technology. The most modern American submarines are already extraordinarily quiet.[40] More important for this discussion, Soviet submarines are becoming increasingly quiet. Indeed, the Soviet Union has made such progress in quieting its submarines that in 1987 one high official from the Department of the Navy declared that the United States faced a "crisis in our antisubmarine warfare."[41] This concern has intensified with time and the continued modernization of the Soviet submarine force. In the spring of 1989, a congressional report expressed serious concern about the future adequacy of United States ASW capabilities. Its conclusions were unambiguous: "Our current antisubmarine warfare capability rests almost entirely on listening for the sounds generated by Soviet submarines. That approach has been successful and our antisubmarine forces have grown potent because the Soviets have traditionally built relatively noisy submarines. But the future of that approach to ASW is now very much in doubt because the Soviet Union has begun to produce quiet submarines ... Unless ways to compensate for the coming degradation in passive sonar can be found, our attack submarines are likely to lose much of their effectiveness in what has been one of their major missions – operations against Soviet submarines."[42] The logical end of trends in submarine quieting, in short, is submarines that are virtually undetectable by current means. As Admiral Kinnaird McKee put it in congressional testimony in 1987: "Submarines will become quieter to the point where they really don't bother one another and can devote their time to other missions."[43] Obviously, in such a world many of the forward operations by attack submarines against the Soviet submarine force would not be feasible and the idea of chasing Soviet SSBNs about the Arctic loses its credibility. In this line of reasoning, then, the strategic importance of the Arctic may decline with the modernization of the Soviet submarine force: the more modern quiet submarines it deploys, the less feasible are contemplated attack submarine operations in the North, and the less incentive the United States will presumably have to undertake them. For those who believe in the edicts of classical stability theory, which equates survivable forces on *both* sides with safety, this is a desirable outcome, quite apart from its implications for the Arctic.

Viewed in isolation, these two factors – the changing fortunes of the United States navy and the growing difficulties associated with ASW – do in fact lead to the conclusion that the Arctic will decline in strategic importance. Set against these factors, however, are others which cut the other way. Moreover, in my view these other considerations suggest that continuity rather than change is the most likely outcome in the medium-term future: the Arctic will remain militarily important.

A *first* point to keep in mind is that the Soviet navy will also shrink in size and capability; not only does it also face budgetary pressures which are, if anything, even more severe than those confronting the United States navy, but it has a much more demanding modernization problem because of the large number of obsolete or obsolescent vessels in its fleet.[44] That the American fleet will be smaller than the Reagan administration's plans called for therefore does not necessarily call into question the feasibility of the operations contemplated under the Maritime Strategy: this smaller force will be going against a smaller rival. Given the difficulties of the Soviet situation, the net result of a superpower naval drawdown could well be that forward naval operations in the Far North by the United States will be more, rather than less, feasible in terms of relative force capabilities. Furthermore, the navy has rarely linked the desirability or feasibility of forward operations to specific force levels; rather, they were operational concepts that could be undertaken by existing forces as well as by the larger force envisioned in the five-year defence plans.[45] It is simply not true that budget pressures and shrinking force levels will necessarily bring to an end the navy's interest in forward operations or render them impracticable.

Second, while the visibility of the Maritime Strategy has diminished and the controversy associated with it has died down, there is no indication that the United States has abandoned counterforce operations as an integral component of its strategic nuclear doctrine. The evidence, in fact, suggests an unwavering commitment to preserve and enhance strategic counterforce options, even when this entails difficult and expensive efforts to cope with new and more survivable Soviet systems, such as mobile missiles.[46] So long as this remains true, it will be incumbent upon the navy to seek to threaten Soviet ballistic missile submarines. It would make no sense whatsoever for the United States to spend billions to acquire the capability to threaten Soviet land-based strategic forces, but to forswear any attempt to neutralize the SSBN force. Therefore, quite apart from the navy's own doctrinal preferences and independent of concerns about the navy's autonomy to pursue those preferences, it is obliged to attempt forward operations against Soviet SSBNs in northern waters *in fulfilment of national strategy.* This will remain true even if the label "Maritime Strategy" disappears entirely from the lexicon of the defence debate, and even if some of the other operations included in the Maritime Strategy are abandoned or modified. Of course, it is true that the navy cannot promise complete or even extensive success in this campaign, but this has been true of other elements of American counterforce capabilities for quite some time. And though a disarming counterforce capability has long been out of sight, the United States has nevertheless pursued a policy of posing as much of a counterforce threat as it could within existing technological and budgetary constraints. Thus, in the context of United States policy, the difficulty of strategic ASW operations is not a convincing reason for not attempting them. It follows that the critical maritime dynamic in the Arctic, the basic source of its strategic importance, will continue to operate: American nuclear-powered attack submarines are going to be hunting Soviet SSBNs until such time as American doctrine changes. While it is true that little can be taken for granted in the present period of dramatic change in international politics, this is one certainty that will persist.

Third, ballistic missile submarines will continue to be important components of the strategic environment and may even become more important in some ways than in the past – especially for the Soviet Union, whose SSBNs operate in the Arctic. This is true in part because the deployment of multiple warheads on submarine-launched ballistic missiles has caused them to become a larger share of deployed strategic nuclear capability. It is also true because of fluctuating confidence in the survivability of other nuclear forces: when these are thought to be highly vulnerable, as is now the case for fixed-site, land-based forces, then sea-based forces, the most survivable component of the deterrent posture, become all the more important. While the deployment of mobile land-based missiles may swing the pendulum back in the other direction, it will be some time before they are extensively deployed, and it remains to be seen how much confidence there will be in the survivability of mobile missiles in the face of determined efforts to threaten them.[47] Finally, reliance on SSBNs may be accentuated as a result of cuts negotiated in the Strategic Arms Reduction Talks (START). While a START agreement along the lines currently under discussion would certainly result in many fewer SSBNs, they could nevertheless, under any number of schemes of compliance with such a treaty, constitute a larger fraction of overall post-agreement forces.[48] In short, SSBNs will at a minimum be just as important as they always have been and may even be more important than in the past. This means that the Soviet Union will continue to have a strong interest in deploying SSBNs in the Arctic, just as the previous point means that the Americans will continue to have a strong interest in hunting them in the Arctic. Here lies the basic reason why I attribute continuing strategic importance to the Arctic.

This line of argument might seem, however, to be strongly undermined by current trends in submarine quieting which look as though they will eventually neutralize existing ASW techniques. At a minimum, they will greatly reduce the range of detection that can be achieved by passive sonars. It is plausible to suggest that my analysis becomes moot if ASW operations are rendered nearly or entirely impracticable. If United States attack submarines cannot find Soviet SSBNs, except by dumb luck, then the interaction between Soviet and American maritime forces in the Arctic becomes uninteresting, the United States incentive for attempting such operations would presumably decline significantly, and the risks associated with United States naval activities in northern waters would be smaller than at present.[49] However, this point is vitiated by a *fourth* consideration: trends in submarine quieting are more likely to *change* the ASW game than to *eliminate* it. The alarm in the United States about the "ASW crisis" has led to calls for a major research effort. There are several lines to be pursued.[50] One is improvements in passive sonars. It may be possible, if expensive, to use more sensitive and sophisticated sensors in more densely packed patterns of deployment to retain some capacity for acoustic detection. A recent discussion of NATO ASW maritime patrol aircraft notes, for example, that their "operations are becoming more expensive since the detection of quietened submarines requires larger numbers of more sophisticated sonobuoys."[51] In addition, ASW tactics are evolving, with more co-ordination among ASW assets, more joint submarine/air training exercises, and so on. These are signs of things to come.

But merely improving existing ASW approaches will, it is widely believed, be insufficient over the long run. As the Advisory Panel on Submarine and Antisubmarine Warfare observed: "We must build what will amount to an entire new ASW capability by the time the Soviet Union has built a significant number of new submarines ... We believe that the Navy must, in effect, 'start over' with new approaches to ASW ... What is needed is an entirely new and aggressive architecture for coping with this immensely serious development."[52] The quest for a new approach to ASW will move in two directions. One is the exploitation of active sensors (sonars) that operate in a manner similar to radar: they send out a beam of energy and listen for the reflection.[53] Because their operation is not connected to the noise generated by opposing submarines, the effectiveness of sonars is not degraded by the trends in submarine quieting. They do, however, have one major liability: they reveal the presence of the hunting submarine because the sonar pulse can be detected by the target. To address this problem, off-board sonars (sensor-loaded torpedoes or submarine-deployable sonobuoys, for example) are being developed that may allow sonars to be exploited without betraying the precise location of the hunting submarine. The second, and more distant, approach is to explore non-acoustic means of ASW detection.[54] This involves efforts to exploit such phenomena as thermal signatures, magnetic anomalies, bioluminescence, vessel exhaust, or such technologies as lasers, to locate submarines. According to the public literature, none of these approaches looks particularly promising at present as the basis for a new ASW infrastructure. But there is no doubt that research will continue in these areas.

In short, while strategic ASW, already a difficult task, will grow more difficult in the future, this does not mean that American efforts to hunt Soviet ballistic missile submarines will be abandoned. Instead, there is likely to be greater attention to ASW, redoubled efforts to discover more effective techniques, and perhaps the need for more, rather than less, in the way of forces and sensors in the Arctic. Just as the United States effort to jeopardize Soviet ICBMs has continued despite the difficulty of the task, despite the inadequacies of present capabilities, and despite sustained Soviet efforts (in hardening and mobility) to neutralize American improvements, so the commitment to strategic ASW is likely to continue despite the growing challenge it presents. So long as this is true, the Arctic will remain an arena in which the superpower navies interact and in which the strategic stakes will be considerable.

A *fifth* point to be taken into account is that we are, for the first time really, entering an era of what might be called Arctic-optimized capabilities. On the American side, the newest generation of submarines (the SSN-21 Seawolf), unlike those of the past, is being designed with Arctic operations in mind, with features which allow the submarine to surface safely through ice and which protect external sensors from ice damage.[55] Newer Soviet vessels, such as the Typhoon strategic submarine, are also thought to have been designed with Arctic operations in mind.[56]

When coupled with the navy-inspired efforts to study the Arctic and the mounting operational experience in the Arctic, this suggests that future naval commanders will venture northwards with more knowledge of, more practice in, and more capable vessels for Arctic deployment. Given the vast sums of money involved in acquiring these submarines, this should be taken as an indication of continued superpower interest in the Arctic.

Thus, although there are some developments that might lead one to think that the Arctic will decline in strategic importance, a number of factors, more compelling in my view, suggest the reverse: that the Arctic will, if not grow in importance, at least remain important in the strategic calculus of the superpowers. This could be true even if there is striking progress towards deep reductions in strategic forces, even beyond those contemplated in START. For a move in the direction of some sort of minimum deterrent, an increasingly fashionable idea these days, would likely preserve some portion of the sea-based nuclear forces because of concerns about the possible future vulnerability of land-based forces and out of respect for the survivability of SSBNs.[57] Barring a change in American doctrine or restraints on ASW activities, the Arctic would retain its strategic character even in a period of more dramatic breakthroughs in East-West relations. In such an environment, the implications of the Arctic as a maritime theatre would probably be much less worrying (if only because war would seem so remote), but they would still exist.

Is Arms Control a Solution?

Are there arms control measures that would change this conclusion?[58] Probably not, for several reasons. First, unless the Soviet Union wants to get out of the maritime power business altogether, which is very unlikely, it has no choice but to exploit the Kola Peninsula and adjacent waters for the deployment of its Northern Fleet and its SSBN force. No arms control agreement can undo this fact. Second, SSBNs continue to be regarded as the cornerstone of deterrence, as the capability whose long-term survivability can most be counted on. Consequently, they are likely to remain in the strategic forces of the superpowers for the foreseeable future. Again, it is extremely unlikely that an arms control agreement will change this fact. It would be contrary to the basic principles of arms control theory to use negotiations to eliminate the most stabilizing weapons and SSBNs are stabilizing in terms of the overall strategic nuclear balance (if not in the context of the Arctic). Finally, and most fundamentally, the main culprits in the militarization of the Arctic are nuclear-powered submarines.

Because submarines are capable of, indeed rely upon, stealth, limits on their activities simply cannot be verified. Therefore, it is not possible to have a meaningful agreement limiting or eliminating their operations in the Far North. Limitations on the numbers of submarines seem more plausible, but so long as the superpowers have not nearly or entirely eliminated nuclear-powered attack submarines and SSBNs from their naval arsenals, the game of hunter and hunted will continue in the waters of the Arctic.[59]

Conclusions

This essay has sought to highlight several themes. It has attempted to show that the Arctic is a distinctive and strategically significant maritime environment. Although many express concern about preventing the militarization of the Arctic, examination reveals that it is, in terms of naval forces at least, already militarized and in some ways growing more so. We have seen that while the implications of the superpower naval competition in the Arctic are unevenly distributed across the Arctic Basin, they are not localized but spread, at least potentially, across the entire region. Further, while some of the factors that affect the strategic maritime role of the Arctic are changing, the strategic importance of the region is not likely to diminish. And, finally, it has been argued that naval arms control is not likely to alter this situation in any fundamental way.

This does not mean that the Arctic must be regarded as a region in crisis or that it is destined to be always an area of *intense* strategic concern. The more hopeful developments (in particular, the apparent survivability of mobile ICBMs and the mounting difficulties of strategic ASW – both, ironically, the byproduct of military modernization), while they do not undo the naval interaction in the Arctic, do muffle its effects (the one by reducing the importance of Soviet SSBNs, the other by reducing their vulnerability). But these developments do not allow an easy escape from the reality that modern technology, when combined with the interests, policies, and doctrines of the superpowers, brings this remote and beautiful part of the world enduringly into the strategic competition between them. For those who are interested in Arctic arms control and who would like to see the region demilitarized as much as possible, this is not a happy conclusion. But I believe it is unavoidable.

Notes

1 This paper has benefited from the author's participation in the ongoing Arctic workshop series of the Tampere Peace Research Institute (TAPRI). It is based on

presentations that were delivered to the International Conference on Arctic Co-operation, Toronto, Canada, October 1988, and to the TAPRI Arctic Workshop, University of Lapland, Rovaniemi, Finland, February 1989.

2 An analysis of the Murmansk speech may be found in Ronald G. Purver, "Arctic Security: The Murmansk Initiative and Its Impact," paper from the conference on "Soviet Foreign Policy at the Crossroads," Carleton University, Ottawa, Canada, September 1988. See also the detailed analysis in David Scrivener, *Gorbachev's Murmansk Speech: The Soviet Initiative and Western Response* (Oslo: Norwegian Atlantic Committee 1989). The speech itself is available in *The North: A Zone of Peace* (Ottawa: USSR Embassy 1988).

3 For a thorough survey of these developments as they affect the Arctic, see David Cox, "Ballistic Missile Defences, Cruise Missiles, Air Defences," in this volume.

4 Exploration of the Arctic commenced soon after the launching of the first nuclear-powered submarine, the USS *Nautilus*. Commissioned in the fall of 1957, the *Nautilus* completed an under-ice crossing of the Arctic Basin from Point Barrow, Alaska, to the Greenland Sea in August 1958. Thereafter, according to the information available on the public record, submarine deployments to the Arctic, often involving more than one boat, took place roughly once a year through the end of the 1970s. For a useful overview of submarine activities in the Arctic, see Capt. Alfred S. McLaren, "Under Ice in Submarines," *US Naval Institute Proceedings* (July 1981), 105-9. McLaren (108) identifies thirteen "principal" Arctic cruises between February 1967 and March 1979.

5 One of the first to recognize the potential maritime importance of the Arctic was Willy Østreng. See notably, his "The Strategic Balance and the Arctic Ocean: Soviet Options," *Cooperation and Conflict,* 12 (no 1, 1977), 41-62.

6 Note, for example, the testimony of Rear Admiral William Studeman, director of naval intelligence, who commented in 1988 that "Soviet operations and testing indicate they intend to operate [in the Arctic] in wartime, seasonal environmental conditions permitting." Testimony before the Seapower and Critical Minerals Subcommittee of the Armed Services Committee of the United States House of Representatives, March 1, 1988, 7.

7 For the most detailed discussion of Soviet bases on the Kola, see Tomas Ries and Johnny Skorve, *Investigating Kola: A Study of Military Bases Using Satellite Photography* (London: Brassey's 1987).

8 This is what some Western analysts describe as the inner defence zone for the USSR in the North. Further south, the waters of the Norwegian Sea, and further north, the more distant waters of the Arctic, are often designated the outer defence zone. See, for example, John Erickson, "The Soviet Northern Fleet: Commitments, Capabilities, Constraints," paper presented at the Oslo Symposium, Oslo, Norway, August 1986; and Michael MccGwire, *Military Objectives in Soviet Foreign Policy* (Washington: Brookings Institution 1987), 146-56.

9 I have dealt with this at length in "The Maritime Strategy and Geopolitics in the High North," in Clive Archer, ed., *The Soviet Union and Northern Waters* (London: Routledge for the Royal Institute of International Affairs 1988), 205-38.

10 MccGwire, *Military Objectives*, 147, stresses the problems of attempting to block the Norwegian Sea.

11 Charles C. Petersen, *Soviet Military Objectives in the Arctic Theater and How They Might Be Attained*, Research Memorandum CRM 86-204 (Arlington VA: Center for Naval Analyses, September 1986), 8. Also on this point, see Anthony R. Wells, "The North Atlantic and Arctic Theaters of Operations," in James L. George, ed, *The Soviet and Other Communist Navies: The View from the Mid-1980s* (Annapolis MD: Naval Institute Press 1986), 199-214. Wells, at 210, suggests that "the Soviet aim is to make a Soviet lake (mare nostrum) of the Arctic." Dissenting somewhat on this issue is Michael MccGwire, who argues that the Soviet Union has abandoned its effort to be able to close off the Arctic because it concluded that it is too costly and too difficult to keep American submarines out. See his "The Changing Role of the Soviet Navy," *Bulletin of the Atomic Scientists*, 43 (September 1987), 35.

12 There are numerous indications of Canadian concern about this possibility. See, for example, Commander Peter T. Haydon, "The Strategic Importance of the Arctic: Understanding the Military Issues," *Canadian Defence Quarterly*, 17 (spring 1988), 27-34; Lt.-Col. John E. McGee, "Call to Action in the Arctic," *US Naval Institute Proceedings* (March 1988), particularly 14, where McGee notes Soviet doctrinal interest in closing choke points in the Canadian Arctic; and especially the Canadian defence white paper, *Challenge and Commitment: A Defence Policy for Canada* (Ottawa: National Defence/Supply and Services Canada 1987), 50, which comments: "Deep channels through the Canadian Arctic offer a means of passing between the Arctic and Atlantic oceans. In a period of tension or war, Soviet submarines could seek to operate off the deep channels of the Canadian Archipelago to intercept Allied submarines entering the Arctic. Moreover, the Soviets might use these channels in war to reach patrol areas in the North Atlantic." This concern was a major part of the rationale for the Canadian government's controversial decision (since abandoned) to acquire a force of nuclear-powered submarines.

13 In this paragraph, I draw on the formative work of Willy Østreng. See his "Strategic Submarines in the Barents Sea," *International Challenges*, 7 (no 1, 1987), 47-5; and Helge Ole Bergesen, Arild Moe, and Willy Østreng, *In Search of Oil and Security: Soviet Interests in the Barents Sea*, Study R:004-1986 (Lysaker: Fridtjof Nansen Institute 1986), 67-102.

14 Bergesen, Moe, and Østreng, *In Search of Oil and Security*, 90.

15 The dynamics of area search, and a detailed analysis of the likelihood of detection, are provided in Mark Sakitt, *Submarine Warfare in the Arctic: Option or Illusion?* (Stanford: Center for International Security and Arms Control, Stanford University, May 1988), 30-40. Sakitt explains (31): "The searching time for an attack submarine to find another submarine depends on the ratio of the area that can be swept per unit time to the total area of deployment that has to be searched."

16 The only circumstance in which this might not be true is if the Soviet Union were highly confident of the survivability of its SSBNs even without wide deployment.

17 Diesel-powered submarines cannot operate in the Arctic because they must 'breathe' regularly which requires reliable access to the ocean surface.

18 See, for example, Maj.-Gen. Edward B. Atkeson (ret.), "Fighting Subs under the Ice," *US Naval Institute Proceedings* (September 1987), 81-7, which proposes that an extensive network of sensors be put in place on the permanent Arctic ice pack, to be supported by helicopters and vertical short take-off and landing aircraft armed with specially designed ASW weapons.

19 Craig Couvault, "Soviet Ability to Fire through Ice Creates New SLBM Basing Mode," *Aviation Week & Space Technology,* December 10, 1984, 16. On this point, see also Tom Stefanick, *Strategic Antisubmarine Warfare and Naval Strategy* (Lexington MA: Lexington Books for the Institute for Defense and Disarmament Studies, 1987), 41-6. Stefanick concludes (41): "In all these ice-covered regions, many of the complex, coordinated tactics of open ocean ASW are much more difficult." Echoing this conclusion is Leonard LeSchack, "Understanding Sea Ice," *US Naval Institute Proceedings* (September 1987), 76: "An ice cover leads to functional problems in hunting, killing, and search and rescue."

20 A brief discussion is Leonard Johnson, "The Arctic Environment," *US Naval Institute Proceedings* (September 1987) 87.

21 As a result there is a serious interest in studying the oceanography of the marginal ice zone. See, for example, Robert H. Bourke and Robert G. Paquette, "Studies of the Marginal Ice Zone along the East Greenland Coast," *Naval Research News,* 39 (no 1, 1987), 19-27, which explicitly links scientific studies of the region to the growing military salience of these waters. For a description of some of the experiments that have been undertaken, see Dean A. Horn, "Winter MIZEX 87: Operations Overview," *Naval Research News,* 39 (no 3, 1987), 15-21.

22 On these points, see Sakitt, *Submarine Warfare in the Arctic,* 47-9.

23 Atkeson, "Fighting Subs under the Ice," 84-5. The passage continues: "Active sonar, besides disclosing the originator's location, would have great difficulty in sorting out the scrambled returns from ice stalactites and up-ended ice 'rafts' along ice pack fissure lines from returns from a submarine hull."

24 George Lindsey, *Strategic Stability in the Arctic,* Adelphi Paper 241 (London: Brassey's for the International Institute for Strategic Studies 1989), 37.

25 These same tactics are available in ice-free waters as well. For discussion of pro-SSBN tactics, see Stefanick, *Strategic Antisubmarine Warfare and Naval Strategy,* 62-6. He notes (66) that "even under very favorable conditions for search, Soviet use of mines and decoys could dramatically shift the exchange ratio in an ASW campaign." Sakitt also discusses decoys, mines, and ambush tactics: see *Submarine Warfare in the Arctic,* 41-4, 54-7.

26 On this point, see Lindsey, *Strategic Stability in the Arctic,* 27. He writes: "The defender can use the ice as a semi-permanent platform, steadier and quieter than a surface ship, from which he can suspend sensors for a detection barrier, the means to signal to defensive SSN and the protected SSBN (and also to trigger anti-submarine mines) and launch anti-submarine torpedos and acoustic decoys or jammers."

27 See W. Harriet Critchley, "Polar Deployment of Soviet Submarines," *International Journal*, 39 (autumn 1984), 855; and Østreng, *The Soviet Union in Arctic Waters*, Occasional Paper 36 (Honolulu: Law of the Sea Institute 1987), 20.

28 See Stefanick's detailed discussion in *Strategic Antisubmarine Warfare and Naval Strategy*, 307-65.

29 For a more detailed treatment of this issue, see Østreng, *The Soviet Union in Arctic Waters*, 16-25.

30 On this point, see, for example, Lindsey, *Strategic Stability in the Arctic*, 31-2. He writes: "Sound transmission, and hence the ability of sonar to detect submarines, is very different in shallow water from that in deep – and different again when the sea is both shallow and covered by ice ... detection ranges are generally considerably less than those achievable in deep ice-covered water." On the difficulties of shallow-water ASW more generally, see U. Ljungdahl, "Submarines and ASW in Coastal Waters," *Naval Forces*, 8 (no 1, 1987), 82-8.

31 Willy Østreng writes, for example, that enormous modern submarines "need space to maneuver, both in the horizontal and the vertical plane ... There have been reports of submarines which have sailed into hollows in the Shelf without any outlet to the deep sea, and have had difficulty getting out, because of ice conditions above the ship – the so-called 'valley of death' problem ... Clearly, ice conditions can in such cases be a question of life or death." Bergesen, Moe, and Østreng, *In Search of Oil and Security*, 85-6.

32 Ibid., 86. A map of depths in the Barents Sea illustrates the point. If one assumes that large submarines (such as Soviet Delta and Typhoon SSBNs) avoid waters of less than 200 metres in depth, then a substantial fraction of the Barents is unsuitable for them.

33 I have discussed this in more detail in S. Miller, "The Northern Seas in Soviet and US Strategy," in Sverre Lodgaard and Marek Thee, eds., *Nuclear Disengagement in Europe* (London: Taylor & Francis for SIPRI 1983), 117-37.

34 For an excellent analysis of the relationship between NATO's dominance of the GIUK (Greenland-Iceland-United Kingdom) gap and naval operations farther north, see Barry R. Posen, "Offensive and Defensive Sea Control: An Assessment," in Charles Glaser and Steven E. Miller, eds., *The Navy and Nuclear War* (Ithaca NY: Cornell University Press, forthcoming).

35 The United States navy, at any rate, seems convinced that the Soviet Union will operate under the ice. See, for example, the testimony of Admiral Kinnaird McKee in United States Congress, House Appropriations Committee, Subcommittee on Defense, *DoD Appropriations for 1987* (Washington: United States Government Printing Office, April 24, 1986), 456-8. Discussing Soviet under-ice capability, McKee comments (457): "It is clear the Soviets are going to work up there [in the Arctic] and if we can work up there, too, that will create more uncertainty for them in a strategic sense."

36 The combination of these deployment options, the availability of a variety of pro-SSBN tactics, and the improvement in Soviet submarines has led many analysts to the conclusion that the strategic ASW mission of the United States navy is not

feasible. But one implication of this analysis is that the best, and perhaps the only feasible, time to attack Soviet SSBNs (most of which are in port on a routine basis) is *before* they have dispersed. This may perhaps account for the strong emphasis in the United States Maritime Strategy on early forward movement of forces (especially submarines) into northern waters. Thus, in the authoritative public articulation of the strategy, Admiral James Watkins stated: "Keys to the success of both the initial phase and the strategy as a whole are speed and decisiveness in national decisionmaking ... Prompt decisions are needed to permit rapid forward deployment of additional forces in crisis." From Watkins, "The Maritime Strategy," in *The Maritime Strategy,* supplement to the *US Naval Institute Proceedings* (January 1986), 9. In the Arctic context, this implies American attack submarines rushing into the Barents Sea in time of crisis, in the hopes of being able to trail Soviet SSBNs as they leave port or, if the war has already begun, to destroy them as they seek to disperse.

37 On the difficulties of attaining and maintaining a force of at least 100 nuclear-powered attack submarines as the navy would prefer, for example, see Caleb Baker, "Report: Navy Options Include Seawolf, Low-Cost Sub Combination," *Defense News,* October 30, 1989, 31.

38 For strong statements of the case for and against the Maritime Strategy, see Linton F. Brooks, "Naval Power and National Security: The Case for the Maritime Strategy," and John J. Mearsheimer, "A Strategic Misstep: The Maritime Strategy and Deterrence in Europe," both in Steven E. Miller and Stephen Van Evera, eds., *Naval Strategy and National Security* (Princeton NJ: Princeton University Press 1988), 16-101. For an overview of the controversy, see my "The Maritime Strategy and Geopolitics in the High North," 205-38.

39 See, for example, Donald C.F. Daniels, "Naval Power and European Security," paper presented to the meeting of the International Studies Association, London, March 28-April 1, 1989, 4. Daniels notes the disinclination of the chief of naval operations, Admiral Trost, to talk publicly about Maritime Strategy options.

40 According to Admiral McKee, the Los Angeles class submarine is so quiet that the energy leakage is the "equivalent of one size D flashlight battery." *DoD Appropriations for 1987,* 457.

41 The assistant secretary of the navy, Melvin Paisley, as quoted in "The Crunch in Submarine Warfare," *New York Times,* April 18, 1987. See also George C. Wilson, "Soviets Score Silent Success in Undersea Race with US," *Washington Post,* July 17, 1987. An excellent overview of the interaction between American ASW sensors and Soviet efforts at quieting is Jonathan B. Tucker, "Cold War in the Ocean Depths," *High Technology* (July 1985), 29-38.

42 *Report of the Advisory Panel on Submarine and Antisubmarine Warfare to the House Armed Services Subcommittees on Research and Development and Seapower and Strategic and Critical Materials,* March 21, 1989, 1, 6-7. See also "Quiet Submarines a Serious Problem," House Armed Services Committee, news release, March 21, 1989. This report attracted considerable public attention. See, for example: George Wilson, "Navy Urged to Focus on Long-Term Soviet Sub Threat," *Washington Post,* March 23, 1989; Richard Halloran, "Navy Advised to Refocus Antisubmarine Studies," *New York Times,* March 22, 1989; and Andy

Pasztor, "Aspin Starts Push on Plan to Counter Soviet Submarines," *Wall Street Journal*, March 21, 1989. For an extended discussion of the implications of what has been called "acoustic parity," see Lt. P. Kevin Peppe, "Acoustic Showdown for the SSNs," *US Naval Institute Proceedings* (July 1987), 33-7; and Richard R. Pariseau and Capt. Lee F. Gunn, "What Quieting Means to the Soviets," *US Naval Institute Proceedings* (April 1989), 46-8.

43 *DoD Appropriations for 1987*, 457.

44 See, for example, the analysis by Shunji Taoka, "East-West Naval Force Comparison," in Richard Fieldhouse and Shunji Taoka, *Superpowers at Sea: An Assessment of the Naval Arms Race* (Oxford: Oxford University Press for SIPRI 1989), especially 58-62.

45 In 1986, for example, Admiral Watkins, wrote: "It is a strategy for today's forces, today's capabilities, and today's threat." From his "The Maritime Strategy," 4.

46 See, for example, Desmond Ball and Robert C. Toth, "Revising the SIOP: Taking War-Fighting to Dangerous Extremes," *International Security*, 14 (spring 1990), 65-92, which details the evolution of American strategic targeting doctrine and policy in the 1980s.

47 See, for example, Michael Brower, "Targeting Soviet Mobile Missiles," *Survival*, 31 (September/October 1989), 433-46, and Robert R. Ropelewski, "Target Mobility, Arms Control Challenge SAC Modernization," *Armed Forces Journal International* (September 1989), 67-72.

48 See, for example, Walter Slocombe, "Force Posture Consequences of the START Treaty," *Survival*, 30 (September/October 1988), especially 406-7; and Lindsey, *Strategic Stability in the Arctic*, 68-70.

49 Soviet SSBNs in port are an exception to this point, because their location is known and their presence would likely constitute a temptation to the United States navy.

50 For a brief overview, see the *Report of the Advisory Panel on Submarine and Antisubmarine Warfare*, 6.

51 Joris Janssen Lok, "The North Atlantic's Listening Force," *Jane's Defence Weekly*, October 21, 1989, 867.

52 *Report of the Advisory Panel on Submarine and Antisubmarine Warfare*, 1-2.

53 On the growing interest in active sensors, see Raymond Cheung, "Towed Array Sonar Developments: Keeping Track of the Tail," *Navy International* (January 1989), 8. On the limitations of sonars, see Lindsey, *Strategic Stability in the Arctic*, 24.

54 See, for example, Simon Elliot, "Non-acoustic ASW Looks to the 21st Century," *Jane's Defence Weekly*, July 1, 1989, 1368-9. Also, James T. Westwood, "Strategic Antisubmarine Warfare," *Journal of Defense and Diplomacy* (February-March 1989), 14.

55 Sakitt, *Submarine Warfare in the Arctic*, 15.

56 See Critchley, "Polar Deployment of Soviet Submarines," 861, and Atkeson, "Fighting Subs under the Ice," 82.

57 See, for example, Harold A. Feiveson and Frank von Hippel, "Post-Start Nuclear Arms Reductions: The Case for Finite Deterrence," an unpublished ms, Center for Energy and Environmental Affairs, Princeton University, October 27, 1989, 14ff.

They write: "Ballistic missile submarines at sea are the only strategic launchers that could be virtually guaranteed to survive for more than a day [in the event of war]."

58 I have discussed this at length in Miller, "Naval Arms Control and Northern Europe: Constraints and Prospects," in Sverre Lodgaard, ed., *Naval Arms Control* (Oslo:Sage for Peace Research Institute 1990).

59 But for a more hopeful view, see Ronald G. Purver, *Arctic Arms Control: Constraints and Opportunities*, Occasional Paper 3 (Ottawa: Canadian Institute for International Peace and Security, February 1988).

16

Ballistic Missile Defences, Cruise Missiles, Air Defences

David Cox

This paper reviews developments in three related areas of strategic force development: ballistic missile defences, particularly as reflected in the evolution of the Strategic Defense Initiative (SDI) or Star Wars programme; strategic cruise missile systems in the context of the Strategic Arms Reduction Talks (START); and air defences, addressing both current improvements to air defence systems and possible future technologies as reflected in the Air Defense Initiative (ADI) research programme. In view of the companion paper on naval interactions, it touches only peripherally on naval force postures as they relate to the Arctic. The paper is intended to outline the military developments which may affect the prospects for arms control in the Arctic.

Missile Defences

When the Strategic Defense Initiative Organization was formed in the United States in 1984, various Ballistic Missile Defence (BMD) technologies were identified for further exploration. The variety of possibilities invited debate about possible deployment and basing modes in the Far North, and, as a consequence, there was considerable apprehension that the Arctic – perhaps especially the Canadian Arctic – might become the forward base for Star Wars operations. In a geostrategic sense, this concern is warranted. If ballistic missiles are fired, their trajectories will cross the polar region, and efforts to intercept them along the course of these trajectories seem more likely than not to involve the northern territories over which they will pass. Without considering the characteristics of any particular system, therefore, it is plausible to argue, as some defence specialists have done, that sooner or later a BMD system will involve northern deployments and, in the case of Canada, possible bases or communications facilities.

At the same time, it is instructive to look back to gain perspective on the actual possibilities of deployments affecting the North. Several years ago there appeared to be a number of sensors and anti-ballistic missile (ABM) components under development which might have raised the issue of northern basing. The components included ground-based lasers and the space-based nuclear-pulsed X-ray laser.

In addition to these exotic weapons systems, two interceptors were also considered to be potentially relevant to northern deployment. Braduskill was designed as a collision-type interceptor which would fly alongside the target rather than rise to meet it head on. This implied that it would be based as far along the flight path as possible, thus giving it maximum time to position itself alongside the incoming intercontinental ballistic missile (ICBM) and effect the kill. ERIS – the Exo-atmospheric Re-entry Vehicle Interception System – is a missile equipped with a heat-seeking hit-to-kill non-nuclear warhead. It may be deployed either in space or on the ground, and because it uses relatively well proven technologies it continues to be favoured if there are early deployments of a limited missile defence. In principle, ground-based ERIS would benefit from a variety of forward basing options because this would increase the time available to attack the ICBM in its mid-course trajectory, thereby allowing more than one opportunity to effect the interception.[1]

Finally, the SDI programme included certain tracking systems which might have benefited from northern deployment. The Airborne Optical System (AOS) is an optical telescope employing long-wavelength infrared. For test purposes it is mounted on a Boeing 767 and will be tested against re-entry vehicles (RVs) flown into a designated test range. Its purpose is to track RVs in the mid-course phase and to relay information to ground-based radar centres for purposes of both mid-course and terminal defence. If the AOS became a part of a deployed ABM system, however, it would need to fly far to the north to track ICBMs on polar trajectories. In times of crisis, it might be assumed that northern basing facilities would be required to support maximum on-station surveillance. The logical complement to AOS is terminal imaging radar (TIR), designed as a long-range ground-based radar able to discriminate between decoys and targets and intended to provide target information to interceptor systems for terminal defence. Insofar as the terminal defence would be a point defence of missile sites or other high-value military assets, TIR appeared to be the system least likely to create pressures for northern deployment. Teal Ruby was a space-based infrared imaging experiment designed to test the feasibility of imaging very small objects close to the earth's surface. Originally intended to test capabilities against cruise missiles, Teal Ruby was absorbed into the SDI programme. Canada supported the programme and had undertaken to provide chase aircraft as part of the Teal Ruby experiment.

From the vantage point of 1990, it is possible to look back and review the trends in the SDI programme. Predictably, technological developments have slowed or stopped some programmes. The X-ray laser has fallen from favour. Braduskill has been dropped. Progress on ground-based lasers has slowed as early optimism has faded and congressional budget restraints have taken hold. Unable to find a launch vehicle after the demise of the *Challenger,* the Teal Ruby spacecraft has been placed in storage, with little interest left in the experiment and some doubt that even the storage costs will be paid indefinitely. Since the Bush administration took office, a more cautious approach has been taken to the SDI programme even though the president has reaffirmed his support for the concept.

Although there can be little doubt that there will be further changes in the SDI programme, the outlines of the debate as described above suggest that it is now much easier to judge the implications of SDI for the Arctic than it was five years ago. First, for the balance of this century the probability is that research on exotic technologies will continue, with some possibility that the ABM Treaty will be threatened by the mid-1990s, but also with the prospect that accommodations will be made with the Soviet Union which will permit certain kinds of testing within the terms of the treaty.[2] For the United States, the more distant the prospects of significant breakthroughs in BMD technologies, the more reason there will be to comply with the treaty.

Second, by the mid-1990s there may be a single-site accidental launch protection system which will be compatible with the treaty and possibly a forerunner to a wider but still limited BMD system. Using relatively well developed technologies, the point defence would probably be based entirely in the United States.

Third, the most optimistic view of SDI proponents is that a Phase I defence, consisting of swarms of small space-based interceptors and the ERIS ground-based interceptor system, could be deployed by 1996-8 at a cost of between $US50 and $US60 billion. If deployed, there is little doubt that such a system would intensify military activity in the Arctic because both the surveillance and the interceptors would benefit from forward basing. In the current Washington environment of budgetary constraints, however, there is little evidence of support for an early Phase I deployment, while in Geneva the two sides have agreed to proceed with START by delinking the controversial question of ballistic missile defences from offensive force reductions.

In sum, fears that SDI would trigger an acceleration of military activity in and over the Arctic have not been realized. On balance, it seems likely that this will be true for the remainder of the decade. Paradoxically, however, strategic arms control negotiations, far from limiting military activity, may well intensify it as far as the Arctic is concerned.

START and Cruise Missiles

At the December 1987 superpower summit, Presidents Reagan and Gorbachev issued a communiqué reporting on agreements reached in principle in the START negotiations. Noting that the negotiators had been able to develop a joint draft treaty text identifying points of both agreement and disagreement, the communiqué listed an agreed framework which has been the basis of subsequent negotiations. The agreements included:
- ceilings of no more than 1,600 strategic offensive delivery systems
- no more than 6,000 warheads on these 1,600 delivery systems
- a sub-limit of 4,900 on the aggregate number of ICBM and submarine-launched ballistic missile (SLBM) warheads within the 6,000 total
- a sub-limit of 154 "heavy" missiles to carry not more than 1,540 warheads
- a limit on the total throw-weight of these delivery vehicles such that, after the prescribed reductions, the aggregate throw-weight of Soviet ICBMs and SLBMs will be approximately 50 per cent less than current Soviet levels, with the new limit not to be exceeded by either side thereafter.

However, the communiqué alluded to, but passed rather lightly over, significant disagreements between the two sides. In regard to ballistic missiles, there was a continuing disagreement over mobile missiles. The United States would prefer to ban them whereas the Soviet Union has already deployed two new types of mobile missile – the single-warhead SS-25 and the ten-warhead SS-24 – which are designed to reduce the vulnerability of their large, fixed land-based ICBMs. Although not apparently relevant to the concerns of non-superpower Arctic states, mobile missiles interact with bombers insofar as they may become the rationale for larger bomber forces. The mission of the B-2 stealth bomber in this regard is discussed below.

Although spokesmen for both sides refer to the START formula as a 50-per-cent reduction in strategic nuclear delivery vehicles, the proposals regarding manned bombers and sea-launched cruise missiles (SLCMs) suggest that the cuts would be far less deep than implied. Furthermore, because the permissive elements in the proposed START formula centre on manned bombers and cruise missiles, the force structures that result from a START agreement may accentuate rather than diminish military activity in the Arctic region.

Because manned bombers equipped with gravity bombs and short-range attack missiles (SRAMs) count as one in both the warhead total and the delivery system total, both sides left themselves with the opportunity to add greatly to their warhead total. One hundred manned bombers each loaded with twenty bombs and SRAMs, for example, would add 1,900 strategic nuclear charges to the strategic inventory over the 6,000 "ceiling." The United States has plans to build over 1,600 SRAM IIs, none of which are accountable weapons in the START context.

The number of air-launched cruise missiles (ALCMs) "attributed" to an ALCM-carrying bomber is also likely to understate significantly the actual numbers that could be carried. The initial American position in START was to attribute 6 ALCMs to each bomber, sometimes modified to "6 to 8." However, the B-52 carries 12 and can be fitted to carry 20, while the B-1B has a larger payload than the B-52 and is able to operate with 24 ALCMs. The Soviet Union has argued that the United States chose a number which conformed to the standard Soviet payload, thereby allowing itself considerably greater flexibility, and countered by suggesting that each type of heavy bomber should be identified *together with* its cruise missile payload. Most recently, informal accounts report that an agreement has been reached to count American bombers with 10 ALCMs and Soviet bombers with 8. In effect, therefore, both sides would understate their ALCM capabilities.

The importance of this dispute is readily understood when placed within the context of the constraints imposed by the 6,000-warhead ceiling. With a sub-ceiling of 4,900 on ballistic missile warheads, there is an implied ceiling of 1,100 on ALCMs. Of these, 100 might be taken up by the residual force of heavy bombers without ALCMs, with each counting as one delivery vehicle and one warhead. With a nominal counting rule of 10 ALCMs per bomber, the United States could then deploy 100 declared ALCM carriers counting for 1,000 warheads under START, but with a capability to carry 2,000.

Statements emerging from the negotiations suggest that there would be no obligation to restrict the actual payload of ALCMs. First, there is little chance of verifying such an agreement; peacetime checks would be meaningless because nuclear bombers do not normally carry a full payload on training flights. Second, in public statements United States defence officials made it clear that, in their view, it was reasonable to "discount" ALCMs because, unlike ICBMs, they could not be used in a disarming first strike and consequently contributed to stability. Larger numbers, therefore, could be tolerated. In 1988 the United States delegation issued a statement on the remaining START issues which confirmed this view and asserted that the number of ALCMs counted in START would be determined by the number of nuclear cruise-missile-carrying heavy bombers multiplied by the number of ALCMs attributed to each bomber.[3]

The Soviet Union has now clearly conceded considerable ground on this point. Insisting throughout the negotiations that the ALCM limit should be higher, they have also drawn attention to the large American reserve of heavy bombers which, if unconstrained, would provide the air force with greatly augmented nuclear capabilities. Insofar as the proposed formula also understates Soviet ALCM capabilities, however, it is apparent that a START agreement, if concluded on the basis described above, will give the Soviet Union a strong incentive to expand its heavy bomber and ALCM capabilities.

The December 1987 communiqué also noted an agreement in principle to place limits on long-range SLCMs, but outside the 6,000-warhead ceiling. In subsequent negotiations the two sides have remained far apart on this point. The Soviet Union pressed for a limit of 400 nuclear SLCMs on two designated types of submarine, later adding one type of surface ship. The United States appeared reluctant to offer a ceiling for nuclear SLCMs. It continued to maintain that there was no effective means of verifying any such quota, a problem compounded by the need to distinguish conventional from nuclear SLCMs. The United States navy, for example, plans to deploy between 3,000 and 4,000 SLCMs, of which about 800 would be nuclear-armed. Although the Soviet Union has offered a number of possibilities for distinguishing conventional from nuclear SLCMs, including a joint experiment to test the practicality of distinguishing a ship with nuclear SLCMs from a neighbouring ship carrying conventional SLCMs, without on-board inspection, the United States navy remained unconvinced. In early 1990 it was still not evident that the two sides had moved closer to a solution to the verification problem.[4] If a quota of around 800 SLCMs were assumed, however, the combination of SLCMs and non-accountable bomber-delivered weapons would move the actual total of strategic weapons well above 9,000 rather than the 6,000 agreed in the negotiations.

In contrast to the treaty on intermediate-range nuclear forces, which banned a complete range of weapon types, the respective START proposals, with the exception of the American suggestion that mobile missiles be banned, permit all existing strategic delivery systems and allow both sides to modernize or replace weapons within the ceilings imposed by the agreement. Spokesmen for the United States have cited the difficulties experienced in earlier negotiations as grounds for deciding not to address the issue of modernization. The Soviet Union does not appear to have commented on this issue. This scheme permits the Soviet Union to continue the development of the SS-X-26 and SS-X-27 ICBMs, the SS-NX-24 SLCM, the Blackjack bomber, the AS-X-16 SRAM, and an advanced cruise missile reported to be in the development stage. The United States will be permitted to develop the rail-mobile MX (assuming Washington is not confounded by its own proposal for a ban on mobile missiles), the Midgetman ICBM, the Trident D-5 SLBM, the B-2 stealth bomber, the advanced cruise missile, and the SRAM II. Both sides will be entitled to develop new warheads for these systems.[5]

This list of strategic weapons systems under development or in the early stages of deployment indicates that, with or without START, both sides are in the process of restructuring their strategic forces and that many of the ballistic missiles and bombers to be given up under a START regime were in any case scheduled for retirement in the five to seven years that it will take to implement an agreement. Nevertheless, the ceilings on delivery vehicles pose certain problems for modernization, particularly in the case of the United States. Essentially, with multi-warhead missiles the ceiling of 6,000 is reached earlier than the ceiling of 1,600 delivery vehicles. To maximize deployments under both ceilings, it is necessary to deploy a considerable number of missiles with one or few warheads. The Soviet Union will be able to do this as long as it continues to deploy the mobile, single-warhead SS-25. The Bush administration has chosen to avoid a final decision on the single-warhead Midgetman, seeking funds for further development but not, at the present time, for deployment. It seems likely, however, that in the last analysis the administration will be forced to acquire either the Midgetman or a modernized version of the Minuteman with two warheads. In either event, the mix of modernized forces seems likely to be a subject of continuing debate within the United States administration.[6]

On the basis of these observations, it is possible to draw out the probable consequences of a START agreement for military activity in the Arctic. In sum, the plausible force structures emphasize that while START would constrain both ICBMs and SLBMs, if the two sides chose to develop the bomber and cruise missile forces currently permitted under the agreement, the real inventory of strategic delivery vehicles on both sides would be closer to 9,000 warheads than to the ceiling of 6,000 identified in the START agreement. The increase would result from non-accountable gravity bombs, nuclear SLCMs, and non-accounted nuclear ALCMs.

Bombers and cruise missiles, therefore, would assume a much greater importance in the nuclear arsenals of the great powers. Of a probable 9,000 deployed warheads, for example, approximately 4,000 would be delivered by bombers and cruise missiles. The likely consequence of this, as is already apparent, will be a greater emphasis on air defences. Because the increasing range of cruise missiles permits the launch platform – either a bomber or an attack submarine – to launch its missiles at much longer ranges, it is apparent that air defences will seek to engage opposing forces at much greater ranges and to attack the more easily detectable bomber before it releases its cruise missiles. In both cases, the consequence would be to extend the combat zone as far north as possible.

Air Defences and ADI

It is sometimes forgotten that both the United States (including Canada for these purposes) and the Soviet Union have extensive experience with deployed air defences. In the case of the Soviet Union, heavy air defences were deployed in the 1950s to meet the threat of American (and other) strategic air attacks, and these were maintained and modernized even after the main strategic threat from the United States took the form of ballistic missiles.

The United States and Canada also deployed heavy air defence after 1955, believing that the Soviet Bear and Bison bombers were the main strategic threat from the Soviet Union. In responding to this threat, the United States first sought early warning to permit its retaliatory forces to leave their bases prior to attack. In addition, under their partnership in the North American Air Defence (NORAD) arrangement, Canada and the United States deployed large numbers of fighters in an attempt to defend against incoming bombers. Then as now, successful defence required the earliest possible interception of the incoming bombers, meaning that in principle the combat zone should be as far to the north as possible. In the 1950s and 1960s, however, there were practical constraints to such an extension northward because the radars deployed for early warning – the Pinetree Line and the Distant Early Warning (DEW) Line – did not have a capability to track incoming aircraft and therefore could not guide interceptors to their targets.[7]

After 1963, NORAD progressively abandoned the effort to shoot down a mass bomber attack and settled instead for early warning, peacetime surveillance, and the ability to intercept stray incursions into North American airspace. And for the most part that situation has persisted to the present. The North Warning System (NWS), for example, is essentially a modernization of the DEW Line rather than a response to perceived future threats. Although it may have improved capabilities against objects as small as cruise missiles, it is best suited for improved detection of bombers and has a modest capability to track such objects through the radar envelope.

Nevertheless, the very existence of Soviet ALCMs carried on new Bear-H bombers is inducing NORAD to attempt interceptions farther and farther to the north. There appears to be a clear pattern of Soviet training flights with cruise missiles. In the recent past Bear-H bombers have flown between Greenland and Iceland to the tip of Newfoundland, to the Aleutian Islands off Alaska, and to the Beaufort Sea, each of which would provide a "window" for the release of cruise missiles. In response, NORAD fighters have attempted to prosecute the bombers outside the cruise missile window: in one publicized case, for example, American F-15s with tanker support intercepted Bear-Hs 2,500 kilometres north of Elmensdorf in Alaska. The over-the-horizon backscatter (OTH-B) radar in Maine permits detection at similar distances so that incoming Bear-Hs can be tracked before they reach Iceland.

Although there have not been comparable public accounts of United States cruise missile windows or launch points into the Soviet Union, there can be no doubt that Soviet air defences face an equal or greater challenge, with a similar need to reach out to detect and track American bombers at the farthest practical point. For example, in May 1988 the United States air force released information about the B-2, the advanced technology bomber whose stealth characteristics make it almost invisible to currently deployed Soviet radars. The B-2 is subsonic, with a top speed of 750 miles per hour, and a range of 7,500 miles. Its missions may include flying deep into the Soviet Union to search out mobile missile bases, command centres, and other elusive targets. In the event of a nuclear war, the Strategic Air Command (SAC) envisages an integrated bomber attack on the Soviet Union: the oldest aircraft, the B-52s, would fly towards the Soviet Union and, from a stand-off launch position, release cruise missiles aimed at Soviet airfields and radars; the stealth bombers would penetrate and launch a combination of SRAM IIs and gravity bombs at withheld Soviet ICBMs and command centres; and the B-1Bs would then attack in a third wave, aiming for military installations, production facilities, and, if required, population centres. The SAC concept for the use of strategic bombers appears to be based on the view that a strategic nuclear exchange might take place over a number of days or even weeks.[8]

In the case of NORAD, neither current nor planned radars can guarantee tracking of the cruise missile itself, and, once launched, the cruise missile is a very difficult target for current-generation aircraft. The Air Defense Initiative, therefore, is intended to address both the tracking and interception of current- and future-generation cruise missiles.

In regard to surveillance systems, three programmes are worthy of note. First, initial ADI programmes have placed considerable emphasis on a follow-on to the current-generation airborne warning and control system (AWACS). A future AWACS will have multiple sensors able to detect and track cruise missiles and a much greater airborne endurance capability. Gliders and airships are two of the platforms being investigated to provide the required endurance. It is evident that such surveillance systems would fly far to the north and require northern base facilities to permit their optimal use. In the case of NORAD, however, it is possible that base facilities would be provided entirely from Alaska unless other allied states chose to enter into agreements to permit basing facilities.

Second, the United States navy is an important participant in the ADI programme. From a northern perspective, the navy is not apparently concerned about Soviet submarine-launched SLCMs from distant Arctic waters but is taken with coastal detection of close-in Soviet SLCM-firing submarines. The minimum requirement, paralleling that in the air defence field, is to be able to identify the launch platform and to locate the point of launch if SLCMs are fired. The navy component in ADI focuses mainly on shallow-water anti-submarine warfare (ASW), with experimental nets of active sonars high on the agenda. It is possible as well that acoustic detection of low-flying cruise missiles may become an element in ADI research. It is apparent, therefore, that interception of SLCMs fired from coastal waters is a distant second in present naval concerns as expressed in the ADI programme: the first and essential requirement is to restore early warning of attack and to provide high-confidence threat assessment. Nuclear SLCMs, in other words, raise the spectre of surprise attack on key military installations in a far more serious way than do ALCMs fired from the Far North.

Third, ADI research proposes to examine new concepts for both short- and long-range unmanned interceptors. In this regard the programme reveals the continuing tension between the attempt to upgrade current forces, as for example in the replacement of older interceptors by F-15s, and the attempt to respond to what increasingly appears as an entirely new atmospheric threat in the mid-1990s. It is not immediately apparent what basing modes might be appropriate for a future generation of unmanned interceptors.

Finally, this brief review of the ADI programme may direct attention to some important aspects of its relationship to SDI. Unlike SDI, whose annual budgets are between US$4 and US$5 billion, ADI budgets are very small. In FY 1988, for example, the ADI budget was $50 million and in FY 1989 it appears to be around $200 million.[9] Nevertheless, ADI may have the greater staying power. In contrast to the uncertainties and shifts of policy over SDI described earlier, the cruise missile challenge to the fundamental requirement of retaliatory nuclear forces – the need for early warning and threat assessment – seems certain to command the continuing interests of United States planners. ADI was begun as a complementary programme to SDI and was intended to produce solutions to the cruise missile problem in the same mid-1990s time-frame that might see the deployment of SDI. But even without SDI, ADI seems likely to continue. As such, it will continue to draw attention to the importance of the Arctic as a key to the detection, tracking, and possible interception of cruise missile carriers, but, as the analysis suggests, the exact nature of future military deployments in the North remains problematic.

Some Specific Canadian Concerns

First, analysis of the main themes in ADI suggests that, on the part of the United States, the prospect of Soviet SLCM-carrying attack submarines patrolling in Canadian Arctic waters and holding at risk important strategic assets is not a major concern – certainly not by comparison with the threat posed by SLCM-carrying submarines in coastal waters. This tends to confirm previous analyses which have suggested that there are few attractive SLCM-firing positions on the Canadian Arctic coast or in the waters of the Canadian Arctic Archipelago.[10] The corollary may be again to cast doubt on the prospect that the Northwest Passage will become a route for Soviet submarines, either in transit to the Labrador Sea or as a patrol area. This analysis would change, however, if future generations of Soviet SLCMs were to have greatly increased range because this would increase the potential for distant patrol areas.

Second, Canada has committed itself to participate in American research on a space-based radar (SBR) and in ADI. Interestingly, SBR does not appear to figure prominently in the ADI programme. United States officials appear sceptical that the funds can be found for a radar which will require a massive initial investment and which faces continuing uncertainty about its capabilities until a demonstration model can be lifted into space. Conversely, ADI programmes involving a shift of emphasis to coastal ASW may be more compatible with Canadian naval policy, given the cancellation of the decision to acquire nuclear-powered submarines. In this context, it is noteworthy that little mention is now made of the single low-cost purchase on which all Canadian commentators seemed once agreed – a passive acoustic system in the Northwest Passage to detect submarine transits of the passage.[11]

Third, the decision to permit the United States to test the advanced cruise missile in the Canadian north may also have long-term implications. Although the advanced cruise has been described as merely a refinement of the ALCM, its significantly greater range indicates the trend of future cruise missile developments and reinforces the view that as the launch point for ALCMs moves farther to the north, so will the attempt to defend against the bomber before it reaches the release point.

Conclusion

In assessing the impact on the Arctic of past and present developments in ballistic missile defences, cruise missile technologies, and air defences, it seems evident that the element of uncertainty must figure prominently in any net assessment. With few exceptions, exotic technologies appear to have very short half-lives, and all too frequently enthusiasts mistakenly shorten the lead time from the scientist's vision to military reality. Nevertheless, this paper has argued that certain trends in strategic force developments are discernible. While their impact on the Arctic region cannot be precisely foreseen, these trends are sufficiently clear to direct attention to areas of concern for those who are interested in a broad approach to Arctic development.

First, the future of SDI is so uncertain that little more than a watching brief is in order. Although there are general reasons to suppose that the Arctic would be an area of confrontation in a strategic defence contest, there are few specific systems within sight which pose immediate questions regarding Arctic deployments. Moreover, it now appears possible to identify a strategic defence time-frame with some confidence: limited United States deployments, beginning with a single-point defence, are possible, but only just so, by the year 2000. Further developments, if any, will await the next century.

Second, paradoxically, success in the START negotiations will greatly increase the significance of the Arctic in the strategic confrontation. Evolving cruise missile technologies are not, like so many SDI technologies, still in the laboratory: they are now a vital element in strategic force structures, and follow-on ALCMs and SLCMs are already well advanced. As the ADI programme acknowledges, the air-breathing threat raises fundamental challenges to the basic strategic requirement for early warning and threat assessment. Both offensively and defensively, therefore, the force structures under negotiation in START will draw attention to northern military developments.

Third, the current situation may nevertheless offer an opportunity to inject into the superpower discourse specific proposals concerning the military future of the Arctic region. The uncertainty in the SDI programme may be seen as a respite from technologically driven programmes. The force structures that will result from a START agreement will not materialize until the mid- to late 1990s. In the meantime, the United States has invited the Soviet Union to suggest the agenda for a follow-on negotiation. It is not implausible to suggest that Canada, perhaps in conjunction with other non-nuclear Arctic states, might seize the opportunity to place Arctic arms control issues on the superpower agenda.

Notes

1 The possibilities for northern deployment of SDI systems were explored in John Pike, "The Technology of the Strategic Defense Initiative," in Dianne DeMille, ed, *Challenges to Deterrence: Doctrines, Technologies and Public Concerns* (Ottawa: Canadian Institute for International Peace and Security 1986).

2 See *Washington Post*, April 25, 1988; *New York Times*, May 21, 1988.

3 For a recent explanation of the agreement on counting ALCMs, see the *Washington Post*, February 13, 1990.

4 Soviet proposals for verifying nuclear SLCMs without boarding naval vessels are described in the *New York Times*, March 4, 1988.

5 For a discussion of the impact of modernization, see R.S. Norris, W.M. Arkin, and T.B. Cochran, "START and Strategic Modernization," Natural Resources Defense Council, Working Paper NWD 87-2, December 1987.

6 An assessment of the survivability and retaliatory capabilities of each side in a post-START environment can be found in S.A. Hildreth, Al Tinajero, and Amy Woolf, "START: A Current Assessment of U.S. and Soviet Positions," Congressional Research Service Report 88-400f, June 1988.

7 These issues are surveyed in David Cox, *Trends in Continental Defence: A Canadian Perspective* (Ottawa: Canadian Institute for International Peace and Security, December 1986).

8 For the comments of the air force chief of staff, Larry Welch, on the B-2 and its relationship to the START negotiations, see *New York Times,* July 27, 1989.

9 The ADI budget is outlined in Secretary of Defense Frank C. Carlucci, *FY 1989 Annual Report to Congress,* February 1988, 240.

10 See Peter Haydon, "The Strategic Importance of the Arctic: Understanding the Military Issues," Strategic Issue Paper 1/87 (Ottawa: Department of National Defence 1987).

11 The Defence white paper promised to deploy fixed sonar systems in the Canadian Arctic: *Challenge and Commitment: A Defence Policy for Canada* (Ottawa: National Defence/Supply and Services Canada 1987), 51.

17

Militarization and Confidence-Building Measures in the Arctic

John Kristen Skogan

This century has witnessed the extension of military activity and rivalry into most of the Arctic region. At the start of the century the Arctic remained largely outside the realm of military operations and interests. Today important military forces operate in the Arctic and parts of the region have become central in some respects to military strategy. The shielding effect of remoteness and climate has been substantially eroded. Lately, however, and probably as a reflection of the recent thaw in East-West relations, military activity in the Arctic has become subject to the current interest in confidence-building measures.

Militarization

The militarization of the Arctic has taken place gradually, starting in the European part of the region where it continues to be the most intensive. Basically, this process has been brought about by improvements in technology. These improvements both extended the effective range of military forces, and their weapons systems, and made it possible to overcome or bypass some of the climatic obstacles to operations in the Far North. This opening of the Arctic to military activity made the region increasingly pertinent to strategic considerations and provided new options which regionally potent powers could not safely ignore and leave to their opponents to explore.

The militarization of the Arctic does not reflect territorial or other kinds of disputes indigenous to the region. As yet, such disputes have not fuelled the process to any notable degree. Rather, it is largely the result of rivalry and conflicts originating outside the region and carried into it by the improved capabilities of military forces and through the operational potentials and requirements of new weapons systems. This may affect the attitudes of people living in the region, making militarization appear to be a plague brought upon them from outside.

During World War I the military relevance of the European Far North became apparent in two ways, and especially to the Russians. The shipment of military supplies from their western allies to the ports of Murmansk and Archangel demonstrated the importance to Russia of its northwesternmost territories and their adjacent waters as a gateway protecting it from being cut off from the west in a war along its western land frontiers in Europe.[1] However, Anglo-French troops who arrived after the separate German-Russian peace treaty, with the purported goal of protecting supplies stored at both ports, subsequently became active supporters of the White counter-revolutionary forces in the area, thereby also illustrating the region's vulnerability to offensive flanking operations from the west.

Several events in World War II served to drive home the military significance of the Soviet White Sea area and the Arctic part of Scandinavia as well as their adjacent waters. Shortly after the outbreak of the war, plans emerged on both the French and British sides for obstructing the transport of supplies of iron ore from the north of Sweden to Germany. As a supplement to this the French proposed landing troops at the Finnish port of Petsamo (now Soviet Pechenga) on the Kola Peninsula in order to assist the Finns in their Winter War against the Soviet Union and, in the process, possibly also complicate German planning. Although the Petsamo part of the plans was dropped, it demonstrated that for powers with no access to the borders of the Soviet Union in eastern Europe, the more exposed Arctic area offered an alternative possibility for making inroads directly on Soviet territory.

After the change in relations between Britain and the Soviet Union following the German attack on the latter, the other dimension of the Soviet northwest's gateway position and the importance of the adjacent northern waterways was made more visible by the Murmansk convoys, once more bringing military supplies from the west to Russia. The heavy losses inflicted by German naval and air attacks out of northern Norway, aiming at – and for a period succeeding in – stopping these convoys also testified to the strategic location of Norway's Arctic territory relative to naval operations in northern European waters. Although unsuccessful, the German campaign for the conquest of Murmansk furthered the full integration of the Fenno-Scandinavian Arctic into war operations.

The range of Arctic operations was also extended westwards. In order to slip more safely into the Atlantic to attack the transatlantic convoys,

German warships on several occasions used the route north of Iceland and out through Denmark Strait. On the basis of an agreement with the local government, the United States, though still neutral, assumed responsibility for the defence of Greenland in the early spring of 1941 – thereby bringing to an end British-Canadian deliberations over the possible undertaking of a joint protective occupation of the island. By invitation, American troops were also stationed in Iceland, replacing the less popular British and Canadian soldiers who had arrived there uninvited in May 1940. Several airfields were constructed in Greenland, and these, in addition to that at Keflavik in Iceland, became important both for the protection of Atlantic convoys and for the ferrying of new aircraft from the United States and Canada to Europe. German attempts to establish observation posts on Greenland's eastern coast were repelled.

After World War II a nuclear dimension was added to the military significance of the Arctic. This aspect of militarization gradually came to have an impact on most of the region. Offering the shortest distance to principal targets for strategic nuclear attack, Arctic air routes became, and remain, attractive to long-range bombers. Accordingly, training flights over Arctic areas became normal practice. On the North American side a string of Distant Early Warning radar stations – the DEW Line – stretching from the Aleutians over Arctic Canada to the eastern coast of Greenland was set up in the 1950s for defence against incoming bombers from the north. In addition, American fighter aircraft were stationed at the newly completed Thule airfield in northern Greenland, both to provide defence against Soviet bombers and to protect the airfield as a possible staging base for American long-range bombers.

The advent of intercontinental ballistic missiles (ICBMs) meant that trajectories directed at a large number of important targets would cross the Arctic. Although no active defence, barring pre-emption, was available against such missiles, the possibility of passive defensive measures, as well as the likely deterrent effect of retaliation, made early warning appear mandatory. This prompted the construction of a Ballistic Missile Early Warning System (BMEWS) station at Thule, operating in conjunction with similar radar stations at Clear in Alaska and Fylingdales Moor in Britain.

The deployment of securely protected second-strike forces and the subsequent American shift to a nuclear strategy based on the concept of mutual capabilities for assured destruction (MAD) made early warning somewhat less critical, though still desirable, and in particular made active defence against strategic attack, whether from ICBMs or by bombers, appear less urgent. Security was now based on the deterrent effect of the capacity under any circumstances to inflict unacceptable damage in retaliation for a strategic nuclear attack. This strategy had a dampening effect on strategic interest in the Arctic. During the 1960s the number of DEW Line stations in the North was radically reduced. And in order to secure this retaliatory capability the Anti-Ballistic Missile Treaty of 1972 prohibited systems for active defence against strategic ballistic missiles. Defence capabilities of this kind might otherwise have produced considerable interest in the Arctic as a location for the construction of detection elements.

In another respect, however, strategic interests and military involvement were on the increase in the European part of the Arctic because of the operational requirements of early Soviet ballistic-missile-carrying submarines. The need to reach waters adjacent to the coast of the continental United States in order to be within range of their targets made safe access to the open seas imperative. However, the narrowness of the straits at the exits of the Baltic and Black seas restricts such egress for Soviet naval vessels to European Arctic waters and those along parts of the Soviet Pacific coast. Reflecting this situation, and possibly also the location of important targets close to the eastern seaboard of the United States, most of the rapidly growing number of Soviet ballistic missile submarines were allocated to naval bases at the Kola Peninsula throughout the 1960s and during the early 1970s. This made the area strategically more significant than ever before to the Soviet Union.

These important submarines, moreover, required protection, both by attack submarines and by surface combatants. This, no doubt, at least partly explains the sharp concurrent increase in the number of such vessels stationed at Kola Peninsula ports. As a result, by the end of the 1960s the Northern Fleet, once the Soviet navy's smallest, had become the largest of its four fleets in terms of submarines and ocean-going surface combatants. It continues to be the largest as well as the most important in strategic terms of all the Soviet fleets. Some 70 per cent of the Soviet submarine-deployed ballistic missile warheads are found on Northern Fleet strategic submarines; today most carry long-range missiles which can reach any target in the United States from European Arctic waters.[2]

Thus, the western part of the Soviet Arctic mainland has become the location of the largest Soviet naval base complex. (It is in fact also the world's largest.) Naturally, this has added to the military significance of that area and to the importance of the open waters next to it – and not only in terms of nuclear strategy. The apparent need to protect the Northern Fleet's ballistic missile submarines does not appear to have been the only motive behind its general augmentation. To some extent the northern Soviet naval build-up is the result of a shift of vessels, especially submarines, from the Baltic to the North. When in the Baltic, these vessels were charged with traditional naval missions and, in the case of some of the long-range submarines, probably naval interdiction beyond the Baltic as well. Today, the relatively few submarines remaining in the Baltic Fleet are hardly fit for such a mission. Yet it would be surprising if this had ceased to be an objective of the Soviet navy. It is far more likely that these and other traditional naval missions are currently assigned to vessels in the Northern Fleet.

In fact, even if the idea of using units of their Northern Fleet for traditional naval objectives such as sea control or sea denial, and in areas well beyond the Barents Sea, might not yet – however unlikely that may be – have crossed the mind of Soviet admirals, it may nonetheless emerge at some later point. The motives of yesterday, as well as today's designs, neither foretell nor constrict the aims of tomorrow, as long as the latter do not exceed capabilities. In any case, the Soviet Northern Fleet, impressive in numbers of ocean-going vessels, is available for whatever purpose might seem fit and is probably sufficient in strength for its masters to conceive (if they do not already cherish) the idea of its use for more than the protection of ballistic-missile-carrying submarines.

The strength and the location of the Northern Fleet, as well as the pattern of its exercises over an extended period of years, has raised questions in the North Atlantic Treaty Organization (NATO) with respect to the ability of the alliance to achieve undisputed sea control in the Norwegian Sea and the North Atlantic. This has also caused concern for the safety of Western sea lanes of communication (SLOC) in these waters. Some have claimed that even if a war cannot be won in the Norwegian Sea, it could well be lost there.[3]

Reflecting such apprehensions, the United States Maritime Strategy of the 1980s has placed increased emphasis on preventing Soviet sea control and fighting Soviet attempts at sea denial in the Norwegian Sea. For this purpose it is envisaged that the operations of United States naval units will need to be extended, even into the Arctic part of the Norwegian Sea. In particular, the established practice of having American attack submarines pursue and threaten Soviet ballistic missile submarines, which are now increasingly patrolling Arctic waters only, is being stressed. The assumption is that this activity will tie down Soviet attack submarines for ballistic missile submarine protection, thereby precluding their use for other missions elsewhere. In this way the conduct of conventional naval operations outside the Arctic has become linked to the operations of strategic naval forces in Arctic waters, with the defensive requirements of the former being put forward as the reason for offensive conduct relative to the latter.

Over the last decade or so, and so far with respect to nuclear strategy, the military significance of other parts of the Arctic has also been on the increase. Recent trends in technology, in nuclear policy and arms reduction negotiations, and in weapons procurement seem to indicate an increase in the military significance of most of the Arctic region.[4]

At least since the early 1980s, and possibly prior to that, Soviet nuclear-powered ballistic missile submarines (SSBNs) have been patrolling the Polar Basin. Operating under the polar ice cap offers several advantages to Soviet SSBNs. They do not have to worry about hostile surface vessels; detection and attack from the air is difficult; the chances of hiding from other submarines are generally better than in open seas; and some of the offensive weapons (Subroc and the planned Sea Lance) on tracking United States attack submarines are not well suited for use under the ice. Moreover, the conditions for receiving very low frequency radio signals are good, and there are always openings in the floating ice through which the submarines can surface, as American, Soviet, and British submarines have proved.[5] The structural features of the new Soviet Typhoon SSBNs suggest that these huge submarines, 25,000 tons each, have been designed specifically for under-ice operations. So far all Typhoons, a total of five, each with 20 multiple-warhead-tipped missiles, have been commissioned to the Northern Fleet.

Soviet SSBNs utilizing the Polar Basin as their patrol area on a regular basis, thereby attracting United States attack submarines, will add to the strategic importance of the central Arctic. This importance may be enhanced if future strategic arms reductions, as proposed by the United States in the Strategic Arms Reduction Talks (START), put stricter numerical limitations on land-based ballistic missiles than on their less vulnerable counterparts carried on submarines. Nor should one exclude the possibility of American SSBNs entering the Polar Basin, though their access to these waters will be more cumbersome and interruptible.

As missile launches from Arctic waters are difficult to monitor from satellites in geosynchronous orbit above the equator, the expansion of SSBN operations into the central Arctic may call for enhanced warning capabilities. The Thule BMEWS radar is already being modernized, though possibly more in response to concerns about the vulnerability of United States land-based ballistic missiles and reduced confidence in pure dependence on MAD. The construction of new warning installations in the Far North may well be considered and in one respect is actually taking place, for the old DEW Line is currently being upgraded and expanded. Plans also exist for the strengthening of active defence over northern Canada.[6] This is probably a reaction to another emerging threat from the polar region: air-launched cruise missiles (ALCMs).

Although behind the United States in modern cruise missile technology, the Soviet Union, too, is developing new longer range sea-launched cruise missiles (SLCMs) and ALCMs. The deep cuts in ballistic missiles being envisaged in the START negotiations may reinforce American and Soviet interest in longer range cruise missiles. So far some 50 Soviet Bear bombers have been equipped with ALCMs of the new AS-15 type, having a reported range of 1600 kilometres or more. It is also likely that the new Soviet Blackjack long-range bomber will carry AS-15s. For these bombers polar air routes may appear attractive, promising a chance of delayed detection by enemy radars and allowing a stand-off missile launch over Canadian territory. Presumably the United States has a similar interest in exploiting air routes over the polar sea. Some 150 of its B-52 bombers are now equipped to carry the AGM-86B ALCM (with a range of 2400 kilometres).

The likely increase in cruise missile ranges will probably make the Arctic even more important. Nor should the future deployment of SLCM-carrying submarines in central Arctic waters be excluded. Extended missile ranges could make it possible to launch SLCMs as well as ALCMs from less exposed positions over, or in, the Polar Basin. Interest in the development of long-range cruise missiles may, moreover, be inspired by the anti-ballistic missile philosophy revealed at the Reykjavik summit, possibly reflecting a concern about ICBM vulnerability and first-strike temptations, and possibly an anti-MAD bias. American plans for defence against ballistic missiles, embodied in the Strategic Defense Initiative, may also give impetus to such developments – and not necessarily on the Soviet side alone.

In trying to look into the future, we should also be aware of the possible development of long-range cruise missiles for the highly accurate delivery of conventional explosives.[7] Such missiles might cause the extension of projected as well as actual conventional military activities from the European periphery of the Arctic right into its centre – perhaps even as an alternative to nuclear options and nuclear-oriented military doctrines.

Confidence-Building Measures

When assessing the prospects for militarily related confidence-building measures (CBMs) in the Arctic, it is important to keep in mind that militarization of the region is not accidental. It is *not* an infection or a disease that just happened to be brought into the area. It is a process and a situation which was brought about and is being maintained by inherent properties of the region itself, such as geography, bathymetry, and climatic and atmospheric conditions. In this sense militarization is not something artificial to the present Arctic. It is the manifestation of military interests reflecting the operational options offered by the region's own particular characteristics. Such options, and the resulting military significance of the region, are also inherent properties of it today. They are integral parts of the present Arctic reality. And like geography, they are inescapable, given the present state of world affairs and current technology. Conceptually viewing militarization as an "infection" not only carries the risk of trying to cure the symptoms of something which is unavoidable, but also opens the way to repression of symptoms which may merely divert the effects of their causes in even less comfortable directions.

Nor should we look upon the militarization of the Arctic as some "nuisance" thrust upon us for purposes which are of no concern to us. Here, as elsewhere in the world, militarization is the result of our employment of military means for ultimate aims which we generally endorse. One such aim is the prevention of the actual use of military means (that is, war) and another is the prevention of their use in ways and for ends which we fear because they may be detrimental to us. Most of us accept that proper preparations for the use of military means in order to achieve the latter aim may actually serve to fulfil both objectives. True, such defence preparations may also entail the risk of war, thus appearing contrary to the former aim. However, by denying the attainment of ends which might otherwise invite the actual use of military means, defence preparations may make such use appear pointless as well as dangerous. No defence preparations, or inadequate ones, may lead to a belief that the use of military means is neither dangerous nor pointless, thereby possibly causing the defeat of both aims.

At least some of the military interests relating to, and causing military activity in, the Arctic arise from concerns over options offered by geography and other features of the region. If left for one side to exploit unopposed, such options might be utilized in ways which would weaken the position of the other and impair its defence efforts. Indeed, if ignored by one side, such options might even tempt the other side, in certain circumstances, to consider actual use of military force in these remote, sparsely populated areas. If left for both sides to seize as the need arises, the possibilities of being able successfully to secure unilateral advantages by the use of military force may bring about a dangerous race for pre-emption in a crisis. Some of the military activities currently being carried out in the Arctic are aimed at precluding such possibilities. In addition, some of the militarization of the Arctic is the result of opportunities offered for military activity in the region which serve to support defence efforts elsewhere. This benefits the people living in the Arctic region as well. Militarization is not entirely disadvantageous and unwanted. It may, however, have unwanted and dangerous features as well as dimensions in excess of prudent requirements. Nevertheless, given present rivalry and disagreements on the world scene, the problem of militarization in the Arctic is not one of eradication. Rather, it is one of management, control, and possible regulation.

When considering the possibility of such regulation, we should note that, conceptually, isolating military activity in the Arctic from such activity outside the region defies reality. As both the history and the present pattern of military activity in the Arctic show, most of it has been, and still is, linked in some way or another to military arrangements and activities outside the region and to military interests beyond it. The effects of the regulation of military activity in the region may not, therefore, be exclusively confined to the region. Misgivings about such effects may generate external opposition to the idea of such regulation, limiting the scope for local regulation. However, as the security of the Arctic is to a large degree both inseparable from, and dependent on, the attainment of security outside the region, certain kinds of externally inflicted side-effects would also be to the detriment of the region itself. Anticipation of such repercussions may also limit the scope for regulations in terms of local acceptability.

The term "confidence-building measures" was first used to denote the measures of notification and observation of military forces and their exercises agreed upon at the Conference on Security and Co-operation in Europe (CSCE), held in Helsinki in 1975. The purpose of these measures was, and is, to prevent the creation of groundless fears as a result of normal peacetime military activities such as large exercises. The underlying idea was that prior notification of such exercises, and on-the-spot observation of their execution, would serve to remove the sense of surprise and reduce uncertainties about intent which occasionally arise from military exercises and which normally arouse undue suspicion. Improved predictability and transparency were to increase mutual confidence.

Today the definition of the term has been broadened to the point where it includes almost any arrangement of multilaterally agreed control and regulation of military forces and their activity. This is especially true with respect to the northern and Arctic areas. When applied to measures in these regions, the term is often simply a substitute for arms control, at least if the latter term is loosely defined as is generally the case today.

Throughout the postwar period several proposals have been made for arms control and restrictions on military activity in the Arctic and its rim areas.[8] As a matter of fact, in 1920 the Arctic islands of Svalbard, situated to the north of the Scandinavian peninsula, were the subject of one of the first multilaterally agreed measures of arms control. In the Svalbard ("Spitsbergen") Treaty of that year, the contracting parties, in order to ensure the "peaceful utilization" of the islands, stipulated that the establishment of any naval base or the construction of any fortification was not to be allowed on the islands and that the islands "may never be used for warlike purposes."[9] The treaty remains in force, its original text unchanged. However, in 1944 the Soviet foreign minister, in a meeting with the foreign minister of the Norwegian government-in-exile, demanded the annulment of the treaty and the cession of the southernmost of the Svalbard islands, Bear Island, to the Soviet Union. In arguing for this change, he pointed to the strategic importance to his country of the adjacent waterways as exemplified by the Murmansk convoys. In its reply to the Soviet demand, which was later turned down, the Norwegian government admitted that the war had shown that the effects of the military restrictions pertaining to the islands were unsatisfactory.[10] This incident should remind us that actual warfare may change the appreciation of arms control and confidence-building measures and that potential arms control measures should always be examined with respect to their effects in war or severe crisis situations.

Until recently, most of the postwar proposals for arms control and restrictions on military activity in northern and Arctic areas have been for nuclear-weapons-free zones (NWFZs) of various kinds.[11] Other proposals have included arrangements for mutual observation and the prohibition of certain kinds of military activity in certain areas.[12] A few unilaterally decreed restrictions have been effected in the North, such as Norway's self-imposed limitations which have barred the stationing of foreign troops in Norway as long as the country is not subject to attack or evident threat of attack and, since 1960, the stockpiling or deployment of nuclear weapons on its territory. Applying specifically to parts of Norway's Arctic border area with the Soviet Union is an additional set of self-imposed restrictions: no overflights by allied aircraft or visits by allied warships in territorial waters, and no military exercises with participation by allied forces.

In at least one case, different arms control measures proposed for the Arctic are conflicting. Proposals for making the central Arctic a nuclear-weapons-free zone are clearly incompatible with proposals for establishing the Polar Basin as a sanctuary area for ballistic-missile-carrying submarines (SSBN sanctuary) by banning by mutual agreement any anti-submarine warfare (ASW) activity in these waters.[13]

This case of incompatible proposed measures probably reflects a conflict between the philosophy of confidence-building and that of arms control strictly defined. At the heart of the former is the peacetime effect of arms arrangements on relations of political conflict. The aim is to reduce the risk of war and to improve relations by reducing the intensity of such conflict. The idea is that its intensity can be reduced by making arms arrangements subject to mutually agreed restrictions which serve to diminish expectations of armed conflict. The original philosophy of arms control, with its particular emphasis on crisis stability, is more concerned about the effects of arms arrangements on military calculations in the event of the impending danger of armed conflict and aims to reduce the incentives for resort to the actual use of military force by making it appear pointless, irrespective of the intensity of political conflict. Moreover, making resort to the actual use of arms appear pointless may not necessarily call for arms reductions, nor does arms control invariably do so.

From the latter perspective there is much to be said in favour of the idea of permitting the Polar Basin to become an SSBN sanctuary (and in the future possibly also a sanctuary for SLCM-carrying submarines) — provided the occurrence of East-West armed conflict cannot be totally ruled out. In the case of such conflict, or its imminence, the safety of ballistic-missile-carrying submarines would render impossible a successful first-strike attack to disarm the opponent strategically. This in turn would both effectively reduce any incentives for pre-emption out of fear of such attack and secure a second-strike capability which would act as a powerful deterrent to the resort to strategic nuclear arms for any purpose. Such a course would clearly serve crisis stability. It might also deter the use of any nuclear weapons.

The fact that even the most ardent local proponents of the idea of a

Nordic nuclear-weapons-free zone have generally refrained from including the Kola Peninsula and the Barents Sea in their proposals probably testifies to their acceptance of the arms control perspective underlying the idea of SSBN sanctuaries. Likewise, the generally accepted importance of an SSBN-based second-strike capability for strategic and crisis stability, and the presumably decisive interests of the Soviet Union in securing the operational needs of its SSBNs, may partly explain why some opponents of a Nordic NWFZ have made demands for reciprocal measures on the Kola Peninsula, even its full inclusion in the zone. Set against each other, interest in an NWFZ is expected to have to yield to the importance of an SSBN-based second-strike capability.

One problem with the idea of a Polar Basin SSBN sanctuary is partly a matter of verification and, with an eye to the future, partly one of emerging competition from non-nuclear utilization of the central Arctic. Another problem is that if such a sanctuary were to be established a great number of Soviet attack submarines now assigned to the protection of SSBNs might be available for other missions.[14] Both problems apply more or less to any sanctuary area for Soviet SSBNs and would be more severe if such a sanctuary were placed in parts of the Norwegian Sea or in the Barents Sea. Not only would attempts at verification encounter new difficulties because of the variety and level of naval activities in these waters, but an SSBN sanctuary in these waters might also turn into a convenient sanctuary for other combatants as well. At the very least, the suspicion of such use might arise.

Although numerous and in some cases of long standing, none of the proposals for northern or Arctic NWFZs have so far come close to being accepted for implementation. The growing military significance of the Arctic may not improve their chances, either. A particular problem with many of these proposals – one that tends to increase on closer examination – is the great number of ambiguities relating to them, especially with respect to scope and verification. This has certainly been the case with the proposal for a Nordic NWFZ.[15] In fact, the ambiguities are so many, and so difficult to resolve in this case, that one wonders whether an actual attempt by the parties concerned to agree on a final NWFZ treaty might not instead increase tensions between them. Moreover, in view of the intractability of these ambiguities, it is likely that even the successful negotiation of a Nordic NWFZ treaty would leave considerable room for, and thus invite, conflicting interpretations as well as charges and countercharges of treaty violations, thereby possibly producing a negative effect on the relations among the parties to the treaty.

The effects of NWFZs in the event of war or severe crisis, although rarely brought to the fore, also deserve particular attention, because some of the proposals for such zones do not really imply much of a change in peacetime. A Nordic NWFZ is a prime example.

The Nordic area proposed for a Fenno-Scandinavian zone is already free of nuclear weapons: in the case of Denmark, Norway, and Sweden because of unilateral declarations by their governments, and in the case of Finland because of a clause contained in its 1947 peace treaty with the Soviet Union. Depending on the stipulations of a Nordic NWFZ treaty, nuclear weapons on ships visiting the territorial waters of the zone countries might also be prohibited. Apart from that, nothing would change with respect to the absence of nuclear weapons in these territories. Accordingly, the value of a Nordic NWFZ ought to be judged in terms of its likely effects in case of war or a threat of war.

In practical terms, the positive guarantees (that is, promises not to allow deployment of nuclear weapons within the zone given by the prospective Nordic zone states) could hardly be more trustworthy in peacetime than their unilateral decisions already banning nuclear weapons on their territories. The negative guarantees (that is, pledges not to use nuclear weapons against targets in the zone given by states outside the zone) would be of interest only in a situation of war or imminent war. So, what would happen then if war were to occur or to appear imminent? Would the negative guarantees remain reliable and be upheld? What might the gains be from breaking them? Would it be possible to fulfil the positive guarantees entirely and without any compromise? What about the effect of suspicions to the contrary? To what extent might provisions of the treaty be swept away by necessities of war? What would be the effect on conventional defence if the treaty text were to prohibit the use of dual-purpose weapons carriers for non-nuclear purposes in the zone? Such questions seem to deserve closer examination – unless NWFZs are intended only for peacetime comfort.

Proposals for NWFZs in other parts of the Arctic might avoid some of the difficulties and ambiguities confronting a Nordic NWFZ. However, other difficulties could prove even more severe, and new stumbling blocks might also arise because other parts of the Arctic are not at present nuclear-weapons-free to the same extent as the non-Soviet Nordic area – or at least not with respect to nuclear weapons transits.

Recently, several new Soviet proposals have been made for restrictions on naval activity in waters adjacent to northern Europe, including Arctic waters. These proposals have been presented partly as an extension to the seas of the confidence-building measures agreed upon on land. The proposals, first presented by Mikhail Gorbachev in his Murmansk speech of October 1, 1987, were confined to northern European waters. Since then the proposals have been spelled out in more detail and expanded on some points by Prime Minister Nikolai Ryzhkov in a dinner speech given during an official visit to Norway in January 1988 and, subsequently, in a *Pravda* article of September 5, 1988, by Marshal Sergei Akhromeev, then chief of the Soviet General Staff.[16] According to the latter the Soviet Union is willing to consider such measures world-wide.

The proposals cover a whole range of different measures, including the establishment of SSBN sanctuaries. Most of the rest are newly proposed measures, although some have previously been suggested in less precise terms by others. Most aim to restrict the conduct of naval and air activities and limit the scale of such activities. The proposals include the banning of naval activity in international straits and in zones of intensive shipping or fisheries, prohibiting the entry of nuclear-weapons-carrying vessels into waters from which the territory of the opponent can be reached by such weapons, restricting the deployment of amphibious forces to reduce the danger of surprise attack from the sea, restricting the number and scale of major naval exercises in certain waters (one every second year in the Baltic-Norwegian-Barents Sea area according to Prime Minister Ryzhkov), pre-notification of such exercises,[17] and limiting by means of mutual understanding the competition in anti-submarine weapons. Additional measures proposed are the invitation of observers to major naval exercises, and mutual inspection of naval exercises.

Measures of the latter kind match well in some respects with the suggestion made by the Norwegian defence minister, Johan Jørgen Holst, for a multilateral agreement for the prevention of incidents at sea, covering the Norwegian Sea and modelled on the Soviet-American agreement of 1972.[18] In his foreign policy address of January 13, 1989, to the Norwegian parliament, the foreign minister, Thorvald Stoltenberg, took up this idea and stated that the government intended to begin work on an agreement to prevent incidents at sea and in the airspace over the seas. He also stated that the government is going to discuss with Norway's allies the possibilities of an East-West exchange of observers during major naval exercises. The practical value of measures of this kind, as well as the Holst plan, may be rather limited because of the existence of such agreements not only between the United States and the Soviet Union but also between the latter and Great Britain and West Germany, respectively.[19] However, their symbolic value should not be underrated in times of political détente.

This is also true of agreements on schemes for inspection and on rules for on-the-spot behaviour covering other parts of the Arctic.

With respect to the first category of measures proposed by the Soviet Union – restrictions and limitations – a particular problem of balance arises, especially from the perspective of countries next to the Soviet Union in the areas involved. Taking Norway as an example, it has never been an aim of this country to achieve a local military balance relative to the Soviet Union. On the contrary, because of their self-imposed restrictions the Norwegians have deprived themselves of the opportunity to reduce the existing local imbalance through the stationing of allied forces in their country. The idea underlying this decision was that this would help to reassure the Soviet Union and keep local tensions within bounds. Instead, Norway has sought to balance Soviet military power through provisions and preparations for the speedy arrival of allied reinforcements in times of war or severe crisis. Most of the measures for restrictions and limitations specified in the recent Soviet proposals would impair the "Norwegian" part of this equation more strongly than the Soviet part. The forces in place on Soviet territory in the area constitute the major element of the Soviet part of the equation. The Norwegian part is critically dependent on allied capabilities for bringing reinforcements to Norway if need be and on allied military training for this task so as to make the arrival of reinforcements a credible element of the equation.

When considering confidence-building, one should not forget that "confidence" in relations of potential conflict between nations is not only "mutual confidence" but also unilateral confidence in one's own ability to prevail in the event that political discord should erupt into armed conflict. A decline in the latter kind of confidence may, moreover, defeat improvement of the former kind of confidence as long as the possibility of armed coercion is not perceived to be totally eliminated.

Confidence-building in the Arctic by regulating military activity in the region does not appear an easy task. Maybe increased mutual confidence in the Far North might prove easier to achieve if less emphasis were to be placed on measures of military limitation and more on co-operation in other fields of common interest. In these fields we should try to avoid letting militarization stand in the way. By insisting on militarily related confidence-building measures, we risk doing exactly that.

Notes

1 Actually, the importance of the northwestern areas in this respect had been brought home to Russia some 250 to 350 years earlier when Turkey, Lithuania-Poland, and,

in particular, Sweden were actively trying to block trading between Russia and west European countries. As a counter to this, Tsar Ivan IV granted trade privileges for the port of Archangel in the White Sea to British merchants, organized as the Muscovy Company, to take advantage of the northern sea route around the Fenno-Scandinavian peninsula. Later, trade with Dutch, French, and Danish merchant vessels arriving at ports along the northern coast of the Kola Peninsula was promoted by Russia. The importance of the peninsula for the supply of commodities from the west to Russia was probably the main motivation behind several Swedish incursions on it during the period. Its importance in this respect was, however, greatly diminished at the beginning of the eighteenth century when Peter the Great defeated the Swedes and gained control of parts of the eastern Baltic coast. See Ivan P. Ushakov, *Kolskaya zemlya* (Murmansk 1971).

2 Since its peak in the mid-1970s, the percentage of ballistic-missile-carrying submarines in the Northern Fleet relative to the Soviet total has declined from close to 80 to some 50 per cent. During the 1980s, however, the Northern Fleet percentage of Soviet submarine-launched ballistic missile warheads – SLBM warheads – has, nevertheless, been increasing because a greater number of such warheads are carried on the newer submarines, most of which have been deployed with the Northern Fleet.

3 See, for instance, Robert G. Weinland, *Northern Waters: Their Strategic Significance* (Alexandria VA: Center for Naval Analyses 1980).

4 This has been noted by Oran R. Young, for one: see his article, "The Age of the Arctic," *Foreign Policy,* no 61 (winter 1985-6).

5 The idea of using the Polar Basin as a patrol area for nuclear-powered ballistic missile submarines was suggested in the 1960s by the Swedish naval captain, R. Thorén. See, for instance, R. Thorén, *Picture Atlas of the Arctic* (Amsterdam, London, New York: Elsevier 1969), 4-5. Later, Willy Østreng of the Fridtjof Nansen Institute in Oslo, in particular, advanced this idea: see Østreng, "The Strategic Balance and the Arctic Ocean: Soviet Options," *Cooperation and Conflict,* 12 (no 1, 1977), 41-62.

6 Oran R. Young, "Canada and the United States in the Arctic: Testing the 'Special Relationship'," *Northern Perspectives,* 15 (May-June 1987), 4.

7 See *Sources of Change in the Future Security Environment,* a paper by the Future Security Environment Group, submitted to the Commission on Integrated Long-Term Strategy (Washington: Pentagon, April 1988), 10. According to the commission, future Soviet-American military competition is likely to focus increasingly on non-nuclear weapons, and advanced conventional systems may come to replace nuclear weapons, even in the strategic force postures of the superpowers.

8 For a brief account of such proposals, see Ron Purver, "The Prospects for Arms Control in the Arctic," in R.B. Byers and Michael Slack, eds, *Strategy and the Arctic* (Toronto: Canadian Institute of Strategic Studies 1986).

9 See article 9 and the preamble of the Svalbard Treaty of February 9, 1920.

10 According to the Soviet minister, his country, which had not become a party to the treaty until 1935, had been opposed to it all the time. It seems, though, that the war had intensified Soviet disapproval of the treaty.

11 Proposals for northern NWFZs have centred, in particular, on the idea of a Nordic zone including the territories of Denmark, Norway, Sweden, and Finland. The idea was first advanced by the Soviet premier, Nikolai Bulganin, in 1958 and taken up by the Finnish president, Urho Kekkonen, in his proposal of 1963. In 1978 he repeated the proposal in a modified form. Once more the response from other Nordic governments was rather negative. However, in the autumn of 1980, Jens Evensen, who had been Norway's law of the sea minister and remained influential, came out in support of a Nordic NWFZ, possibly reflecting strong misgivings about NATO's 1979 "two-track" decision on intermediate-range nuclear forces and the planned pre-positioning of equipment in Norway for a United States amphibious brigade. After some internal strife in the governing Labour party, the prime minister, Odvar Nordli, lent his support to the idea, provided that a Nordic NWFZ were to be part of a broader European arrangement. The latter reservation was not welcomed by the truly enthusiastic Nordic supporters of the idea. Nevertheless, from now on, and promoted by new Soviet initiatives, the idea became a subject of discussion on the Nordic governmental level, leading to the establishment in 1987 of an intra-Nordic group of governmental experts to study the concept of a Nordic NWFZ. Some of the zealous proponents of such a zone fear, though, that this may turn out to prove once more the truth of the Devil's device for non-action on a proposal: put it to a committee!

12 The first postwar proposal for a multilateral arms control measure designed specifically for the Arctic was a Western proposal of 1957-8 for an Arctic aerial inspection zone modelled on the Eisenhower "open skies" proposal which had earlier been rejected by the Soviet Union as was this one. Proposals for restrictions on military activity in the Arctic include, among others, suggestions for total or partial demilitarization of parts of the region: see, for instance, Franklyn Griffiths (A Northern Foreign Policy, Wellesley Papers 7 [Toronto: Canadian Institute of International Affairs 1979]), on the prohibition of ballistic missile submarine patrols close to enemy territory (stand-off zones) and on banning anti-submarine warfare in certain waters with the objective of making these waters sanctuaries for ballistic missile submarines.

13 In the Arctic, the Barents Sea – along with the Sea of Okhotsk and the Gulf of Alaska just outside the Arctic – have also been mentioned as possible SSBN sanctuaries. The more recent suggestion of the Polar Basin as a suitable and politically more acceptable candidate was made in W. Østreng, "Strategic Developments in the Norwegian and Polar Seas: Problems of Denuclearization," Bulletin of Peace Proposals, 13 (1982), 108-11.

14 However, to a certain extent NATO will face this problem in any case. Even without the formal establishment of a Polar Basin SSBN sanctuary, Soviet SSBNs will need less protection from other vessels when operating under the polar ice cap. Consequently, the demand on Soviet attack submarines for SSBN protection will diminish as more Soviet SSBNs designed for under-ice operations are launched and these boats come to represent an increasing proportion of the total Soviet SSBN fleet.

15 For an instructive overview of the Nordic NWFZ proposals, their history and problems, see Ronald G. Purver, Arctic Arms Control: Constraints and

Opportunities (Ottawa: Canadian Institute for International Peace and Security 1988).

16 For the Murmansk speech, see *Pravda,* October 2, 1987; for the Ryzhkov speech, see *Foreign Broadcast Information Service,* Sov-88-011, January 19, 1988; for Akhromeev's article, *Pravda,* September 5, 1988.

17 Advance announcement of naval manœuvres in the northeast Atlantic was suggested in 1977 by Johan J. Holst, now Norway's defence minister. In addition he suggested a mutual agreement not to carry out naval exercises or major naval movements closer than 50 to 100 nautical miles from the coast of non-participant states and not to stage amphibious landing exercises closer than 50 to 100 kilometres from the territories of adjacent states. See Holst, "Prospects for Conflict Management and Arms Control in the North Atlantic," in J. Bertram and J.J. Holst, eds, *New Strategic Factors in the North Atlantic* (Oslo: Universitetsforlaget 1977), 137-8. These suggestions were made at a time of considerable uneasiness in Norwegian circles over the expansion of Soviet naval activity in the Norwegian Sea.

18 See for instance Johan Jørgen Holst, "Norwegian Security in Light of the Maritime Development in the North Atlantic and the Norwegian Sea," in E. Ellingsen, ed, *NATO and US Maritime Strategy* (Oslo: Norwegian Atlantic Committee 1987), 75-6.

19 Yet another incidents-at-sea agreement is being prepared between France and the Soviet Union.

18

Gorbachev's Murmansk Initiative

Evgenia Issraelian

In his Murmansk speech of October 1, 1987, Mikhail Gorbachev, the general secretary of the Communist Party of the Soviet Union, put forward a wide-ranging programme for radical reduction of military confrontation in the North, and for the replacement of mistrust and suspicion with confidence, peaceful co-operation, and reciprocity.

The Murmansk initiative did not appear out of a vacuum. It was the result of a detailed and laborious effort to comprehend the role of the North in the modern world, to analyse factors and tendencies of its development and their interrelation and to link them with European and world events. Nor was it the first time that the Soviet Union had focused its attention on northern problems.[1] In 1949 when Norway, Denmark, and Iceland joined the North Atlantic Treaty Organization (NATO), the question of northern security became acute for the USSR. That is why the Soviet government became active in this sphere in the 1950s. In January 1957 the USSR stated that given the refusal of Norway and Denmark to have nuclear weapons on their territory and the absence of such weapons in Sweden and Finland, there were good grounds on which to make northern Europe a nuclear-weapons-free zone (NWFZ). The idea of turning the Baltic Sea into the sea of peace was put forward at the same time.

New elements in the Soviet position on a Nordic NWFZ appeared in the 1970s and especially in the 1980s. It is widely admitted that the Soviet Union showed realism and flexibility during these years. In 1974 the USSR agreed to provide guarantees for a Nordic NWFZ. In 1981 it stated its readiness to give such guarantees unilaterally and also its desire to discuss some measures which could be applied to its own territory adjacent to the nuclear-weapons-free zone and would strengthen the nuclear-weapons-free status of such a zone. In his answers to questions from representatives of public organizations in Finland in 1983, Y.V. Andropov underlined the readiness of the Soviet Union to register its commitment not to use nuclear weapons against the countries of northern Europe that became participants in a NWFZ. That same year the USSR proposed for discussion the question of nuclear-weapons-free status for the Baltic Sea.

The Murmansk initiative also absorbed many ideas, points of views, and proposals which had been expressed in various northern countries. There is a direct connection with such significant proposals as that put forward by the Finnish president, Urho Kekkonen, in 1963 on a Nordic NWFZ, and the Swedish initiative developed by Olof Palme in 1980 concerning the establishment of a corridor in central Europe that would be free of nuclear weapons. The latter proposal was an important complement to the idea of a Nordic NWFZ. The ideas of Denmark and Norway and the conclusions of the interparliamentary commission of the Nordic countries were also studied.

The ideas of limiting naval activities in northern waters and of pursuing confidence-building measures were also raised by the Western countries: for example, by the Finnish president, M. Koivisto, when he spoke in Helsinki in 1986. The Norwegian ministers, K. Frundenlund and J. Holst, developed the idea of a multilateral incidents-at-sea regime, covering the Norwegian Sea and modelled on the Soviet-American agreement. Concern over military activities in the northern Atlantic has also been expressed by Iceland.[2]

While it incorporates many constructive ideas from previous years, the Murmansk initiative is not, however, a simple summation of these proposals. It is representative of the application of new political thinking to the problems of northern security and co-operation. It is not by chance that the initiative is concerned with more than military and military-political problems. Universal as well as northern security is considered in all its interconnected dimensions – military, political, ecological, economic, and humanitarian.

The Murmansk initiative reflected the basic principles elaborated by the 27th Party Congress in 1986. In the first place, congress documents emphasized the interconnectedness of contemporary international relations: "The modern world is complicated, diverse and dynamic, and shot through with contending tendencies and contradictions. It is a world of the most difficult alternatives, anxieties and hopes."[3] It was also pointed out that the need to solve humanity's most vital problems must move us towards greater interaction, must awaken hitherto unseen powers of self-preservation. The course of history, of social progress, ever more insistently requires that there be constructive and creative interaction between the states and peoples of the world. Such interaction is necessary to address global problems, which must be resolved jointly in the interests of all concerned. The dialectics of present-day development consists in a combination of competition and confrontation between the world's two social systems and a growing tendency towards the interdependence of all countries.[4] One of the problems requiring such interaction and co-operation is the management of the Arctic.

The military-political part of the Murmansk initiative is based on the Soviet concept of international security. The main principles of this concept are the following. First, the character of present-day weapons leaves no country with any hope of safeguarding itself solely with military and technical means – for example, by building up a defence system – even the most powerful ones. Security cannot be built endlessly on fear of retaliation, in other words, on the doctrines of containment or deterrence. Ensuring security is increasingly seen as a political task, and it can be attained only by political means. Second, in the context of relations between the USSR and the United States, security can only be mutual, and if we take international relations as a whole, it can be only universal. The highest wisdom of the state is not in taking care exclusively of itself, especially to the detriment of the other side. It is vital that all should feel equally secure, for the fears and anxieties of the nuclear age generate unpredictability in politics and concrete actions.[5] And, third, security should be comprehensive, including within its purview all spheres: military, political (including, for example, strict respect in international practice for the right of each people to choose the ways and forms of its development independently), economic (in particular, renunciation of economic blockades and sanctions unless by the recommendations of the world community, a joint quest for a just settlement of the debt problem), humanitarian (namely, co-operation in disseminating the ideas of peace, disarmament, and international security, greater flow of objective information, and broader contacts between peoples in order to learn more about each other).

The concept of reasonable sufficiency also has an application in resolving problems of northern security. Mass realization is rapidly growing in the world that further multiplication of the weapons of mankind's self-destruction has practically lost all military and political meaning. At the same time the constant build-up of armaments has given rise to serious doubts concerning the ability of military-strategic parity to ensure an acceptable level of strategic stability indefinitely. With a continuing unlimited arms race, the maintenance of parity at ever higher levels, far from ensuring mutual deterrence and stability, constantly reduces the guarantees that a conflict will not break out. The mounting threat of a clash or a war as a result of a mistake or a fault in technical systems increasingly weakens the stabilizing role of parity. In the second half of the eighties, it became ever clearer that to avoid a catastrophe, it is necessary to lower the levels of confrontation, to reduce military potentials, and to move in the direction of reasonable sufficiency. Economic doctrines moving in the same direction made themselves felt more and more acutely. The arms race causes tangible and growing damage to the economies of the West, the East, and the developing countries. Asymmetries in the economic limits of the arms race do not mean that there are no such limits at all. They become more and more evident with every decade. Moreover, the conception of reasonable sufficiency, when put into practice, will ensure a favourable political-military situation in addressing the problem of the security of each state and of global security as a whole.

While reflecting the security interests of the USSR and its allies, the Murmansk initiative gives no less consideration to the interests of the other circumpolar states by strictly observing the principle of equality and equal security. It is important to note that these initiatives were supplemented and developed during Nikolai Ryzhkov's official visit to Norway and Sweden in January 1988.

In his Murmansk speech Gorbachev stated that the North represents a security problem for the USSR at its northern borders.[6] The military activities of the United States and NATO in the areas adjacent to the Soviet polar regions are increasing. This build-up and operational use of the naval forces is based on the Maritime Strategy of the United States. It aims to increase the attack capabilities of naval forces, to ensure naval superiority by the further development of naval strike forces, and to establish control in all the "vitally important" regions of the world. American naval forces, according to this strategy, should be ready to attack Soviet territories from adjacent seas and to inflict strikes on targets located deep within Soviet territory. These plans cause deep concern in the Soviet Union. Moreover, the conclusion of the treaty on intermediate-range nuclear forces led to plans and attempts to compensate for the elimination of Pershing and cruise missiles by the future deployment of sea-launched cruise missiles in the North Atlantic. Such measures would have a destabilizing effect on the situation in Europe and negative consequences for global stability.

Turning to northern security, we should take into consideration the geostrategic factors, which in many respects determine the Soviet position. First of all, about half the total land territory of the USSR lies north of 60°

North and half of the Soviet coastline is on the Arctic Ocean. Thus, in the Arctic the Soviet Union is quite open to the fleets and weapons of opponents. Second, in the North Atlantic and the Arctic, the USSR is confronted by the naval forces of the West European countries, the United States, and Canada, which control the straits and narrows adjacent to northern Europe. And, third, the coastal zone of the USSR is very shallow and the only place where the USSR has access to the open sea is the area of the Kola Peninsula.

Soviet as well as Western experts admit that the strategic importance of the North has been increasing in recent decades. If we view a map of the world not from the west to the east but from the North Pole, as some Western experts suggest, we see that northern Europe, the traditional flank of military activities in the period of the First and Second World Wars, has become the main route for any potential exchange of nuclear strikes between the United States and the USSR. Here is the shortest aerial distance between the main industrial and population centres of the great powers and, accordingly, the shortest routes for intercontinental ballistic missiles, submarine-launched ballistic missiles, and long-range bombers. The military-strategic significance of the Arctic has grown in recent years because of the introduction of long-range air-launched cruise missiles and new strategic bombers. These developments raised the requirement for earlier detection and interception, thus extending the combat zone northwards to the Arctic. Even more significant was the development of sea-based weapons which has given submarines carrying nuclear missiles an increasingly important role.

In discussions of northern security, some Western experts point to the fact that NATO and the Warsaw Treaty Organization (WTO) have significantly different structures. If the Warsaw pact is mainly continental, NATO is more naval-oriented. That is why, in their view, any limits on the activities and size of naval forces in the North, and any confidence-building measures there, will give unilateral advantages to the Soviet Union and undermine the possibility of the transfer of American forces to Europe in time of crisis. According to data given in 1988 by the chief of the Soviet General Staff, Marshal Sergei Akhromeev, NATO exceeds the WTO in the number of naval personnel by a ratio of 5:4, in the number of the ocean-going ships by 7:6, and in combat aircraft by 4:2. The WTO has an advantage in submarines at 2:1, and in coastal ships at 6:1. In general, therefore, the naval supremacy of the United States and NATO over USSR and WTO is considerable.[7]

The problem of limiting naval arms and armaments is becoming an inescapable factor in East-West relations. As the process of strategic arms reduction and limitation of armed forces in Europe continues, the problem of cuts and confidence-building in the sphere of naval forces will gain in importance. The Soviet Union has more than once stated its readiness to discuss all the aspects of the problem of the limitation and reduction of naval activities at any level, in any forum, in a global or a regional context. The USSR believes that the limitation and reduction of naval armaments is possible. It can be begun in areas where there now are, or may in future appear, elements of mutual understanding: for example, guaranteeing the security of sea lanes of communication and confidence-building measures (CBMs) for naval forces. The Murmansk initiative put forward a wide programme of naval CBMs.

The imperatives of the modern world prove that international security and confidence-building are indivisible. Security and stability cannot be achieved without confidence. The arms race is generated by fear, mistrust, and suspicion. At the same time the arms race is turning into an independent creature driven by its own internal logic. As such, it rules out the very possibility of confidence-building. A vicious circle is formed as mistrust causes the arms race and the arms race in its turn increases suspiciousness.

CBMs are a relatively new phenomenon in international relations. They became the subject of broad international discussion only in the 1970s, but in the contemporary interdependent and interwoven world their significance is steadily growing.

The Murmansk initiative is a significant contribution to the overall process of confidence-building. An important element of this programme is the Soviet proposal to limit the number of large exercises carried out by the naval and air forces in northern seas to one a year. Though the activities of land forces are already subject to CBMs under the Stockholm agreement, all attempts to include naval activities in this agreement have thus far failed. At the same time there is a persistent growth in naval activities. For example, during the first half of 1988, the United States and NATO increased the number of their military activities almost twofold. In the same period, the USSR sharply reduced its equivalent activities. It conducted only one military manœuvre in the Northern Fleet and only one in the Baltic and Leningrad Military Districts.[8] The USSR has also suggested an agreement to notify others about large naval exercises, to invite observers to inspect manœuvres, and to limit the number of large exercises in every ocean and naval theatre of operations. The Soviet Union also took an unprecedented step in 1988 by inviting official observers from northern countries to one of its exercises. Regrettably, this invitation was not accepted – only journalists were present. Taking into consideration the wishes of Scandinavian countries, the USSR has declared its readiness to include not only the Greenland Sea, the Arctic Ocean, and the Norwegian and Baltic seas, but also the Barents Sea in a zone of confidence.

The other CBM proposed at Murmansk is the limitation and eventually the elimination of rivalry between the USSR and the United States in anti-submarine warfare. This idea was put forward in 1986 by President Koivisto of Finland. The USSR proposes to start with the creation of agreed areas in the northern and western Atlantic where anti-submarine activities would be banned. The geographical scope of this zone could be made more precise and supplemented in future. It is agreed now that there is no efficient anti-submarine technology adapted to Arctic conditions. This is a new challenge and vast resources would be needed to address it. But if the problems of anti-submarine warfare in the Arctic were indeed solved, the world would face a situation in which submarine survivability would be threatened in ice-covered or northern ice-free waters. A new round in the nuclear arms race would start. The proposed measure therefore stands to contribute to a climate of mutual trust and confidence.

From the Soviet point of view, it would be desirable to include questions of the limitation and reduction of military activities in the Arctic in the agenda of the second stage of the Conference on Confidence- and Security-Building Measures and Disarmament in Europe. As a preliminary measure, consultations could be held between the WTO and the NATO countries with the participation of Finland and Sweden. At the same time, consultations on a bilateral basis would also be helpful as well as meetings between military experts representing NATO and the Warsaw pact. All such meetings should seek to work out reasonable compromises and common approaches.

The Murmansk initiative offers a new approach to the reduction of naval activities in international straits, such as the Baltic Sea, Denmark Strait, the English Channel, and the region comprising Iceland, the Faeroes, and Scandinavia. It would be desirable to prevent the concentration of naval forces in international straits and the approaches to them. The number and classes of ships subjected to such limitation should be discussed.

To return to the issue of a Nordic NWFZ, the northern countries have pointed out that nuclear-weapons-free status for the European north cannot be effective without the participation of the nuclear powers. This is a complicated problem with two main aspects. The first deals with guarantees on the part of the nuclear powers as to the status of the zone. That means that the nuclear powers would not use, and would not deter another's use of, such weapons against the nuclear-weapons-free states. The Soviet Union has without hesitation stated its readiness to offer such a guarantee. It has declared that it is ready to be a unilateral guarantor and to give bilateral or unilateral guarantees in any agreed form. The other side of the problem is much more complicated and is linked to Soviet nuclear weapons deployed on the Kola Peninsula. Can special requirements be demanded of a nuclear power on the grounds that its territory is adjacent to a probable nuclear-free zone? Should any of its regions be included in a zone created only by non-nuclear states? Here the Soviet Union took an unusual decision. In 1986 it dismantled all the launchers for medium-range missiles on the Kola Peninsula and most of the launchers for such missiles in the rest of the territory of the Leningrad and Baltic Military Districts, and it moved several battalions of operational tactical missiles out of those districts. It also declared that in case of an agreement on a Nordic NWFZ, the USSR would also withdraw all ballistic-missile-carrying submarines from the Baltic Fleet. (About six submarines with eighteen ballistic missiles have been on station in the Baltic since 1978.) The USSR has also proposed that Sweden be the co-ordinator of all efforts in this area.

The Murmansk initiative should not be considered as a static, completed scheme. It is not the last word, but an invitation to discussion because the problems are complicated and sensitive for all the countries involved. Changes are possible, new ideas are appearing, and more will appear in the future. That is why the key message of the Murmansk initiative is the appeal to co-operation. The initiative demonstrates that, despite the strategic importance of the Arctic, the USSR is open to broad discussion, to a search for compromise and mutual concession. Such co-operation and interaction, based on a balance of the interests of all the states concerned, will create a new political atmosphere that will facilitate the resolution of the most acute problems of the North.

The Soviet Union desires to conduct a constructive dialogue with all circumpolar states on global, regional, and bilateral problems. One of the active participants in these discussions of Arctic problems will be Canada. Soviet-Canadian co-operation in the North, including scientific contacts, will contribute to the creation of confidence. It will help to turn the North into a zone of peace.

Notes

1 *Mezhdunarodnaya zhizn*, no 5 (1988), 36.
2 Ibid.
3 Mikhail Gorbachev, *Political Report of the CPSU Central Committee to the 27th Party Congress* (Moscow: Politizdat 1986), 9.
4 Ibid., 26.
5 Ibid., 82.
6 *Pravda*, October 2, 1987.
7 *Pravda*, September 5, 1988.
8 *Vestnik MID*, no 3, 1988, 15.
9 *Pravda*, January 12, 1988.

Epilogue: Civility
in the Arctic

Franklyn Griffiths

How best to check and reverse the militarization of the Arctic? To what extent can the peoples and states of a militarized region engage in international co-operation on non-military or civil issues of common concern? Can civil co-operation, pursued on its own merits, also prepare the way for military confidence-building and arms reduction agreements in the circumpolar North? Might the militarization of the Arctic be reduced with the acceptance and use of an integrated conception of security – one in which military requirements are combined with an awareness of the need to act for ecological, economic, cultural, and social security as well? Such are the questions which gave rise to this book. They bring us to a wide-angle view of the region's problems in which military uses of Arctic spaces are viewed in broader context. They invite us to reconsider the meanings of and the pathways to security as such. This epilogue considers how the two main propositions of reliance on civil co-operation and the utility of an integrated security concept have fared in the light of the initial presentations in this volume – and of events affecting the region to early 1992. With so much of great moment happening in the world today, we should not be surprised if a major overhaul of our assumptions is in order.

Arctic Alternatives

Not that long ago, say thirty years, it was customary for southerners to think of the circumpolar Arctic as a region in which not a lot happened outside the various areas of national jurisdiction administered by Canada, Denmark (Greenland), Finland, Iceland, Norway, the Soviet Union, Sweden, and the United States – the Arctic Eight. Nuclear-powered submarines had only just begun to venture under the Arctic ice in the early 1960s. Public concern over transpolar bomber attack and air defence needs was starting to dwindle as the Soviet Union and the United States began to invest heavily in land-based intercontinental ballistic missiles (ICBMs). Cold War imperatives served to keep the Soviet Union, the Arctic member-countries of the North Atlantic Treaty Organization (NATO), and the two non-aligned states, Finland and Sweden, on guard. Cold War policy requirements also served to deny the thought of collaboration among adversaries even on Arctic non-military or civil issues, lest the opponent gain some advantage. The Soviet Union was momentarily arrested in the economic exploitation and settlement of its vast portion of the region, and commercial quantities of oil and natural gas had yet to be discovered in Arctic North America or off the shores of Norway. Alaska had just become a state, Greenland had only recently ceased to be a colony, and Canada's Arctic aboriginal peoples had just received the right to vote. Recognition of the greenhouse effect was still far off. Few had even heard of the biosphere or an ecosystem. It was another world, gone forever now.

A Circumpolar Perspective
Today it is increasingly recognized that the Arctic's physical environment and social affairs are best understood and managed on a circumpolar and indeed a global basis. The Arctic Ocean, itself a complex whole, forms part of the world's ocean transport system: dump organic chemicals into the sea off South Africa and they will appear in the Arctic, as Max Dunbar tells us in his contribution to this volume; send heavy metals down a Soviet Arctic river and traces will eventually make their way to the Indian Ocean. Similar interconnections apply to the region's atmosphere and to ocean-air interactions as ozone depletion and the thinning of pack ice in the Arctic demonstrate: both phenomena are caused by human activity far removed from the region and are potentially capable of affecting not only the global environment but the human condition in return. The movements of caribou, whale, birds, polar bears, and many other forms of Arctic wildlife do not respect national frontiers. Nor do the airborne and other pollutants that concentrate in Arctic animals and fish and thereby affect the health of aboriginal peoples pursuing a renewable-resources or subsistence way of life.

To view the Arctic primarily in terms of sovereignty and national defence against foreign intrusion is thus to be woefully behind the times. Countless silent border crossings occur daily in a region whose environment forms a whole and is closely tied to extra-regional and global processes. It will require extensive collaboration among the circumpolar countries and others if it is to be looked after properly. Nor is humanity alone here. The Arctic environment is itself a mute but eloquent actor. We have an obligation to express and to act on what it tells us. But that expression is sure to be imperfect if it is shaped primarily by the outlook of populations and states centred on a southerly way of life or by the levelling effects of a global perspective, however benign.[1]

Experience in the fields of economic development, administration of justice, delivery of health services, transportation, land-use planning, constitutional development, and any number of like matters makes it all too clear that the transference of national priorities and practices derived from a southerly way of life and the experience of southern majorities invites disappointment and disaster if adaptations are not made to the special conditions that prevail in the Arctic. Owing to the pervasive effects of climate, culture, remoteness, and cost, these conditions are, again, strikingly similar throughout the region. They make for great commonality in the policy agendas of the Arctic countries right down to the local level. Still other parallels are to be seen in the management of the commons, as represented by the Arctic atmosphere and ocean areas, and in efforts to deal with transboundary processes that neither originate nor can be handled in one jurisdiction alone. States, territorial governments, and small communities throughout the region are striving for solutions to what are common problems. Indeed, they are finding solutions. But at what rate, at what expense, and with what duplication of effort?

The Arctic is a distinct domain. It needs to be understood and approached in the round. To conceive of our Arctic purpose essentially in terms of what might be accomplished behind lines of national jurisdiction is no longer adequate. The exercise of sovereignty, to say nothing of the pursuit of national security by military means, must be tempered by an awareness of the interdependence that prevails in the Arctic and in its relationships with the surrounding world.

Fortunately, a readiness to close the circle in the Arctic has begun to appear in recent years. Aboriginal peoples were the first to recognize that the sovereignty principle and a north-south conception of Arctic alignments do not confer unalloyed benefits. Not merely to subsist but to survive in separate national jurisdictions governed by southern interest, they found it necessary to band together in international non-governmental organizations (NGOs) such as the Inuit Circumpolar Conference, Indigenous Survival International, the Nordic Saami Council, and the World Council of Indigenous Peoples. As well, in March 1990, the twenty-six aboriginal peoples of the then Soviet Union joined together in the Association of Small Peoples of the Soviet North. And an Arctic aboriginal leaders' summit, held outside Copenhagen in June 1991, has led to the formation of a new network for co-ordinated action by the diverse aboriginal peoples of the region.[2] The same need to work across formal lines of jurisdiction is to be observed in the activities of the International Union for Circumpolar Health, the International Permafrost Association, and other Arctic NGOs and standing conferences. Meanwhile, territorial governments within the Arctic countries have also become increasingly active in pursuit of transnational collaboration.

The heightened role of territorial governments as Arctic actors is to be seen in the development of relationships between the government of the Northwest Territories and the Greenland Home Rule government and between the Yukon government and the state of Alaska, and in the extraordinary outburst of co-operation between Alaska and far eastern regional governments in the former Soviet Union. A gathering of Arctic territorial governors, held at Anchorage in September 1990, produced a declaration of intent to create a Northern Forum or circumpolar institution at the territorial level.[3] Among the signatories of that statement were governors and ministers from Alaska, Alberta, British Columbia, Chukhotka, Greenland, Heilongjiang (China), Hokkaido, the Jewish Autonomous Region (Russian federation), Lapland (Finland), Magadan, the Northwest Territories, Sakhalin, Tröndelag (Norway), Västerbotten (Sweden), and Yukon. In November 1991 the Northern Forum was formally established.

Viewed in the ensemble, the boundary-crossing activity of the aboriginal NGOs, non-aboriginal associations, and territorial governments attests to the growing need for a comprehensive approach to the region's affairs. Gone for good is the time when countries could expect to meet their responsibilities in the Arctic without engaging in international collaboration that embraces the peoples of the region, without acknowledging the inherent inter-relatedness and similarity of the Arctic's physical and social processes. In fact, the eight Arctic states have themselves begun to act on the need for region-wide co-operation on civil issues.

New Inter-State Co-operation

The emergence of collaboration at the inter-state level is to be seen in two pathbreaking Arctic international negotiations. One led to the establishment, at Resolute in August 1990, of an International Arctic Science Committee (IASC),[4] the subject of an essay by E.F. Roots in this volume. The second negotiation began in response to a Finnish initiative of

January 1989 on behalf of an accord to protect the Arctic environment. Though the IASC has been constituted as an international non-governmental organization answering to national science establishments, the talks that led to its creation were carefully monitored and in some instances conducted by the foreign ministries of the regional states. As to the Arctic environmental negotiation, known as the Rovaniemi process after the Finnish town in which the first round of consultations was held, it yielded in June 1991 a regional environmental protection strategy and a series of specific commitments to monitor and conserve the Arctic's physical environment and living resources.[5]

In this setting of intensified inter-state collaboration, the government of Canada announced, on November 28, 1990, that it would seek the creation of an Arctic Council or central institution for circumpolar co-operation. Its view of an Arctic Council was essentially as follows: "The agenda of an Arctic Council should be flexible, allowing for growth with success, as confidence grows. In addition, the Government believes that it is crucial that an Arctic Council allow the voice of Northern people to be heard so that they may contribute to decisions affecting their lives and interests. Finally, an Arctic Council should be designed to include some appropriate input from non-member countries from outside the region who have interest in the Arctic and whose activities can affect that region – for better or worse."[6] Negotiations among the Arctic states to set up such an organization are to begin in Canada in the spring of 1992. When established, an Arctic Council should provide a much-needed forum for discussion and collective action on critical problems of the region and its peoples.

Without wishing in any way to minimize the significance of pan-Arctic collaboration at the NGO and territorial government levels, especially its capacity to address local needs, I find it difficult to overemphasize the importance of the breakthrough that has been achieved in circumpolar inter-state relations during the last two or three years. If we set aside the Polar Bear Convention of 1973, which is self-administered by the signatories, and the Svalbard Treaty of 1920, which demilitarized the Spitsbergen archipelago while affirming the sovereign rights of Norway there, it is only in the late 1980s and early 1990s that the Arctic states have been willing to contemplate the negotiation of region-wide multilateral agreements and the creation of permanent pan-Arctic institutions. The situation as it exists now in Arctic inter-state relations is unexpectedly novel and unexpectedly promising.

Why the onset of inter-state civil co-operation as the 1990s begin? For one thing, thinking about the needs of the Arctic in southern centres of decision has gradually come to accept the existence of regional and regional-global interdependencies such as we have discussed. Second, the growth of mass environmental awareness throughout the industrialized countries has reached a point where political decision-makers cannot but respond. Third, the Soviet Union began not merely to reform but to transform its ways with the advent of Mikhail Gorbachev to the leadership in 1985. Speaking in Murmansk in October 1987, the Soviet leader broke abruptly with decades of Soviet practice by denying an opposed-forces view of circumpolar affairs and calling for collaborative action to address the Arctic's military, scientific, environmental, resource development, marine transportation, and other problems.[7] The effect of his remarks was to do away with prior Soviet resistance to all but selective bilateral co-operation on problems specific to the Arctic. They made the Soviet Union into a potential partner in circumpolar multilateral arrangements. They transformed the calculation of what was possible in Arctic international relations. And now, as of early 1992, the irrevocable end of the Cold War and Russia's astonishing rise from the ruins of the Soviet communist order have altered the Arctic international calculus in ways that we have only just begun to appreciate.

Meanwhile, the United States and its allies gradually came to view changes in Soviet politics and policies as authentic and worthy of support, even as NATO persisted in its endeavour to deter and negotiate reductions in the military power remaining in Soviet hands. In the Arctic, the altered approach of the NATO countries to the Soviet Union came to mean step-by-step multilateral negotiations to meet the civil interests of all concerned, a continued posture of strategic deterrence, and a guarded readiness in principle to discuss arms control and confidence-building measures that bear on the region – but to work such measures out only in extra-regional negotiating forums. A variety of developments occurring outside and then within the region (including the efforts of Finland and Sweden) have thus served to open the way for multilateral civil co-operation and institution-building in the Arctic. But, significant as today's breakthrough may be in the history of the region, the way is not yet fully open to greater co-operation in circumpolar affairs.

An Arena for Military Competition
Though the value of the Arctic as an arena for military operations was in decline thirty years ago, technology, geography, and politics were

conspiring to create new strategic uses for the region. The Soviet Union led the way, and Russia, as the prime successor state to the USSR, retains by far the largest concentration of forces in this part of the world. Finding itself unable to project naval power through the narrow straits that close the Baltic and Black seas, the USSR opted for a vigorous build-up of its northern surface and submarine fleet based on the Kola Peninsula to the east of northernmost Norway. Then, as of 1972, ballistic-missile-firing submarines (SSBNs) were deployed, and subsequently improved and defended, to allow attack on North American and European targets from Arctic launch points in and about the Barents Sea and in the central Arctic Basin if necessary. Additional positions of strategic naval strength were also constructed and fortified in far eastern Arctic waters centred on the Sea of Okhotsk. For their part, the United States and in lesser measure the non-Arctic and Arctic NATO allies responded by the mid-1980s with energetic anti-submarine and related naval deployments designed to attack the offshore SSBN bastions and onshore strategic assets of the Soviet Union in and from Arctic waters. In contrast to the situation in the early 1960s, the Arctic had been transformed into a major theatre for potential strategic naval warfare by the beginning of the 1990s.

Starting in the 1970s, a revolution had also occurred in cruise-missile technology as both the Soviet Union and the United States, the latter leading this time, began to deploy progressively more accurate nuclear-tipped sea- and air-launched cruise missiles (SLCMs and ALCMs) with ranges of up to 3,000 kilometres. Despite asymmetry in the structure of American and Soviet strategic forces, Arctic airspace and waters offered a number of potential cruise missile launch points against targets on both sides. In turn, the perceived need for air defences against cruise missiles and strategic bombers in the Arctic appreciated for the Soviet Union, and for the United States and Canada. For Canada, for example, the results were all too well known: Arctic testing of American ALCMs, including the advanced cruise missile (ACM) for use over comparable Soviet Arctic terrain; modernization of the Distant Early Warning (DEW) Line; construction of Arctic bases for forward deployment of interceptors; and, in pursuit of wider NATO purposes, low-level flight training at Goose Bay over the protests of the Innu.

Nor did the militarization of the Arctic seem likely to be checked, much less reversed, by means of arms control as practised to mid-1991. On the contrary and in a perverse twist of fortune, nuclear and conventional arms reduction agreements concluded without reference to the Arctic threatened to increase the strategic value of the circumpolar region relative to others. Consider, for example, the counting rules and exemptions employed by Moscow and Washington in the strategic arms reduction (START) treaty signed in July 1991: while they did serve to reduce the number of warheads carried on ballistic missiles, as David Cox notes in his chapter, they left the way open for intensified competition in strategic bombers and thus for heightened Arctic operations. Consider as well the nuclear and conventional force reductions in Europe which were agreed in November 1990: while very welcome, their effect was nevertheless to make the Arctic a refuge for military activity that was unacceptable closer to "home." Norway in particular is concerned over the displacement of Soviet and now Russian forces from the central front to more northerly areas including the Kola Peninsula as a consequence of the European force reduction process. Or consider the related question of nuclear weapons testing. Denied the use of its test site in the central Asian republic of Kazakhstan where environmental and anti-war sentiment reached truly formidable proportions, the USSR transferred its testing to the uninhabited Arctic islands of Novaya Zemlya. As of October 1990, the champion of the Arctic as a zone of peace was the only state to test in the region.

Despite these down-side effects, political change in the Soviet Union, subsequently in Russia and the Commonwealth of Independent States (CIS), and inevitably in global political-military relations could not but influence the Arctic. In September-October 1991 and then in January 1992 Washington and Moscow announced a series of unilateral arms reduction and confidence-building initiatives. Though not conceived with the Arctic in mind, they did begin to alter if not markedly to reverse the militarization of the region. The details of these moves, countermoves, proposals, and counterproposals are complex.[8] Suffice it to say here that the United States, while ceasing to deploy tactical nuclear weapons on its surface ships, submarines, and naval aircraft, sought to move the Soviet and CIS/Russian strategic nuclear force from land out to sea, which is to say into the Arctic Ocean and adjacent waters. For its part, Moscow undertook to remove tactical nuclear weapons from surface ships and submarines, to eliminate a third of its sea-based and one-half of its airborne tactical nuclear weapons, to cease the production of existing submarine-launched ballistic missiles (SLBMs) and ALCMs, to scrap all SLCMs, to stop developing its advanced cruise missile if the United States did the same, and to abide by a unilateral moratorium on nuclear weapons testing for one year as of October 1991.

All of these actions stopped far short of a full recognition of the reality that, as of early 1992, not only the Cold War but the Soviet Union was over. Much of the weaponry that was in the Arctic region, or that might move into and through it in the event of a now scarcely imaginable crisis or war, was still intact. As well, the vigour with which the new Russia contested Ukraine's desire for control over the Soviet Black Sea fleet suggested that Moscow could well continue to attach high value to its naval assets including, of course, those located on the Kola Peninsula. In fact, if Russia were denied most of the naval facilities on the Black Sea, Kola could become still more important as a future base of operations. Moreover, on February 27, 1992, the Russian president issued a decree authorizing site preparation for two to four underground nuclear tests on Novaya Zemlya in the event of termination of the existing unilateral moratorium.

The overall conclusion is unavoidable. The Arctic today is subject to persistent military activity even as demilitarization becomes the rule in Europe and in the global American-Russian strategic interaction. The Arctic is being treated in prejudicial fashion by national security decision-makers determined to maintain the global forces and freedom of action thought necessary for defence in the event of crisis and war, however unlikely these may now be. But while the circumpolar Arctic continues to be subject to discriminatory military uses relative to other regions of the world, it is also clear that the outlook for demilitarization has begun to improve. Arctic-specific measures of confidence-building and arms control, seemingly far-fetched in the eyes of officialdom as recently as 1991, could yet serve as a means of co-ordinating the transition of American and Russian military policy to new purposes which once again accord a diminished strategic role to the northern circumpolar region. And beyond confidence-building there lies the increasingly obvious need to establish and progressively widen a demilitarized zone in the central Arctic Basin.[9]

In the meanwhile, the eight Arctic states have an immediate obligation to begin to discuss the military problems particular to the region and to carry any common understandings forward into extra-regional talks. Their obligation stems from their collective responsibility as stewards of a part of the world that can only suffer when a competitive southern user's mentality is paramount in national action.

The Choice
More could be said about the changing state of the globe and of the Arctic as it bears on the need for new forms of civil and military collaboration in the circumpolar north. But the essential points should be clear. In recent

decades the evolution of the Arctic as a region has proceeded along two divergent paths. On the one hand, we observe deep-seated but weakening processes that have driven the ice states to seek military-strategic advantage in highly competitive behaviour. At the same time, awareness has been growing among the Arctic countries that the civil affairs of the region must be addressed by joint action if they are to be dealt with effectively. As the millennium approaches, the Arctic countries are faced with an increasingly clear choice as to the kind of region they wish to have.

The Arctic can become a region of enhanced co-operation and civility, a region in which southern majorities and the governments that speak for them accord progressively greater respect and attention to one another, to their circumpolar environment, and to their Arctic populations – aboriginal populations first and foremost. Alternatively, the evolution of the region can continue to be marked by improvised civil collaboration in the midst of seemingly interminable if waning military-strategic opposition whose excesses are addressed elsewhere by southerners preoccupied by other matters. In my view, the choice is crystal clear. Co-operation must prevail in a region which constitutes a whole and which cannot remain a home to a military competition increasingly viewed as intolerable elsewhere. How then might the Arctic become a domain of enhanced civility?

Civil-Military Interaction in the Arctic

Several assumptions about the interconnection between international civil and military matters underlie the series of questions that opened this chapter and, by the same token, the propositions advanced in the introduction to this book. In probing these assumptions we may gain a more exact understanding of how best to advance the cause of civility in circumpolar affairs. And not only should we evaluate these notions as they stand. We should also enquire whether they may have been overtaken by events in very recent times, indeed since August 1991.

The assumptions to be considered first concern civil-military interaction in Arctic international relations to mid-1991. We have assumed, on the one hand, that the civil and military realms can be decoupled to permit the peoples and governments of a militarized, and hence politically divided, region to achieve widening co-operation on civil issues of common concern. And yet, on the other hand, we have assumed that international civil co-operation pursued on its own merits can be linked to military and political competition in ways that attenuate the latter.

Put these two sets of assumptions together and we would seem to envisage a one-way or arbitrary freedom to link: whereas civil collaboration is to be decoupled from and to unfold with diminishing effect from military-political competition, this same competition is also to be linked to and progressively constrained by joint action in the civil sphere. To what extent are these varied propositions workable in practice?

Decoupling

As of the late 1980s and early 1990s, the remarkable surge of multilateral civil collaboration and institution-building among Arctic states, territorial governments, and international NGOs provides ample verification of the decoupling assumptions made here. No longer is the question why collaborate on non-military matters in the Arctic; now the question is how best to co-operate on which issues. Furthermore, Canada's Arctic Council initiative promises to take us well beyond ad hoc co-operation. It presents the regional states with an opportunity to organize a means for the collective identification of and joint action on pressing Arctic problems.[10]

But if the assumption and indeed a strategy of decoupling have clearly been proven workable, we should still inquire whether perceived military-strategic and hence opposed-forces political requirements have set limits to civil collaboration in the region. At issue here is the degree to which decoupling has worked in practice. Also at issue is the more fundamental question of the extent to which *Arctic-specific* civil co-operation – multilateral ventures among the Arctic countries on non-military matters specific to the region – can escape constraints that originate in *extra-Arctic* competition – in mistrust and rivalry whose sources are to be found outside the region.

As one who has followed Arctic international relations closely in recent years, it seems to me that political-military considerations have indeed figured as a real if dwindling constraint on circumpolar civil collaboration at the inter-state level to mid-1991. Among the NATO military establishments there have been informal expressions of concern over the potential of collaborative arrangements to constrain military operations in the region; in particular, the Soviet Union was viewed by military planners in the United States as threatening to acquire an enhanced capacity to inhibit Western naval access to the Arctic by converting the area into a "zone of peace" through sponsorship of non-military co-operation there. For its part, the Soviet military, which was taken aback by Gorbachev's Murmansk speech of October 1987, is said by observers within the country to have resisted international arrangements that would grant foreigners greater access to the Soviet Arctic. Furthermore, as typified by the Canadian briefing paper reprinted as chapter 3, the military-diplomatic establishments of the NATO countries and the Soviet Union alike evinced a strong common concern to avert a course of events that might lead to negotiations among Arctic governments on Arctic military matters. Such matters, to rephrase the argument, were (and still are) defined as extra-Arctic in their origins and substance and thus were to be dealt with only in non-Arctic negotiating forums.

The net effect of such thinking and of the institutional forces associated with it has been to inhibit but not to prevent inter-state civil collaboration in the region. In essence it has imparted caution and a "go-slow" quality to talks on civil co-operation among the Eight. Combined with other considerations – for instance, the remoteness of Arctic issues in the minds of southern majorities and the pervasive shortage of funding for new Arctic undertakings – political-military factors have also helped to keep Arctic international co-operation low on the list of national priorities. Though they do not appear to have imposed significant constraint on civil collaboration among Arctic territorial governments or among aboriginal NGOs, they have clearly stood in the way of the Inuit Circumpolar Conference and other non-state actors such as the government of the Northwest Territories which seek the demilitarization of the region.[11]

Political-military constraints have, however, proved on the whole to be a waning force in the process of civil collaboration. The latter was for a time greatly retarded relative to change occurring elsewhere in East-West relations as a consequence of the continued military-strategic significance of the region and of the Soviet preference for bilateral Arctic-specific co-operation until 1987. Nevertheless, in due course Arctic international relations came to resemble more closely the larger pattern of East-West interaction in which collaboration on economic, scientific, environmental, and other civil matters mingled somewhat uneasily with continuing military-strategic opposition. The word uneasily is employed advisedly: just as East-West relations from the 1970s to the early 1990s retained the potential for deterioration in which a renewed emphasis on conflict and the use of sanctions could lead to the suspension or dismantling of established co-operation on non-military matters, so also in the Arctic the decoupling of civil and military affairs remained vulnerable to a renewal of political-military tension whose origins could well have had little or nothing to do with the Arctic as such.

As of August 1991, therefore, the evolution of Arctic-specific civil co-operation continued to be much influenced by extra-regional forces. Basically they served to endow Arctic governments and peoples with a wider but still constrained opportunity to achieve joint gains in the non-military sphere. Of primary importance here, as Willy Østreng makes clear in his contribution to the volume, was the gradual waning of hegemonic conflict between East and West. It enabled Arctic states and non-state actors to contemplate and, in due course, to act on the potential for civil collaboration among adversaries. Though political and geostrategic factors continued to bar Arctic-specific co-operation on military matters, the door was opened to what may be termed inhibited multilateral civil collaboration. As of mid-1991, the partial decoupling of civil and military activity in the Arctic was on its way to becoming established practice.

But it should also be noted that in pursuing civil co-operation, Arctic states and non-state actors chose to act primarily on the merits of the matter at hand. They did not seem greatly interested in the use of civil co-operation as a means of contributing to the demilitarization of the region. Though an awareness of the constraining effects of political-military conflict was by no means lacking in the region's capitals, Arctic states found that an agenda of civil collaboration had much to offer in its own right. There is something to carry forward here as we turn now to our assumptions about the utility of civil co-operation in reducing the militarization of the region.

Linking
The Arctic states have yet to engage in negotiations for region-specific confidence-building, arms control, and disarmament measures. Nor have they been guided by an evident intent to employ civil collaboration as an indirect route to demilitarization of the region. But ours is a time of unusually rapid change in international relations. Could it be that, despite outward appearances, multilateral civil co-operation had begun to create preconditions for international military collaboration in the region by mid-1991? Similarly, might Arctic-specific civil co-operation have already begun to exert a moderating effect on political-military interaction outside the region? To consider these questions is to probe the assumption that civil co-operation, progressively decoupled from the military domain and pursued on its own merits, can also serve the purpose of regional demilitarization. Though the short answer is that it is still too early to tell, civil collaboration may already have started to affect the course of political-military interaction in the region as of August 1991. Military-

technical thinking and operations proved immune to countervailing effects
from circumpolar civil co-operation, but the situation appeared somewhat
different on the political plane.

Though we remain very largely in the realm of inference here, it is fair
to say that acceptance of the utility of a circumpolar perspective on the
region's affairs began to grow with the onset of civil co-operation. The
effect was to qualify, but by no means to displace, long-standing
conceptions of the Arctic as an arena for the unfettered pursuit of extra-
regional functions and purposes, including military ones. The intellectual
milieu of those professionally concerned with the Arctic in government
and outside it thus showed signs of marginally greater receptivity to the
thought of regionally based responses to the region's military problems.
For the government of Canada, for example, it became possible in 1991 to
"discuss" if not yet to "negotiate" Arctic military matters with other
regional states. Though the onset of Arctic-specific arms bargaining could
still be some time away, the gathering influence of a circumpolar outlook
would seem to be lending new legitimacy to arguments for military
collaboration in the region. As well, it stands to strengthen the case of
those from around the region, and from southern metropolitan centres, who
favour direct talks or unilateral action to end the practice whereby Arctic
spaces are used for military purposes deemed unacceptable in other regions
of the world.

Still other effects, also for the most part incipient, could be observed in
the influence of civil collaboration on regional political-military interaction
by mid-1991. For one thing, the Arctic international agenda had become
more diversified as non-military considerations were added to the long-
standing preoccupation with strategic military affairs. No longer was the
region an arena for political-military opposition alone. On the contrary, the
growth of civil co-operation attested that the regional states had much in
common; it imparted new elements of reassurance and trust to their
interactions; and it served to create new constituencies for improved
political relations. The combined effect of these changes in the substance
and quality of Arctic international relations could have been to inject a new
and essentially political dimension of confidence into the affairs of the
region – to be specific, into the dealings of the then Soviet Union, on the
one hand, and the Western Seven, on the other. Though the gap between
political and military confidence-building remained large within the
region, international experience in other contexts suggests that purely
political measures that make for greater confidence serve to create

background conditions for military confidence-building and arms reduction arrangements.

This much said on how linkage might work to the detriment of militarization in the Arctic, it should be apparent that it is hard to come by hard evidence of constraints on regional political-military interaction which stem directly from regional civil co-operation. Interviews with policy-makers and informed observers in the circumpolar countries might confirm some of the inferences made here, and possibly produce still others. But it is in fact too early to tell, for Arctic multilateral civil collaboration has only just begun. Accordingly, while our decoupling assumptions are effectively confirmed by the circumpolar record, the case for linkage had yet to be validated in the *regional* practice of Arctic states and non-state actors to August 1991, and for that matter to early 1992. And if demilitarizing linkage processes are not readily evident in regional practice, what of the view that Arctic-specific political-military behaviour is in principle the result of *extra-Arctic* considerations and therefore cannot be addressed on an Arctic-specific basis?

Where force posture, doctrine, and operations were concerned, military uses of the circumpolar North to 1991 did indeed continue to be heavily dependent upon extra-regional and global strategic requirements. But the situation would seem to have been different in the case of underlying political calculations. Outside the Arctic, as hegemonic conflict decayed, a cleavage opened up between the military-technical and the political dimensions of basic national security policy. Then, as enmity yielded to a progressively rapid admixture of amity in the 1980s, collaborative and unilateral action in Europe (in Eastern Europe in particular) and in Third World conflict situations contributed to the growth of mutual confidence and trust in overall political relations between what still passed for East and West. Regional political developments thus added to the declining force of conventional adversarial assumptions in the behaviour of states large and small. Though the onset of multilateral co-operation in the Arctic region after 1987 may not have counted for much in the larger scheme of things as viewed from national capitals, it is difficult to believe that it had no effect whatsoever on the political dimension of national security polity. That something of significance was occurring here, as it was in other regions of the world, was surely noted in Moscow, Ottawa, and in the various Nordic centres of decision.

The point I am driving at is that, as of August 1991, it was no longer appropriate to conceive of Arctic political-military interaction as being

wholly derived from extra-regional and global requirements. Dependence
continued to be great in the military-technical realm. But where the extra-
Arctic political rationale for opposed-forces behaviour in the Arctic was
concerned, the relationship between the circumpolar region and its
surround was already one of *interdependence*, not of dependence of the
former on the latter. However modest the contribution, multilateral civil
collaboration in the Arctic had also begun to influence the extra-regional
political setting in ways that could, in turn, work against continued enmity
and mistrust within the region.

If this analysis is correct, the linkage between civil collaboration and
Arctic demilitarization may have begun to operate in two rather different
ways as of mid-1991. On the one hand, within the region the creation of
background political conditions for Arctic-specific military confidence-
building and arms reduction measures might already have been set in
motion. At the same time, civil co-operation within the region, facilitated
by change in the external political environment, contributed in turn to the
wider erosion of opposed-forces behaviour on which regional
militarization depended. Though here, too, we lack confirmation, it could
be that the demilitarizing effects of Arctic-specific civil collaboration were
considerably more circuitous than direct: whereas military uses of the
Arctic seemed resistant to regional civil collaboration, which the Eight also
preferred to decouple from the military sphere, they might more readily
have been influenced as the result of a regional contribution to the larger
decline of adversarial assumptions on which Arctic militarization relied.

To conclude these remarks on civil-military interaction in the Arctic to
August 1991, we may state that whereas our initial assumptions in favour
of decoupling the civil and military domains are broadly substantiated, the
case for linkage to the detriment of militarization remains very largely
hypothetical. Though linkage processes as envisaged here could yet
unfold, the record suggests that collaborative action in the civil sphere was
more inhibited by sustained political-military conflict than the other way
around. In short, the notion of one-way freedom to link is not borne out in
the period under review. If there is a lesson to be had here, it is simply that
civil collaboration is best pursued on its own merits and without the
additional intent to further the demilitarization of the region. If multilateral
co-operation on Arctic civil issues also serves to generate constraints on
regional political-military rivalry, so much the better. But such effects
seem likely to be diffuse in nature and ill suited to co-ordinated action.
Better, on balance, to seek beneficial civil collaboration and to let the side-
effects take care of themselves.

Outlook

In the wake of the failed putsch of August 1991 in Moscow, the collapse first of communism in the Soviet Union and then of the Soviet Union itself has altered the structure and processes of the international system, of the Arctic as a regional subsystem, and of the inter-relationship between system and subsystem. To be sure, forces for qualitative change in international relations had already gathered in many quarters well before the August 1991 events in Moscow. But with the disappearance of Soviet communism, hegemonic conflict has finally vanished as an ordering force in world affairs. The Arctic in particular is now an arena for strategic military interaction whose former political basis is all but blown away. Today's situation accordingly requires a still more searching review of our assumptions about civil-military interaction in the Arctic. Above all, we need to reconsider the value of a strategy of indirection in checking and reducing the militarization of the region.

When the planning was done for this book, the force of East-West political-military conflict still seemed sufficient to frustrate any appeal for immediate Arctic measures of military confidence-building, arms control, and disarmament. In these circumstances, circumpolar civil co-operation appeared to offer a promising new point of departure in weakening the impulse to exploit Arctic spaces for military purposes. The underlying assumption, that military and civil activities in the region were in some way interdependent, certainly held to mid-1991. But as of early 1992 we have crossed the threshold into a new era in which the very notion of civil-military interaction has been overtaken by events, in which the problem of Arctic militarization is open to frontal as distinct from indirect attack.

Whatever the prospects of the Commonwealth of Independent States, the appearance of a structurally weakened post-communist Russia as the principal successor to the Soviet Union signals the end of adversarial relations as we have known them. The condition of bipolarity exacerbated by ideological conflict has been replaced by a situation in which the United States, pre-eminent in military capability, is faced with increasingly severe economic and political challenges from a uniting Europe and from Japan. Small wars still abound, but the potential for nuclear crisis to spring from local conflict in the Third World has all but vanished. Notwithstanding the START agreement of July 1991 and the unilateral reductions subsequently announced by the United States and the Soviet Union/Russia in September-October 1991 and in January 1992, strategic nuclear weapons also abound, including those in former Soviet republics. But now it is truly difficult to provide a rationale for their retention except as backing for diplomacy or as counters to be bargained away. Meanwhile, as the industrialized countries seek ways to shore up the staggering economies and polities of the successor states to the Soviet Union, non-military questions of economic competitiveness, North-South economic disparity, sustainable development, and global change are coming to displace political-military affairs as the predominant issues of the international agenda.[12]

Though a renewal of preferences for international assertiveness within Russia cannot be excluded, the country is in no position to maintain nuclear and conventional forces on a scale comparable to that of the old Soviet Union. Instead, post-communist Russia seems poised for still more rapid unilateral reductions in its strategic nuclear capabilities as it strives for acceptance as a viable member of the community of nations. Despite uncertainties that continue to surround the security policies of the new Commonwealth and of Russia in particular, the threat system that served so long to orient so much international behaviour has been deprived of virtually all its energy.

Fundamental transformations in the political and military environment of the Arctic cannot but affect the nature of civil-military interaction within the region. The shift from military-political to civil priorities in the global agenda seems certain to reinforce processes of multilateral civil co-operation in the Arctic. More immediately, the withdrawal of political-military threats should result in further decoupling of civil and military matters in the region to the point where residual constraints on the former are all but eliminated. Civil-military interaction will be replaced by separate activity in two all-but-autonomous spheres. Whatever might be accomplished through civil collaboration to create background conditions for military co-operation among adversaries, it now declines in significance relative to new opportunities for direct action by the Arctic countries for unilateral and negotiated Arctic-specific arms measures.

Though Arctic conventional force cuts, particularly naval ones, may take time to achieve, the moment has arrived for the Eight to co-operate in the military sphere by injecting Arctic-specific requirements into extra-regional arms talks; to establish and then enlarge a demilitarized zone in the Arctic Ocean; to create a joint space-based surveillance system for scientific and environmental as well as arms control verification purposes; to restrict the movement of nuclear-powered attack submarines in Arctic waters; to make the deployment of air force capabilities consistent with requirements of non-offensive defence; to elaborate common military doctrines guiding legitimate military activity in the region; and to enact

Arctic-specific confidence-building measures including data-sharing, limits on naval and amphibious exercises, and exchanges of military observers.[13] All of this and more is within reach; some of these measures may no longer be necessary if Boris Yeltsin's appeal for Russia to be treated not as the partner but as an ally of other countries is vindicated. Nor does such action need any longer to await political priming by means of civil collaboration in the region.

In sum, civil-military interaction in the Arctic is no longer exempt from the momentous changes now unfolding elsewhere in the world. Decoupling, not linkage, has become the order of the day in the region. The way is open to intensified civil co-operation on the merits of the issue at hand, and to measures of Arctic-specific confidence-building, arms control, and disarmament. While a great deal of unfinished military business remains to be done in the region, the future of international co-operation in the Arctic, as in the world at large, lies principally with an expanding civil agenda that deserves to be pursued in its own right.

Greater civility in Arctic international relations is thus to be had through the achievement of civil collaboration and through actions that directly reduce the uncivil practice whereby states threaten one another's populations and environment with nuclear annihilation and war. Last and not least, the interment of the Cold War as a global phenomenon gives a new lease on life to collective action at the regional level. No longer is regional political development so subordinate to extra-regional imperatives. In so far as they are able to achieve greater civility within the region, the peoples and governments of the Arctic may succeed in offering new benefits to the world at large. All of which brings us to a final set of considerations.

On Civility

Much has been said and written in recent years about the meanings of security. To the vast lore on its political-military dimension – everything ranging from alliance, balance of power, and collective security through deterrence, arms control, and disarmament, to United Nations peacekeeping, and now common security – new notions of environmental or ecological, economic, energy, and food security have been added. Nor should we fail to note the steadily mounting attention being given to the demographic threat to the human condition, and to the need to defend human rights to life, liberty, and security of the person. The proliferation of contemporary understandings of security at the global, national, and subnational levels reaching down to the individual, attests further to the fact that political-military understandings of security are no longer the pre-eminent international concern they once were. Still other but, as we shall see, less compelling indications of the obsolescence of a political-military focus are to be seen in efforts to knit the various dimensions of security into an integrated or comprehensive concept that better meets the needs of our time.

New thinking about security was very much in the air when planning for this book first began in 1987; it therefore seemed appropriate to initiate discussion of an integrated conception of security adapted to the particular requirements of the circumpolar North. The underlying intent was essentially to change the subject for the better in the Arctic. If only little could be accomplished by way of a direct attack on the phenomenon of regional militarization, progress might still be accelerated by redefining the central problem in ways that might guide international practice away from an inordinate and unprofitable preoccupation with military conflict. Given as well our assumptions of civil-military interaction and of the potential for civil collaboration to ease the way to demilitarization, it appeared quite in order to broach a discussion of comprehensive security in which civil and military considerations were combined to yield new and better options for governments still very largely locked in Cold War thinking.

All of this seemed reasonable not so long ago. But is a comprehensive conception of security likely to meet today's needs? And if not, is there an alternative?

Disabilities of Comprehensive Security

The effort to construct an integrated conception of security proves to be triply misguided. It fails to meet the practical requirements of international co-operation in the circumpolar Arctic. It promises to fail under the pressure of considerations so varied and numerous that they cannot be contained by a single concept with operational policy significance. And it will fail because the notion of security is inherently incapable of capturing the essence of the problem in the Arctic or, for that matter, globally.

Willy Østreng has provided us with a telling critique of the utility of an integrated conception of security in Arctic international practice to the late 1980s. He finds that under conditions of acute hegemonic conflict, international relations in the circumpolar region were guided by a fully integrated multidimensional security concept in which the linkage between military and civil spheres was virtually absolute. Subsequently, a comprehensive decoupled conception of security came into being and provided a real basis for collaboration as civil co-operation arose side by side with continuing military-strategic conflict. Though it is debatable whether the outcome was a comprehensive rather than a disintegrated concept, the point here is that we once had an integrated conception of security in the Arctic and have been moving away from it to the benefit of all concerned.

In so far as decoupled co-operation continues to point the way ahead, the creation of an integrated conception of security can only be at variance with the practical needs of statecraft in the region. Although in future the Eight could recognize the need for an overarching conception to lend direction and coherence to Arctic international co-operation, an integrated notion of security is quite out of keeping with their requirements today.

Aside from its lack of fit with current state practice in the region, the attempt to elaborate and apply an integrated security concept is almost certain to be confounded by the variety and interdependence of the issues at hand. So far as I am able to determine, discussions of comprehensive security at the global level have yet to offer much more than a high-altitude pass over the intellectual problem of ordering economic, environmental, social, human rights, military, institutional, international legal, and other salient variables in a framework that gives us a reliable understanding of cause and effect.[14] Nor are the results greatly more impressive when the focus is narrowed to the environment, or to environment and economy.[15] And while some point to a renaissance of international security studies keyed to a political-military agenda, the emergence even here of new understandings that might provide an improved basis for collective and unilateral action is still along way off.[16]

Though the substantive problems to be dealt with are reduced when the development of an integrated security concept is focused on the Arctic, the inherent difficulties of the task are still very imposing. Nor can this be regarded primarily as an intellectual enterprise. A security concept appropriate to the region will have early policy relevance only if it is generated in a process that produces consensus on the problem and the implications for collective action. We are in effect contemplating an Arctic security equivalent of the Brundtland Commission, with the difference that considerably more than two key variables would need to be addressed. At a time when the Eight are inclined to decouple the civil and military spheres, the political as well as intellectual outlook for the creation and use of an integrated conception of Arctic security is decidedly unpromising.

If all of this were not enough, there are intrinsic difficulties with the notion of security as such. The dictionary meaning of the term is to be safe against danger, untroubled by apprehension, certain or sure that something will not fail or give way. The word connotes a condition and indeed a feeling that resides within an individual or a collectivity. Implying something that may be had or possessed by an actor or unit, it directs our attention to the unit and its state of mind, as distinct from the relationship between the unit and its human or physical surround. It also highlights actual and potential threats perceived by the unit, as distinct from unit-unit or unit-surround transactions as perceived from an autonomous point of view. In so doing, it orients us not so much to accommodation but to resistance and opposition aimed at preserving the self intact and transferring the burden of change to others or to the surrounding environment. The main problem here is that it is *we* who are the prime danger to ourselves where overpopulation, unsustainable development, global warming, ozone depletion, and many other non-traditional threats to "security" are concerned. A concept that alerts us essentially to danger emanating from elsewhere is no longer appropriate to the needs of humankind. Nor is an understanding that biases action towards resistance rather than accommodation. What we require is an organizing concept that is more properly *relational* in orienting us to human interaction and to interaction between humans and their physical surroundings. We are in need of a notion that is less egotistical and that engenders a more accommodating view of ourselves as part of the problems we face.

Civility as a Guiding Concept

The disabilities of an integrated conception of security may be such as to warrant our declining to create one, but we could still do with an overarching notion to lend direction, energy, and efficiency to the diverse activities of states and non-state actors in the circumpolar Arctic. Put another way, if we cannot yet be coherent about what we want to achieve and how to achieve it in a changing region embedded in a changing global surround, we are in a position to generalize about the process that so far has enabled the Arctic countries to discover a way ahead. If we are to have a guiding concept here, it must be derived from current policy concerns. It must be simple and easily understood. Further, if it is not to succumb to complexity, it should convey a currently under-represented attitude or predisposition rather than imply an understanding of causation by highlighting a desired outcome or final result. To have any chance of being taken as a guide to action, it must also reveal something of what many are already thinking and doing but have yet to identify.

I suggest that a concept of civility meets all of these requirements.[17]

The idea here can be made simple. It represents a widespread latent predisposition in the region. In providing an answer to the question "How do we proceed?" it is capable of imparting a larger sense of purpose to the process of Arctic international co-operation. And, if shown to yield real benefits in the circumpolar North, a concept of civility could ultimately help to better the human condition elsewhere.

Looking into the *Oxford English Dictionary*, we find that the word *civility* has been in use in English since at least 1380 and has gained and lost a great many meanings. Among these we find the art of civil government, courteousness or politeness, a community of citizens, a good polity or social order, conformity to principles of social order, behaviour befitting a citizen, the state of being civilized, decent respect, and so on. Not a few of these meanings are shared with the adjective *civil* which, in an unfortunate sign of our times, is coming to signify "not actually rude" where courteousness is concerned. We are not however concerned here with civility in the sense of politeness or courtesy, which would hardly take us far in guiding Arctic international practice. What then might be meant by civility?

Without at this point attempting to provide a fully fledged presentation of civility as central concept, let me first demonstrate that the notion is indeed latent in the affairs of the Arctic. In so doing I seek to create an empirical basis for a judgment on just what the term might mean for the circumpolar North and for the world at large.

It is obvious, to begin, that civil co-operation is now a prime concern of the Arctic countries in their multilateral relations. Interest in the affairs of the citizen as distinct from the military is on the rise and promises to become still more prominent.

It is equally apparent that in the military realm itself the circumpolar countries are moving towards more civilized forms of behaviour as previously alert forces are stood down, weapons are separated from delivery platforms, and decisions made to cease building new platforms such as attack submarines. There is an opportunity here to reduce still further what is in reality the barbaric practice of retaining nuclear and conventional arms that threaten not only opposed military forces but civilians and their physical environment even as political reasons for such behaviour evaporate. In such circumstances the continued presence of offensive weapons and force postures is doubly offensive: not only do such weapons evoke fear and apprehension, but to maintain them today is the equivalent of pointing a knife at someone's face when seated together at the dinner table. By the same token, a transition to conventions of non-offensive or defensive defence in the Arctic, as elsewhere, can only provide reassurance that one is indeed in civilized company where fights are unlikely to break out. Needless to say, weapons and the possibility of their legitimate use will long be with us in the Arctic. And yet by instituting Arctic-specific measures of confidence-building and disarmament we stand to create new conventions of mutual consideration and respect. In unilateral and collaborative action to constrain menacing and peremptory military behaviour, the Arctic countries may all come to feel not only more secure against being caught off guard but also able to get on with other things of greater moment.

Two other current concerns of the Arctic countries also attest to the need for greater respectfulness in matters relating to the military. For one thing, in the performance of defence tasks the Arctic states have dealt with the region's physical and biological environment in harsh and arrogant fashion. Whether it be nuclear weapons testing on the islands of Novaya Zemlya, the release of PCBs into the food chain from DEW Line stations in Canada, or simply the debris abandoned at military sites throughout the Arctic, insults have been freely administered to a singularly vulnerable natural environment which all along should have commanded our respect and consideration. Though the severity of these assaults varies from country to country and from community to community within them, we have here a common need for greater sensitivity both in curtailing the military propensity to run roughshod and in repairing damage already done.

Further, as military activity begins to diminish around the region, conversion to a more decidedly civil economy is becoming a significant problem for Arctic communities whose livelihood has in larger or smaller measure come to depend upon the presence of defence forces. Though the difficulty here is part of the far larger problem of military conversion in the wake of the Cold War, it will be experienced with especial force in circumpolar communities with little autonomous capacity for economic adaptation. Decision-makers to the south and the majorities they represent will need to show new regard for certain of their Arctic communities, if the latter are not to suffer still greater marginalization in failing to make the transition to a civil economy. Ultimately, southerners will have to end the uncivil practice, observable with variations around much of the region, of treating their Arctic areas as internal colonies whose resources are to be extracted without full and proper regard for local residents and their need for economic and political self-sufficiency.

If any group of Arctic citizens has been marginalized, it is surely the region's aboriginal peoples whose civil and other human rights are still to be fully acknowledged and honoured. And if there is any one consideration that takes precedence over others in the achievement of international co-operation which is fully adapted to the needs of the region, it is the vindication of aboriginal civil rights. When full respect is accorded to those of us who are most vulnerable, who live in the most intimate and respectful of relations with the vulnerable natural environment we seek to protect, all of us will have taken a significant step towards doing things right in the Arctic.

As yet the voices of aboriginal peoples in decisions affecting their vital interests and continued existence as communities are still to be heard as in justice they should be. We to the south seem unready to listen to what they have to say about living lightly on a land we have all too often been willing to ravage for our own purposes. If this were not enough, aboriginal cultures have been savaged not only by an unsustainable southern industrialism, but also by the grossly inconsiderate actions of southern anti-fur and animal-liberation movements which have severely disabled the renewable-resources life ways of aboriginal peoples.

Rough treatment like this is not only uncivilized but self-defeating. It must end if Arctic governments and peoples are to make good on the promise of international co-operation. We to the south need to act on the following assessment which, *mutatis mutandis*, could be applied to many of the circumpolar countries:

The objectives of Canadian Arctic policy, if set in broad national terms of politics, economics, defence, science or environment, could very easily find little or no scope for Inuit concerns. Canada could pursue peace and security in the Arctic as if it were an uninhabited world, which much of it is. But if we did, we would fail in our moral obligation to the Inuit people. And we would also end up, I would submit, with a hollow policy: inadequate, without credibility internationally and doomed to fail in the long run for lack of any sound base in Canada's domestic North.

I suggest to you that we cannot have a successful policy for the international Arctic if we do not have population in the Canadian Arctic that is self-reliant, self-respecting and self-directing.[18]

To fail to honour in full the civil and other human rights of Arctic aboriginal peoples is without doubt to invite the failure of circumpolar collaboration.

When we turn to the Arctic's physical and biological environment, we find that the prejudicial effects of military activity pale in comparison with the destruction wrought by a conquering and predatory industrialism. Environmental considerations have certainly gained greater currency in resource development decisions, but the fact remains that hydrocarbon, hydroelectric, pulp and paper, mining, and other northern megaprojects are continuing to attack the ecosystems of the region. Nor of course does this adversity stem from Arctic-specific resource exploitation alone. This is one area of the world that will be among the hardest hit by global warming. Wildlife and wilderness experience multiple assaults from the long-range transport of air- and waterborne pollutants. Insults are being delivered to the renewable resources on which aboriginal communities and cultures depend. The need for greater enlightenment and consideration in the relationship of humankind to its natural surroundings is reaching crisis proportions in the Arctic.

Finally, in the special circumstances of Russia, many of the requirements for more civil behaviour are expressed in acute form. As a principal victim of the Soviet experiment, Russia is the first major country in the world to face the consequences of unsustainable development. If anywhere in the Arctic, it is in Russia's portion of the region that the environmental effects of a disrespectful industrialism, indeed military-industrialism, are most evident. Northern aboriginal peoples of the Russian federation have truly been reduced to dire straits.[19] In the Russian North as elsewhere in the federation, there is an urgent need to create a civil society in which autonomous private and public organizations such as interest groups, political parties, and the means of communication serve to mediate relations between the citizen and the state. In this regard Russia offers but an extreme instance of the more widespread situation in the circumpolar region whereby the citizen is more or less bereft of the elaborate social and political structures which do stand between the individual and the state in the south. As to Russia's foreign affairs, the Arctic included, it is Moscow's present aim to return to the civilized world, to rejoin the international community not as a vanguard but as an ordinary member of the family of nations.

Put all the signs together, and we obtain the following hints of a latent unifying predisposition in the domestic and international affairs of the Arctic: mounting attention to a civil international agenda; initial unilateral reductions in the uncivil practice of threatening destruction with armed force; potential for active pursuit of mutual reassurance through non-offensive defence in the region; appearance of the need to facilitate the transition from a military to a civil economy in the North; growing demands of citizens to end and repair industrial and military insults to the Arctic's physical and biological environment; perceived need to honour and respect the civil and other rights of Arctic aboriginal peoples; and efforts being made in Russia, and in different ways throughout the region, to proceed with democratic development in building more civil societies. Separately and taken together, these varied concerns are of critical importance to the future of the Arctic as a region. They indicate a gathering commitment to more civilized behaviour in what southern majorities have long regarded as a frontier region where roughness is to be expected.

Civility being a capacious notion, I suggest that we do indeed employ the term in endeavouring to understand what is happening and what is needed in the Arctic as the region's countries set out on a new voyage of international co-operation. Earlier in this chapter civility was defined as a process in which southern majorities and the governments that speak for them accord progressively greater respect and attention to one another, to their circumpolar environment, and to their Arctic populations – aboriginal peoples first and foremost. This characterization suffices as a guide to action, but we should look for deeper meaning in what is under way in the region.

In my view we are witnessing the emergence of a sense of circumpolar community as the Arctic countries begin to conceive of and to deal with the region in the round. There can be no community without shared values and conventions. These engender a sense of solidarity as well as safety by protecting all against the roughness and greed of some amongst them.[20] The emergent values of a circumpolar community would seem to centre on attributes of citizenship which transcend national jurisdictions. They unite collectivities as well as individuals in acceptance of joint responsibilities of stewardship for a human and physical domain which cannot be well managed in segmented fashion.

The circumpolar citizen behaves with respect and consideration towards others and towards Nature. A conquering attitude, rudeness, intolerance, arrogance, and the like have no valid place in a part of the world which itself demands respect, which has the power to force a reconsideration of practices derived from other circumstances. The realities of life in an Arctic setting require an acceptance of differences, an ability to accommodate and share, a readiness to listen and learn. They also engender processes of consensual decision-making which accord a leading role to those whose circumstances and way of life are likely to be most directly affected by collective action. Though sharing and an incipient sense of community are more prevalent among residents around the Arctic than between northerners and their compatriots to the south, southern majorities are also coming to countenance and show greater respect for their Arctic domains. This is evident in their varied efforts to mitigate and prevent the damage of a presuming industrialism, to further the cause of northern and aboriginal self-government, and, starting with the Rovaniemi process, to accord aboriginal and other northerners a place at the table in Arctic inter-state negotiations.

Needless to say, conflict and the potential for conflict are in no way excluded in a domain governed by civility. Without conflict, why aspire to civility? Disputes and conceivably even warfare cannot be ruled out in future relations among Arctic countries or among them and others. All should certainly respect the Arctic's physical and biological environment, but certain attitudes and actions will always be ineligible for respect. Nor can norms of civility be used to banish or otherwise deny a hearing to those perceived as renegades or troublemakers. But politeness and inhibition are not what civility is about. Rather we are contemplating common values and conventions that provide a framework for peoples and governments to deal more readily with their differences and passions in achieving shared gains.

In the emergence of civility as a predisposing attitude in the Arctic we therefore have more than the latent propensity to act with respect and consideration. We also have the manifestation of a nascent community which unites the peoples and governments of the region in an acceptance of new standards of civilized behaviour and understandings of what is uncivil. In short, new ideas of citizenship and civilization would seem to be crystallizing in the Arctic.

The word civility stems from the Latin *civilitas*, itself a translation of the Greek equivalent. The root of both refers to communities gathered in cities and towns where civilization and citizenship first flourished. Outside was chaos and barbarity. In the global village that is taking shape today there is less and less of an outside. Nor are frontier areas unable to contribute to civilization and citizenship. Whereas in yesterday's world the Arctic explorer or missionary could presume to "civilize" aboriginal peoples, in their exemplary accommodation with Nature aboriginal peoples are now revealed to be bearers of civilization to metropolitan centres in search of pathways to a livable world. Today's Arctic may be less of a physical frontier than once it was but it remains a frontier of human discovery, a place where the physical setting can still push the imagination to its limit.

Attitudes towards the Arctic are representative of attitudes towards Earth as a whole. In their spontaneous elaboration of new notions of good citizenship and civilized behaviour, the peoples of the Arctic find themselves at the outer edge of the human endeavour to learn how to do things better together. Pursued with greater awareness, the fledgling circumpolar practice of civility – not security, demilitarization, sustained economic growth, or other such – has the potential to reveal new and more enlightened meanings of citizenship on the planet Earth.

Notes

1 Franklyn Griffiths and Oran R. Young, "Impressions of the Co-Chairs: Protecting the Arctic's Environment," Working Group on Arctic International Relations (Hanover NH: Institute of Arctic Studies, Dartmouth College, 1990), 18-19.

2 "Arctic Leaders Summit, Copenhagen, June 17-20, 1991" (Montreal: Inuit Circumpolar Conference 1991).

3 *Cooperation in a Changing World: Third Northern Regions Conference, Anchorage, Alaska, 1990: Summary Proceedings* (Anchorage: Office of International Trade 1990); and *The Northern Forum: The Founding Meeting, November 6, 7 and 8, 1991, Anchorage, Alaska* (Anchorage: Office of International Trade 1991).

4 See "Founding Articles for an International Arctic Science Committee (IASC)," final edition, August 1990, available in *Arctic Research of the United States*, 4 (fall 1990), 65-9.

5 "Arctic Environmental Protection Strategy," available in *Arctic Research of the United States*, 5 (fall 1991), 29-35.

6 Canada, External Affairs and International Trade, Statement 90/68, "Notes for a Speech by Secretary of State for External Affairs, the Right Honourable Joe Clark, PC, MP, at a Conference on Canadian-Soviet Relations at the Government Conference Centre," Ottawa, November 28, 1990, 9.

7 "Rech' tovarishcha Gorbacheva M.S." [Speech of Comrade M.S. Gorbachev], *Izvestia*, October 2, 1987.

8 Other developments having a less direct bearing on the Arctic and its military uses included the following. For the United States: its strategic bomber force of B-52s was stood down from 24-hour alert, as were land-based ICBMs designated for destruction under START; the new Seawolf nuclear-powered attack submarine programme was cancelled, with only one boat to be built; the B-2 strategic bomber programme was cut from 75 to 20 aircraft; production of new warheads for SLBMs was stopped as was production of the ACM and, if the Commonwealth of Independent States were to eliminate land-based multiple-warhead ballistic missiles, the United States would cut its SLBMs by one-third and convert a substantial portion of its strategic bomber force to carry conventional weapons. See "Remarks by President Bush on Reducing U.S. and Soviet Nuclear Weapons," *New York Times*, September 28, 1991; "Text of Bush's Message," *New York Times*, January 29, 1992; and Andrew Rosenthal, "Bush and Yeltsin Propose Deep Cuts in

Atomic Weapons," *New York Times*, January 30, 1992. As to Russia and the Commonwealth of Independent States, heavy bombers, and 600 land- and sea-based ICBMs came off alert; 130 ICBM launchers had been or would be eliminated, as would missile launchers on six ballistic-missile-firing nuclear submarines; production of two types of heavy bomber was to cease, as would exercises involving more than 30 heavy bombers; half of the warheads available for use on anti-aircraft missiles would be eliminated; and a global ballistic missile defence system was proposed. See Serge Schmemann, "Gorbachev Matches U.S. on Nuclear Cuts and Goes Further on Strategic Warheads,' *New York Times*, October 6, 1991, and John Gray, "Yeltsin Offers Nuclear Weapons Cuts on Eve of Visit," *Globe and Mail*, January 30, 1992.

9 David Cox and Tariq Rauf, *Security Cooperation in the Arctic: A Canadian Response to Murmansk* (Ottawa: Canadian Centre for Arms Control and Disarmament, October 24, 1989). For other views, see A.I. Arikaynen and O.A. Kossov, *Problemy voennoi bezopasnosti v Arktike* [On Military Security in the Arctic] (Moscow: Institute for Systems Studies 1990); and Steven E. Miller, "The Superpowers and Nordic Security in Post-Cold War Europe," in Bo Huldt and Gunilla Herolf, eds, *Yearbook 1990-91: Towards a New European Security Order* (Stockholm: Swedish Institute of International Affairs 1991), 293-311.

10 Franklyn Griffiths and Rosemarie Kuptana, *To Establish an International Arctic Council: A Framework Report* (Ottawa: Canadian Arctic Resources Committee, May 1991).

11 *Northwest Territories Government Discussion Paper on Military Activity in the North and Establishment of a Circumpolar Zone of Peace and Security* (Ottawa: Office of the Government of the Northwest Territories, November 1, 1990).

12 Franklyn Griffiths, "The CSIS, Gorbachev and Global Change: Canada's Internal Security and Intelligence Requirements in Transition," in A. Stuart Farson et al, eds, *Security and Intelligence in a Changing World: New Perspectives for the 1990s* (London: Cass 1991), 140-64.

13 John M. Lamb, "Arms Control in the North: A Post-Cold War Agenda," *Barometer* (fall 1991), 2.

14 See, for example, United Nations, Department of Disarmament Affairs, *Report of the Secretary-General: Concepts of Security* (New York: United Nations 1986); and V.F. Petrovsky, "Comprehensive Security and Cooperation: The Northern Dimension," News Release 74 (USSR Embassy in Canada, October 23, 1989). Consider also the more reflective discussions in Richard H. Ullman, "Redefining Security," *International Security*, 8 (summer 1983), 129-53; Jessica Tuchman Mathews, "Redefining Security," *Foreign Affairs*, 68 (spring 1989), 162-77; and Lincoln P. Bloomfield, *International Security: The New Agenda* (Minneapolis: Hubert Humphrey Institute of Public Affairs 1991).

15 On environmental security see, for instance, Eduard Shevardnadze, "Ekologiya i diplomatiya" [Ecology and Diplomacy], *Literaturnaya gazeta*, November 22, 1989, 9-10; and Arthur H. Westing, "The Environmental Component of Comprehensive Security," *Bulletin of Peace Proposals*, 20 (no 2, 1991), 129-34. The leading presentation on environment and the economy is of course World Commission on

Environment and Development (Brundtland Commission), *Our Common Future* (London: Oxford University Press 1987).

16 Helga Haftendorn, "The Security Puzzle: Theory-Building and Discipline-Building in International Security," *International Studies Quarterly*, 35 (March 1991), 5-17; Stephen M. Walt, "The Renaissance of Security Studies," ibid., 35 (June 1991), 213-39; and Barry Buzan, *People, States, and Fear* (Brighton: Wheatsheaf 1983).

17 For an earlier discussion, see Franklyn Griffiths, "Summation," in Thomas R. Berger et al, *The Arctic: Choices for Peace and Security* (Vancouver: Gordon Soules 1989), 271-7.

18 Gordon Robertson, "The Human Foundation for Peace and Security in the Arctic," in Berger et al, *The Arctic: Choices for Peace and Security*, 89. Also of interest is Louis-Edmond Hamelin, "Une politique autochtoniste: suggestions aux non-autochtones," paper presented at the colloquium, Environnement, Développement et Nations autochtones, Institut Interculturel de Montréal, 2 juin 1991. Nor, of course, should we idealize aboriginal peoples in stressing their singular capacity to impart valuable knowledge to industrial societies in search of pathways to sustainable development: see, for example, "Watching America's Grisliest Home Videos," *Globe and Mail*, February 24, 1992.

19 For instance, see A. Pika and B. Prokhorov, "Bol'shie problemy malykh narodov" [The Big Problems of the Small Peoples], *Kommunist*, 18 (September 1988), 76-83.

20 The thought here – as do some other points in this section – comes from Margaret Visser, *The Rituals of Dinner* (Toronto: HarperCollins 1991), 69.

Contributors

Aleksandr Arikaynen is Head of Labratory, All-Union Research Institute for Systems Studies, Russian Academy of Sciences, Moscow.

Terence Armstrong is Reader, now Emeritus, in Arctic Studies at the Scott Polar Research Institute, University of Cambridge, England.

Arkady I. Cherkasov has been a Senior Research Fellow at the Russian Academy of Sciences, Moscow, since 1985 and is currently Senior Researcher in the Canadian Department of the Academy's Institute of the USA and Canada. He also lectures in the Department of Geography at Moscow State University.

Melvin A. Conant is editor of the journal, *Geopolitics of Energy*, in Washington, DC. His interest in Arctic affairs began with the publication of his book, *The Long Polar Watch*, in 1962.

David Cox is Professor of Political Studies, Queen's University, Kingston, Ontario, Canada.

M.J. Dunbar is Emeritus Professor of Oceanography, Department of Atmospheric and Oceanic Sciences, and former Director of the Institute of Oceanography, McGill Univeristy, Montreal, Quebec, Canada.

Milton M.R. Freeman is Henry Marshall Tory Professor of Anthropology at the University of Alberta, Edmonton, and Senior Research Scholar, the Canadian Circumpolar Institute.

Franklyn Griffiths is Professor of Political Science, University of Toronto, Ontario, Canada. Editor of *Politics of the Northwest Passage* (1987), he is currently co-chair of the Arctic Council Panel, a private Canadian group seeking the creation of a central intergovernmental forum for the circumpolar North.

Jost Heintzenberg is Associate Professor in the Department of Meteorology, University of Stockholm, with a special interest in the physics and chemistry of atmospheric trace substances.

Evgenia Issraelian is a Senior Research Fellow at the Institute of the USA and Canada of the Russian Academy of Sciences, Moscow.

Anders Karlqvist is the Director of the Swedish Polar Research Secretariat, Stockholm, and Adjunct Professor in Systems Analysis at the University of Umeå.

Aqqaluk Lynge, who lives in Nuuk, Greenland, is Vice-President (Greenland) of the Inuit Circumpolar Conference.

Steven E. Miller is currently a Senior Research Fellow at the Stockholm Peace Research Institute, Stockholm, Sweden, and editor of the journal, *International Security*.

Jens Misfeldt, a specialist in community medicine, has been the Chief Medical Officer in Greenland since 1986. He is a member of the Nordic Council for Arctic Medical Research and has written on public health issues, occupational medicine, and health conditions in Greenland.

Willy Østreng is the Director of the Fridtjof Nansen Institute, Oslo, Norway. His interest in polar affairs has led, most recently, to the publication of an edited volume, *The Antarctic Treaty System in World Politics* (with Arnfinn Jørgensen-Dahl, 1991).

E.F. Roots is Science Advisor Emeritus, Department of the Environment, Government of Canada, Ottawa, Ontario.

Mary Simon of Canada is President of the Inuit Circumpolar Conference.

John Kristen Skogan is a specialist in international security affairs at the Norsk Utenrikspolitisk Institutt (Norwegian Institute of International Affairs), Oslo, Norway.

Anders Stigebrandt is Professor of Oceanography in the Department of Oceanography at the University of Goteborg, Sweden.

Oran R. Young is Research Professor of Government, Senior Fellow of the Dickey Endowment for International Understanding, and Director of the Institute of Arctic Studies at Dartmouth College, Hanover, New Hampshire, and Senior Fellow of the Center for Northern Studies, Wolcott, Vermont, USA.